# Macro-financial Linkages in the Pacific Region

T0271902

Growth perspectives in emerging market economies are increasingly dependent on international capital flows in recent decades because of their influence on business cycles. In fact, volatile international capital flows have been one of the main concerns for the macroeconomic policy authorities. Focusing on emerging economies in the Pacific region, this book reveals how they are different from those in other regions in terms of international macro-financial linkages to the global capital market and domestic financial development.

The book also discusses how these characteristics have interacted with their macroeconomic policy regimes and their macroeconomic performance throughout the two major international financial crises in the preceding more than two decades. It suggests facts that have strengthened the resilience of these emerging economies in the Pacific region against the global financial crisis along with the intensified intra-regional economic integration through trade and investment. The book also examines their macroeconomic management, focusing on monetary policy regimes, and suggests that their factual unorthodox policies with exchange rate management and capital controls have contributed to their resilience against the intrinsic volatility of the international capital market and financial flows.

**Akira Kohsaka** has been affiliated with School of International Studies, Kwansei Gakuin University, Nishinomiya, Japan, since 2011. He received his PhD in economics from Stanford University in 1984. He has worked for the Institute of Developing Economies, Tokyo (1975–88), Kyoto University (1988–94) and Osaka University (1994–2011). His major research fields include international economics and development economics. He has also taken on other roles such as President of the East Asian Economic Association (2012–), editor of *Asian Economic Journal* (2001–6) and international steering committee member of the Pacific Forum for Trade and Development (1998–).

# Macro-financial Linkages in the Pacific Region

Edited by
Akira Kohsaka

Routledge
Taylor & Francis Group

LONDON AND NEW YORK

First published 2015
by Routledge
2 Park Square, Milton Park, Abingdon, Oxfordshire OX14 4RN

and by Routledge
711 Third Avenue, New York, NY 10017

First issued in paperback 2017

*Routledge is an imprint of the Taylor & Francis Group,
an informa business*

*British Library Cataloguing in Publication Data*
A catalogue record for this book is available from the British
Library

*Library of Congress Cataloging-in-Publication Data*
Macro-financial linkages in the Pacific region / edited by Akira
 Kohsaka.
   pages cm
 Includes bibliographical references.
 1. Finance—Asia.  2. Finance—Pacific Area.  3. Monetary
policy—Asia.  4. Monetary policy—Pacific Area.  5. Capital
market—Asia.  6. Capital market—Pacific Area.  I. Kohsaka,
Akira, editor.  II. Kohsaka, Akira. Macro-financial linkage and
financial deepening. Container of (work):
 HG187.A2M325 2015
 332'.042095—dc23
 2014027475

ISBN 13: 978-1-138-06696-0 (pbk)
ISBN 13: 978-1-138-80653-5 (hbk)

Typeset in Galliard
by Apex CoVantage, LLC

# Contents

# Figures

# Tables

# Contributors

**Chaiyasit Anuchitworawong** is a Research Specialist at the Thailand Development Research Institute.

**Tomoyuki Fukumoto** is the Chief Representative of the Representative Office in Beijing, Bank of Japan.

**Miranda S. Goeltom** is a Professor of Economics at the University of Indonesia.

**Sheng-Cheng Hu** is an academician at the Academia Sinica and Taiwan Institute of Economic Research.

**Solikin M. Juhro** is a Senior Economist at Bank Indonesia and Lecturer in the Graduate Program of Economics at the University of Indonesia.

**Akira Kohsaka** is a Professor of Economics in the School of International Studies at the Kwansei Gakuin University.

**Dongmin Liu** is the Deputy Director for the Institute of World Economics and Politics at the Chinese Academy of Social Sciences.

**Peter J. Morgan** is a Senior Consultant for Research at the Asian Development Bank Institute.

**Kumiko Okazaki** is a Senior Economist of the International Department, Bank of Japan

**Cayetano W. Paderanga, Jr.** is a Professor of Economics at the University of the Philippines.

**Shigenori Shiratsuka** is the Branch Manager of Kanazawa Branch, Bank of Japan.

**Zhenxin Zhu** is an Analyst in the Research Department of China Minsheng Securities.

# Introduction

*Akira Kohsaka*

The International Monetary Fund (IMF)'s *World Economic Outlook* (2014) started by stating, "*Global activity strengthened during the second half of 2013 and is expected to improve further in 2014–15. The impulse has come mainly from advanced economies. . . . Growth in emerging market economies is projected to pick up only modestly.*" They worried "*because capital inflows could slow or reverse.*" Indeed, how to tame international capital flows has been one of the most important policy concerns to the policy authorities of emerging economies, including those in the Pacific region. We must note, however, that emerging economies are heterogeneous in terms of their financial and macroeconomic linkages to advanced as well as other developing economies to a great extent. Focusing on emerging economies and their macro-financial linkages to other economies in the Pacific region as well as the rest of the world, this book is going to reveal how they are different from other emerging economies in other regions and to discuss how these characteristics are related to their macroeconomic performance and financial development throughout the two major international financial crises in the previous more than two decades.

In the Asian financial crisis in 1997–8, because of *sudden stops* and/or reversals in foreign capital inflows, emerging economies in the Pacific region experienced nightmarish economic downturns collectively for the first time in the past two decades. Their virtual dollar peg system of exchange rates collapsed, and their domestic financial systems were forced to implement structural reforms. In contrast, in the global financial crisis in 2008–9, these economies were far less affected by sudden stops of foreign capital flows and were able to regain handsome economic growth quickly as compared to advanced economies, which suffered from sudden stops of capital flows and prolonged economic downturns thereafter.

Why these differences exist and what causes the resilience of some emerging economies concern many economists in academic, media and policy circles. Focusing on the Pacific region as a main target, this book examines their increasing macro-financial linkages to the international capital market and their interactions with their macroeconomic and financial developments. Emerging economies in the Pacific region are demonstrated to be very different from other emerging economies, such as Brazil, India, Russia, and others, in terms of financial linkages to the international capital market as well as macroeconomic balances in sectoral saving and investment and financial deepening.

In this book, we will show that the difference has been widening since the late 1990s between emerging economies in the Pacific region and those in other regions and suggests that this fact must have strengthened the resilience of these emerging economies in the Pacific region against the global financial crisis along with the intensified intra-regional economic integration through trade and investment. Furthermore, we will examine their macroeconomic management, focusing on monetary policy regimes, and suggest that their factual unorthodox policies with exchange rate management and capital controls have contributed to their resilience against the intrinsic volatility of the international capital market and financial flows.

The most recent slowdown in emerging market economies as a whole shows that their quick recovery from the global crisis comes from favorable but ultimately transitory external factors such as high commodity prices and cheap credit on the one hand and their wise macroeconomic policies and strategies on the other. In the case of the emerging economies in the Pacific region, we will show that the external demand shocks of the crisis affected their growth seriously through trade channels; nevertheless, they have been less prone to capital flow volatility because of the nature of their macro-financial linkages and monetary policy regimes. These emerging economies in East Asia demonstrate to us that developing economies should be liberated from the conventional mantra "the freer the market, the better" and that they should start rethinking in their own way how to reconcile their relatively immature markets with relatively weak institutions and governance.

This chapter gives the general background of the book, describing what the macro-financial linkages are, how they relate to macroeconomic development and domestic financial systems and how they interact with the macroeconomic policy framework. Then it highlights some moot points to be deepened in the following chapters showing macroeconomic developments in terms of some relevant macroeconomic data for global, regional and individual economies. Then it summarizes each chapter and maps the chapters within the general context of the book.

This book contains updated versions of selected outcomes from the two Pacific Economic Outlook projects, i.e. *Macro-financial Linkages and Financial Deepening in the Pacific Region* (2009–10) as well as *Monetary Policy Regimes in the Pacific Region* (2011–12) under the Pacific Economic Cooperation Council, respectively.

## Part I: macro-financial linkages and financial deepening

Part I looks into macro-financial linkages to the international capital market and their interactions with macroeconomic and financial developments in the Pacific region, focusing on emerging economies in East Asia.

Emerging economies, including those in East Asia, have intensified their financial linkages to the international capital market so that the recent global financial crisis has undoubtedly had large negative impacts on them. In this respect, a contrast between the external balances of emerging economies in East

Asia and Europe before the crisis is particularly noticeable, i.e. surpluses in the former and deficits in the latter. Some (for example, IMF 2008), assert that the surpluses came from financial repression and the deficits from financial liberalization. How are these contrasting external balances possible in terms of macro-financial linkages to the international capital market?

Part I tries to answer the following questions: First, how are the macro-financial linkages of East Asian emerging markets characterized in terms of international capital flows, and how are they related to the impact of the global financial crisis on the region? Next, to what extent are the capital flows important to their domestic flow of funds, and how are the domestic financial developments related to them? Furthermore, how does the global financial crisis affect international capital flows in the region and its domestic financial developments, and what policy implications does the economic recovery after the Asian as well as the global financial crises have for macroeconomic management and regional financial cooperation regimes?

## Regional overview

*Chapter 1 by Akira Kohsaka* sets a conceptual framework to examine the theme and, along with it, gives an overview of the region.

The chapter shows, first, how the macro-financial linkages of East Asian emerging markets are characterized in terms of international capital flows and how they are related to the impact of the global financial crisis on the region, focusing on the composition of capital flows. The composition of capital inflows changed broadly before and after the Asian crisis, i.e. relatively persistent and stable foreign direct investment (FDI) became dominant. In addition, intra-regional flows from old emerging to new emerging economies began to play a larger role than those from the United States, European Union and Japan.

Second, the chapter scrutinizes to what extent the capital flows are important to emerging markets' domestic flow of funds and how the domestic financial developments are related to this, highlighting financial intermediation to the private sector. East Asian emerging markets are found to be significantly less dependent on foreign capital flows and to demonstrate higher degrees of financial deepening than other emerging markets. Looking at the role of their domestic financial sectors in investment financing for the private sector, however, since the Asian crisis, financial intermediation through credits has remained retrenched and their securities markets, regarded as an alternative channel, did not develop enough to substitute for credits. In other words, the recovery of their domestic financial systems since the crisis has been far less proportional to their real economic performance.

Finally, the chapter discusses how the global financial crisis affects international capital flows and domestic financial developments and what policy implications the economic recovery after the Asian as well as the global financial crises has for macroeconomic management and regional financial cooperation regimes. The current global financial crisis is very unlikely to impose a large negative impact on East Asian emerging markets as a whole as in the Asian crisis. This is probably because of the previously mentioned changes in financial linkages, not because of their developments in their domestic financial systems after the Asian crisis. Furthermore, post-crisis domestic macroeconomic policies as well as the framework of regional financial cooperation can play only limited roles in preventing the negative impacts of the global crisis. Current policy challenges will be, rather, to reestablish flexible macro-monetary policy regimes in the short run that can cope with growing market risks, and to seek domestic financial systems in the longer run that can cope with changing investment risks, beyond the conventional dichotomy between bank-based or market-based systems. This will lead to the theme of our Part II, i.e. *Monetary policy regimes.*

## China

As China's economic integration with the global economy deepens, the amount of capital flow to/from China has been increasing significantly, particularly since it joined the World Trade Organization. *Chapter 2 by Kumiko Okazaki and Tomoyuki Fukumoto* first reviews the factors that have made the Chinese economy and financial markets less vulnerable to the global financial crisis and analyzes the recent changes in China's macro-financial linkages overseas, by focusing on the movement of cross-border capital transactions. Relatively strict capital controls, a large accumulation of foreign exchange reserves and the recapitalized banking systems are pointed to as contributing factors, in addition to active stimulative policies under sound fiscal positions and abundant domestic savings.

Then the chapter discusses the challenges that the Chinese financial system reform faces in furthering the sustainable development of the economy. As often pointed out, too much reliance on bank intermediation between state-owned banks and enterprises and underdeveloped securities markets have remained as sources of inefficient resource allocation. In addition, the extremely high domestic savings rate reflects disproportionately high capital income shares and inadequate public support for health care, education and pensions.

On the horizon, the factors that protected the Chinese economy during the crisis also seem to carry with them substantial risks and challenges for its sustainable growth. China's primary task will be to change the market dominance of state-owned sectors, to liberalize financial intermediaries and develop securities markets, to adjust the extremely high domestic savings rate and to reduce the risk of the foreign exchange reserves on the central bank's balance sheet. Furthermore, the chapter points to the importance of monitoring international capital flows and properly sequencing the opening up of capital accounts.

## The Philippines

The 2008–9 global economic crisis proved that emerging economies in Asia were "decoupled" from the US economy only to a certain extent. *Chapter 3 by Cayetano W. Paderanga, Jr.,* identifies channels through which the global economic crisis affected the Philippine economy and then points to reasons why the impact of the crisis on the Philippine financial sector was negligible. While financial sectors avoided a direct hit from the US subprime crisis, the resulting worldwide credit crunch led to falling export demand by developed economies. This holds true for the Philippines.

On the one hand, the crisis affected the Philippine economy through five channels: first, through the impact on confidence and purchasing power, particularly owing to asset losses on the part of rich people; second, through the added losses resulting from the flow-out of portfolio investments, leading to lower asset values and, in turn, to greater difficulty in mobilizing investment in the equity and credit markets; third, through the difficulty of raising FDI in developed markets; fourth, through the impact on exports; and, finally, through the feared impact on overseas Filipino worker (OFW) deployment, whose remittances are the main engine of Philippine economic growth.

On the other hand, the negligible impact of the global economic crisis on the Philippine financial sector could be attributed to two factors: first, the conservative behavior of local firms during the run-up to the crisis and, second, stricter standards imposed by regulators as part of post-1997 financial sector reforms. In the period preceding the crisis, and during the crisis, the sector was in a healthier state.

Finally, the chapter draws two major lessons for the Philippines from the macroeconomic and macroprudential nature of the global crisis. First, there is an urgent need for emerging markets such as the Philippines to monitor not only their own financial markets but also international financial markets, given the increasing integration and interdependence between the two. Second, the global financial crisis has shown that macroprudential lapses in some countries can have a significant impact on other countries. Cautious behavior in some countries may not fully prevent disequilibrium arising from these lapses.

## *Thailand*

*Chapter 4 by Chaiyasit Anuchitworawong* explores how resilient the Thai economy is in the face of a number of setbacks. The chapter tries to answer three main questions: (a) whether the current crisis changed the structure of macro-financial linkages, (b) whether the crisis affected domestic financial deepening in regional emerging market economies, and (c) how regional financial cooperation can strengthen their economic immunity.

Overall, the US subprime mortgage crisis that spread to Europe and Japan tended to affect the Thai economy more through trade channels than through financial channels because there was a fairly strong spillover effect on Thai exports from external demand shocks from the United States, Japan and European countries. The export sector was hit hard, which adversely affected production, employment and incomes. The government introduced a fiscal stimulus package to ensure economic recovery and sustainable long-term growth.

A relatively strong financial system in place before the latest crisis was a key factor for Thailand to weather the impacts of the crisis. The financial sector had been in good health, and the banks, on average, had strong capital bases and low exposure to problem loans. There was not a great deal of concern about external vulnerability because Thailand had enjoyed a current account surplus for several years and had accumulated a large amount of international reserves, which led to an improved international investment position.

Looking ahead, there will be an increase in the complexity and international linkages of financial systems. As the linkages through financial activities become increasingly complex, there will certainly be a need for better development in terms of global regulatory and supervisory frameworks to handle cross-border implications. The potential solution to ensure macroeconomic and financial stability is to promote greater regional financial cooperation and integration.

### Chinese Taipei

*Chapter 5 by Sheng-Cheng Hu* first describes Chinese Taipei's financial deepening process and its impacts on key macro-financial variables. Then it sheds light on the channels through which the contagion of the crisis took place, and thus on the nature of the macro-financial linkages.

Chinese Taipei's financial deepening has taken the form of financial liberalization, improvement in asset quality, globalization and expansion of securities markets. While early liberalization in the 1990s resulted in excessive competition and a decline in banking asset quality, the financial system had been restructured by the time of the global financial crisis. During the restructuring process, the financial sector has been globalized substantially, opening up for foreign banks and for both inward and outward international financial transactions.

Chinese Taipei's financial sector was relatively stable throughout the global financial crisis. The main effect of the crisis on the financial sector was a decline in stock prices and a loss in the value of its holdings of overseas assets. The real effect of the decline in asset value appears to be less powerful than the decline in exports. First, while securitized products played an important role in the spread of the financial crisis to other advanced countries, they still represented only a small fraction of Chinese Taipei's financial markets. Second, its banks had not been highly leveraged. Third, the central bank was able to effectively counter the attacks of capital flows, thanks to its large holdings of foreign exchange reserves.

Chinese Taipei's infection with the financial crisis was mainly through the non-financial channel, particularly through the decline in exports. The deep recession was also in stark contrast to what happened to the economy during the 1997 Asian financial crisis. At that time, Chinese Taipei suffered only a relatively minor economic downturn, mainly because, unlike the situation in the current crisis, the 1997 crisis-hit countries were not major export markets for Chinese Taipei, while the United States, Chinese Taipei's most important export market, was still maintaining a respectable growth rate.

Even as the global economy has recovered from the global financial crisis, the macroeconomic causes of the crisis have not been eliminated. Solutions must be found to these problems in order to prevent another asset bubble or financial crisis. While each country must solve its own fiscal problems and contain hot money, an international cooperative approach, at both global and regional levels, including a regional financial stability fund, may be necessary to prevent the contagion of crises or the sparking of friction among countries.

## Part II: monetary policy regimes

Part II discusses monetary policy regimes suitable to cope with financial business cycles, i.e. business cycles caused by financial turmoil, in conditions of increasing macro-financial linkages, focusing mainly on emerging economies in the Pacific region.

In light of the current global turmoil, the macroeconomic policy trilemma among the three policy goals, i.e. exchange rate stability, free capital mobility and monetary autonomy, has been reexamined. Recently, even the IMF admitted, albeit reluctantly, that capital controls and monetary policy discretion could be useful in some circumstances (IMF 2013). As a first step, we review our diverse experiences in the region since the 1990s and then pursue a new perspective on monetary policy regimes. Again, we need to take into account the new realities that we found under the name of financial deepening and globalization.

The above observations lead us to discuss the following questions: The current crisis has seriously affected domestic financial systems and macroeconomic developments in the region. How have the policy authorities coped with these, and how can we assess their efforts to date? Then, does the above examination suggest that we should change the framework of monetary policy management or monetary policy regimes in terms of monetary policy independence, exchange rate stability and capital mobility?

### *Regional overview*

*Chapter 6 by Akira Kohsaka* provides a conceptual framework needed to examine the theme and, along with it, gives an overview of the region.

Reviewing the diverse experiences in the region, this chapter confirms the diverse monetary policy regimes and their developments but also identifies a few common facets worthwhile to learn for more robust monetary policy regimes. First, facing financial globalization, emerging market economies need to cope with increasing volatile foreign capital flows. Meanwhile, prudential policies regarding the financial sector need to be better coordinated with macroeconomic stabilization policy under the name of macroprudential policy, which is much discussed mainly in the context of advanced economies. In fact, however, through the series of financial crises in the 1990s, emerging economies in the Pacific region continued to resort to unorthodox but traditional instruments, i.e. a combination of foreign exchange market intervention and capital controls. Conventional wisdom, such as the macroeconomic trilemma and/or corner solutions within it, was challenged, and the emerging economies settled on non-corner solutions to address the new global economic environment.

8   *Akira Kohsaka*

Second, the region consists of surplus economies that have expanded their linkages with the global financial market on a "gross" basis, i.e. both hosting foreign investment and investing abroad themselves. Moreover, the composition of capital inflows has been dominated by FDI, not by restless portfolio and other flows. Nevertheless, domestic financial deepening appears to have stagnated. In the 2000s the non-financial corporate sector came to rely less and less on financial intermediation (bank credits) and more on self-financing as well as on FDI (*financial internalization*).

Third, regarding assessments of policy outcomes, emerging economies in the Pacific region have successfully coped with the destructive force of volatile foreign financial flows, using unorthodox policy tools. This time is very different from that of 1997. These economies have minimized their reliance on foreign financial resources and diversified across categories toward less volatile flows. Remarkably, their private sectors have also done the same through their financial internalization. Their domestic financial systems are not so deep as those of advanced economies but not as shallow as those of emerging economies in other regions, which enables their policy mix. Resulting changes in domestic demand may need to be reexamined, though.

Fourth, with regard to sustainability from a global perspective: while it is often argued that emerging economies have appeared to be far more resilient than advanced economies during the global financial crisis, they are far from immune to some new types of risks. With the prolonged recession in advanced economies, emerging economies may have to confront more destabilizing capital flows in the short run, and trend currency appreciation along with accelerated income convergence in the long run. These risks are inevitable anyway. The real concerns over the long run are macroeconomic rebalancing in domestic demand and financial development in these economies. Significant declining trends in domestic investment, persistently high savings and persistently low household consumption are notable. Whether or not they are sustainable and appropriate for long-run growth remains to be seen.

## Asia

Reviewing the history of Asian monetary policy frameworks since 1990, *Chapter 7 by Peter J. Morgan* describes current monetary policy frameworks, including the issue of price versus financial stability for a central bank and the policies a central bank can use to manage financial stability. Defining financial stability is not an easy task because it has multiple dimensions and is related to complex financial systems. Nevertheless, central banks have various tools to support financial stability, including standard and "unconventional" monetary policy tools, currency market intervention tools and, in some cases, supervisory authority, macroprudential tools and capital flow management tools. Asian central banks have in fact frequently resorted to such tools to safeguard financial stability and reduce the volatility of capital flows.

The chapter then examines the monetary policy transmission mechanism based on financial linkages and financial deepening, and provides assessments of policy outcomes including inflation targeting and responses to the "Impossible Trinity".

Overall, monetary policy frameworks in the region appear to have worked well in achieving low and stable inflation coupled with economic growth. However, the standard characterizations of monetary policy frameworks focusing on the use or non-use of explicit inflation targeting are probably too simplistic. The chapter points to the availability of a large number of policy tools, including unconventional policies, macroprudential measures and capital flow measures that help to deliver financial and economic stability.

East Asian central banks also appear to have coped well with the constraints of the trilemma hypothesis, gravitating toward an "interior solution" with an independent monetary policy, partial financial openness and partly managed currencies. Although currency flexibility in recent years is higher than it was before the Asian crisis, these currencies are far from freely floating. Finally, the chapter suggests giving greater weight to financial stability as a policy objective and strengthening institutions for regional policy coordination, including the Chiang Mai Initiative.

## *China*

*Chapter 8 by Dongmin Liu and Zhenxin Zhu* first gives a brief history of the Chinese monetary policy regime and then discusses monetary policy targets and policy transmission mechanisms. In particular, multi-target decision-making has been a typical model for China's monetary policy regime, focusing on targets "'such as inflation control, employment incentivization, economic growth, collaboration with fiscal policy to expand domestic demand, guaranteeing of increases in foreign reserves, and stabilizing the exchange rate.'" The chapter concludes that the People's Bank of China (PBOC) must be ready to switch to a different core target as the situation requires.

On policy transmission, despite the potential inefficiency risk of a non-market approach such as administrative guidance to commercial banks, the chapter determines that the PBOC has helped well-performing private companies to get loans, and the banks have profited from these arrangements so far. Nevertheless, the chapter admits that such planning-style monetary tools are not appropriate for sustainable economic development over the long term and that, with financial deepening, the PBOC will steadily move away from these planned-economy approaches.

While highly praising the achievements of the monetary policy since the global financial crisis in terms of liquidity provision for economic growth, inflation controls, containment of real estate bubbles, national welfare and renminbi (RMB) internationalization, the chapter points to some challenges ahead for monetary policy regimes, such as the opening up of the capital account and interest rate liberalization. It asserts that opening of the capital account need not be conditional on liberalization of the interest rate and the exchange rate, and that promotion of RMB internationalization should strengthen capital account opening and stimulate liberalization of the exchange rate and the interest rate at the same time.

## Indonesia

The aftermath of the financial crisis of 1997–8 was a period when the monetary policy regime was directed to the inflation targeting framework (ITF) in emerging economies, including Indonesia. In a climate of high global uncertainty, the global financial crisis significantly affected not only the domestic financial systems and macroeconomic developments in the region but also the ways monetary policy should be implemented there.

*Chapter 9 by Solikin M. Juhro and Miranda S. Goeltom* shows that in a small open economy like Indonesia, the multiple challenges to monetary policy imply that the monetary authorities should undertake unconventional monetary policy and employ multiple instruments. In the case of Indonesia, monetary policy is tactically directed not only toward controlling inflation but also toward managing the exchange rate within a specified range, in line with macroeconomic fundamentals, through quite active interventions in the foreign exchange market and simultaneously management of international reserves at safe levels. The chapter also shows that the monetary policy framework in Indonesia since the global financial crisis is characterized by "enhanced" ITF, where ITF looks not only at the inflation target but also at other factors, including financial sector stability as well as the dynamic of capital flows and the exchange rate.

The change in the framework will have a number of significant implications for the institutional mandates of Bank Indonesia. Monetary policy requires the support of macroprudential policy in order to ensure its effective implementation, since it is generally hard to separate monetary policy from macroprudential policy. Therefore, strengthening policy coordination between Bank Indonesia and the government in maintaining monetary and financial system stability is essential. Policy coordination can also be carried out from a broader perspective. In a crisis management context, coordination or cooperation among central banks in the region can be established in order to formulate a kind of international financial safety net.

## Macroprudential perspective

*Chapter 10 by Shigenori Shiratsuka* explores a policy framework for central banks from a macroprudential perspective, to pursue price and financial system stability in a consistent and sustainable manner. First, it reviews the basic concept of an asset-price and credit bubble, as a symptom of financial imbalances in the run-up to a crisis. Second, it presents a selective review of the current discussions on designing macroprudential policy tools in addressing two key externalities in the financial system: intertemporal procyclicality and cross-sectional spillover effects. Third, it explores how to design a policy framework for central banks from a macroprudential perspective, with special emphasis on the interactions between monetary and macroprudential policies.

Financial crises are generally preceded by a period of a benign economic and financial environment with a prevailing euphoric sentiment. Behind the scenes, financial imbalances are built up, typically seen as an asset-price and credit bubble, and the subsequent unwinding of such imbalances produces significant adverse effects, potentially leading to prolonged economic stagnation. Crises are fundamentally endogenous to the financial system and arise from exposure to common risks among financial institutions, underpinned by complicated incentives at both the micro and macro levels.

The recent crisis shed light on crucial deficiencies in the regulatory and supervisory framework in maintaining the stability of the financial system as a whole. Based on our experience during the recent crisis, however, the soundness of individual financial institutions does not necessarily assure the stability of the financial system as a whole. Note that achieving higher financial system stability purely by more stringent microprudential regulations tends to result in lower efficiency in financial intermediation.

Pursuing both price and financial system stability in a consistent and sustainable manner requires a combination of monetary and prudential policy, especially macroprudential policy. Macroprudential policy is indeed a missing element in the current policy framework. Given the close interaction between monetary and macroprudential policies, it is crucial for central banks to consider an overall policy framework for central banking, encompassing both policies. To that end, this chapter proposes to extend *constrained discretion* for monetary policy, proposed as the conceptual basis for flexible inflation targeting, to overall central banking, encompassing monetary and macroprudential policies, which are designed to pursue price stability in the medium to long term while responding flexibly to shocks in the short term.

## References and Further Readings

International Monetary Fund (IMF), 2008, *World Economic Outlook*, October, Washington, DC: International Monetary Fund.

———, 2013, *World Economic Outlook*, October, Washington, DC: International Monetary Fund.

———, 2014, *World Economic Outlook*, April, Washington, DC: International Monetary Fund.

Kohsaka, Akira, ed., 2011, *Macro-financial Linkages and Financial Deepening in the Pacific Region*, Osaka: Japan Committee for Pacific Economic Outlook.

———, 2013, *Monetary Policy Regimes in the Pacific Region*, Osaka: Japan Committee for Pacific Economic Outlook.

# Part I

# Macro-financial linkages and financial deepening

# Part I

# Macro-financial linkages and financial deepening

# 1 Macro-financial linkages and financial deepening

## An overview

*Akira Kohsaka*

## Introduction

Focusing on East Asian emerging markets as main targets, this chapter examines countries' macro-financial linkages to the international capital market and the interactions with developments in their domestic financial systems. The global financial crisis since 2007 has played a significant role in pursuing this line of examination. Moreover, considering the Asian economic crisis of more than ten years ago, it would be interesting, from the above viewpoint, to examine the developments between the two crises. This not only will be relevant for the East Asian and other emerging markets but will also further our understanding of the dynamics of the international capital market and assist in future courses for domestic financial system development.

Among developing economies, emerging markets, including those in East Asia, are those that have intensified financial linkages to the international capital market, and the current global financial crisis will undoubtedly have had large negative impacts on them. Above all, since the current crisis was triggered by the banking crisis in the United States and Europe, it is not difficult to imagine that those emerging markets that have strong linkages through bank loans would suffer heavily (International Monetary Fund [IMF] 2009).

From the viewpoint of emerging markets' linkages to the international capital market, of particular note is the contrast in the external balance between East Asia and Europe. Conventional economic growth theory predicts that international capital will flow from advanced to emerging market economies as water flows from high to low in pursuit of higher marginal product of capital; as a result, expenditures would exceed income (alternatively, investment exceeds savings), generating current account deficits in the recipient countries.

However, in the 2000s the contrast between conventional current account deficits in emerging markets in Europe and unconventional surpluses in East Asian countries is conspicuous. According to IMF (2008), a part of the contrast comes, first, from the usual structural factors – namely, large current account deficits in European emerging markets that resulted from liberalization of the financial sectors and enhanced growth prospects due to their accession to the

European Union (EU), while surpluses in East Asia resulted from insufficient liberalization of the financial sector and capital account and currency undervaluation with accumulation of foreign exchange reserves. However, the analysis cannot fully explain how undervaluation of East Asian currencies and/or huge foreign exchange reserves are related to their current account surpluses. In addition, we cannot help but be skeptical about the sustainability of unprecedented large persistent current account deficits in European emerging markets. Furthermore, we wonder whether their fixed exchange rates and capital account liberalization can be continued with a possible *sudden stop* of foreign capital inflow.

Before the Asian economic crisis in 1997, the most important focus of financial deepening in East Asia appeared to be savings mobilization. In fact, despite exceptionally high domestic savings rates, vigorous domestic investment demand required foreign savings beyond domestic savings. In the process, the efficiency of fund allocation deteriorated, investment risks ballooned, and then came the currency crisis. After the crisis, the focus shifted to allocative efficiency and risk diversification/management. Analyzing changes in financial structures in East Asia, Gill and Kharas (2007) argue that in order to sustain regional trade and investment growth, East Asia should further develop securities markets, which have advantages in pricing risks and attracting foreign savings. In reality, however, the current global financial crisis generated serious doubts about the ability of securities markets in evaluating risks, as will be discussed later.

This overview attempts to answer the following questions. First, how are the macro-financial linkages of the East Asian emerging markets characterized in terms of international capital flows, and how are they related to the impact of the global financial crisis on the region? Second, to what extent are the capital flows important to these countries' domestic flow of funds, and how are the domestic financial developments related to it? Furthermore, how does the global financial crisis affect international capital flows in the region and domestic financial developments, and what policy implications does the economic recovery, after the Asian as well as the global financial crises, have for macroeconomic management and regional financial cooperation regimes?

Our findings to these questions can be summarized as follows:

- If we look at the macro-financial linkages between East Asian emerging markets and the international capital market in terms of international capital flows, the composition of capital inflows changed broadly before and after the Asian crisis. For example, in terms of categories of capital flows, foreign direct investment (FDI), which is persistent and stable relative to other types of capital flows, became dominant, and intra-regional flows from old emerging to new emerging economies began to play a larger role than those from the United States, the EU and Japan.
- With regard to domestic financial systems in the East Asian emerging markets, it is confirmed that they are significantly less dependent on foreign

capital flows and are experiencing greater financial deepening than in other emerging markets. Moreover, structural reforms in the East Asian financial and corporate sectors witnessed some progress. In looking at their role in investment financing for the private sector, however, since the Asian crisis, financial intermediation remains retrenched, and their securities market, regarded as an alternative market, did not develop enough to serve as a substitute. As a result, the recovery of their domestic financial systems since the crisis has been far from remarkable compared to their real economic performances.

- Having said this, the current global financial crisis is very unlikely to impose large negative impacts on the East Asian emerging markets, as the Asian crisis did. This is probably because of the above-mentioned changes that have occurred in financial linkages and not because of post-Asian crisis development of the domestic financial systems in these countries. Furthermore, post-crisis domestic macroeconomic policies as well as the framework of regional financial cooperation can play only limited roles in preventing negative impacts from the global crisis.
- Current policy challenges will be, rather, to reestablish flexible macro-monetary policy regimes in the short run that can cope with growing market risks, and to seek domestic financial systems in the longer run that can cope with changing investment risks, beyond the conventional dichotomy between bank-based or market-based systems.

## 1. Macro-financial linkages and transmission of financial crises

The global financial crisis, which began with the burst of the U.S. housing market bubble in 2006, affected not only the United States but also Europe, where financial institutions held a large amount of securitized products related to U.S. subprime loans; this, in turn, led to global stagnation and then to the emerging market crises. Specifically, along with increasing integration of the international capital market, the linkages among national capital markets witnessed financial distresses almost comparable to those that occurred in the Great Depression of the 1930s.

Figure 1.1 shows financial stress indices[1] that measure asset market price volatilities in both advanced and emerging market economies.[2] The figure shows that the indices of the two groups moved together through the various crises, i.e., the emerging market financial crisis in 1997–8, the information technology bubble crisis in 2000–1, and the global crisis in 2007–9. In addition, we note that the stress in the emerging markets preceded that in advanced economies in the first case. However, it was the other way around in the second and third cases, when advanced economies pulled a trigger and their stresses were far larger and were transmitted to emerging markets with some significant time lags.

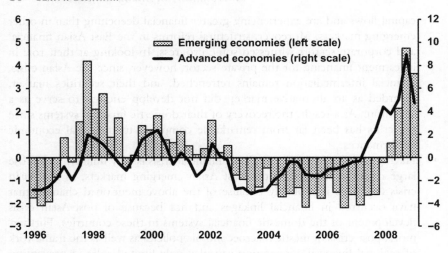

*Figure 1.1* Financial stress in emerging and advanced economies (levels of index, weighted GDP)

Source: International Monetary Fund, *World Economic Outlook*, April 2009, fig. 4.6.

With regard to capital flows to emerging markets before the global crisis, Figure 1.2 shows the financial exposure of emerging markets to advanced economies. Outstanding amounts of bank (and other) loans and portfolio (bonds and equities) investment flows are shown as a ratio to emerging market gross domestic product (GDP) from advanced to emerging market economies by region of emerging markets. On one hand, Asia was the largest recipient of bank loans, while Latin America was second and Europe was negligible before the Asian crisis. However, after the crisis and up until the mid-2000s, while Asia and Latin America showed a declining trend, Europe by contrast enjoyed some increase. On the other hand, the inflow of portfolio investment steadily increased in Asia, was stagnant in Latin America and began to increase from an initially low level in Europe. As such, the pattern of inflows varied significantly by category of capital and across regions.

Figures 1.3a and 1.3b show the regional patterns of the same capital flows from the investors' perspective. The upper panel of Figures 1.3a and 1.3b shows the outstanding amounts of investment as a ratio to investors' GDP for the three advanced economy regions. Bank loans remained relatively small in North America and declined sharply from significant levels in Japan after the Asian crisis. In contrast, for Europe, bank loans increased despite the emerging market crisis, particularly after the mid-2000s. As shown in the lower panels of Figures 1.3a and 1.3b, with regard to portfolio investments, the United States has been the largest investor, followed by Europe, and Japan and Australia are relatively

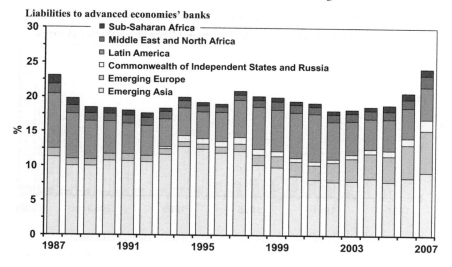

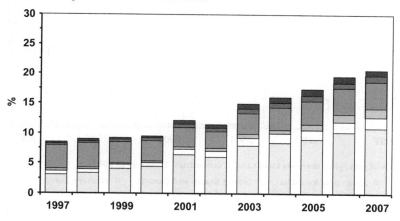

*Figure 1.2* Financial exposure of emerging markets to advanced economies (% of emerging economies' GDP)

Source: International Monetary Fund, *World Economic Outlook*, April 2009, chap. 4, fig. 4.9.

insignificant. Both the United States and Europe showed strong increasing trends, particularly since the 2000s.

These differences and/or contrasts in investment behaviors by investor country/region become clearer when reviewed by both investor and recipient. According to the lower panel of Figures 1.3a and 1.3b, advanced economies in Europe have not only an overwhelming share of bank loans in emerging

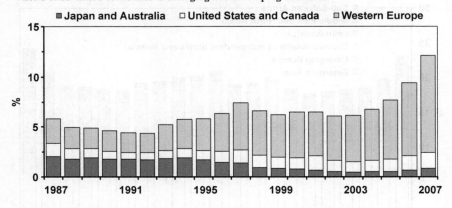

**Assets of advanced economies in emerging and developing economies**

**Portfolio exposure of advanced economies to emerging and developing economies**

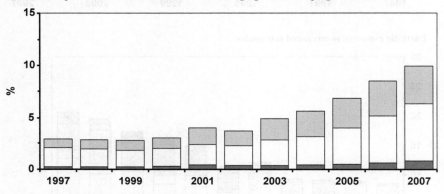

**Liabilities of emerging markets to advanced economies' banks as of 2007**

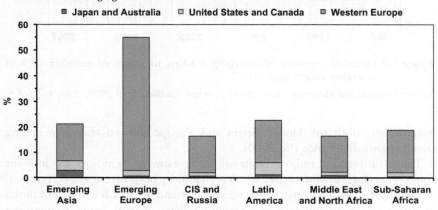

*Figure 1.3* Financial linkages between advanced and emerging economies: (a) % of advanced economies' GDP and (b) % of emerging economies' GDP

Source: International Monetary Fund, *World Economic Outlook*, April 2009, chap. 4, fig. 4.10.

Note: CIS: Commonwealth of Independent States.

Portfolio exposure of emerging markets to advanced economies as of 2007

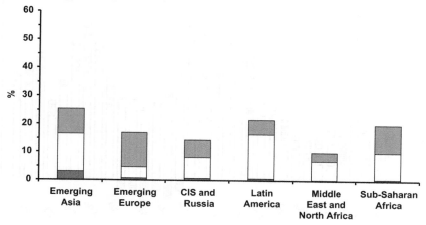

*Figure 1.3* (Continued)

markets in Europe but also a significant share across every emerging market in terms of recipients' GDP. In terms of portfolio investments, however, the United States is the largest investor in Latin America and the Middle East/North Africa; both the United States and Europe are competitive large investors in emerging markets in Asia, the Commonwealth of Independent States and Russia, and Africa, and Europe is the largest only in European emerging markets. Thus, we reconfirm that the relationship between investors and recipients varies both across regions and across categories of capital. Similar to investment decisions in general, international investments are a product of complex decisionmaking based on multiple factors, including risks and information asymmetry, which leads to diverse investment patterns across regions and categories of capital.

## 2. The changing patterns of international capital flows in East Asia

Recall that bank loans and portfolio investments are only part of the total foreign capital flows to emerging markets. Figure 1.4 shows foreign capital inflows to East Asia as a ratio of GDP by category of capital. Since the Latin American currency crisis in 1982, the share of bank and other loans has declined; instead, FDI has become the principal component. While portfolio bond and equity have become major players since the late 1990s, FDI has maintained the overwhelming share of capital flows. In addition, while bank loans and portfolio investments showed volatile movements (including sudden stops in 1997–8, 2000–1 and 2007–9 when internal and external financial stresses accumulated), FDI remains persistent as well as stable.

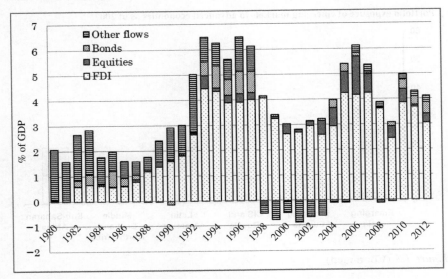

*Figure 1.4* Financial inflows to East Asia (% of GDP)

Source: Adapted from World Bank, *World Development Indicators* (http://databank.worldbank. org/data/views/variableSelection/selectvariables.aspx?source=world-development-indicators).

Note: FDI: foreign direct investment.

Figure 1.5, which shows foreign capital flows by category in Latin American and European emerging markets, clearly illustrates these characteristics. In Latin America, the following characteristics of the categories of capital appeared more clearly. First, the sudden stop of bank loans, which was the main category until the Mexican crisis, was one of the main factors that generated the lost decade of the 1980s. Second, the role of FDI was relatively minor, contrasting with East Asia. Third, the role of portfolio flows was relatively large in recovering capital inflows in the 1990s. Fourth, the quantitative importance of foreign capital flows was relatively large. In terms of this last point, the capital flows/GDP ratio in East Asia is at most 4 percent and is significantly lower than in Latin America, where it is around 7 percent; this is in contrast to the domestic savings rates of the two regions: domestic savings rates are higher in East Asia than in Latin America. We will discuss the meaning of this point in more detail later.

In the case of European emerging markets, foreign capital inflows have surged since the beginning of the 1990s when the transition to market economies began. Foreign capital began to enter in the form of public flows and FDI, and then increased along with the privatization of state enterprises. This was followed by portfolio flows, and, finally, bank loans began to increase from the latter half of the 1990s and then surged in the 2000s along with

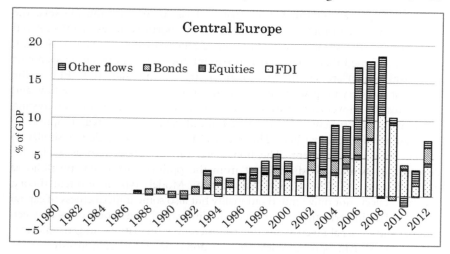

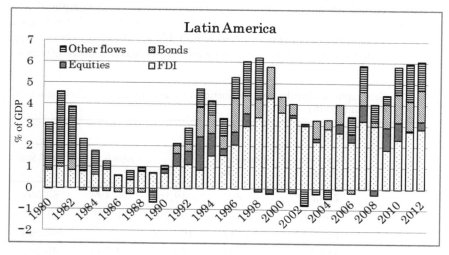

*Figure 1.5* Financial inflows to emerging markets (% of GDP)

Source: Adapted from World Bank, *World Development Indicators* (http://databank.worldbank.org/data/views/variableSelection/selectvariables.aspx?source=world-development-indicators).

Note: FDI: foreign direct investment.

the liberalization of the financial sector. While we will not go into detail, these developments come from the fact that their domestic financial systems relied on foreign banks, which differs from the cases of East Asia and Latin America.[3] In fact, their reliance on foreign capital was higher than 10 percent of GDP before the global financial crisis, far higher than in East Asia and Latin America.

To sum up, we confirmed, first, that in East Asian emerging markets, the principal category of foreign capital flows is FDI; portfolio investments replaced bank loans as the second-most important category of foreign capital. Second, we also confirmed that while FDI is persistent and stable, portfolio investments (and bank loans) are sensitive to financial stresses and that while FDI is the dominant category in quantity, portfolio investment is the most volatile flow and dominates the movement of capital flows. Finally, we confirmed an interesting fact that the investment behaviors of advanced economies by region appear to show an explicit regional bias. This regional bias can be regarded as similar to a home bias in investment. The home bias can be referred to as a bias for domestic investment products apart from the optimal investment portfolio as deduced from a CAPM (Capital Asset Pricing Model)–type investment theory. The bias reflects not only limited rationality but also some imperfectness of capital markets. The imperfectness might include differential transaction costs between internal and external investments due to differential regulations and/or information on investment opportunities between domestic and foreign investors.

Imperfect and asymmetric information often depends on geographical and time distances. In fact, the regional bias in investment in East Asian emerging markets is conspicuous in portfolio investment. Table 1.1 shows the outstanding amounts of international portfolio equity investment between countries/regions

*Table 1.1* Geographical distribution of portfolio equity investment (US$ millions, year end 2008)

| Destination | Investors | | | | |
| --- | --- | --- | --- | --- | --- |
| | Total value of investment | Emerging East Asia | EU15 | Japan | United States |
| China | 226,873 | 107,792 | 49,161 | 5,499 | 53,269 |
| Hong Kong | 165,473 | 22,091 | 56,900 | 8,915 | 61,483 |
| Japan | 626,077 | 16,713 | 197,226 | — | 347,600 |
| Korea | 112,278 | 7,591 | 39,259 | 6,799 | 45,287 |
| Malaysia | 25,278 | 7,173 | 7,162 | 529 | 6,673 |
| Philippines | 7,574 | 717 | 2,055 | 165 | 4,279 |
| Singapore | 60,188 | 4,408 | 20,430 | 3,074 | 24,028 |
| Chinese Taipei | 79,948 | 5,546 | 26,294 | 1,631 | 41,195 |
| Thailand | 24,211 | 3,215 | 8,477 | 683 | 6,670 |
| United States | 1,486,907 | 54,476 | 741,220 | 159,163 | — |
| Emerging East Asia | 701,822 | 158,533 | 209,739 | 27,295 | 242,884 |
| **Total value of investment** | 9,848,594 | 484,995 | 4,214,632 | 394,678 | 2,748,428 |

Source: Adapted from International Monetary Fund, Coordinated Portfolio Investment Survey (http://cpis.imf.org/), accessed in 2010.

at the end of 2008. International investment in East Asian emerging markets amounted to US$700 million, out of which US$240 million came from the United States, US$210 million from Europe (EU15, i.e., the major 15 member economies of the EU) and US$160 million from the East Asian emerging market itself. In other words, we should note that East Asian emerging markets have become a major investor in the region, next to Europe. While the share of the region as an investment destination remains slightly less than 10 percent of the world total, it is nevertheless worth noting that the region has appeared as a remarkable investment destination among emerging market regions. The fact that intra-regional investment is increasing dynamically is a notable new development when thinking about the region's future growth-finance.

As a matter of fact, increasing intra-regional investments are not limited to portfolio flows. Rather, this holds true for FDI, which, as discussed before, has been the major category of capital flows to East Asian emerging markets. There, the major investors are the ANIEs (Asian Newly Industrialized Economies, i.e., Hong Kong, Korea, Singapore and Chinese Taipei). Of course, we can see some intra-regional flows in Latin America, but to a lesser degree, and they are minimal in Europe. In other words, as far as East Asian emerging markets are concerned, in order to examine their linkages with the international capital market, it is not adequate just to look at their linkages with advanced economies, but it is necessary to note the role of *old* emerging markets as intra-regional important investors.

Finally, examining the linkages to the global capital market, in addition to foreign capital flows, it is also important to note the accumulation of official foreign exchange reserves. Since the Asian economic crisis in 1997, there has been a great deal of debate on the huge accumulation of official foreign exchange reserves in emerging markets, including East Asia.[4] In each region, the increase in reserves is far greater than before, and it is particularly remarkable in East Asia in terms of scale, timing and speed. In addition, various combinations of economies concluded foreign exchange swap agreements in the region, so that their provision of foreign exchange liquidities is far higher than official reserve accumulations in other regions.

From the above, we can summarize the changes in the linkages between the global capital market and East Asian emerging markets since the Asian crisis as follows:

- With regard to foreign capital inflows, non-debt-creating FDI has been the primary category and is stable and persistent, and intra-regional investors have recently become one of the significant groups of investors. Relevant factors explaining these developments include opening-up policies of capital accounts as well as sustained industrial growth in the region.
- Bank loans and portfolio investments are sensitive to developments in the capital market and often show volatile movements that magnify business cycles. We can point to the inherent imperfectness of capital markets lying in the background, and we should therefore note the increasing presence of intra-regional investments as a stabilizing factor.

- The accumulation of official foreign exchange reserves in emerging markets since the Asian crisis has been remarkable, particularly in East Asia, and it appears to have helped in coping with capital market stresses. Nevertheless, whether the accumulation of foreign exchange reserves is excessive or not is debatable.

## 3. Financial developments in emerging markets

How have these changes in financial linkages affected domestic finance? More concretely, we wonder how external finance is linked to the functions of domestic financial systems. First, we examine how important foreign capital is to sustain factor accumulation for economic growth and observe the developments of investment and savings balances.

Figure 1.6 shows the investment and savings ratios (as a percentage of GDP) in emerging markets in East Asia and Europe. In East Asia, while both investment and savings rates show an upward trend over the 1980s and 1990s, investment fell sharply in the face of the Asian crisis and recovered slowly; as a result, savings were significantly larger than investment for quite a while, and, in particular, the gap expanded before the global financial crisis. While both investment and savings amounted to as much as 35 to 40 percent of GDP for the regional average, domestic investment could be more than financed by domestic savings without relying on foreign capital or savings, at least in net terms.

European emerging markets contrast with those of East Asia. First, their investment rate has continued to exceed their savings rate, so that net foreign

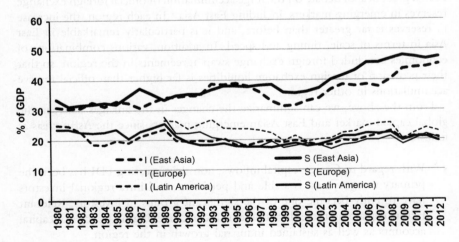

*Figure 1.6* Savings (S) and investment (I) (% of GDP)

Source: Adapted from World Bank, *World Development Indicators* (http://databank.worldbank. org/data/views/variableSelection/selectvariables.aspx?source=world-development-indicators).

capital inflows are indispensable to maintain the regional investment rate.[5] The savings rate is around 20 to 25 percent of GDP, far below that of East Asia, which is more than 40 percent. Note, however, that European emerging markets are not an exception among developing economies in this regard. In fact, Latin American emerging markets have similarly low savings rates, and their current investment rates are barely supported by net external inflows.

Next, we look at how and to what extent these domestic savings are used to finance domestic investment. Investment is internally financed through retained earnings and/or externally financed through borrowing or bond issuance, which is usually the case in developing economies, including emerging markets. External finance comes mainly from financial intermediation rather than from the securities market. Reflecting the degree of financial intermediation, Figure 1.7 shows banks' credits to the private sector as a ratio of GDP. According to the figure, financial intermediation in East Asia has maintained a strong increasing trend since the 1980s, and its outstanding amount became equal to the GDP on average (though there was some stagnation since the Asian crisis). By contrast, those measures in European emerging markets reached at most 60 percent of GDP despite their rapid increases since the mid-2000s. As to the degree of financial deepening, East Asia is again an exception among developing economies.

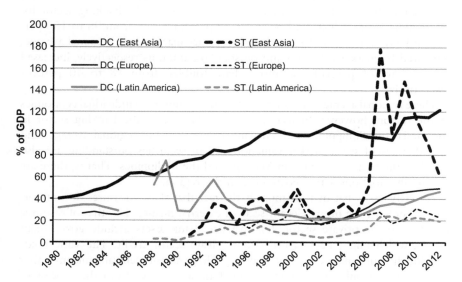

*Figure 1.7* Financial depth (% of GDP)

Source: Adapted from World Bank, *World Development Indicators* (http://databank.worldbank. org/data/views/variableSelection/selectvariables.aspx?source=world-development-indicators).

Note: DC: domestic credit to the private sector; ST: stock market turnover.

To sum up, in view of the linkages to the international capital market, the contrast between emerging markets in East Asia and those in regions elsewhere can be summarized as follows:

- The reliance on foreign capital flows in East Asian emerging markets is far smaller than in other developing countries. In fact, East Asian emerging economies are net creditors to the rest of the world.
- In view of the intermediation within domestic financial systems, the amount of financial intermediation not only is larger in East Asia as compared with other regions but has expanded in a sustained way, thereby leading to greater financial deepening.

## 4. Development of domestic financial systems in East Asia

These factors noted in the previous section above may or may not suggest that the financial system in East Asia can be said to have recovered against the headwinds from the Asian economic crises.

External financing has three channels: (i) the banking sector, (ii) the stock market and (iii) the securities market. Table 1.2 shows the size of the three channels in terms of outstanding amounts (in U.S. dollars) and in terms of the ratio to GDP in East Asia in 1997 and 2005, as reported by World Bank (Gill and Kharas 2007). Measured by asset size, the size of the banking sector for the regional average increased by about 50 percent, rising from 95 to 150 percent of GDP. The size of the stock and securities markets, as a regional average, measured by market valuation and outstanding amounts respectively, increased from 37 to 71 percent and more than doubled from 18 to 40 percent respectively.

These regional averages mask large differences among the individual economies in the region, however. In fact, growth in the size of the banking sector in Indonesia, the Philippines and Thailand is less than the regional average, and growth rates of stock market valuation and of securities outstanding are also less than the regional average in Malaysia and the Philippines. That is, there are significant variations across economies in the region.

Nevertheless, what matters more is the fact that these measures do not correctly represent the most relevant scale of external finance, i.e., that of resource transfers to the private sector. For instance, bank assets include government bonds, which might have crowded out private sector credit. The same holds true for the outstanding amount of bonds. Government, central bank and other public bonds would crowd out part of domestic savings from the process of resource transfers to the private sector.

Thus, let us look at Table 1.3, which shows direct measures of financial intermediation to the private sector including private credit for the banking sector and private bonds outstanding that are separated from public bonds for six East Asian economies (China, Indonesia, Korea, Malaysia, the Philippines

Table 1.2 Domestic financial systems of East Asia

| | Bank assets | | | | Equity market capitalization | | | | Bonds outstanding | | | |
|---|---|---|---|---|---|---|---|---|---|---|---|---|
| | US$ billions | | % of GDP | | US$ billions | | % of GDP | | US$ billions | | % of GDP | |
| | 1997 | 2005 | 1997 | 2005 | 1997 | 2005 | 1997 | 2005 | 1997 | 2005 | 1997 | 2005 |
| China | 1,125.7 | 3,692.2 | 124.6 | 163.1 | 101.4 | 401.9 | 11.2 | 17.8 | 116.4 | 552.0 | 12.9 | 24.4 |
| Indonesia | 74.1 | 140.0 | 31.1 | 49.8 | 29.1 | 81.4 | 12.2 | 28.9 | 4.5 | 55.2 | 1.9 | 19.6 |
| Korea | 196.4 | 736.1 | 37.9 | 93.5 | 41.9 | 718.0 | 8.1 | 91.2 | 130.3 | 599.8 | 25.2 | 76.2 |
| Malaysia | 100.9 | 208.5 | 100.9 | 159.4 | 93.2 | 180.5 | 93.2 | 138.0 | 57.0 | 115.1 | 57.0 | 88.0 |
| Philippines | 46.5 | 62.2 | 56.1 | 63.2 | 31.2 | 39.8 | 37.7 | 40.4 | 18.5 | 36.1 | 22.4 | 36.7 |
| Thailand | 120.3 | 183.0 | 79.7 | 103.6 | 22.8 | 123.9 | 15.1 | 70.1 | 10.7 | 72.1 | 7.1 | 40.8 |
| Hong Kong | 361.6 | 790.1 | 205.1 | 444.6 | 413.3 | 1,055.0 | 234.5 | 593.6 | 45.8 | 82.9 | 26.0 | 46.6 |
| Singapore | 117.0 | 216.4 | 122.0 | 185.4 | 106.3 | 257.3 | 110.8 | 220.4 | 23.7 | 79.8 | 24.7 | 68.2 |
| Total | 2,142.5 | 6,028.5 | 94.6 | 149.5 | 839.2 | 2,857.8 | 37.0 | 70.9 | 406.9 | 1,593.0 | 18.0 | 39.5 |

Source: Gill and Kharas (2007).

*Table 1.3* Domestic financial systems: intermediation to the private sector (ratio to GDP)

| Country | Year | Private credit | Private bonds | Public bonds | Stock market capitalization |
|---|---|---|---|---|---|
| China | 1992 | 0.00 | 0.03 | 0.03 | 0.02 |
| | 1997 | 0.00 | 0.03 | 0.04 | 0.17 |
| | 2002 | 0.00 | 0.08 | 0.12 | 0.34 |
| | 2007 | 0.00 | 0.15 | 0.29 | 1.32 |
| Indonesia | 1992 | 0.44 | 0.00 | 0.00 | 0.07 |
| | 1997 | 0.54 | 0.02 | 0.01 | 0.28 |
| | 2002 | 0.18 | 0.01 | 0.26 | 0.14 |
| | 2007 | 0.23 | 0.02 | 0.17 | 0.41 |
| Korea | 1992 | 0.97 | 0.34 | 0.14 | 0.31 |
| | 1997 | 1.21 | 0.33 | 0.10 | 0.18 |
| | 2002 | 1.29 | 0.63 | 0.27 | 0.43 |
| | 2007 | 1.01 | 0.59 | 0.48 | 1.02 |
| Malaysia | 1992 | 0.89 | 0.18 | 0.45 | 1.29 |
| | 1997 | 1.39 | 0.40 | 0.25 | 2.02 |
| | 2002 | 1.20 | 0.53 | 0.35 | 1.29 |
| | 2007 | 1.01 | 0.55 | 0.36 | 1.56 |
| Philippines | 1992 | 0.22 | 0.00 | 0.31 | 0.25 |
| | 1997 | 0.54 | 0.00 | 0.27 | 0.69 |
| | 2002 | 0.37 | 0.00 | 0.33 | 0.53 |
| | 2007 | 0.28 | 0.01 | 0.34 | 0.60 |
| Thailand | 1992 | 0.89 | 0.06 | 0.03 | 0.42 |
| | 1997 | 1.54 | 0.08 | 0.01 | 0.41 |
| | 2002 | 0.97 | 0.12 | 0.21 | 0.33 |
| | 2007 | 0.83 | 0.16 | 0.35 | 0.69 |

Source: Adapted from World Bank, Financial Development and Structure Database. (http://econ.worldbank.org/WBSITE/EXTERNAL/EXTDEC/EXTRESEARCH/), accessed in 2009.

and Thailand). The data, covering the periods before and after the financial crises, reveal several points. First, only China recovered the pre-crisis level of private credits after the Asian financial crisis. The level of private credits in the other five economies continued to be stagnant after the crisis, particularly in Indonesia, the Philippines and Thailand (in fact, their private credits remained as low as half of their 1997 levels). In examining private bonds outstanding, while China, Korea and Malaysia have observed comparatively rapid increases, they are not yet large enough to offset decreases in private credit. Moreover, in the case of Indonesia and the Philippines, no symptom of growth in private bonds can be found. Rather, we see remarkable increases only in public bonds in the region except for Malaysia and the Philippines after the crisis, which may or may not have crowded out private bonds.

In sum, the strong growth of bank assets and bonds outstanding in Table 1.2 resulted mainly because banks provided credits not to the private sector but to governments by buying government bonds, and the public sector issued bonds to remedy the banking sector and financing fiscal deficits. The economic growth after the Asian crisis was not underpinned either by banks' financial intermediation to the private sector or by the securities markets' offering of themselves as an alternative conduit of resource transfers to the private sector.

Nevertheless, the often discussed and well-known vulnerabilities of domestic financial systems have been restructured significantly thus far. As a matter of fact, there seems to be some evidence of optimization of bank size through bank consolidation, strengthening of bank capital bases through injection of public funds and restructuring of nonperforming loans, and resolution of excess leverages of nonfinancial firms.[6] However, there has been little or no progress on the front of institutional development in private bond markets.

Furthermore, an additional new development is the recent rise in the corporate savings rate. Actually, in both advanced and emerging markets, including East Asia, an upward trend in the corporate savings rate has been commonly witnessed since around 2000.[7] This implies that compared to the past, the corporate sector as a whole tends not to distribute dividends but rather retains its earnings for internal finance.

From the above observations, our preliminary assessment of the domestic financial systems in East Asia is as follows:

- The recovery of the domestic financial systems after the Asian crisis is far from complete. In fact, they have not returned to their pre-crisis levels yet, in contrast to the recovery and dynamism of their real economies.
- Particularly notable are the retrenchment of private credits on one hand and the slow growth of private bond markets on the other.
- Probably because of the above, growth of the real economy appears to be underpinned less by external financing through the domestic financial system and more by FDI (foreign savings) and own finance (corporate savings), both of which can be regarded as internal financing.

Having said the above, however, we should note that if we compare East Asian emerging markets with those in Latin America and Europe, financial development in the latter regions is far retarded in the long run as well as stagnant now in the short run. As a matter of fact, countries who are facing possible sudden stops of international capital flows triggered by the global financial crisis are not in East Asia nor Latin America but rather in the European emerging markets, who could suffer from their lost decades from now on.

## 5. Policy implications

In this final section, some policy implications are drawn from the above observations. First, we discuss immediate policy issues that are of concern to the economic policy authorities in the region. Subsequently, some alternative policy frameworks are pursued. Finally, we reexamine the conventional views on development of domestic financial systems in the longer run.

### 5.1. Immediate policy issues

Worrisome issues to domestic policy authorities relate to three aspects. First, what matters is the direction of exchange rates and capital inflows in the very short run. The shrinkage of capital markets owing to the global crisis has destabilized international capital flows. Losing sight of which destinations offer quality investments, the capital flows are likely to rush into emerging markets, including East Asia, which appear to be the only growth pole left intact. Because of elevated general risk perceptions, however, the capital flows tend to be sensitive to any news. Consequently, at this moment, currency appreciation resulting from capital inflows – rather than either sudden stops or capital outflows – is likely to undermine the real economy.

Second, international business cycles are worrisome and are potentially affected by several factors including how fast the recovery of advanced economies will be, whether capital flows will change greatly when the United States graduates from monetary easing, how likely it is that China and East Asian emerging markets will be forced to follow monetary tightening to combat inflation, and whether international capital flows tend to magnify business cycles.

Third, with respect to financial systems, worrisome are the issues regarding domestic financial systems that were revealed by the Asian crisis, i.e., financial disintermediation, high domestic savings rates and stagnant domestic investment and consumption.[8] Facing the global imbalances, East Asia intends to rebalance toward domestic demand; however, since their trade and investment structure relies on exports, particularly extra-regional markets, the longer the stagnation of EU and the United States, the more difficult the realization of their rebalancing will be.[9]

### 5.2. Policy frameworks for macro-financial linkages

Furthermore, in order to cope with foreseeable volatile exchange rates and international capital flows, both domestic policies and medium-term regional cooperation frameworks will have to be reexamined.

First, in terms of domestic policies, macro-prudential policy and foreign exchange reserve policy must be reexamined. Review of the former is needed to harmonize monetary policy with financial system stability, and one of the new issues is to what extent the policy should weight exchange rates, product price inflation and asset price inflation.[10] Although we managed to control product inflation beforehand, it has become difficult to neglect the influence of volatilities of exchange rates and/or asset prices on business cycles. Conventional wisdom appears to dismiss the need to regard asset product inflation as a stability target, but is this true? In fact, some studies using the financial conditions index show significant impacts of asset price movements on the real economy in advanced economies.[11]

We need to pursue a more flexible approach to macroeconomic policy management, taking account of multiple nominal anchors instead of a single anchor such as product inflation or exchange rate stability. Then we have to adopt highly sophisticated discretionary policy management, setting up some sophisticated nominal anchor based on continuous monitoring of multiple asset price movements on one hand, and taking structural changes in policy transmission mechanisms into account on the other hand. While rule-based policy management may cope with business cycles that are well characterized as repetitive games, we may have to prepare for faster structural changes in macroeconomic systems through accelerated technological progress and factor accumulation in both advanced and emerging market economies.

On the other hand, foreign exchange reserve policy can also play a significant role. We have already touched on the numerous debates on whether foreign exchange reserves in East Asia are excessive or not. If emerging markets are not immune from the original sin, and then from external debt crises, their policy authorities understandably consider it indispensable to monitor external debt and accumulate foreign exchange reserves for exchange rate stability. Unfortunately, the effectiveness of foreign reserve accumulation in attaining exchange rate stability is doubtful, however. In fact, these countries had to face severe exchange rate volatilities in the midst of the global financial crisis despite their good macroeconomic fundamentals and ample foreign exchange reserves.[12]

Second, because currency crises tend to be contagious to neighboring economies, a framework of regional cooperation has been pursued. The Chiang Mai Initiative is a regional policy framework comprising swaps of foreign exchange liquidity, macroeconomic policy dialogue and monitoring of capital flows. The Asian Bond Market Initiative is a framework to develop a regional market for regional currency–denominated bonds. The goal of the former is to try to build a regional safety net for both crisis prevention and crisis management, namely, a regional macro-prudential policy framework. The latter, by easing issuance of regional currency–denominated bonds, enables international financing without being influenced by exchange rate fluctuations among major currencies, thereby becoming immune from original sin problems and promoting bond market development under regional initiatives.

Foreign exchange swap agreements, however, have an intrinsic dilemma: economies may hesitate to use the swap because it gives a negative signal about their credibility to the international capital market. As a result, the swap arrangements may or may not fully play the role of lender of last resort. Moreover, the ultimate goal of exchange rate stabilization in the region heavily depends on exchange rates among major currencies, which are not within the realm of the Chiang Mai Initiative. In fact, in the current global financial crisis, foreign exchange swap arrangements do not seem to have been effective in stabilizing currency values.[13]

With regard to the Asian Bond Market Initiative, we have already observed that financial disintermediation has prevailed in some domestic financial markets and that the momentum to restructure and/or develop domestic bond markets has not been met. In addition, the private corporate sector has strengthened internal rather than external finance, and multinational corporations have strengthened intra-firm financing with their headquarters at home. Moreover, as investment rates themselves have remained stagnant, the private sector's needs for bond financing are lacking momentum to proceed with the Asian Bond Market Initiative. That is, insofar as the needs for institutional reforms of domestic bond markets are not strong enough to shake the status quo of domestic financial systems, there are reasons why we do not see vigorous momentum for growing domestic bond markets; in fact, the growth of a regional bond market appears to be far-fetched.

Ultimately, one real outcome of the post-crisis regional economic cooperation might be that the countries have successfully reduced information asymmetry through regular policy dialogues and peer monitoring. While this may have been an unexpected outcome, it reflects important progress. In the private sector, multinational corporations have minimized information asymmetries across borders through their networks, but without a regional framework for economic cooperation, national governments may have had limited opportunities to exchange and share information. If this is the case, the fact that many policy authorities have spared a lot of time and energy in various frameworks of international and regional cooperation can be understood as producing international and/or regional public goods through creating information and/or minimizing information costs.

### 5.3. Future course for financial deepening

Finally, let me touch on the future course of domestic financial systems in the long run. Securitization has been closed up as an alternative to bank financial intermediation because the latter is regarded as disadvantageous in financing risky investment such as venture capital. In addition, in the literature on financial development, there are pros and cons with regard to two types of financial development, i.e., bank based as in continental Europe and Japan versus market based as in Anglophonic economies.[14] While it is clear to us that governments often fail, it has been also become clear that markets are not good at looking into the future either. As a matter of fact, through a series of recent crises, we know that markets tend to support herd behavior in the short run and tend to predict future behaviors via a simple extrapolation of the past and present. Good examples of this are the recent asset market bubbles where self-fulfilling expectations led to a repeated series of bubble bursts.

Information on risky investment opportunities is generally not certain even for actual investors. It is more difficult, therefore, for a third person to price risks using a variety of indirect information. Generally, information on investment opportunities is intrinsically individual and specific so that it should be known to be only partially commonalized and standardized. In this sense, it should be noted that securitization is far from being a panacea for capital market failure, and the trend toward securitization needs to be reexamined.

In this respect, what interests us most is the recent upward trend in corporate savings rates or the regression to internal financing that started since the 2000s. The rise in FDI as well as retained earnings suggests that those who know best about investment opportunities have increased self-finance. If this is the case, financial disintermediation of the banking sector and the slow growth in bonds markets found in East Asia are part of this trend change and are nothing to worry about. We are not sure, however, that this observation holds true only for advanced economies but may also hold true for emerging markets in East Asia.

## Notes

1 Financial stress indices are calculated as a weighted average of price volatilities of multiple asset markets including long-term and short-term financial markets, the corporate stock market, the bond market, the credit market and the foreign exchange market. For a detailed explanation, see IMF (2009, Appendix 4.1).

2 The seventeen advanced economies are Australia, Austria, Belgium, Canada, Denmark, Finland, France, Germany, Italy, Japan, the Netherlands, Norway, Spain, Sweden, Switzerland, the United Kingdom and the United States. The twenty-six emerging market economies are Argentina, Brazil, Chile, China, Colombia, the Czech Republic, Egypt, Hungary, India, Indonesia, Israel, Korea, Malaysia, Mexico, Morocco, Pakistan, Peru, the Philippines, Poland, Russia, the Slovak Republic, Slovenia, South Africa, Sri Lanka, Thailand and Turkey.

3 In the literature on financial development, it is often argued that the entry of foreign banks generally contributes to financial development in developing economies through external economies created by the foreign banks' advanced financial know-how. When their activities depend on economic conditions in their home economies (i.e., the activities are independent of host economies, for instance, as in the current global financial crisis, when these banks were forced to retrench the credit supply in host economies because of financial meltdowns in their home economies), however, the presence of foreign banks generates external diseconomies to hosts. European emerging markets started their transition to a market economy with vulnerable domestic banking systems that were part of their socialist centrally planned economies; as a result, these countries had no choice but to rely on foreign banks. This resulted in an overwhelming presence of foreign banks in the emerging European markets. In contrast, in East Asia, domestic banks have dominated the domestic financial markets, and their post-crisis efforts to open up to foreign banks did not produce any significant changes in their market structure.

4 The accumulation of foreign exchange reserves in East Asia since the Asian crisis is notable both historically and in comparison with other economies. It is conventionally argued that there are two main motives for foreign reserve accumulation, i.e., self-insurance against currency crises out of precautionary motives for one and undervaluation of currencies with *mercantilism* to maintain international

competitiveness, to which Aizenman et al. (2011) add exchange rate stability as a third motive.

5 In assessing macro-financial linkages of European emerging markets to the international capital market, before the global financial crisis, their current account deficits were argued to have promoted their economic growth and contributed to their income catching up with advanced economies (Abiad et al. 2007). The winds have changed 180 degrees, however, and the post-crisis literature has been toned down to argue the risk of financial integration (e.g., Fabrizio et al. 2009).

6 According to Gill and Kharas (2007), the prudence of the banking sectors in East Asia has been significantly improved through restructuring and consolidation, bank regulation and supervision have been strengthened, the corporate sector has been deleveraged and has improved its balance sheets, and the banking sectors have expanded their profit basis by strengthening consumers' credit.

7 For advanced economies, increases in corporate savings are commonly found, particularly since the information technology bubble burst. The IMF (2005) and others argue that this is not a temporary phenomenon to simply adjust excess liabilities and capital formation in the 1990s but may be the result of more significant structural changes, including (i) profits enhanced by low interest rates and tax reduction, (ii) lower relative prices of capital goods through technological progress, (iii) the shift to overseas capital formation, and (iv) the increased optimal levels of liquid assets because of increased management risks and growing importance of knowledge capital. Moreover, even East Asian emerging markets, including China, have shown some upward trend in the corporate savings rates. In particular, although it is often argued that low dividends in state-owned enterprises and weak corporate governance are to blame for the high corporate savings in China, Bayoumi et al. (2010) argue that factors related to high corporate savings rates in China are common with the above global trend.

8 Prasad (2009) argues that slow consumption in China is in tandem with its high household savings rate. In particular, he emphasizes the importance of financial reforms aimed at expanding domestic demand from the household sector. He argues that households have remained severely constrained in terms of their access to the domestic financial market even though they were severed from the social safety nets since the 1978 opening up of the economy.

9 Examining the degree of international industrial linkages using international input–output tables, Pula and Peltonen (2009) showed that the development of production networks in East Asia has deepened their linkages to advanced economies such as the EU and the United States, while their trade figures tend to exaggerate their reliance on these advanced economies.

10 Monetary policy regimes in advanced economies have been analyzed in such contexts as dynamic inconsistency of monetary policy, independence of central banks, nominal anchors for (product) inflation, etc. Meanwhile, monetary regimes in emerging markets have been left outside these contexts; this is because they are merely price-takers in the international market, they are not immune from the original sin problem, and their institutions are characterized by information asymmetry, default risks, moral hazard and other kinds of market failure. The global financial crisis revealed that these market failures can be intrinsic to capital markets of advanced economies as well as the international capital market. In fact, Frankel (2010) argues for reexamination of monetary policy regimes for both advanced and emerging markets.

11 The financial conditions index attempts to comprehensively capture the business cycle effect of changes in multiple financial markets, reflected in such variables as long-term and short-term interest rates, stock prices, exchange rates and credit market conditions. In the case of Japan, while the financial bubble burst in the

early 1990s is well known, the analysis using the financial conditions index reveals that the role of financial channels is as large in the global financial crises as it was in the 1990s (Shinkai and Kohsaka 2010).

12 A typical example is Korea, which experienced the largest exchange rate depreciation in East Asia despite apparently sufficient fundamentals and ample foreign exchange reserves. Korea is also known to have opened up its financial accounts most actively in East Asia since the Asian crisis.

13 Examining whether swap lines substitute for foreign exchange reserves based on precautionary motives, using cross-country data, Aizenman et al. (2011) found that the substitution effect depends on the scale of foreign exchange reserves and is fairly limited. They also found that the feasibility of bilateral swap lines is highly limited to cases where suppliers have high credibility (such as the Federal Reserve of the United States) on one hand and where applicants have an excellent macroeconomic stability record on the other; on top of this, there are close interests between these two groups, such as the large presence of U.S. banks. Here again we can see the basic tradeoff that prerequisites for swap lines are too difficult to utilize for those countries that need them.

14 Recent literature has become less supportive of this dichotomy between bank-based and market-based financial development (Levine 1997). Rather, Demirgüç-Kunt and Levine (2008) have summarized empirical studies as follows: (i) economies with developed financial systems tend to grow faster whether their financial systems are bank or market based; (ii) this is not because of the simultaneity between real growth and financial development; and (iii) financial systems tend to relax external finance constraints on corporate firms as well as industries.

## References and Further Readings

Abiad, Abdul, Daniel Leigh and Ashoka Mody. 2007. International finance and income convergence: Europe is different. International Monetary Fund Working Paper, WP/07/64 (March). International Monetary Fund, Washington, DC.

Aizenman, Joshua, Yothin Jinjarak and Donghyun Park. 2011. International reserves and swap lines: substitutes or complements? *International Review of Economics and Finance* 20, Volume 20 (1), January, pp. 5–18.

Bates, Thomas W., Kathleen M. Kahle and Rene M. Stulz. 2009. Why do U.S. firms hold so much more cash than they used to? *Journal of Finance* 64 (5), September, pp. 1985–2021.

Bayoumi, Tamim, Hui Tong and Shang-Jin Wei. 2010. The Chinese corporate savings puzzle: a firm-level cross-country perspective. National Bureau of Economic Research Working Paper 16432 (October). National Bureau of Economic Research, Cambridge, MA.

Demirgüç-Kunt, Asli and Ross Levine. 2008. Finance, financial sector policies, and long-run growth. (March.) World Bank, Washington, DC.

Detragiache, Enrica, Thierry Tressel and Poonam Gupta. 2006. Foreign banks in poor countries: theory and evidence. International Monetary Fund Working Paper 06/18. International Monetary Fund, Washington, DC.

Fabrizio, Stefania, Daniel Leigh and Ashoka Mody. 2009. The second transition: Eastern Europe in perspective. International Monetary Fund Working Paper, WP/09/43 (March). International Monetary Fund, Washington, DC.

Frankel, Jeffrey A. 2010. Monetary policy in emerging markets: a survey. National Bureau of Economic Research Working Paper 16125 (June). National Bureau of Economic Research, Cambridge, MA.

Gill, Indermit and Homi Kharas. 2007. *An East Asian renaissance: ideas for economic growth.* World Bank, Washington, DC.

Hsu, Hsiufen and Akira Kohsaka. 2010. Common monetary policy in East Asia? Counterfactual experiments of its implementation. Paper presented at the JSPS EU-Japan Joint Workshop on Spillover Effects and Cycle Effects of Regional Integration: East Asia and EU, Catholic University Leuven, Belgium, January 29–30.

International Monetary Fund (IMF). 2005. Awash with cash: why are corporate savings so high? In *World Economic Outlook*, Chapter 4. International Monetary Fund, Washington, DC.

International Monetary Fund (IMF). 2008. Financial stress and economic downturns. In *World Economic Outlook,* Chapter 4. International Monetary Fund, Washington, DC.

International Monetary Fund (IMF). 2009. How linkages fuel the fire: the transmission of financial stress from advanced to emerging economies. In *World Economic Outlook*, Chapter 4. International Monetary Fund, Washington, DC.

Jeanne, Olivier. 2007. International reserves in emerging market countries: too much of a good thing? Brookings Papers on Economic Activity 1. Brookings Institution, Washington, DC.

Levine, R. 1997. Financial development and economic growth: views and agenda. *Journal of Economic Literature* 35(2), June 688–726.

Prasad, Eswar S. 2009. Rebalancing growth in Asia. National Bureau of Economic Research Working Paper 15169 (July). National Bureau of Economic Research, Cambridge, MA.

Pula, Gabor and Tuomas A. Peltonen. 2009. Has emerging Asia decoupled? An analysis of production and trade linkages using the Asian International Input–output table. European Central Bank Working Paper No. 993 (January). European Central Bank, Frankfurt am Main.

Shinkai, Jun-ichi and Akira Kohsaka. 2010. Financial linkages and business cycles of Japan: an analysis using financial conditions index. Osaka School of International Public Policy Discussion Paper, DP-2010-E-008 (October). Osaka University, Osaka.

# 2 Macro-financial linkage and financial deepening in China[1]

*Kumiko Okazaki and Tomoyuki Fukumoto*

## 1. Introduction

During the recent global financial crisis, the Chinese economy demonstrated a tolerance to shocks from overseas or a potential power to continue its high growth. Although the economy displayed a rapid slowdown in the latter half of 2008, with a severe decline in the demand from its major international trading partners, it escaped falling into a deep recession. Boosted by the government's stimulus policies, it picked up quickly from the second quarter of 2009.

Several conditions enabled China to keep its economy less vulnerable and realize a quick recovery. Few domestic financial markets were directly affected by the turbulence in the foreign financial markets. The relatively strict control of cross-border capital transactions, the large accumulation of foreign exchange reserves, and the recapitalized banking system acted as bulwarks against the shock of the crisis that originated outside of the country. The sound fiscal position and abundant domestic savings became sources of the government's aggressive stimulus policies. To date, the domestic banks, as a whole, have functioned well, mobilizing the savings for the country's strong economic recovery.

However, the factors that protected and stimulated China's economic growth seem to carry with them substantial risks and challenges to the economy. Too much reliance on the banking sector and less developed capital markets distorts the efficient use of domestic funds. The dominance of the state-owned sector in formal financial markets drives private enterprises into informal financial markets in the country. The extremely high domestic savings rate is largely the result of a disproportionately high capital share and insufficient public support for health care, education, and pensions; it also raises a serious discussion about the global imbalance among major countries. As economic globalization continues to develop in China, the volume of cross-border capital transfer is also growing significantly. In addition to the huge current account surplus and massive foreign direct investment (FDI), capital inflows through securities and other investment accounts are growing substantially. It has become increasingly difficult for the Chinese authorities to manage the rapidly accumulating foreign exchange reserves safely and efficiently.

In this study, we first review the factors that have made the Chinese economy and financial markets less vulnerable to the global financial crisis and analyze the recent change in China's macro-financial linkage overseas, by focusing on the movement of cross-border capital transactions. Then we discuss the challenges that the Chinese financial system reform faces in furthering the sustainable development of the economy.

## 2. Underlying conditions that have made the Chinese economy less vulnerable

### 2.1. Similarities and differences between the Asian financial crisis and the recent crisis

During the Asian financial crisis, China possessed some advantages that shielded it from the negative effects of the crisis. Lardy (1998) pointed out that the inconvertibility of the Chinese currency for capital account transactions, massive inflows of FDI, lower dependence on short-term borrowings, sizable trade surpluses, and increased foreign exchange reserves helped to maintain a relatively stable Chinese financial market in 1997. In addition, the Chinese government's guarantee on bank deposits as well as its intervention in the decision-making process of banks largely eased the credit crunch in the second half of 1998 (Fernald and Babson, 1999). Many of these factors continue to be relevant.

On the other hand, there is a significant difference between the periods of the Asian financial crisis and the recent global crisis. Today, the flow of private capital has become larger and more volatile (as discussed in the next section). A larger capital flow implies that China is subject to larger external shocks. Hence, it would have been more difficult for China to maintain a stable economy without the following fundamentals.

### 2.2. Strong economic and financial fundamentals

During the recent global financial crisis, some factors worked favorably in keeping the Chinese economy relatively stable. Among them, (a) the favorable external position, (b) the healthy fiscal position, (c) modest leverage, (d) a high amount of domestic savings, and (e) a stable banking system were especially effective, although they were not in a perfect condition for a sustainable economic development in a longer perspective.

### a. Favorable external position

China's external position has improved remarkably since the late 1990s. Its dependence on external debt declined and its foreign exchange reserves surged, while its current account surplus expanded rapidly until 2007 (Figure 2.1). Regarding its international investment position, China is a net surplus country.

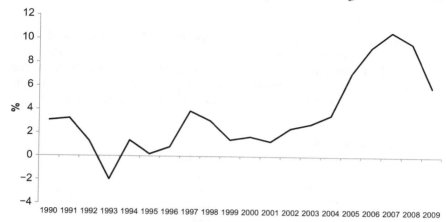

*Figure 2.1* Current account balance in China (% of nominal GDP)
Source: International Monetary Fund (2010).

*Table 2.1* China's external debt and foreign exchange reserves (US$ billions)

|  | December 1998 | December 2007 | December 2008 | December 2009 | June 2010 |
|---|---|---|---|---|---|
| External debt | 146.0 | 373.6 | 374.7 | 428.7 | 513.8 |
| Foreign exchange reserves | 149.8 | 1,534.9 | 1,953.3 | 2,399.2 | 2,454.3 |

Source: "Data and Statistics" section of the website of the State Administration of Foreign Exchange (http://www.safe.gov.cn).

The outstanding current Chinese foreign exchange reserves are about five times as large as its external debt (Table 2.1). The high amount of foreign exchange reserves is widely regarded as a kind of guarantee for external debt payment.

### b. Healthy fiscal position

As the recent examples of some European countries have shown, market participants regard the health of a fiscal position as a final backstop to support the country's financial system. As for official statistics, China has kept its fiscal position in good shape. The ratios of the fiscal deficit to China's gross domestic product (GDP) and of the government debt to the GDP are both much more moderate than the ratios of other emerging countries. So far the Chinese government has been successful in keeping its fiscal health appealing to market participants.

## c. Modest leverage

The recent global financial crisis shows that financial turbulence is likely to become catastrophic with high leverage on the part of economic entities. In this regard, investment and consumption in China are modestly leveraged (Figure 2.2). Although bank loans soared in the first half of 2009, the proportion of bank loans as a source of funds was still low compared to that during

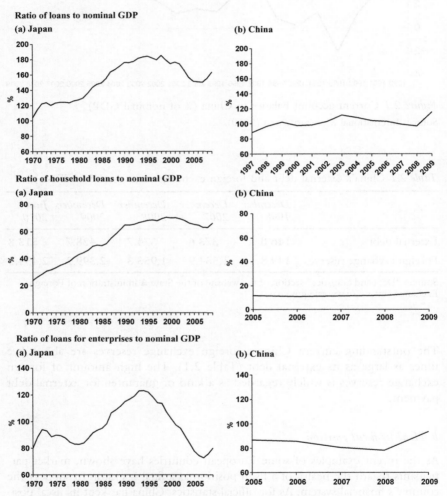

*Figure 2.2* Comparison of leverage between Japan and China

Source: Bank of Japan (http://www.stat-search.boj.or.jp/index.html), Ministry of Finance of Japan (http://www.mof.go.jp/pri/reference/ssc/results/index.htm), Cabinet Office of Japan (http://www.esri.cao.go.jp/jp/sna/data/data.html), National Bureau of Statistics of China (http://data.stats.gov.cn/workspace/index?m=hgnd), and People's Bank of China (http://www.pbc.gov.cn/publish/diaochatongjisi/133/index.html).

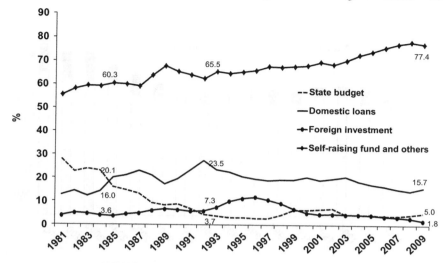

*Figure 2.3* Sources of funds for fixed asset investment in China
Source: National Bureau of Statistics of China (2009, 2010).

past investment booms (1985 and 1993; Figure 2.3). Since the leverage of Chinese households and enterprises has been modest, the negative impact of the global market turmoil, which is a shrinkage in external demand, was not as fatal as in other countries with high leverage.

### d. High domestic savings

Behind the aforementioned factors lies a more essential factor. China's savings rate is extraordinarily high. The ratio of China's gross savings to the GDP stood at more than 50 percent in 2007, the highest among the world's major countries (Figure 2.4). The high savings rate has lessened China's dependence on external debt. It has also resulted in excess domestic savings (savings minus investment), which seems to have been partly responsible for its large current account surplus. In order to offset the pressure of the currency appreciation arising from the current account surplus, the Chinese Central Bank has been buying massive amounts of foreign currencies. As a result, China has accumulated the world's largest foreign exchange reserves. The relatively low leverage is also a result of China's high savings rate. Kujis (2006) argues that high enterprise savings and capital transfers from the government generally play a much larger role in the financing of enterprises than does borrowing from financial institutions.

### e. Stable banking system

The Chinese banking system in 2008 was more stable than in the 1990s. During the Asian financial crisis, many Chinese banks were widely suspected to be

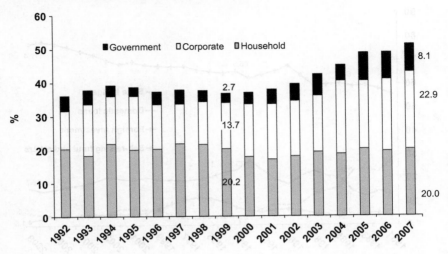

*Figure 2.4* China's savings rate (% of national disposable income)
Source: Zhou (2009a).

technically insolvent. Afraid of the detrimental effects that the crisis would have on some countries in the region, the Chinese leaders realized the importance of financial stability. In late 1997 they decided to promote the banking system reform more intensively. China's accession to the World Trade Organization (WTO) in 2001 also accelerated the reform since the Chinese government committed to completely opening the banking market to foreign competitors within five years after accession.

In order to help or encourage banks to improve solvency and governance, the government introduced a series of measures such as capital injections, tax exemptions, special arrangements for disposal of nonperforming loans (NPLs), introduction of foreign funds, and enforcement of transparent disclosure rules.[2] By September 2007 four out of the five state-owned commercial banks (SOCBs)[3] had finished restructuring and listed their shares in the Hong Kong and Shanghai stock exchanges, before the influence of the US subprime loan crisis expanded to a global scale.[4]

Since the reform, Chinese commercial banks have maintained relatively good performances without suffering serious damage from the global financial crisis. The major listed commercial banks[5] have enjoyed favorable operating results in the last three years (Figure 2.5). The NPL ratios of the major banks have largely declined (Figure 2.6), and their capital adequacy ratios have remained at 10 percent or higher. The banks were less subject to the negative effects of the crisis and willingly provided loans for foreign trades and infrastructure construction in the country (while the surge in loans raises new concerns in the market regarding loan quality).

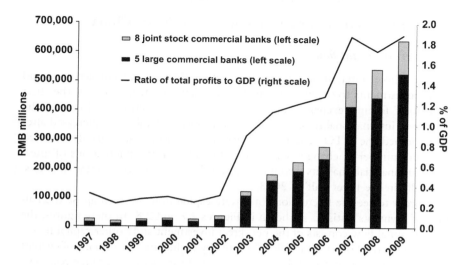

*Figure 2.5* Profits of the major listed commercial banks (before income tax)

Source: Annual reports of the Industrial Commercial Bank of China, Agricultural Bank of China, Bank of China, China Construction Bank, Bank of Communications, China Merchants Bank, China CITIC Bank, Shanghai Pudong Development Bank, China Minsheng Banking Corp., Industrial Bank, China Everbright Bank, Huaxia Bank, Shenzhen Development Bank, and the Almanac of China's Finance and Banking Editorial Board (1998, 1999, 2000, 2001 and 2002).

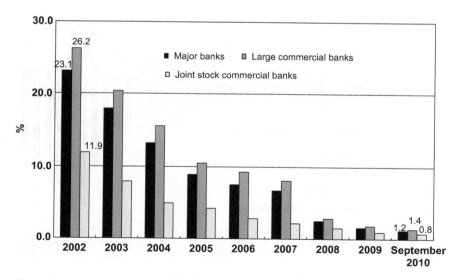

*Figure 2.6* Ratios of NPLs to total loans for major commercial banks in China

Source: China Banking Regulatory Commission (2010).

## 3. The recent cross-border capital flow to/from China

### 3.1. Overall capital flow

On the whole, international transactions other than on current accounts and direct investments to/from China had been relatively small owing to the strict control of foreign exchange on capital account transactions.[6] However, the volume of international transactions related to foreign bank loans increased after China joined the WTO. The movements of portfolio investments also showed a certain number of changes since 2002. In addition, the fluctuations of international financial markets brought substantial impacts to Chinese markets, especially in the latter half of 2008.

In order to see the fluctuations of private capital flow, we recompose the balance of payments statistics as shown in Figures 2.7 and 2.8. In these figures, the private capital flow consists of the net direct investment and "other capital flow". We calculate the "other capital flow" simply by deducting the amount of current account surplus and net FDI from the increase of the foreign exchange reserves.[7]

When the Asian financial crisis occurred in 1997, there was a growing anticipation of China's currency depreciation. The non-deliverable forward (NDF) rate of the Renminbi (RMB) was lower than the cash RMB rate in the late

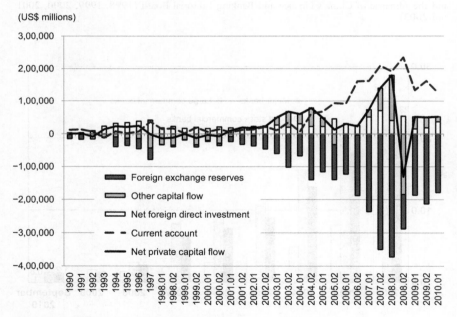

*Figure 2.7* Trend of international capital flow into China

Source: The balance of payments statistics compiled by the State Administration of Foreign Exchange (http://www.safe.gov.cn).

Note: 01: the first half of the year; 02: the second half of the year.

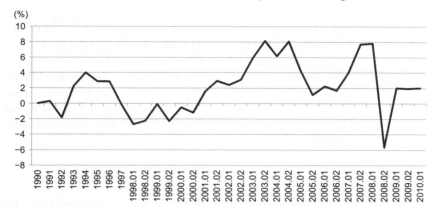

*Figure 2.8* Net private capital flow in China (% of GDP)

Source: The balance of payments statistics compiled by the State Administration of Foreign Exchange (http://www.safe.gov.cn).

Note: 01: the first half of the year; 02: the second half of the year.

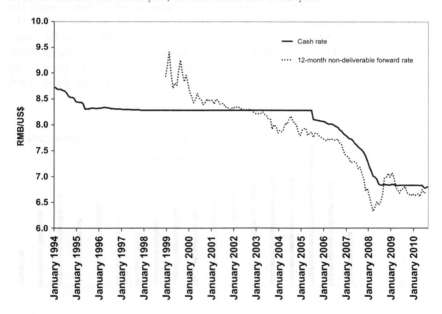

*Figure 2.9* Trend of RMB exchange rate to US dollars

Source: Bloomberg Database by Bloomberg Data Services.

1990s (Figure 2.9), and private capital outflow was seen from 1998 to 2000. In 2001 the tide turned. Private capital flow became positive in China, and the non-deliverable forward rate became higher than the cash RMB rate. In the first half of 2008, the net private capital flow surged to US$180 billion, which was 7.8 percent of the country's GDP. As the global financial crisis became more severe, the second half of 2008 showed a sudden net private capital out-flow of nearly 6 percent of the GDP. However, in the first half of 2009, the private capital flow became positive again. In sum, the impact of the crisis was substantial, but China was capable of absorbing it.

Although the Chinese government is still cautious about the further liberalization of capital transactions, the amount of cross-border transactions in recent years is not negligible, and certain movements have been affected by the global financial crisis. Hereafter, we investigate the details of the shifts of cross-border capital transactions affected by the crisis.

### 3.2. Direct investment

China has kept attracting FDI, making it one of the largest destinations for FDI in the world in recent years.[8] Figure 2.10 shows the trend of direct investment to/from China as shown in the balance of payments (BP) statistics published by the State Administration of Foreign Exchange (SAFE FDI/BP) and the statistics of the Ministry of Commerce (FDI/MOFCOM). The amount of FDI in China was significant in the 1990s and continued to increase after China joined the WTO (while the proportion to the nominal GDP had been decreasing). The pace slowed from 1998 to 2000 (mainly because of the Asian financial crisis), in 2003 (influenced by severe acute respiratory syndrome in China), and in 2009.

The difference between the FDI/BP and FDI/MOFCOM grew from 2005 in comparison to previous periods. As for the difference from 2005

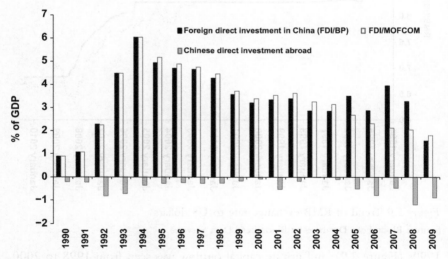

*Figure 2.10* Direct investment to/from China

Sources: The balance of payments statistics compiled by the State Administration of Foreign Exchange (http://www.safe.gov.cn) and the direct investment statistics compiled by the Ministry of Commerce (http://data.mofcom.gov.cn/channel/wzsj/wzsj.shtml, http://data.mofcom.gov.cn/channel/dwjjhz/dwjjhz.shtml).

to 2009, the official report explains only that the disparities reflect differences in reporting sources and definitions. We suppose that behind the data for 2007 and 2008, there might have been some movements in the service sector where the reporting system was not yet sufficient. The net inward direct investment dropped by 47 percent on the FDI/BP in 2009. The SAFE official report shows a few reasons for this, such as foreign banks' withdrawal of their investments from Chinese banks and foreign non-financial enterprises' withdrawal of loans from their subsidiary companies. The amount of US$10.4 billion was counted as capital outflow because of the foreign banks' withdrawal of direct investment from Chinese banks (SAFE, 2010a). According to the FDI/MOFCOM statistics, the inward direct investment decreased by only 2.6 percent in 2009, and it has recovered, showing a 20.1 percent increase during the first seven months in 2010. To date, it has been widely believed that the majority of foreign enterprises still maintain a strong willingness to invest in China.

Meanwhile, Chinese direct investment abroad has been increasing rapidly since 2005, in accordance with the policy change to encourage Chinese enterprises to "go global" and pursue energy resources, high technology, and popular global brands. In recent years, Chinese enterprises have become more aggressive for mergers and acquisitions abroad, supported by bank lending.

### 3.3. Portfolio investment

The Chinese bond market is small and closed especially to foreign investors (an issue to be discussed later), and portfolio investment in China is carried out mainly through the stock markets (Figure 2.11). In the 1990s both foreign individuals and institutional investors could invest only in the so-called B shares: special foreign currency–denominated shares for non-residents. In order to develop stock markets, China launched the Qualified Foreign Institutional Investors (QFII) scheme in November 2002. The scheme allowed foreign institutional investors to trade RMB-denominated A shares listed in the Shanghai and Shenzhen stock exchanges, T-bills, and convertible bonds, so long as the investment size did not exceed the quotas primarily approved by the China Security Regulatory Commission and SAFE. As a result, the amount of capital inflow through stock markets has been increasing. However, its overall impact on the capital flow to/from China has been limited. In 2009 US$31.2 billion of inflow and US$2.4 billion of outflow were seen in the non-residents' portfolio investment account. The shares of the total capital flow in the financial account were 4.2 percent and 0.4 percent, respectively.

The amount of Chinese portfolio investment abroad is also small, but activities have been developing, motivated by the government's "go global" policy. However, in the wake of the global financial crisis, Chinese banks exercised caution in holding foreign bonds. When the global bond markets shook heavily in 2008 and 2009, the Chinese banks sold foreign bonds and instead increased foreign currency loans to domestic customers in 2009 (SAFE, 2010a).

a. Into China

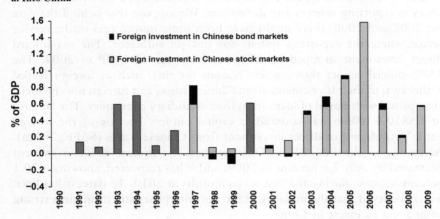

b. Out of China

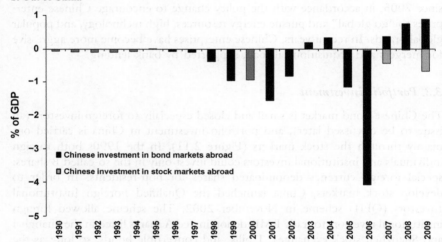

*Figure 2.11* Portfolio investment into and out of China

Source: The balance of payments statistics compiled by the State Administration of Foreign Exchange (http://www.safe.gov.cn).

Note: The data from 1990 to 1996 and for 2000 show only the aggregate amount of the portfolio investment abroad for the year.

### 3.4. Other capital transactions

Capital movements through other channels are still limited. However, the paths fluctuated largely during the global crisis. In the latter half of 2008, a large amount of withdrawal occurred in the foreign trade finance and bank loans (on the liability side of China's balance of payments statistics), which caused sudden net capital outflows in China. This was a clear influence of the global crisis on

*Table 2.2* Capital account transactions in China under the global crisis (US$ billions)

| | | 2008 | | 2009 | |
|---|---|---|---|---|---|
| | | *First half* | *Second half* | *First half* | *Second half* |
| Direct investment | Net | 40.8 | 53.6 | 15.6 | 18.7 |
| | Outward | (33.3) | (20.1) | (13.3) | (30.6) |
| | Inward | 74.1 | 73.7 | (28.9) | 49.3 |
| Portfolio investment | Net | 19.8 | 22.8 | 20.2 | 18.5 |
| | Assets | 14.8 | 18.0 | 7.7 | 2.2 |
| | Liabilities | (5.1) | 4.9 | 12.5 | 16.3 |
| Other investment | Net | 9.7 | (130.8) | 23.9 | 44.0 |
| | Assets | (83.1) | (23.0) | 29.1 | (19.7) |
| | Liabilities | 92.7 | (107.7) | (5.2) | 63.7 |
| Breakdown | | | | | |
| Trade credit | Net | 11.2 | (24.4) | (23.0) | 0.7 |
| | Assets | (4.2) | 10.1 | (16.3) | (38.1) |
| | Liabilities | 15.4 | (34.4) | (6.7) | 38.8 |
| Loans | Net | 47.6 | (62.4) | 0.4 | 16.4 |
| | Assets | (5.4) | (13.1) | 6.4 | 6.6 |
| | Liabilities | 53.0 | (49.3) | (6.1) | 9.8 |
| Errors and omissions | Net | 17.1 | (43.2) | (9.5) | (34.0) |

Source: The balance of payments statistics compiled by the State Administration of Foreign Exchange (http://www.safe.gov.cn).

Note: Parentheses indicate a negative number.

China. The trend did not last long, and the flows became positive in the latter half of 2009 (Table 2.2).

Chinese bank loans abroad had been growing until 2008, but in 2009 the channel showed net capital inflow. This was primarily because the Chinese banks withdrew overseas short-term interbank lending, in accordance with the increasing credit risks and declining interest rates in the markets abroad (SAFE, 2010a).

## 4. Challenges for a more market-oriented economy

### 4.1. Current stage of the financial system reform

The Chinese government has gradually implemented the financial system reform, bearing in mind the economic development of the country and social acceptability of the changes (Figure 2.12). China took a large step toward a more market-oriented economy after it joined the WTO in 2001. A wide range of reforms showed rudimentary but significant successes before the recent global financial crisis.[9] These efforts resulted in the establishment of such strong financial fundamentals as those explained in Section 2 of this chapter.

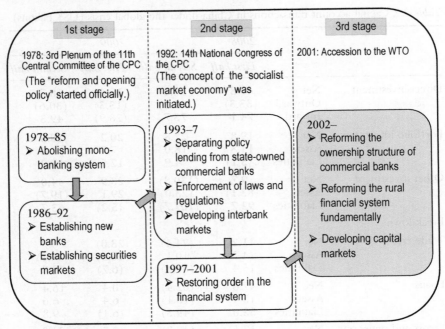

*Figure 2.12* Outline of the banking system reform in China
Source: Okazaki (2007).

However, the current situation of the Chinese financial system is far from ideal. The reform process has yet to establish a more market-oriented economic system. Worse still, some areas of the reform seem to be suspended or reversed, in an attempt to overcome the global financial crisis. In addition, some of the favorable factors that protected the Chinese economy during the crisis currently pose substantial risks and challenges to the country's sustainable growth.

The Chinese financial system as a whole is not deep or diversified enough to allocate funds effectively and thus to guarantee long-term sustainable economic growth. In the following sections, we discuss several challenges that China will have to face to promote further economic development and cope with global economic integration.

## 4.2. Toward efficient fund allocation

The fact that bank loans hold a dominant position in the external funding of the corporate sector does not always mean that fund allocation is inefficient. If bank governance is healthy and the market mechanism is working well, banks can act as superb financial intermediaries to realize efficient fund allocation. However, at least currently, Chinese banks do not seem to allocate funds very efficiently. Although the Chinese banks' governance has improved remarkably

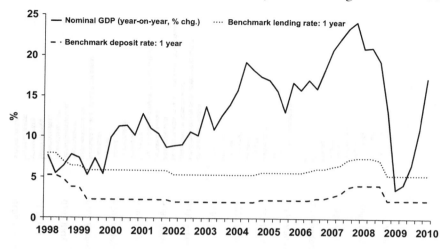

*Figure 2.13* Nominal GDP growth and interest rates in China
Source: Database compiled by CEIC Data (http://www.ceicdata.com).

since they invited foreign strategic investors and enhanced transparency through listing bank shares, the banks are still subject to the government's de facto interventions in terms of increasing the pace of lending and allocation of loans.

The presence of window guidance enabled the government to control the increase of bank loans without flexibly modifying the interest rates. Figure 2.13 shows that the lending and deposit rates stayed relatively unchanged compared to the fluctuations of the nominal GDP. Window guidance is a useful tool to control the amount of credit where financial markets are underdeveloped and interest rates do not function well. However, the government's "visible hand" does not always lead to efficient fund allocation (Fukumoto, Higashi, Inamura, and Kimura, 2010).

When the Chinese government decided to stimulate the economy in the fourth quarter of 2008, commercial banks quickly responded and provided loans very actively. In the first quarter of 2009, the net increase of bank loans amounted to 4.6 trillion RMB, which was nearly the equivalent of that for the whole year of 2008 (Figure 2.14). Medium- and long-term loans made up 41 percent of the total loans. This was because the banks followed the government's guidance to support infrastructure investment and technological innovation. The increase in infrastructure loans constituted 50 percent of the total medium- and long-term loan increases. Such a rapid increase in infrastructure loans helped the economy to recover quickly. Nevertheless, now that bank loans to local-government investment vehicles, which are responsible for the funding of infrastructure construction, have become an issue, many suspect that some of the bank loans were used in inefficient projects.

In China the difficulty for small and medium-sized enterprises (SMEs) to access bank loans has been a serious problem since the 1990s. As of mid-2006,

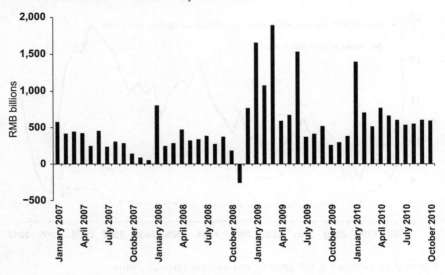

*Figure 2.14* Net increase of RMB bank loans (monthly) in China

Source: "Survey and Statistics," People's Bank of China website (http://www.pbc.gov.cn/diaochatongjisi/133/index.html).

less than 1 percent of all loans extended by SOCBs went to private businesses, which employ over 200 million people in total and account for about 50 percent of the country's GDP (Tsai, 2006).[10] The private sector, which is replete with SMEs, has largely relied on informal finance. The government has been encouraging banks to supply loans to profitable private enterprises, and the People's Bank of China relaxed the commercial banks' lending rate ceiling in October 2004. However, the loan pricing environment has not yet changed, for the following reasons: the slow implementation of changes in sizable SOCB operations, the low priority of interest rate differentiation in an environment of abundant liquidity, and the banks' decision to avoid charging higher interest rates when it would worsen the clients' conditions (Podpiera, 2006).

Under the recent global crisis, a lending bias toward state-owned enterprises (SOEs) seems to have exacerbated again. When we analyze the changes in the corporate lending sector, we find that the percentage of lending to infrastructure sectors such as transportation and utilities increased rapidly from 2003 to the first half of 2009. Large SOEs play a dominant role in these sectors. In addition, when the People's Bank of China strictly limited the increase in bank lending in the fourth quarter of 2007, SMEs were crowded out by commercial banks. According to Li Zishan, chairman of the SMEs Association, the proportion of bank loans for SMEs to the total amount of outstanding loans dropped from 22.5 percent to 15 percent after the central bank tightened the monetary policy (Hexun 2008). The Zhejiang Office of the CBRC reported that according to survey results from the Wenzhou enterprises financing sources, the proportion of bank loans declined from 24 percent in 2006 to 18 percent in 2008.[11]

We recommend several policy measures to improve fund allocation. First, promote financial market infrastructure. In particular, it is advisable to expand and deregulate corporate bond and commercial paper markets. As shown in Table 2.3, bank loans play a dominant role among the sources of external funding for Chinese enterprises. The growth of Chinese capital markets has been relatively slow (Figures 2.15 and 2.16). The Chinese authorities have been cautious about the enterprises' ability to repay, and the permission for bond issuance is still very limited. Although corporate bond issuance has been surging over the past five years, most short-term and medium-term corporate bonds are issued in interbank markets where limited investors, such as banks and institutional investors, can purchase them. The issuance of corporate bonds that various investors can buy is desirable. In addition, to improve the functioning of corporate bond markets, it is imperative to establish a reliable credit-rating system and a more transparent accounting system.

*Table 2.3* Proportion of external funding sources for domestic non-financial corporations in China (%)

|  | *2006* | *2007* | *2008* | *2009* |
| --- | --- | --- | --- | --- |
| Bank loans | 87.9 | 81.6 | 83.8 | 85.9 |
| Stocks | 6.0 | 13.6 | 5.9 | 4.1 |
| Bonds, etc. | 6.1 | 4.8 | 10.2 | 10.1 |

Source: People's Bank of China (2006, 2007, 2008, 2009a).

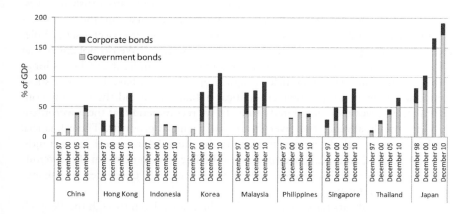

*Figure 2.15* Outstanding bonds in Asia (% of nominal GDP)

Source: Asian Development Bank, Asian Bonds Online (http://asianbondsonline.adb.org/regional/data.php#bond_market_indicators).

Note: In this figure, the category "government bonds" consists of bonds issued by the central government, other government entities, and the central bank.

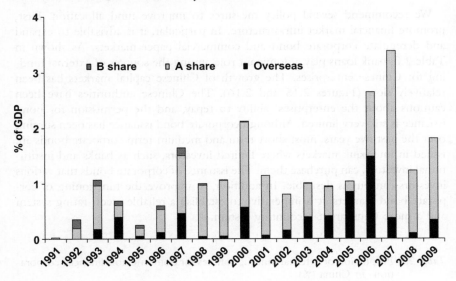

*Figure 2.16* Size of stock issuance by Chinese corporations (% of GDP)

Source: Almanac of China's Finance and Banking Editorial Board (2002) and the security markets monthly data compiled by the China Securities Regulatory Commission (http://www. csrc.gov.cn/pub/newssite/sjtj/zqscyb/index_6html).

Second, diversify financial products. This point is closely related to the first one. In China the financial products that people can invest in are still very limited, and stocks and properties are the only choices that people can consider for investment. More often than not, both domestic and foreign investors rush to invest in stocks and properties, resulting in bubbles and bursts in these markets (Figures 2.17 and 2.18). For instance, in recent years, concerns over asset bubbles especially in the property market in China have increased. We do not think that China's property price will undergo serious adjustments in light of China's long-term growth potential. Nonetheless, high property prices have become a social issue that might eventually weaken political stability. To avoid the extreme concentration of investment in limited products, we recommend that the government should carefully advance the diversification of financial products. These financial products might include money market funds, mutual funds, real estate funds, corporate bonds, and local government bonds. The government can also carefully introduce asset-backed securities. Securitization itself is a good idea to enhance the efficiency of finance.

Third, gradually liberalize deposit and lending rates. Even though the People's Bank of China is conducting open market operations, the interbank rates have a small influence on deposit and lending rates because of the presence of strict regulations. The government might consider other factors such as negative impacts on bank profits. However, we think that gradual liberalization in tandem with the improvement of bank management and governance would be feasible.

Fourth, further improve bank governance. We recommend the further diversification of bank ownership. In order to support private businesses, it is

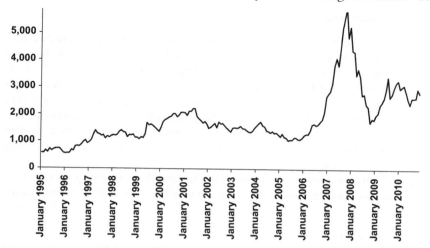

*Figure 2.17* Price index of Shanghai stock exchange

Source: Annual and Monthly Reports of the Shanghai Stock Exchange (http://www.sse.com.
cn/researchpublications/publication/yearly, http://www.sse.com.cn/researchpublications/
publication/monthly).

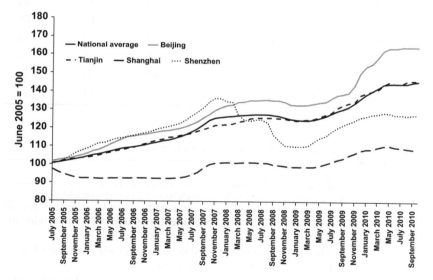

*Figure 2.18* Trend of property prices in major cities (primary residence)

Source: Sales Price Indices of Residential Buildings in 70 Large and Medium-Sized Cities,
compiled by the National Bureau of Statistics of China (http://data.stats.gov.cn/).

advisable to establish privately owned banks. In addition, it is worth allowing
private enterprises to own part of state-owned or state-controlled banks so
that these banks act as strategic investors. In any case, the prerequisite is that
the decision-making process is fair and transparent with a more developed
disclosure system.

### *4.3. Reasonably lower savings rate*

As shown in Figure 2.3, the proportion of external funding (bank loans, government budgets, and FDI) as a source of fixed asset investment is low, and self-funding is on the rise and is by far the largest source in China.[12] The high percentage of self-funding is in line with China's high corporate and household savings rate. In particular, large SOEs accumulated a huge amount of reserves throughout the 2000s, largely owing to the government's preferential treatment. Table 2.4 indicates that corporate investment is increasingly funded by corporate savings. In addition, Table 2.5 shows the reasons for China's increase in savings since the late 1990s.

Considering the current developmental stage and the country's growth potential, China has good reasons to maintain a reasonably high savings rate to finance

*Table 2.4* Investment and savings (% of GDP)

|  |  | *1996* | *2000* | *2004* | *2005* |
|---|---|---|---|---|---|
| Households | Investment | 6 | 5 | 6 | 6 |
|  | Savings | 20 | 15 | 16 | 16 |
| **Corporations** | Investment | 29 | 26 | 32 | 31 |
|  | Savings | 13 | 15 | 19 | 20 |
| Governments | Investment | 2 | 3 | 3 | 4 |
|  | Savings | 5 | 6 | 6 | 6 |
| Total | Investment | 38 | 34 | 41 | 40 |
|  | Savings | 37 | 35 | 41 | 44 |

Source: Kuijs (2006).

*Table 2.5* Reasons for China's increasing savings rate since late 1990s

| *Savings sectors* | *Reasons for increasing savings* |
|---|---|
| Corporation | • The government reduced state-owned enterprises (SOEs)' responsibilities for employees' health care, education, pensions, and housing, which allowed them to maintain larger liquidity in their own accounts. |
|  | • The government allowed SOEs to retain their profits, leaving their own dividends at nearly nothing. |
| Government | • The government's income from taxation increased greatly, and fiscal income as a percentage of the gross domestic product (GDP) rose significantly. |
|  | • However, government consumption has been relatively restrained. |
| Household | • The anticipation of future expenditures for education, health care, and housing causes households to increase their savings. |

Sources: Zhang Ming (2009); Kuijs (2006); Chamon and Prasado (2008).

domestic investment, especially in infrastructure. However, the downside risks of keeping such high savings rates in the current manner should not be under-estimated. The high proportion of self-funding does not always promise efficient fund allocation. For example, it is often pointed out that cash-rich SOEs some-times invest their reserves in areas that are not their strengths, such as real estate, and end up incurring losses. In addition, the high corporate savings have been accompanied by a drop in the labor share of the national income, which has made China's long-term economic growth less sustainable. Externally, China's savings rate has created a massive number of global imbalances and has thus enlarged China's capital inflow.

The governor of the Central Bank explains that the Chinese authorities have a clear policy intention to reduce the savings rate but that in-depth studies are needed to identify the factors influencing the savings rate, its elasticity with respect to these factors, and the specific adjustment measures to assume (Zhou, 2009c). The measures include expanding the government's expenditure on public support for education, health care, and housing; improving employees' wages and labor conditions; and decreasing capital transfers to SOEs, requiring higher dividends from the SOEs. Some of these measures have already been planned or partly implemented. The government began to require higher divi-dends from the SOEs, though they were still very low. In addition, 14 percent of China's recent 4 trillion RMB economic stimulus package is to be spent on assistance for health care, education, and housing. It would be better for China to promote these policies further.

### 4.4. Effective foreign exchange reserves management

In addition to the need for domestic financial reform, China has to tackle other challenges owing to the deepening of its macro-financial linkage overseas. Pro-moting effective management of foreign exchange reserves would be one of the primary tasks of the Chinese government.

China's large foreign exchange reserves act as a buffer to absorb external shocks. However, holding large amounts of foreign currency implies that the Chinese government is subject to large currency fluctuation risks. Currently, more than 80 percent of the Central Bank's assets are foreign currency assets. The SAFE explains that one of the tough challenges for them today is reducing the imbalance among the foreign currency assets holders. It admits that an excess of foreign currency assets is concentrated in the government account and not in the private "reservoir" (SAFE, 2010b). Against this background, the central government is gradually easing the control of cross-border capital trans-actions in recent years.

The Chinese government realized that its excessive dependency on the US dollar in foreign trade, international capital flows, and management of foreign exchange reserves carries huge risks; therefore, ideas about the internationaliza-tion of the RMB, regional monetary cooperation, and the reconstruction of the international monetary regime have become issues for discussion (Zhang, 2009).

Although the definition is not very clear, the idea of the "internationalization of the RMB" has become a hot topic in China. Gao and Yu (2009) introduced the framework by Chinn and Frankel (2005), explaining that an international currency has to be capable of storing value, acting as a medium of exchange, and serving as a unit of account for both residents and non-residents. The internationalization of the RMB is expected to decelerate China's accumulation of foreign exchange reserves and thus mitigate the risks of its management.

In December 2008 the Chinese government announced a pilot project permitting the use of the RMB in cross-border trade settlements. The government has been gradually expanding the number of provinces where companies are able to settle international trade and services transactions in RMB instead of US dollars. In addition, with regard the internationalization of the RMB, Hong Kong is expected to serve as a place for offshore RMB settlements.

Meanwhile, the government is still very cautious about the effects of wide use of the national currency globally, and it has yet to officially use the phrase "the internationalization of the RMB". As Gao and Yu (2009) pointed out, the internationalization of a currency needs low-inflation credibility, a reasonable interest and exchange rate, and full convertibility of the currency. It would take time to establish the ideal environment for wider use of the RMB, even if the Chinese government becomes more willing to promote it.

As for regional monetary cooperation, China joined the 10+3 (the countries of the Association of Southeast Asian Nations, plus China, Korea, and Japan) currency swap framework (the Chiang Mai Initiative) in 2001. Among China's six bilateral currency swap agreements based on the Chiang Mai Initiative, in three agreements (China–Japan, China–Korea, and China–the Philippines) China commits to provide RMB; in the other three agreements (China–Indonesia, China–Malaysia, and China–Thailand) it commits to provide US dollars to make up for a liquidity shortage in the counterpart country.

Responding to the recent global financial crisis, China has newly committed to bilateral local currency swap agreements with Korea, Hong Kong, Malaysia, Belorussia, Indonesia, Argentina, Iceland, and Singapore. The Central Bank explains that these new practices will promote bilateral trade and direct investment and drive economic growth (People's Bank of China, 2009b). The local currency swap agreement is expected to promote the use of the RMB as a payment currency.

While the reconstruction of the international monetary regime seems to be a medium- or long-term issue, China is trying to strengthen its voice in the global financial community, backed by its rising economic power and large foreign exchange reserves. In March 2009 the governor of the People's Bank of China published a note entitled "Reform the International Monetary System" (Zhou, 2009c), in which he proposed wider use of Special Drawing Rights (SDRs), the creation of financial assets using its denominations, and changes in its valuation and allocation. This was followed by a speech by the Chinese president Hu Jingtao at the Group of 20 (G20) Financial Summit held in London in early April 2009. President Hu did not talk about the issue in detail, but he called for the advancement of reform in the international financial system. Kwan (2009) analyzes the aims of Zhou's note as follows: China is indicating its willingness to establish a new international financial order in which the dominance of a certain country's currency would be corrected, and it wants to reorganize its structure of foreign exchange reserves.

As for the SDR, there are still many hurdles in using it as a reserve currency. Zhou pointed out the issues to be improved on as follows: setting up a settlement system between the SDR and other currencies, promoting the use of the SDR in international trade, creating financial assets denominated in the SDR, and improving the valuation and allocation of the SDR.

## 5. Concluding remarks

The Chinese financial system is more robust than it was a decade ago. It has worked as a bulwark for China to withstand the external shocks caused by the recent global financial crisis. The relatively strict control of cross-border capital transactions has also protected the Chinese financial markets from the contagion of the negative effects of the crisis. However, the factors that have supported economic growth also carry with them substantial risks, and China faces several challenges for the further development of its economy. The primary tasks should be to change the market dominance of the state-owned sectors, weaken government intervention in commercial banks, develop capital markets, adjust extremely high savings rates, and reduce the risks of the foreign exchange reserves in the Central Bank's account.

The widening and deepening economic integration between China and the world is bringing about a massive pressure of cross-border capital transactions even under strict capital control. For example, when the expectation of RMB appreciation is strong, a number of overseas investors attempt to make their money flow into China through official and/or unofficial routes. Since China has benefited significantly from the economic globalization and is willing to continue pursuing overseas markets to sell its products and to gain natural resources, higher technologies, and worldwide brands, cross-border capital transactions to/from China will significantly increase in the future. For sustainable economic development, it is important for the Chinese government to grasp movements of international capital flow and adjust the financial markets with more market-oriented measures.

Having witnessed the recent financial debacle and its ramifications in Western countries, China seems to be much more cautious about utilizing market mechanisms in the domestic financial markets in the short term. However, to improve the economic structure or introduce fair competition, the establishment of market mechanisms is critical.

On the other hand, because of the differences in the extent to which the economy is transformed from a planned one to a market-oriented one, there are huge differences in the condition of economic development across business sectors and regions in the country. The implementation of a financial market reform requires a well-considered sequence. Moreover, the reform process should be followed up and revised carefully. It is true that China's gradualism in the economic reform process has worked very well thus far. However, gradual reform does not imply slow reform. The pace of the reform should be checked frequently, and necessary reform measures should be carried out consistently and should not be delayed.

In accordance with the economic development, China is increasing its economic influence over other countries in the world. The policy changes introduced by the Chinese government greatly influence the world's financial markets. The market participants already consider the Chinese economy to be one of the most important contributors to the world economy. The successful development of the Chinese financial system is integral to the stable growth of the world economy.

With these situations in mind, we would like to expect China to act as a responsible country, implementing the necessary economic reforms in order to enhance its economic structure, thereby enhancing the robustness of the global economy as a whole. At the same time, we expect market participants outside China to understand the economic and financial conditions of China more carefully, without any prejudice or bias. Information sharing, exchanges of opinions, and mutual understanding are growing in importance.

## Notes

1 This chapter was prepared for the research project of the Pacific Economic Outlook (PEO) in 2010. We thank Akira Kosaka, Helen Chan, Ichiro Otani, Kazuo Ogawa, and the participants of the two PEO Structure Specialists Meetings held in March and September 2010 for their comments and discussions. The views expressed in this chapter are those of the authors and do not necessarily reflect the official views of the Bank of Japan.
2 For detailed information on the Chinese banking system reform from 1997 to 2007, see Okazaki (2007).
3 In the 1990s the SOCB category included four banks: the Industrial Commercial Bank of China, Agricultural Bank of China, Bank of China, and China Construction Bank. Under the 2002 reform plan, the Bank of Communications was frequently called an SOCB and was provided government support similar to what the other SOCBs received.
4 The Agricultural Bank of China was the last SOCB to list its stocks in the Hong Kong and Shanghai stock exchanges in July 2010.
5 The Chinese regulatory authority, the China Banking Regulatory Commission (CBRC), defines the five SOCBs and twelve JSCBs as "Joint Stock Commercial Bank". Of these, the SOCBs and eight JSCBs are listed. After listing their shares in the stock exchanges, the SOCBs are categorized as "large commercial banks".
6 In 1996 China notified the International Monetary Fund that it was in full compliance with the Fund's Charter Article VIII, confirming the full convertibility of the domestic currency on the current account transactions. China still strictly controls transactions on the capital and financial accounts, except that it has actively invited FDI into China.
7 We adjust the amount of the increase in foreign exchange reserves according to Tsuyuguchi (2009). In his analysis of the recent movements of foreign exchange

reserves in China with the balance of payments statistics, he adjusts the following three factors: the influence of the Central Bank's currency swap trade, movement of the commercial banks' reserve requirement of foreign currency, and capital injection into the China Investment Corporation using foreign exchange reserves.

8 According to the United Nations Conference on Trade and Development's *World Investment Report*, China has been among the world's top five destinations for FDI since 2002, except in 2007 (when it fell to sixth place); it was the second largest in 2009.

9 In addition to the commercial banks' reform (briefly mentioned in Section 2.2e), Chinese authorities promoted various reforms in the rural financial system (rehabilitating more than 40,000 rural credit cooperatives and establishing new types of financial institutions), the stock market (unifying the non-tradable and tradable shares), the foreign exchange market (implementing a new floating exchange-rate mechanism), the corporate bond market, and so on.

10 It should be noted that in China there are various definitions of SMEs. Based on the official definition, the People's Bank of China announced that loans for SMEs accounted for 53 percent of the total corporate loans in 2009. However, the official definition of an SME denotes an enterprise with fewer than 2,000 employees in the case of manufacturing, whereas that number is 500 in the United States and 300 in Japan.

11 According to the People's Bank of China, the amount of bank loans for SMEs increased by 31 percent in 2009, led by the government's strong guidance.

12 Because of some technical reasons related to the statistics' compilation, the self-funding includes a certain amount of bank loans and funding in capital markets. Nevertheless, on the basis of our rough calculation using the Central Bank's other bank lending statistics, we assume that the proportion of bank lending to the total fund resources for fixed asset investment is not very high either (less than 30 percent at the maximum in 2009).

## References and Further Readings

Almanac of China's Finance and Banking Editorial Board, ed. 1998, 1999, 2000, 2001, and 2002. *Almanac of China's Finance and Banking 1998, 1999, 2000, 2001, and 2002*. Beijing.

Cao Fengqi, ed. 2006. *Zhongguo Shangye Yinhang Gaige Yu Chuangxin* [*China's commercial banks reform and innovation*]. Beijing: China Financial Publishing House.

Chamon, Marcos and Eswar Prasad. 2008. "Why Are Savings Rates of Urban Households in China Rising?" International Monetary Fund Working Paper WP/08/145. Washington, DC: International Monetary Fund.

China Banking Regulatory Commission. 2010. *Annual Report 2010*. Beijing: China Banking Regulatory Commission. http://www.cbrc.gov.cn/Chinese/home/docViewPage/110007.html

Chinn, Menzien and Jeffrey Frankel. 2005. "Will the Euro Eventually Surpass the Dollar as Leading International Reserve Currency?" National Bureau of Economic Research Working Paper 11510. Cambridge, MA: National Bureau of Economic Research.

Fernald, John G. and Oliver D. Banson. 1999. "Why Has China Survived the Asian Crisis So Well: What Risks Remain?" In Baizhu Chen, J. Kimball Dietrich, and Yi Feng, eds., *Financial Market Reform in China: Progress, Problems, and Prospects*. Boulder, CO: Westview Press.

Fukumoto, Tomoyuki, Masato Higashi, Yasunari Inamura, and Takeshi Kimura. 2010. "Effectiveness of Window Guidance and Financial Environment – in Light of Japan's

Experience of Financial Liberalization and a Bubble Economy." Bank of Japan Review 2010-E-4. Tokyo: Bank of Japan. http://www.boj.or.jp/en/research/wps_rev/rev_2010/data/rev10e04.pdf

Gao Haihong and Yu Yongding. 2009. "Internationalization of the Renminbi." Bank of Korea-Bank for International Settlements Seminar Presentation Paper. Basel: Bank for International Settlements. http://www.bis.org/repofficepubl/arpresearch200903.05.pdf?noframes=1

He Xinghua and Cao Yonghu. 2007. "Understanding High Savings Rate in China," *China and World Economy* Vol. 15, Issue 1, pp. 1–13.

Hexun. 2008. "Zhongxiao Qiye Xiehui Huizhan: Dui Zhongxiao Qiye Jiaqiang Jiandu he Zhixing Lidu" [Chairman of the SMEs Association: Strengthen the Monitoring and Policy Implementation to SMEs]. http://news.hexun.com/2008-11-21/111513025.html (originally a CCTV interview).

International Monetary Fund. 2010. *World Economic Outlook Database.* October. Washington, DC: International Monetary Fund. http://www.imf.org/external/pubs/ft/weo/2010/02/weodata/index.aspx

Kuijs, Louis. 2006. "How Will China's Saving-Investment Balance Evolve?" World Bank Policy Research Working Paper 3958. Washington, DC: World Bank.

Kwan Chi Hung. 2009. "Stepping Up Efforts toward Renminbi Internationalization," in "China in Transition" section of the Research Institute of Economy, Trade and Industry website. http://www.rieti.go.jp/en/china/09040601.html?stylesheet

Lardy, Nicholas R. 1998. *China's Unfinished Economic Revolution.* Washington, DC: Brookings Institution Press.

Muto, Ichiro, Miyuki Matsunaga, Satoko Ueyama, and Tomoyuki Fukumoto. 2010. "On the Recent Rise in China's Real Estate Prices." Bank of Japan Review 2010-E-3. Tokyo: Bank of Japan.

http://www.boj.or.jp/en/research/wps_rev/rev_2010/rev10e3.htm/

National Bureau of Statistics of China, ed. 2009. *China Statistical Yearbook 2009.* Beijing: China Statistics Press.

National Bureau of Statistics of China, ed. 2010. *China Statistical Abstract 2010.* Beijing: China Statistics Press.

Okazaki, Kumiko. 2007. "Banking System Reform in China: the Challenges of Moving toward a Market-Oriented Economy." Rand Corporation Occasional Paper 194. Santa Monica, CA: Rand Corporation.

http://www.rand.org/pubs/occasional_papers/OP194.html

People's Bank of China. 2006. "China Monetary Policy Report Quarter Four, 2006." Beijing: People's Bank of China. http://www.pbc.gov.cn/publish/english/989/1951/19518/19518_.html

———. 2007. "China Monetary Policy Report Quarter Four, 2007." Beijing: People's Bank of China. http://www.pbc.gov.cn/publish/english/988/1952/19523/19523_.html

———. 2008. "China Monetary Policy Report Quarter Four, 2008." Beijing: People's Bank of China. http://www.pbc.gov.cn/publish/english/3004/2048/20485/20485_.html

———. 2009a. "China Monetary Policy Report Quarter Four, 2009." Beijing: People's Bank of China. http://www.pbc.gov.cn/publish/english/3005/2010/20100521103242520199079/20100521103242520199079_.html

———. 2009b. "Strengthen Regional Financial Cooperation and Actively Conduct Currency Swap." March 31. Beijing: People's Bank of China. http://www.pbc.gov.

cn/publish/english/955/2009/20091207090515983654214/20091207090
515983654214_.html
Podpiera, Richard. 2006. "Progress in China's Banking Sector Reform: Has Bank
Behavior Changed?" International Monetary Fund Working Paper WP/06/71.
Washington, DC: International Monetary Fund.
State Administration of Foreign Exchange. 2010a. "Guoji shouzhi baogao 2009"
[Balance of Payments Report 2009]. Beijing: State Administration of Foreign
Exchange.
———. 2010b. "Waihui guanli zhengce redian wenda" [Questions and Answers on
the Hot Issues of Foreign Exchange Control Policy]. News. July 2. Beijing: State
Administration of Foreign Exchange. http://www.safe.gov.cn/
Tsai, Kellee S. 2006. "Testimony before the US-China Economic and Security
Review Commission on China's Financial System." Hearing Transcript from the
U.S.-China Economic and Security Review Commission on August 22–3. http://
origin.www.uscc.gov/sites/default/files/06_08_22_23_tsai_kellee_statement.pdf
Tsuyuguchi, Yosuke. 2009. "The Recent Flow of Hot Money in China." Bank of
Japan Review 2009-E-3. Tokyo: Bank of Japan. http://www.boj.or.jp/en/
research/wps_rev/rev_2009/rev09e03htm/
United Nations Conference on Trade and Development. 2003–9. *World Investment
Report* 2003, 2004, 2005, 2006, 2007, 2008 and 2009. http://unctad.org/en/
Pages/DIAE/World%20Investment%20Report/World_Investment_Report.aspx
Zhang Ming. 2009. "China's New International Financial Strategy amid the Global
Financial Crisis." *China and World Economy* Vol. 17, Issue 5, pp. 23–35.
Zhou Xiaochuan. 2009a. "Address at the Global Think-tank Summit, Governor
Zhou Xiaochuan, People's Bank of China, July 3, 2009, Beijing." July 3. http://
www.pbc.gov.cn/publish/english/956/2009/20091229122954330948779/
20091229122954330948779_.html
———. 2009b. "Zhou Xiaochuan: On Saving Ratio." People's Bank of China.
March 24.
http://www.pbc.gov.cn/publish/english/956/2009/20091229104810768831191/
20091229104810768831191_.html
———. 2009c. "Zhou Xiaochuan: Reform the International Monetary System."
People's Bank of China. March 23.
http://www.pbc.gov.cn/publish/english/956/2009/20091229104425550619706/
20091229104425550619706_.html

# 3 Macro-financial linkage and financial deepening in the Philippines

*Cayetano W. Paderanga, Jr.*

## 1. Introduction

One question about the recent global financial crisis is how it could have happened. At the time, we were focused on controlling our foreign indebtedness and our fiscal deficits in order to obviate the factors that had caused the Asian financial crisis of 1997–1998 and the Latin American debt crisis in the early 1980s. This time, however, it was our credits (not debts) and investments abroad that had an immediate adverse impact, which became much deeper as export markets contracted as a result of asset losses in importing countries. As a side effect of increased global financial integration, cross-border interaction among financial markets had increased. Because the size of the market had increased tremendously, volatility was much more intense, and what would previously have been minor fluctuations had become larger than individual countries could absorb or mitigate on their own. While prudential structures were designed, the exact form of vulnerability had not been fully specified, so preventive mechanisms were difficult to devise.

By most accounts, this was the worst financial crisis since the Great Depression given the depth and breadth of its effects. It affected several of the most economically and financially important countries. By February 2009 the United Kingdom, Japan, and the United States had suffered absolute gross domestic product (GDP) declines of 0.5 percent, 11 percent, and 1.5 percent, respectively. Meanwhile, China's rapid growth rate was expected to decelerate to 6.5 percent from a one-time high of 11 percent. Other countries suffered similar, if not worse, fortunes. For a crisis of such depth, length, and breadth, we would probably have to go back to the 1930s to find close parallels.

## 2. How the global crisis reached the Philippines

Many wonder what and how great the impact of the U.S. recession has been on other countries, including the Philippines. Some nations relied on America as their largest export market, not only for goods but also for services. U.S. companies have investments and subsidiaries in Asian countries that provide employment and financing to those countries. U.S. investors had also included emerging market stocks in their portfolios in order to diversify their holdings, investing in riskier assets for potentially higher returns. Volumes of the domestic assets of other countries were held by U.S. investors, and the reverse was also true. These interrelationships made a lot of countries vulnerable to the U.S. economic situation.

There has been discussion on the degree of "decoupling" – whether or not other economies have reduced their dependence on the U.S. economy to such an extent that adverse impacts of U.S. downturns are diminished. When the United States went through a recession in 2001, China's growth fell by less than a percentage point; it kept growing at 7.3 percent because strong domestic demand helped cushion the huge decline in exports. In 2007 Asian countries enjoyed healthy growth even as the U.S. housing sector slumped and the sub-prime mortgage crisis exploded. Local currencies strengthened against a weakening U.S. dollar while stock markets rallied.

On the one hand, developing Asia was still strongly affected by the U.S. recession, and developing nations had not decoupled from the U.S. economy. As the recent declines in the stock indexes of Asian countries illustrated, the subprime mortgage crisis had spillover effects on markets outside of the United States. Investors fled from risky assets to safer ones, and the sell-off led to declines in Asian stock market indexes. The drastic reductions in exports by Asian countries reinforced this. Meanwhile, financial markets around the world, including Asian institutions, that did not have substantial exposures to soured collateralized debt obligations and mortgage-backed assets were strongly affected by asset price movements in developed economies.

On the other hand, some of these countries were somehow insulated from the impact of the U.S. recession. Some private commentators share this view. Growth rates forecast for emerging markets in Asia, though expected to be slower paced than in the pre-crisis years, were more than double those for developed countries. This insulation is puzzling in an era of globalization. The economies of developed and developing nations are interrelated to a greater extent than in the past. Then again, globalization and decoupling may not be totally incompatible. In the past, emerging economies were more coupled with developed economies, especially that of the United States, and less with the rest of the world. Today, emerging countries have become more globalized; that is, they have expanded their relationships with other economies, especially those of neighboring countries. This stemmed partly from a restructuring of global trading arrangements that saw emerging economies trading among themselves and creating new markets in the process.

This is certainly true of Asia. Globalization has allowed economies to decouple from the U.S. economy in at least two ways. First, globalization has resulted in stronger trade relationships among Asian countries. In the case of the Philippines (see Figure 3.1), the share of exports to the United States has declined from 30 percent to less than 20 percent since 2000. Demand from other

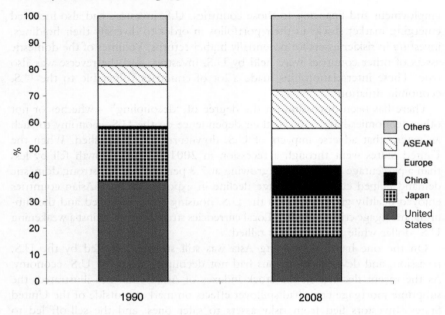

*Figure 3.1* Major trading partners of the Philippines, 1990 and 2008

Source: Bangko Sentral ng Pilipinas (BSP) Statistics (online via BSP website, http://www.bsp.gov.ph/statistics/efs_bop2.asp#bpm6).

Note: ASEAN: Association of Southeast Asian Nations

neighboring countries helped offset the decline in exports resulting from sluggish U.S. consumer demand. Also, China has become a rising force in the region's trading activities. BCA Research reports that emerging markets, as a group, now export more to China than they do to the United States. At the same time, China's internal growth is now expected to result in a reduction in its dependence on exports to the United States. This partly explains the degree of Chinese growth during the crisis despite a deep slide in exports to the United States and Europe.

Second, globalization has helped support the growth of the middle class. With the growth of industries, higher production and income generation have led to strong consumer spending. Growth in Asian countries is gradually but increasingly becoming internally driven by domestic consumers. In turn, increased purchasing power helps to spur investments and capital growth, as businesses emerge to meet domestic demand.

With respect to the Philippines, although the United States remains its biggest trading partner, the decline in export dependence suggests that it is gradually decoupling from the U.S. economy. The same could be said for other emerging markets. Although we are unable to fully quantify the effects, we can expect this trend to continue, especially in light of the growth of large economies such as those of China and India. The progress of this decoupling may ultimately determine how emerging markets will respond to future shocks emanating from other parts of the world.

That said, during the global crisis, the Philippines was adversely affected through the loss of exports due to the slowdowns in developed economies. Its financial sector was not as intensively involved with the financial markets in developed economies as were those of other countries, such as Japan. The immediate impact on the Philippine financial sector was therefore relatively muted. Domestic banks and other financial institutions such as insurance companies were adversely affected by asset losses, but those write-downs were comfortably absorbed by available hedges and capital cover.

On the other hand, macroprudential lapses in the United States, Europe, and other advanced economies led to real economy slowdowns. These real economy effects, in turn, had a major impact on the Philippine real economy. When the financial sectors in the developed economies collapsed, their own real consumption and investment activities declined drastically. These real economy effects led to shrinking of the export markets for export-oriented emerging economies like that of the Philippines.

## 3. Impact on the Philippines

The impact on the Philippines flowed through five channels: first, through the damage to confidence and purchasing power because of the asset losses of members of the higher-spending ranks of the population, magnified by the losses suffered by banks; second, through the added losses to the investing public as portfolio investments flowed out, leading to lower asset values within the country, which in turn led to greater difficulty in mobilizing investment resources in the equity and credit markets; third, through difficulty in raising direct investment capital (foreign direct investment) in the overseas developed markets (to persist over the next few years); fourth, through the impact on exports as our overseas markets contracted (in October down to −37 percent); and, finally, through the feared impact on deployment of overseas Filipino workers (OFW), with the resulting adverse effect on the main engine of Philippine economic growth, OFW remittances. This last impact turned out to be less of a factor as remittances slowed down but did not decline in absolute terms. A closer look at the demand side of the Philippine macroeconomy indicates that the fourth channel constituted the largest impact on the economy.

Figure 3.2 shows how the Philippines was affected. Before the crisis and its attendant uncertainty struck in the latter part of 2007, the GDP growth rate in the Philippines was on a perceptibly upward trend, beginning in the very early part of the decade (around 2001). There was a hesitation in 2004–2005, indicating a tapering off of the growth trend. However, there was a growth spurt in 2006, indicating a recovery of the growth trend. All of these indicators

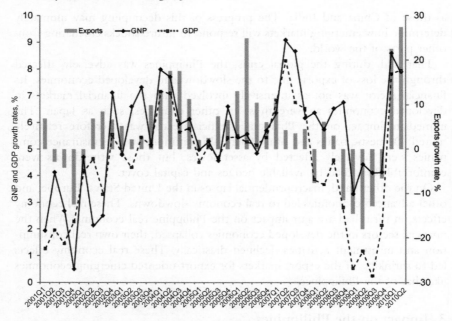

*Figure 3.2* Philippines quarterly output and exports growth rates, 2001Q1 to 2010Q2

Source: National Income Accounts – National Statistical Coordination Board (NIA-NSCB), online data (http://www.nscb.gov.ph/sna/DataCharts.asp).

suddenly reversed as the growth rate dropped dramatically at the onset of the crisis in early 2007. Fortunately, the country narrowly avoided an outright decline in GDP, posting GDP growth of 1.1 percent for 2008. It has since recovered, expanding at an almost historic high growth rate in the first two quarters of 2010.

These gyrations in GDP merely reflected the substantial decline in manufactured exports that started in late 2007 when uncertainties in financial markets were initially felt. The recovery in overall GDP growth in the fourth quarter of 2009 is a continuation of the merchandise exports recovery and is also indicated by the growth in imports, which precedes industrial growth by three to six months, especially in semiconductors and electrical machinery.

In Table 3.1 we show how growth in the Philippine export sector was affected by four main variables: overall appreciation/depreciation of the exchange rate, GDP growth in the United States, GDP growth in Japan, and growth in the import sector. Based on regression results, U.S. GDP growth was the most significant variable determining exports growth (or slowdown).

We then use the 2000 input–output table to trace the sectoral impact of the export slowdown in other parts of the economy. Based on a 2.03 percent export contraction in 2008 – uniform for all subsectors – the slowdown shaved 1.04 percentage points off the country's GDP for that year. Of this,

*Table 3.1* Regression results for export sector growth (%)

| Dependent variable: exports growth | |
| --- | --- |
| Period: 1987:1 to 2010:4 | |
| Exogenous variables | |
| Growth of exchange rate (Php/US$, year-on-year) | −0.2822 |
| | (−3.4251) |
| U.S. GDP growth | 0.0180 |
| | 5.6504 |
| Japanese GDP growth | 0.0068 |
| | 2.1299 |
| Imports growth (−1) | 0.1827 |
| | 2.2822 |
| Adjusted R-squared | 0.7326 |
| Durbin Watson (DW) Statistic | 1.9793 |

Source: Author's calculations.

Note: Moving average (MA) and autoregressive (AR) terms are omitted from the table. GDP: gross domestic product.

0.71 percentage points were borne by the manufacturing subsector, followed by the agriculture, fishery, and forestry subsector at 0.1 percentage points (see Table 3.2).

Next, we look at the country's labor force before and during the global economic crisis. Except for the jump in first quarter of 2009 – when the unemployment rate rose to 7.7 percent from 6.8 percent in the previous quarter – there was no significant change in the number of unemployed in succeeding quarters. From October 2008 through March 2009, a Department of Labor and Employment estimate indicates that around 109,000 workers were displaced because of the crisis (Sy 2009). This estimate was markedly lower than the 950,000 estimate provided by the Asian Development Bank for the same period (Son and San Andres 2009). By regional standards, the impact of the crisis on the Philippine labor markets was relatively small. However, this is not a sign of strength because the impact was effectively muted by the already small size of the industrial sector.

Even as the export, import, and capital formation subsectors contracted from the first quarter up to the third quarter of 2009, domestic consumption continued to hold up. For that period, growth was supported mainly by private spending and later by government pump-priming in the second half of 2009. More importantly, the small number of local equity investors meant that the economy avoided experiencing a significant slowdown in consumption due to negative wealth effects; this was in stark contrast to the United States, where consumption remains stubbornly weak as consumers, devastated by falling asset

*Table 3.2* Simulation results using 2000 input–output table

| | Change in Y (Php thousands) | Change in X (Php thousands) | % Change in X | % Contribution |
|---|---|---|---|---|
| Agriculture, fishery, and forestry | –597,673 | –7,261,195 | –1.06 | –0.1 |
| Mining and quarrying | –115,483 | –2,939,821 | –7.78 | –0.04 |
| Manufacturing | –31,981,241 | –53,607,654 | –1.62 | –0.71 |
| Construction | –87,024 | –165,078 | –0.06 | 0.00 |
| Electricity, gas, and water | — | –1,622,372 | –0.82 | –0.02 |
| Transport, communication, and storage | –1,054,793 | –2,319,065 | –0.45 | –0.03 |
| Trade | –816,692 | –5,271,351 | –0.66 | –0.07 |
| Finance | –130,985 | –964,275 | –0.32 | –0.01 |
| Real estate and ownership of dwelling | — | –186,291 | –0.06 | 0.00 |
| Private services | –2,253,279 | –3,716,279 | –0.56 | –0.05 |
| Government services | –33,195 | –33,195 | –0.01 | 0.00 |
| | 0 | | –1.04 | –1.04 |

Source: Author's own calculations.

prices on their housing and equity investments, now spend less and save more. In fact, the ratio of private consumption to GDP was on a sharp uptrend in 2009, indicating that the GDP experienced deeper slowdowns compared to private consumption for the period.

### 3.1. Remittances and liquidity

Both the run-up to and the height of the global financial crisis led to a marked deceleration in OFW deployment and, consequently, remittance inflows. Overseas deployment decelerated sharply from mid-2008 up until December of that year, when it finally contracted by 9 percent (see Figure 3.3). With the U.S. economy by then mired in a deep recession – believed to have started in December 2007 – manufacturing companies based in South Korea and Taiwan started laying off foreign workers in response to falling U.S. demand. Further adding to their woes was rising uncertainty over the depth and length of the recession, which was projected to affect most if not all of the developed economies, providing no insulation for export-oriented economies.

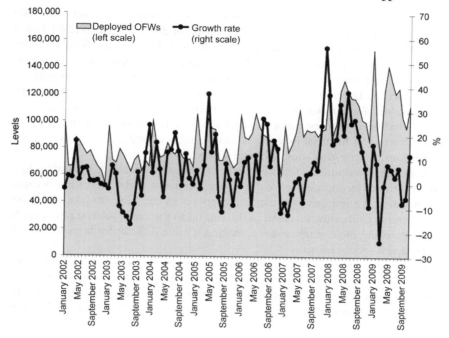

*Figure 3.3* Overseas-deployed Filipino workers (OFWs), January 2002 to November 2009

Source: Philippine Overseas Employment Agency (POEA; http://www.poea.gov.ph/stats/statistics.html).

Before this deceleration, OFW deployment was actually growing at its fastest rate (on a monthly basis) since 2002, peaking at 56 percent in December 2007. In the first half of 2008, the growth rate of deployment easily exceeded 10 percent, although by mid-2008 it had begun to decelerate. The slowdown finally bottomed out in March 2009, when deployment actually contracted by 23 percent. The situation only began to stabilize almost a year after the start of the deceleration, as overseas job placements began to expand once more, albeit at a decidedly slower pace, rising by double digits in November 2009, to 11 percent.

While it was reasonable to expect that remittance inflows would also decline (albeit with a certain lag) as a natural consequence of the decline in deployment, the economy avoided a substantial contraction of inflows owing to the diversifying profile of its overseas workers and labor markets. First, skilled workers and professionals were leaving the country to look for jobs abroad, on either a temporary or a more permanent basis. Second, although OFWs were still concentrated in their traditional markets, such as Taiwan and the Middle East, overseas workers could now be found in more countries than before, allowing them to ride out the global downturn and wait for recovery. Other reasons included their placement in recession-proof industries such as the healthcare and education sectors, and the premiums placed by foreign employers on Filipino employees in general.

As Figure 3.4 shows, remittance inflows narrowly avoided a contraction in 2009 and still managed to expand to US$12.65 billion in 2009, from US$12.64 billion in 2008. With remittances falling, this naturally spilled toward the financial sector because the robust remittance inflows had now replaced export receipts as an important source of foreign exchange and driver of liquidity in the monetary system.

The decline in remittances led to subsequent declines in the country's total liquidity, net foreign assets, and net domestic assets. At the same time, the global decline in interest rates in the United States encouraged the entry of more short-term financial inflows into emerging economies such as that of the Philippines, as investors sought higher yields.

Although the domestic finance subsector was still expanding at double-digit rates up to the second quarter of 2008, risk aversion was also increasing because of unanswered questions over the true exposure of the U.S. financial system to the worsening subprime markets. In the run-up to the crisis, interest rate spreads were becoming increasingly volatile, making it more difficult for firms to finance their capital requirements.

By the time the global financial crisis was inescapably apparent in September 2008, investors had rapidly abandoned the emerging markets, which were now deemed too risky, in an effort to keep their assets as liquid as possible. In response, the world's major central banks, led by the U.S. Federal Reserve

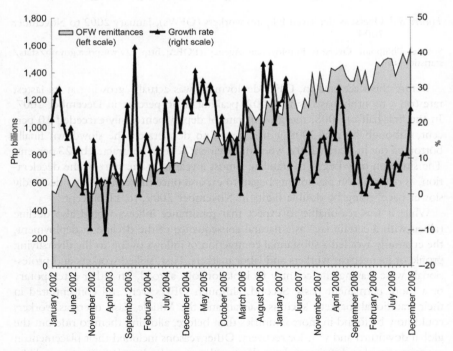

*Figure 3.4* Remittances from overseas Filipino workers (OFWs), January 2002 to December 2009

Source: Bangko Sentral ng Pilipinas (BSP) Statistics (online via BSP website, http://www.bsp.gov.ph/statistics/efs_bop2.asp#bpm6).

Board, launched a coordinated approach of infusing massive emergency liquidity into their financial systems in an attempt to stave off an impending credit crunch.

Subsequent policy actions focused on providing additional monetary stimulus to the systems, first in the form of policy rate cuts (with interest rates already hitting the 0 to 1 percent band for the United States and Japan) and then through ongoing implementation of quantitative easing.[1] Subsequent policy actions, such as interest rate cuts and quantitative easing by major central banks, helped to normalize global markets, as indicated by the easing of global market interest rates and credit default swaps (see Figure 3.5).

Even though the current interest rate spreads between two-year and ten-year government bonds were at significantly higher levels than the pre-crisis levels, the yield volatility also remained low, indicating steady market conditions.

Figure 3.6 shows the flow of portfolio investments in 2008 and 2009. From late 2008 through mid-2009, hot money was flowing out of the country, which was similar to the situations in other countries as investors were influenced by "flight to safety" at that time. Since then, portfolio investments have been volatile, driven partly by related developments in other economies, such as the Euro Crisis.

Surprisingly, the country's sovereign risk ratings remained steady during the global crisis. Unlike in previous crises, the economy was in a better position to respond owing to its stronger fiscal fundamentals (at that time) and its improved balance of payments position. This occurred because of the heavy remittance inflows that raised investor confidence in the economy's ability to pay its foreign liabilities and to sustain its growth track.[2]

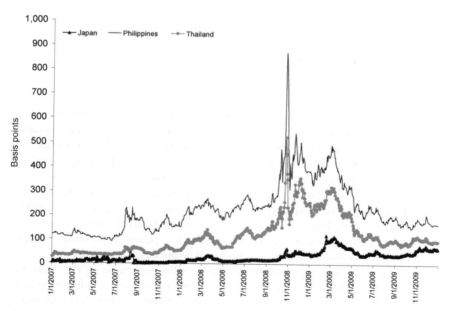

*Figure 3.5* Credit default swaps for selected Asian countries, senior five-year, January 2007 to December 2009

Source: Asian Development Bank, Asian Bonds Online (http://asianbondsonline.adb.org/, accessed September 3, 2010).

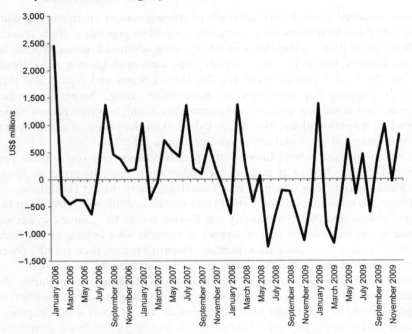

*Figure 3.6* Portfolio investments in the Philippines, January 2006 to December 2009

Source: BOPM5 Concept – Bangko Sentral ng Pilipinas (online via BSP website, http://www.bsp.gov.ph/statistics/efs_bop2.asp#bpm6).

## 4. Impact on the financial sector

### *4.1. Banking sector*

As mentioned earlier, the direct impact of the global crisis on the financial sector was relatively muted since the banking system, accounting for almost 81 percent or Php6.03 trillion of the financial system's estimated Php7.48 trillion value (as of end-December 2008), had no significant exposure to the U.S. subprime mortgage markets that were at the heart of the crisis.[3] While a few banks are thought to have been exposed to some of these troubled U.S. financial firms, primarily through "counterparty exposures", Bangko Sentral ng Pilipinas (BSP), the country's central bank, estimated its exposures at US$1.5 billion, or roughly 1.4 percent of total banking resources, which thus posed no imminent threat to the broader financial system (International Monetary Fund 2009).[4]

Apart from its low exposure to the U.S. subprime markets, the banking system's resilience has also been credited to the regulatory reforms implemented from the mid-1990s to 2000s by the BSP in the wake of the Asian financial crisis (Gunigundo 2006; Manlagnit and Lamberte 2004). These reforms included redefining non-performing loans to align with international standards and general loan loss provisions, adopting a risk-based capital requirement in line with the

Basel 2 recommendations, defining unsafe and unsound banking practices, and advocating greater transparency and disclosure requirements among banks. The new reforms, together with the likely conservative banking behavior prompted by them, helped the banking sector to avoid engagement in the excesses of the global financial crisis. Based on its asset quality indicators, it appears that the banking system had enough resources to withstand the worst effects of the global financial crisis. First, its ratios of non-performing loans (NPL) to total loans and of non-performing assets (NPA) to gross assets were already on a downward trend in the second half of 2008 – hitting 4.13 percent and 5.03 percent respectively in September 2008 (see Figure 3.7).

Contrary to initial expectations, the decline continued in 2009 as both ratios were brought down to 3.66 percent and 4.48 percent respectively in December 2009.[5] Second, the asset levels that the banking system sets aside for possible bad loans also saw a corresponding rise in 2009. From 83.33 percent in September

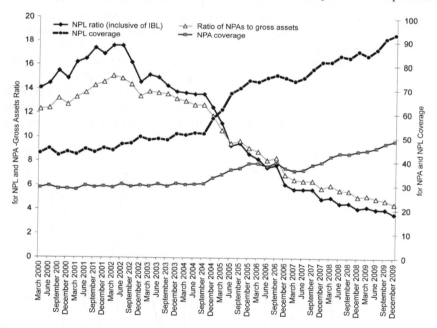

*Figure 3.7* Selected asset quality indicators for the banking system, 2000Q1 to 2009Q4 (%)

Notes: (1) Gross assets refers to: total assets, net of due to head office/branches/agencies + allowance for credit losses-loans + allowance for credit losses – sales contract receivable + allowance for losses of Real and Other Properties Acquired (ROPA) + accumulated depreciation of ROPA – loans classified as loss fully covered by allowance for credit losses; (2) Non-performing assets (NPAs) refers to non-performing loans (NPLs) + ROPA, gross; (3) NPLs refers to loans classified as past due and already non-performing + items in litigation – loans classified as loss fully covered by allowance for credit losses; (4) NPA coverage refers to the ratio of allowance on NPAs to NPAs (IBL = interbank loans receivable); (5) NPL coverage refers to the ratio of allowance for credit losses – loans to NPL.

Source: Bangko Sentral ng Pilipinas (BSP) Statistics and Glossary (online via BSP website, http://www.bsp.gov.ph/statistics/efs_bop2.asp#bpm6m, http://www.bsp.gov.ph/banking/glossary.asp).

2008, its NPL coverage increased to 93.13 percent by end-December 2009. For the same period, its NPA coverage also grew, albeit at a smaller magnitude, from 43.34 percent to just 48.69 percent. Third, the banking system is more than sufficiently capitalized, as indicated by its current capital adequacy (CA) ratios, which are above the BSP's prescribed 10 percent requirement and even higher than the 8 percent ratio set under the international Basel Accord. As of end-December 2009, its CA (consolidated) ratio hit 15.8 percent, from 15.5 percent a year earlier, and its total capital accounts-to-total assets ratio reached 11.1 percent, from 10.6 percent for the same period in the preceding year.

### 4.2. Non-banking sector

The case of the non-banking sector, particularly the insurance subsector, was different because the global financial crisis once again triggered questions about the sector's overall health, an issue that slowed down the industry in 2005–2006.[6] Its strong recovery in 2007 was cut short the following year as deteriorating conditions abroad led to a drop in insurance demand due to the public suspending investment and turning to cash holdings as an emergency measure. From a peak of Php1,080 in 2007, the country's per capita insurance expenditure plunged to Php859.5 in 2008 before settling at Php845.4 in 2009.

This was also evident in the insurance subsector's gross value added (GVA), which, after a bullish 35.48 percent growth in 2007, contracted by 7.52 percent in 2008 and by another 0.84 percent in 2009 (see Figure 3.8). Reduction in

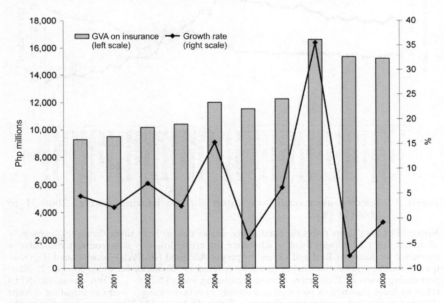

*Figure 3.8* Gross value added (GVA) on insurance and growth rate, 2000–2009

Source: National Income Accounts – National Statistical Coordination Board (NIA-NSCB), online data (http://www.nscb.gov.ph/sna/DataCharts.asp).

insurance coverage could have reflected (i) a drop in asset values and/or (ii) a decline in appetite or ability to pay insurance premiums as revenues suffered; industry observers attribute the slowdown more to the latter. Hence, it comes as no surprise that the country's estimated life insurance coverage remained low. At 13.9 percent in 2009, this was still far below the nine-year high of 18.31 percent back in 2003.

## 5. Lessons from the global financial crisis

There are some lessons that can be gleaned from the global financial crisis. Here we concentrate on the macroeconomic and macroprudential aspects of crises. The implications of the global financial crisis for the development and industrial strategies of countries, or the implications for domestic financial regulation, are not discussed here. These topics have been well covered in other discussion forums. Our focus is on the international finance and macroeconomic aspects.

The first lesson relates to the changing characteristics of international crises. From the more traditional merchandise export and exchange rate crisis that used to be prevalent, the pattern for crises has gradually evolved toward one of more financial and asset collapses, a process that may have originated in the developing country debt problems of the late 1970s and early 1980s, up to the Asian financial crisis, from which countries discovered that it was not sufficient to be well behaved in fiscal and trade terms. Because cross-border flows have come to be dominated by financial and capital flows, changes in asset prices anywhere in the world can substantially affect the international finance and macroeconomic interests of particular countries, especially those without deep capital and financial markets, such as emerging economies. Consequently, it is no longer safe to simply concentrate on good housekeeping in the fiscal, trade, and industrial sectors. It would be prudent for countries to also monitor financial markets around the world, as offshore events could affect the values of their own financial assets and liabilities. The intertwining of financial markets has made countries more interdependent. This has been of immense benefit because capital and financial flows have allowed countries to circumvent some resource bottlenecks and have even served as crisis-dampening mechanisms. However, certain events have also demonstrated potential to cause disequilibrium; accordingly, care needs to be exercised.

Second, the global financial crisis has taught us that macroprudential lapses (admittedly unintended) in some countries also have the potential to exert tremendous impact on other countries. Furthermore, the disequilibrating force can come from any direction. This lesson is particularly apt for Asian countries, which were already watchful as to the indebtedness of their public and private sectors, even as they exercised prudence with regard to their fiscal budgets and trade flows. However, that prudence did not totally insulate them against the effects of the global financial crisis; some countries were adversely affected by the changing values of their assets. The drastic drops in the values of assets invested in the developed economies affected the investment and consumption behaviors of their own constituents and those of other countries. In the case of the Philippines, the decline in prices of its international assets had only minimal impact because more conservative regulation and risk aversion on the part of its citizens prevented large-scale exposure to international financial markets. However, it still suffered substantially when its exports to developed markets shrank as the asset values of developed economies adversely affected the consumption and investment behaviors of their citizens.

Thus, given the ongoing integration of financial markets and increased use of financial techniques to ease real economy activities such as investment and production, exporting countries must monitor not only the real economy events of their trading partners but also their financial markets. The implications for macroeconomic and industrial development strategies related to diversifying markets and products are discussed elsewhere. What is taken up here is the need for countries to be mindful of not only their own macroprudential mechanisms but also those of their trading partners, and even beyond.

Summarizing the two lessons outlined above, we are led to the conclusion that the modern, globalized world is much more complicated than many may have ever imagined. While this new reality has put more instruments and techniques within our reach, it has also increased the risks with which we could be confronted. There is a need for further analytical work to find out how to maximize the benefits of the mechanisms and techniques while minimizing the potential hazards.

## Notes

1   The U.S. Federal Reserve Board's first round of quantitative easing began in December 2008 and lasted until March 2010. It initially targeted purchases of US$600 billion in assets but later expanded this to US$1.7 trillion in Treasury debt, mortgage-backed securities, and Fannie Mae– and Freddie Mac–backed assets. In November 2010 the U.S. Fed's Federal Open Market Committee announced a second round of quantitative easing worth US$600 billion until March 2011 to provide more monetary stimulus and counter possible deflation.
2   For a more comprehensive discussion, please see "The Macroeconomic Impact of Remittances in the Philippines" by Dr. Cayetano W. Paderanga, Jr. (2009).
3   At an exchange rate of Php44.4746 to US$1 in 2008, total resources for the country's financial system reached US$168.07 billion, with the banking and non-banking systems being worth US$135.76 billion and US$32.33 billion, respectively.
4   Initial reports by the BSP state that around seven to ten banks – led by Banco de Oro Unibank at US$134 million and the Development Bank of the Philippines at US$90 million – had a combined exposure of US$386 million to failed U.S. investment giant Lehman Brothers.
5   Five years after the onset of the Asian financial crisis, the banking system was still overburdened by its NPAs. In March 2002 its NPL ratios and NPA-to-gross asset ratios hit their worst levels, at 17.6 percent and 15.1 percent, respectively. To spur the offloading of these NPAs and NPLs, the BSP pushed for critical legislation, namely, the Special Purpose Vehicle Act of 2002 and its extension in 2004, which granted tax incentives to asset management companies and/or special-purpose vehicles.

6 This arose from the still-unresolved problems affecting the pre-need sector, one of the more popular savings schemes in the country. In September 2005 one of the largest pre-need companies – the College Assurance Plan – filed for corporate rehabilitation. It was followed down this path by other pre-need firms such as Pacific Plans, PET Plans, Platinum Corporation, and TPG Corporation (Goboleo 2008).

## References and Further Readings

Aldaba, R.M. 2008. SMEs in the Philippine Manufacturing Industry and Globalization: Meeting the Development Challenges. Philippine Institute for Development Studies Discussion Paper (PIDS DP) 2008-15, May. Makati City, the Philippines: Philippine Institute for Development Studies (PIDS).

Goboleo, D.D. 2008. Reforming the Pre-need Industry: A Review. Congressional Planning and Budget Department, House of Representatives Policy Advisory 2008-07. Quezon City, the Philippines.

Gunigundo, D. 2006. The Philippine Financial System: Issues and Challenges in the Banking System in Emerging Economies. How Much Progress Has Been Made? Bank for International Settlements Paper 28 295. Hong Kong: Bank for International Settlements (BIS).

International Monetary Fund (IMF). 2009. Philippines: Selected Issues. Country Report 09/63, February. Washington, DC: International Monetary Fund.

International Monetary Fund (IMF). 2010. Philippines: Financial System Stability Assessment Update. Country Report 10/90, April. Washington, DC: International Monetary Fund.

Kawai, M. and G. Wignaraja. 2011. Asia's Free Trade Agreements: How Is Asia Responding? Manila: Asian Development Bank (ADB) and ADB Institute with Edward Elgar Publishing.

Manlagnit, M.C.V. and M.B. Lamberte. 2004. Evaluating the Impacts of Competition Policy Reforms on the Efficiency of Philippine Commercial Banks. Philippine Institute for Development Studies Discussion Paper (PIDS DP) 2004-46, December. Makati City, the Philippines: Philippine Institute for Development Studies (PIDS).

Paderanga, C.W. 2009. The Macroeconomic Impact of Remittances in the Philippines. University of the Philippines School of Economics (UPSE) Discussion Paper 0903, June. Quezon City, Philippines: University of the Philippines School of Economics.

Son, H. and E. San Andres. 2009. How Has Asia Fared in the Global Crisis? A Tale of Three Countries: Republic of Korea, Philippines and Thailand. Asian Development Bank Working Paper 2009-174, October. Mandaluyong City: Philippine Institute for Development Studies (PIDS).

Sy, M. 2009. DOLE: RP Labor Headed for Rebound. *Philippine Star*, March 29.

Yap, J.T., C.M. Reyes, and J.S. Cuenca. 2009. Impact of the Global Financial and Economic Crisis on the Philippines. Philippine Institute for Development Studies Discussion Paper (PIDS DP) 2009-03. Makati City, Philippines.

# 4 Macro-financial linkage and financial deepening in Thailand

*Chaiyasit Anuchitworawong*

## 1. Introduction

The most recent financial crisis originating in the United States has attracted considerable attention from policymakers, economists, and the financial media. The crisis was a massive failure of the banking system that affected all corners of the financial markets and real sectors in various countries. Its impacts have been transmitted worldwide; however, they are relatively country specific depending on the intensity of financial linkages with the crisis-hit countries.

Research into the causes of financial crises, for example, the work of Reinhart and Rogoff (2008), has documented that previous financial crises shared several common causes, such as credit booms, currency speculation, asset price bubbles, and large and persistent capital flows. Comparing the 2007 U.S. subprime mortgage crisis with the 1997 Asian financial crisis, we see that the impacts of the recent crisis differed in terms of scale and scope. Strikingly, this latter event was the result of financial innovation that endangered the financial stability of large economies and would lead to significant underestimation of credit and liquidity risk exposure.

In retrospect, Thailand has experienced financial difficulties several times in the past. The most painful was when the Thai economy was hit by a series of currency attacks during late 1996 and mid-1997, leading to devaluation of the Thai baht and driving massive increases in the liabilities of Thai firms that, before the onset of the crisis, had substantially relied on short-term loans from international markets to finance long-term and illiquid investment. Consequently, these firms suffered significantly from a steep depreciation of the baht, illiquidity, and tremendous losses. Further, many financial institutions encountered liquidity and insolvency problems, some were closed down, and others were beset by substantial non-performing loans, which weakened the quality of their loan portfolios. The situation was aggravated by the cross-border transmission of the crisis and shocks, which hit other Asian countries and had a feedback effect on the Thai economy (Tinakorn, 2006). However, the lessons learned from that crisis sparked a number of important policy reform initiatives, all of which were aimed at reinforcing robustness and risk management discipline in domestic financial systems. For example, the Bank of Thailand introduced a macro-prudential framework and risk-based supervision to strengthen the risk management practices of financial institutions. Several preventive measures were introduced, such as limits on the loan-to-value ratio for luxury mortgages, higher minimum payment requirements for credit cards and personal loans, and higher non-performing loan provisions through the fair valuation standards of the International Accounting Standard 39 (IAS 39). There were also some improvements in financial and legal infrastructures, including enactment of new legislation such as the Deposit Protection Act, establishment of a National Credit Bureau, enactment of a Financial Sector Master Plan, etc. As ongoing globalization links Thailand more closely with other countries through trade and financial activities, it is important to examine how resilient the Thai economy was in response to the most recent financial crisis.

This chapter aims to answer three main questions: (a) whether or not the global financial crisis of 2008 changed the structure of macro-financial linkages, (b) whether or not the crisis affected domestic financial deepening in regional emerging market economies, and (c) how regional financial cooperation can be achieved in order to bolster the economic community. The rest of the chapter is organized as follows: Section 2 analyzes the macro-financial linkages and impacts of the global financial crisis on macroeconomic performance to determine if the Thai economy was able to weather the impacts of the crisis. Section 3 analyzes the effects of the crisis on financial deepening in Thailand. Section 4 addresses the importance of regional financial cooperation in East Asia and ways to strengthen such cooperation. The author's conclusions are provided in Section 5.

## 2. Macro-financial linkages and impacts of the global financial crisis on macroeconomic performance

To analyze the extent to which Thailand has been affected by the global financial crisis that hit the world in 2008, this section first provides an overview of the Thai economic structure, describing economic and financial ties to foreign economies through trade and financial transactions, and goes on to show the impacts of the financial crisis on Thailand's macroeconomic performance, particularly in the financial and asset markets but also in the real sector.

A series of trade and financial liberalization actions played an important role in shaping Thailand's current economic structure. By formally accepting the obligations under Article VIII of the Articles of Agreement of the International Monetary Fund (IMF), Thailand underwent complete liberalization of current account transactions and reduction of restrictions on capital flows, and also entered into free trade agreements, at both bilateral and regional levels. To examine how the economy interacts with the wave of financial and trade liberalization, we analyze the degree of financial and trade openness, which, to some extent, demonstrates the impact of the global crisis on the Thai economy through financial and trade linkages with the rest of the world. The financial and trade openness indicators are defined as the sum of foreign assets and liabilities and the sum of exports and imports, respectively, as percentages of the gross domestic product (GDP). It can be seen that the economy has relied heavily on cross-border trade and financial activities (Figure 4.1). The degree of financial and trade openness has witnessed a significant rise since the late 1980s, particularly after the end of the 1997 financial crisis. However, when the global financial crisis struck in 2008, it affected Thai financial markets drastically in the short run as there was a substantial amount of capital flight to safer countries, leading to a drop in the degree of financial openness. However, the economic conditions of the crisis-hit developed countries continued to be bleak, while the economies of countries like Thailand and other Asian countries that were not directly hit by the crisis started to recover gradually and tended to provide better opportunities for foreign investors to earn an attractive return on their capital. Hence, a substantial amount of money began to flow back into Thailand. As a result, the degree of financial openness grew substantially in 2009. This was driven largely by remarkable foreign inflows, particularly in the form of portfolio equities.

With respect to the trade openness indicator, there had been a rise in the level of international trade, due mainly to the government's export-promotion policies, relocation of production facilities from industrial countries, and a shift in the official exchange rate regime. However, the degree of trade openness dropped remarkably in 2009, suggesting how badly a crisis could hurt domestic economic activities when foreign demand for Thai products dropped considerably as a result of sluggish global economic conditions.

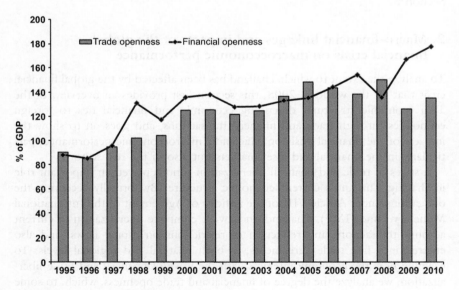

*Figure 4.1* Financial and trade openness

Source: Author's calculations based on data from the Bank of Thailand and Office of the National Economic and Social Development Board.

In sum, the process of liberalization of trade and investment has helped to create global networks in production, trade, and finance, giving rise to an interconnected world. However, this interlinking of local networks with global networks comes with benefits and risks, in particular the risk of contagion. The U.S. subprime problem that came to light in 2007 is a good example of contagion because it sparked severe economic repercussions and worldwide deleveraging. Clearly, there was a massive flight to quality during the period, with investors flooding out of risky markets to more secure ones in pursuit of protection against potential losses from the ongoing economic downturns. As foreign investors sold assets and withdrew their investments, such sales eventually accelerated downturns in local markets.

Events to date with respect to the current global financial crisis clearly illustrate the power of the financial sector to amplify business cycle dynamics. An adverse feedback loop exists in which disruptions in financial markets will restrain economic activities. Weaker economic activity is likely to exacerbate financial strains, causing a further deterioration in the macroeconomic status in the form of falling asset prices, worsening balance sheet positions for borrowers, and higher likelihood that a financial disruption could cause further contraction of the real economy (Bernanke, Gertler, and Gilchrist, 1999). Tanboon et al. (2009) argued that there exists a financial accelerator in Thailand whereby businesses and lenders are financially constrained. Such financial constraint is not limited to firms and banks; households and government are similarly affected. Using the 2007 Industrial Census, the authors showed that about 70 percent of total investment in the manufacturing sector was made by firms that relied on external finance. Although Thailand was not at the center of the global financial crisis, the crisis did to some extent affect the performance of the country's local industries as adverse financial conditions intensified negative shocks and brought about a downward spiral for the economy. Tanboon and colleagues also postulated that the risk premium rather than a network shock helped to explain a rise in the external finance premium in Thailand. In the following sub-section, therefore, we attempt to investigate further the extent to which Thailand's real and financial sectors may have been affected by the two most recent crises.

## 2.1. Impacts of crises on the real sector

Comparing the two most recent crises, it becomes apparent that the magnitude of the impact of the recent global crisis on the Thai economy was quite different from what had been experienced in the earlier situation. Specifically, following the 1997 Asian financial crisis, it took at least four years for Thailand's GDP to recover to near pre-crisis level, whereas this time it took only about one year to recover from the 2008 global financial crisis. Plotting the economic growth rates of various countries over the period 1990–2010 clearly shows that the Group of Seven advanced economies (G7) and European Union (EU) countries were not affected by the 1997 Asian financial crisis because their growth rates continued to improve, whereas a group of countries in the Association of

Southeast Asian Nations (ASEAN) and the newly industrialized economies were substantially affected, although to a much lesser extent in the case of the latter (Figure 4.2). On the other hand, during the subprime mortgage crisis period the Thai economy contracted at a rate that was almost comparable to the rates in the crisis-hit G7 and European countries. Worse, the economy showed poor economic performance in comparison with the average performance across the ASEAN-5 countries (Indonesia, Malaysia, the Philippines, Vietnam, and Thailand), while China showed strong growth over the same period.

*Business cycle synchronization*

With the rapid progress of globalization and improvements in cross-border information and capital flows, the economic policies of a country tend to affect other countries to varying degrees as a result of shocks from one country being transmitted across borders. To check whether the Thai economy has a high degree of business cycle correlation with others, we analyzed the co-movement of international business cycles, or business cycle synchronization, employing the rolling time series method with a time span of 16 quarters to measure the correlation of GDP growth among Thailand, major advanced countries, and Asian countries. The rolling time series method computes correlations that update each period within a given time frame.

Figure 4.3 shows that during the recent crisis there was fairly high and positive international business correlation between Thailand and all major selected industrial economies except for the United Kingdom, and also between Thailand and all selected Asian economies excluding the Republic of Korea. This happened because these crisis-hit economies were major export destinations for Thai products. Hence, the collapse of external demand in these markets certainly affected the Thai

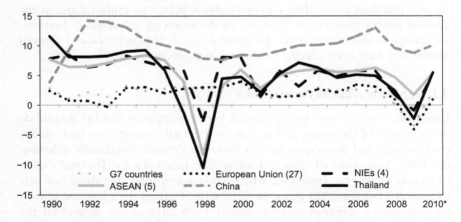

*Figure 4.2* Annual percentage growth rates of the GDP by country group/countries

Source: International Monetary Fund (2010), *World Economic Outlook, Rebalancing Growth, World Economic and Financial Surveys*, Washington, DC.

(a) Between Thailand and major advanced economies

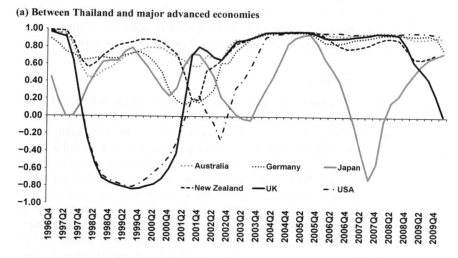

(b) Between Thailand and selected Asian economies

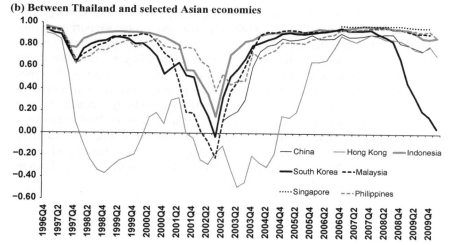

*Figure 4.3* Co-movement correlation between Thailand and other countries

Source: Author's calculations based on data from International Monetary Fund, *International Financial Statistics.*

economy, at least in the short to medium term. The same reasoning applies to the Asian economies: because these countries were engaged in similar economic and export activities, they were exposed to similar global economic shocks. Nonetheless, the pattern is different from what was evident during the Asian financial crisis. That crisis did not affect advanced economies, other than that of Japan. Specifically, there was an apparently negative business cycle correlation between Thailand on the one hand and the United States, United Kingdom, and Hong Kong on the other (Figure 4.3a), whereas there was a quite strong and positive correlation between Thailand and all of the selected Asian countries (Figure 4.3b). These results support the findings of earlier studies that countries with intensive trade links and close proximity are likely to have similar business cycles.

## Government responses to the crisis

Since the impacts of the subprime mortgage crisis were not foreseeable at that time, the Thai government, fearing that the crisis would be prolonged and that sluggish external demand would continue to hold back economic expansion and even trigger a deep economic downturn, responded by developing massive fiscal stimulus packages, as had been done in most countries, expecting that these would help in resisting the effects of the 2008 global financial crisis and the expected slow growth in its aftermath.[1] More specifically, the government unveiled its first stimulus package of about US$5.8 billion in January 2009 and followed up with a second package of US$4.2 billion in June 2009. According to the Fiscal Policy Office, implementation of the "Strong Thailand 2012" economic stimulus program of around US$10 billion was designed to be used in such areas as food and energy security, basic public services development, tourism development, public health development, education, community and quality of life programs, and income support programs. As of April 23, 2010, the disbursement rate was about 33.28 percent.

Figure 4.4 suggests that the strong government spending was the main driver that helped to prevent a larger contraction of the economy during the crisis. However, using fiscal stimulus to tackle the slow growth and economic downturn worsened the country's fiscal balance by causing a record budget deficit of about 349 billion baht, representing a negative 4 percent of GDP in 2009, worsening from 0 percent in 2008. More importantly, the ratio of public debt to GDP rose dramatically to 45 percent in 2009, despite the fact that the ratio fell gradually from 56–7 percent during the 1997–8 Asian financial crisis to bottom out at 37 percent in 2008 (Figure 4.5).

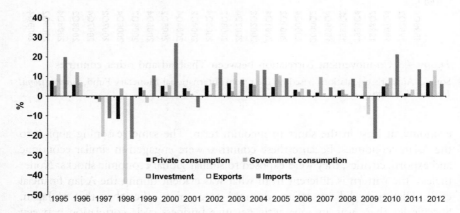

*Figure 4.4* Annual percentage growth rates of GDP components

Source: Author's calculations based on data from Office of the National Economic and Social Development Board, *Quarterly Gross Domestic Product* tables.

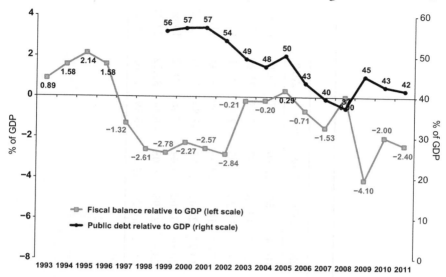

*Figure 4.5* Fiscal balance and public debt

Source: Author's calculations based on data from the Fiscal Policy Office and Public Debt Management Office.

## Export performance and sluggish external demand

A sharp decline in export growth was observed after the subprime mortgage crisis took effect. On an annual basis, exports from Thailand declined drastically from US$178 billion in 2008 to US$152 billion in 2009, accounting for a negative growth rate of 14 percent. In order to explore the extent to which the situations in crisis-hit countries affected Thailand's international trade performance, the next few paragraphs analyze the geographical breakdown of exports to determine the risks and pressures they exerted on domestic production.

The breakdown of total Thai exports by major destination in Table 4.1 suggests that the economy has relied heavily on exporting to major trading partners, including Japan, the United States, Europe, and ASEAN countries during the past few decades, accounting for more than 54 percent of total exports during 1996–2009 (Table 4.1). To examine how sensitive Thai exports were to the economic conditions of trading partners, Poonpatpibul et al. (2009) measured the elasticity of Thai export volume in relation to trading partners' GDPs and found very high elasticity, meaning that Thai exports, particularly high-tech exports, would be substantially affected during economic downturns among trading partners.

Since the Thai economy was closely connected with these major countries through trade, their deteriorating demand amid slow economic growth was likely the principal factor that led to negative growth of exports to those

*Table 4.1* Concentration and growth of Thai exports by major destination

| | % share | | | | | | | % growth | | | | | | |
|---|---|---|---|---|---|---|---|---|---|---|---|---|---|---|
| | 1996 | 2002 | 2006 | 2008 | 2009 | 2010 | 2011 | 1996 | 2002 | 2006 | 2008 | 2009 | 2010 | 2011 |
| Japan | 16.82 | 14.60 | 12.63 | 11.30 | 10.32 | 10.51 | 10.72 | -1.13 | 0.04 | 8.59 | 10.90 | -21.75 | 29.16 | 17.53 |
| United States | 17.97 | 19.82 | 14.99 | 11.40 | 10.93 | 10.45 | 9.79 | -0.51 | 2.34 | 14.43 | 4.42 | -17.83 | 21.25 | 7.83 |
| Europe | 16.60 | 15.55 | 13.90 | 13.19 | 11.93 | 11.30 | 10.87 | -0.79 | -2.95 | 19.25 | 7.90 | -22.41 | 20.11 | 10.75 |
| ASEAN | 21.64 | 19.91 | 20.83 | 22.59 | 21.32 | 22.93 | 24.28 | -1.72 | 7.69 | 10.79 | 22.45 | -19.08 | 36.41 | 21.94 |
| Middle East | 3.83 | 3.60 | 4.41 | 5.34 | 5.74 | 4.98 | 4.65 | -15.92 | 13.97 | 28.01 | 26.88 | -7.84 | 10.09 | 7.47 |
| Australia | 1.51 | 2.41 | 3.35 | 4.49 | 5.63 | 4.85 | 3.59 | 8.11 | 20.56 | 37.02 | 34.44 | 7.46 | 9.22 | -14.65 |
| China | 3.35 | 5.22 | 9.04 | 9.11 | 10.58 | 11.11 | 11.79 | 13.80 | 23.72 | 27.93 | 9.05 | -0.44 | 33.22 | 22.24 |
| Hong Kong | 5.82 | 5.41 | 5.52 | 5.65 | 6.22 | 5.82 | 5.37 | 10.91 | 11.52 | 16.25 | 15.54 | -5.59 | 18.62 | 6.25 |

Source: Author's calculations based on data from Bank of Thailand, *Trade Classified by Country (US$)*.

Note: ASEAN stands for Association of Southeast Asian Nations.

countries, falling from around −17 percent to −22 percent in 2009. However, the question is why ASEAN countries imported less from Thailand despite the fact that they were not at the center of the crisis. The underlying reason was that most ASEAN countries have been integrated into global production networks to supply intermediate inputs and final products to world markets. Since their export performance was tied to final demand in major advanced economies, those countries experienced both direct exposure to slowdowns in exports to the United States and Europe and indirect exposure through China, which itself experienced a decline in exports to the United States and Europe.[2] This helps to explain why Thai exports fell dramatically during the crisis period.

### 2.2. Impacts of the crisis on financial and asset markets

By analyzing the amount of value added from the production side, we were able to observe that the current global crisis did not affect the Thai financial sector to anywhere near the same extent as did the 1997–8 Asian financial crisis. Figure 4.6 shows that the growth rate for real value added in the financial sector has been positive since 2001, following several years of highly negative growth during 1997–2000. And the sector was resilient enough to withstand external shocks from the current global turmoil. Thus, financial sector growth remained in the positive zone with a growth rate of 3.98 percent being recorded in 2009, thanks to the policy reform initiatives taken after the 1997 financial crisis that helped to strengthen the fundamentals of the Thai banking system. In addition to the reforms made in several areas in the wake of the earlier crisis, Thai banks have been more cautious about their

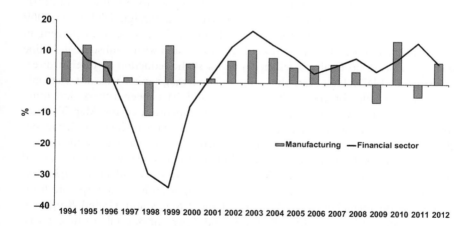

*Figure 4.6* Annual percentage growth rates of value added in manufacturing and financial sectors

Source: Author's calculations based on data from Office of the National Economic and Social Development Board, *Quarterly Gross Domestic Product* tables.

lending and investment policies and procedures. This helps explain why there was very low direct exposure of Thai banks to foreign assets, which made up only 1.2 percent of total assets as of August 2008, of which 0.04 percent was associated with subprime-related collateralized debt obligation (CDO) investments. Furthermore, since Thai banks depended more on deposit funding than on external funding, the sector was not greatly affected by the turmoil abroad.

Following the analytical framework using the balance sheets of various sectors, including household, corporate, financial, and government sectors, we can observe how each sector is interlinked through capital structure and is possibly linked with foreign countries, leading to more complicated risk transmission patterns. In practice, financial risk can be transmitted in different patterns and can sometimes cause serious feedback problems to the economy—for example, from the corporate sector to the financial sector and to the public sector, similar to what was experienced in the 1997–8 Asian financial crisis, or from the financial sector to the public sector, as in the current global financial crisis. The magnitude of financial impacts depends largely on the level of international financial linkage between the country concerned and the crisis-hit countries. In this regard, this section analyzes the international investment position and asset price movements in the stock and bond markets.

*International investment position*

Table 4.2 presents a breakdown of external assets and liabilities into functional investment categories, which include direct investment, portfolio investment, financial derivatives, other investments, and reserves. In general, total outstanding foreign assets in 2009 were about four-fold higher than the level in 2001, ending at a record high of US$219 billion, while total foreign liabilities in 2009 were 2.1 times the level in 2001 but had shrunk by almost 12.5 percent in 2008. The fall in total liabilities in 2008 was associated with a substantial decline in foreign portfolio equity investments and a slight reduction in foreign direct investment (FDI). However, the subprime mortgage crisis was not the only factor responsible for the decline. There could have been others, including political uncertainty and the potential risk of suspension of the Map Ta Phut industrial estate project, which made investors reluctant to invest in Thailand. Regarding external debt, although not reported, the statistics showed that the financial sector's dependence on external financing was relatively low compared to that of the corporate sector. Moreover, private firms had been relying on long-term rather than short-term debt. More importantly, Thai corporate firms relied less on financing raised from the United States and United Kingdom, which accounted for only about 8 percent and 7 percent of total private external debt, respectively (Table 4.3). To summarize, Thai financial institutions and corporate firms did not suffer much from the subprime mortgage problems compared to their counterparts in countries that were closely linked with the crisis-hit countries.

Table 4.2 Annual international investment position of Thailand (US$ billions)

| | 2001 | 2002 | 2003 | 2004 | 2005 | 2006 | 2007 | 2008 | 2009 |
|---|---|---|---|---|---|---|---|---|---|
| Total assets | 54.32 | 58.73 | 64.19 | 81.86 | 92.19 | 120.93 | 163.61 | 179.73 | 218.94 |
| Direct investment | 2.63 | 2.86 | 3.40 | 3.73 | 5.07 | 6.40 | 9.99 | 13.36 | 18.21 |
| Portfolio investment: equity securities | 0.08 | 0.08 | 0.43 | 0.69 | 1.02 | 1.78 | 3.30 | 2.18 | 3.30 |
| Portfolio investment: debt securities | 0.74 | 1.61 | 2.40 | 0.93 | 2.46 | 3.01 | 11.89 | 11.24 | 20.08 |
| Financial derivatives | 0.14 | 0.28 | 0.61 | 0.64 | 0.47 | 0.71 | 1.57 | 4.60 | 3.36 |
| Other investment (trade credits, loans, etc.) | 17.68 | 14.97 | 15.20 | 26.03 | 31.11 | 42.05 | 49.40 | 37.34 | 35.57 |
| Reserve assets | 33.05 | 38.92 | 42.15 | 49.83 | 52.07 | 66.99 | 87.46 | 111.01 | 138.42 |
| Total liabilities | 105.03 | 103.24 | 118.77 | 132.82 | 146.07 | 177.10 | 216.80 | 189.79 | 220.81 |
| Direct investment | 33.27 | 38.45 | 48.94 | 53.18 | 60.41 | 76.95 | 94.11 | 93.50 | 106.15 |
| Portfolio investment: equity securities | 10.24 | 12.26 | 24.32 | 26.62 | 32.98 | 38.50 | 56.94 | 25.84 | 45.32 |
| Portfolio investment: debt securities | 6.84 | 5.49 | 4.77 | 5.49 | 7.35 | 9.06 | 7.09 | 8.27 | 9.21 |
| Financial derivatives | 0.51 | 0.54 | 0.77 | 0.84 | 0.60 | 0.57 | 1.15 | 4.10 | 3.19 |
| Other investment (trade credits, loans, etc.) | 54.17 | 46.50 | 39.97 | 46.69 | 44.73 | 52.01 | 57.50 | 58.10 | 56.94 |
| Net international investment position | −50.70 | −44.52 | −54.58 | −50.97 | −53.88 | −56.17 | −53.19 | −10.06 | −1.88 |
| Direct investment | −30.64 | −35.59 | −45.54 | −49.46 | −55.34 | −70.55 | −84.12 | −80.14 | −87.94 |
| Portfolio investment: equity securities | −10.16 | −12.18 | −23.89 | −25.92 | −31.97 | −36.73 | −53.64 | −23.65 | −42.02 |
| Portfolio investment: debt securities | −6.10 | −3.89 | −2.37 | −4.56 | −4.89 | −6.06 | 4.80 | 2.97 | 10.88 |
| Financial derivatives | −0.37 | −0.26 | −0.15 | −0.20 | −0.13 | 0.14 | 0.42 | 0.50 | 0.17 |
| Other investment (trade credits, loans, etc.) | −36.49 | −31.54 | −24.78 | −20.65 | −13.62 | −9.96 | −8.10 | −20.75 | −21.37 |
| Reserve assets | 33.05 | 38.92 | 42.15 | 49.83 | 52.07 | 66.99 | 87.46 | 111.01 | 138.42 |

Source: Bank of Thailand, *Thailand's International Investment Position Statistics*.

*Table 4.3* Proportion of external debt by creditor country

| Country | 2004 | 2005 | 2006 | 2007 | 2008 | 2009 |
|---|---|---|---|---|---|---|
| Singapore (%) | 13 | 15 | 18 | 18 | 22 | 23 |
| Japan (%) | 17 | 15 | 14 | 14 | 16 | 16 |
| Hong Kong (%) | 10 | 11 | 11 | 11 | 14 | 14 |
| United Kingdom (%) | 11 | 6 | 6 | 5 | 7 | 8 |
| United States (%) | 24 | 26 | 22 | 19 | 11 | 7 |
| Cayman Islands (%) | 0 | 0 | 0 | 4 | 3 | 4 |
| Germany (%) | 6 | 6 | 5 | 5 | 4 | 3 |
| Others (%) | 20 | 19 | 23 | 24 | 24 | 25 |
| Total private non-bank external debt(in billions of bahts) | 24.79 | 24.18 | 30.10 | 32.82 | 34.48 | 32.54 |

Source: Author's calculations based on data from Bank of Thailand, *Report on Thailand's External Debt Outstanding as of end-December 2009.*

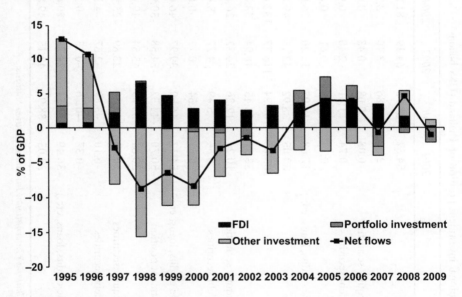

*Figure 4.7* Net capital flows

Source: Author's calculations based on data from Bank of Thailand, *Balance of Payment Statistics.*

This section further illustrates the pattern of net capital flows in Thailand with a longer time span between 1995 and 2009. Figure 4.7 highlights an improvement in the amount of external indebtedness and the debt structure, partly resulting from the post-1997 structural reforms that helped to enhance capital flows into the Thai economy. The share of net capital flows to GDP began improving gradually after the 1997 Asian financial crisis, thanks to continuous inflows of FDI and the improved external debt position. Following the economic recovery, the soundness of the country's macroeconomic fundamentals attracted speculative capital inflows, boosted by the market's expectation of baht appreciation. Therefore, net flows of foreign portfolio investment rose significantly during 2005–6. This spurred the Central Bank of Thailand to intervene in the foreign exchange market. But the official intervention failed to work effectively because the pressure of baht appreciation continued to rise. Consequently, the central bank had to impose a 30 percent unremunerated reserve requirement on short-term foreign capital inflows with less than one-year maturity, resulting in net outflows of portfolio investment. However, the measure was subsequently lifted in March 2008.

Regarding sources of FDI, Japan remained the largest contributor of FDI in Thailand in 2009, accounting for 35 percent of total FDI stock, followed by Singapore (13 percent) and the United States (9 percent) (Table 4.4). However, the role of the ASEAN community has gained in importance over time, at a slow but steady pace. FDI was mainly concentrated in the manufacturing sector (58 percent), followed by financial institutions (13 percent), real estate and hotels (8 percent), trade (6.6 percent), and services (5.9 percent). However, the advent of the global financial crisis in 2007 adversely affected confidence among foreign investors, resulting in a negative growth rate for FDI stock from Singapore, the United States, and Hong Kong.

As for foreign portfolio investment, its scale had been somewhat small compared to that of FDI, but it had been on the rise in recent years, showing an average annual growth rate of 25.6 percent during 2001–7. The country breakdown for foreign portfolio investment indicated that investors in the United Kingdom, Singapore, and the United States had played dominant roles in the Thai equities market. However, the current crisis was likely to cause the stock of foreign portfolio equity investment to drop by half, from US$30 billion in 2007 to roughly US$14 billion in 2008 (Table 4.5). The substantial decrease was due in part to considerable deterioration in market prices for equities and also to worldwide panic in financial markets that caused foreign investors to pull back their investments and capital out of concern about the rising degree of financial turmoil and the possibility of the contagion spreading to Thailand.

Overall, although the net international investment position (NIIP) remained a net foreign liability position with a smaller deficit of $4.8 billion in 2009, there still existed an asset-liability mismatch, particularly in the private non-bank sector. In other words, the assets were mostly in the form of debt, while the liabilities were in the form of equities. More importantly, the primary factor underlying the improved NIIP came from an increase in reserve assets, which recorded a high of US$138 billion in 2009. The ongoing increase in reserve assets stems from the fact that Thailand's current account surplus has continued to expand over the past 10 years. Figure 4.8 depicts movement in the NIIP and the cumulative current account balance as percentages of the GDP. It can be seen that both lines generally moved in the same direction, except during the crisis period of 1997–8, when the two indicators can be seen to diverge.

*Table 4.4* Foreign direct investment (FDI) into Thailand by major countries

| | 2001 | 2002 | 2003 | 2004 | 2005 | 2006 | 2007 | 2008 | 2009 |
|---|---|---|---|---|---|---|---|---|---|
| Total FDI (in billions of bahts) | 25.51 | 29.71 | 40.94 | 44.64 | 46.88 | 62.74 | 75.97 | 75.25 | 87.42 |
| (a) Proportion (%) | | | | | | | | | |
| Japan | 33.96 | 36.58 | 32.81 | 36.46 | 37.77 | 35.44 | 35.47 | 37.55 | 34.98 |
| Singapore | 10.62 | 9.45 | 13.04 | 13.67 | 12.86 | 14.82 | 13.33 | 11.45 | 13.11 |
| United States | 14.47 | 12.17 | 11.02 | 11.78 | 12.43 | 9.89 | 10.50 | 9.69 | 9.05 |
| Netherlands | 7.81 | 6.85 | 8.40 | 9.25 | 8.24 | 6.96 | 6.90 | 7.40 | 7.57 |
| Hong Kong | 4.25 | 6.12 | 6.60 | 5.90 | 6.09 | 5.78 | 5.71 | 5.46 | 5.77 |
| Others | 28.90 | 28.84 | 28.13 | 22.93 | 22.62 | 27.11 | 28.10 | 28.44 | 29.52 |
| Total | 100.00 | 100.00 | 100.00 | 100.00 | 100.00 | 100.00 | 100.00 | 100.00 | 100.00 |
| (b) % change | | | | | | | | | |
| Japan | | 25.46 | 23.59 | 21.17 | 8.81 | 25.58 | 21.18 | 4.87 | 7.89 |
| Singapore | | 3.62 | 90.27 | 14.33 | -1.20 | 54.14 | 8.91 | -14.89 | 33.99 |
| United States | | -2.09 | 24.82 | 16.60 | 10.74 | 6.52 | 28.57 | -8.56 | 7.15 |
| Netherlands | | 2.11 | 69.03 | 20.13 | -6.51 | 13.16 | 19.94 | 6.30 | 20.10 |
| Hong Kong | | 67.71 | 48.68 | -2.52 | 8.35 | 27.01 | 19.64 | -5.23 | 6.66 |
| Others | | 16.21 | 34.40 | -11.12 | 3.60 | 60.45 | 25.48 | 0.25 | 20.58 |
| Total | | 16.45 | 37.80 | 9.04 | 5.03 | 33.84 | 21.08 | -0.95 | 16.17 |

Source: Author's calculations based on data from Bank of Thailand, *Report on Thailand's International Investment Position as of end-December 2009.*

Note: The data cover only investments in Thai private non-bank companies.

*Table 4.5* Foreign portfolio investment in equity securities in Thailand by major countries

| | 2001 | 2002 | 2003 | 2004 | 2005 | 2006 | 2007 | 2008 | 2009 |
|---|---|---|---|---|---|---|---|---|---|
| Total foreign equityinvestment (in billions of bahts) | 7.65 | 8.48 | 14.73 | 15.74 | 17.36 | 20.32 | 30.05 | 14.07 | 23.22 |
| (a) Proportion (%) | | | | | | | | | |
| United Kingdom | 21.40 | 31.99 | 28.61 | 41.63 | 34.70 | 30.53 | 26.10 | 34.79 | 38.85 |
| Singapore | 18.45 | 29.65 | 36.17 | 14.15 | 13.00 | 10.92 | 18.06 | 18.40 | 17.69 |
| United States | 11.92 | 13.19 | 13.38 | 18.88 | 17.61 | 19.63 | 19.96 | 16.18 | 15.47 |
| Luxembourg | 0.90 | 1.24 | 0.71 | 4.27 | 6.01 | 6.54 | 7.12 | 4.68 | 5.02 |
| Japan | 4.13 | 3.50 | 3.56 | 3.56 | 3.12 | 3.27 | 3.08 | 4.30 | 2.96 |
| Others | 43.20 | 20.43 | 17.57 | 17.50 | 25.56 | 29.11 | 25.69 | 21.65 | 20.01 |
| Total | 100.00 | 100.00 | 100.00 | 100.00 | 100.00 | 100.00 | 100.00 | 100.00 | 100.00 |
| (b) % change | | | | | | | | | |
| United Kingdom | | 65.67 | 55.46 | 55.46 | -8.10 | 2.99 | 26.44 | -37.61 | 84.39 |
| Singapore | | 78.17 | 111.97 | -58.19 | 1.30 | -1.68 | 144.48 | -52.28 | 58.67 |
| United States | | 22.59 | 76.30 | 50.84 | 2.79 | 30.53 | 50.36 | -62.04 | 57.77 |
| Luxembourg | | 52.17 | 0.00 | 540.00 | 55.21 | 27.33 | 60.99 | -69.22 | 77.20 |
| Japan | | -6.01 | 76.43 | 7.06 | -3.57 | 22.74 | 39.31 | -34.49 | 13.53 |
| Others | | -47.58 | 49.48 | 6.41 | 61.02 | 33.32 | 30.50 | -60.54 | 52.53 |
| Total | | 10.84 | 73.79 | 6.85 | 10.25 | 17.06 | 47.89 | -53.18 | 65.03 |

Source: Author's calculations based on data from Bank of Thailand, *Report on Thailand's International Investment Position as of end-December 2009.*

Note: The data covers only investments in Thai private non-bank companies.

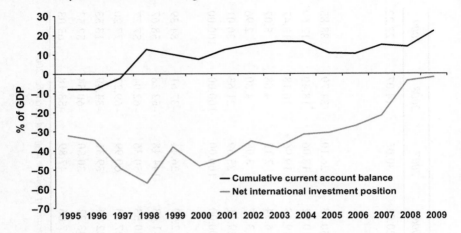

*Figure 4.8* Cumulative current account balance and net international investment position

Source: Author's calculations based on data from Bank of Thailand, *Balance of Payment and Thailand's International Investment Position Statistics.*

Nevertheless, after the economy began to recover from the crisis, the ratio of the cumulative current account balance to the GDP grew steadily from 2000 through 2004, then dipped in 2005 before moving back to the 2003–4 level in 2007, while the NIIP ratio on average improved much faster during the past five years. The NIIP ratio became less negative as Thailand had higher reserve holdings and was able to maintain current account surpluses over several years; it also held more external debt. The higher reserve holdings could be regarded as a precautionary measure against short-term capital flow reversals.

## Asset price movement

A financial crisis can have major effects on equity and bond markets. Typically, when a financial meltdown spills over into the global credit markets, risk premiums will increase rapidly and illiquidity becomes prominent. Once financial markets realize and expect that a credit crunch is likely to affect the economy at large, a typical response of less diversified investors in the equity markets is to sell risky shares and withdraw their investments from the markets in which they are prone to high risk exposure and economic uncertainty. However, with national economies now more closely linked, the impact of a crisis in one country will certainly spread to several others. In the literature, international stock market linkages have been extensively studied, suggesting that correlation between international stock markets becomes higher during those periods in which markets are highly volatile.

Normally, the sale of a large amount of equities on a stock market would translate to a substantial drop in stock prices and market capitalization. Comparing the percentage change in stock price indices between the Thai stock market on the one hand and those in advanced economies and countries in the East Asian region on the other, Figure 4.9 shows that Thailand's stock price index

**(a) Thailand compared to selected advanced economies**

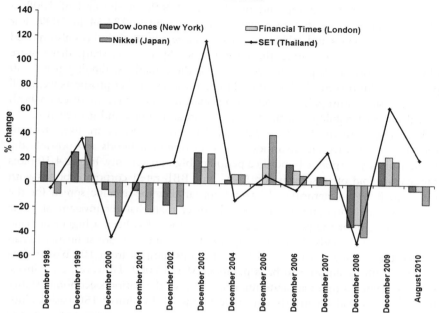

**(b) Thailand compared to selected asian economies**

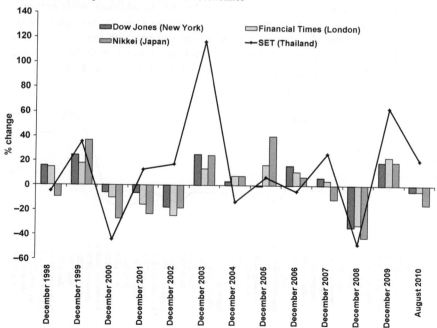

*Figure 4.9* Percentage change in stock price indices

Source: Author's calculations based on data from Bank of Thailand, *SET and External Stock Market Indices.*

dropped from 858.1 at the end of 2007 to 449.96 at the end of 2008, a 47.5 percent decrease, before moving back to stand at 734.54 in 2009. For advanced economies and other countries in the region, their indices also moved in a similar direction during the crisis period. Specifically, sharp drops were observed in the stock price indices in all of these markets, ranging from –30 percent to –50 percent during 2008. However, stock market prospects were still uncertain since Europe's bad-debt problems came into play to threaten both global financial stability and the future of Eurozone unity and governance.

With regard to the bond markets, fixed income investors are likely to shift their investments to safe securities such as government bonds and possibly the highest-quality corporate bonds in a period of high uncertainty. Figure 4.10 plots the average bid-offer spreads for AAA- and BBB-rated corporate bonds with three- to five-year maturities. It would appear that the average spread for the highest-quality corporate bonds is much lower than that for investment-grade bonds throughout the period, suggesting that there has been a higher demand for high-quality bonds. It further appears that during the global financial crisis period, the average spread for BBB-rated bonds jumped from 100 basis points in June 2008 to almost 350 basis points in March 2009. However, once investors had gained a more accurate understanding of the nation's economic status, the average spread for investment-grade bonds fell by almost 150 basis points. Moreover, the difference in average spread between these two types of corporate bonds appears to have widened during the period of global financial turmoil to a greater extent than would be seen in normal times. In addition, some nervousness in the financial and credit markets pushed up not only the average yield on corporate bonds but also the average yield on government bonds, while the average rate for risk-free treasury bills has been pushed down since the beginning of the subprime mortgage problems in the U.S. market (Figure 4.11).

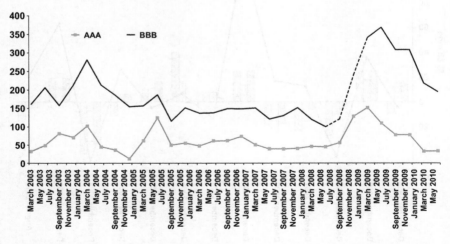

*Figure 4.10* Average spread for AAA and BBB corporate bonds with three- to five-year maturities (basis points)

Source: Thai Bond Market Association, *Price and Yield Data.*

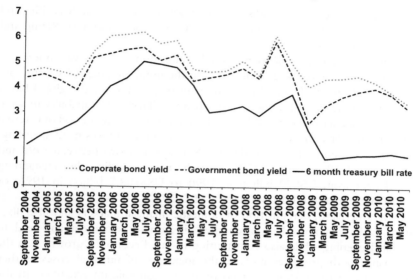

*Figure 4.11* Average yields of government and corporate bonds (% per annum)
Source: Thai Bond Market Association, *Price and Yield Data*.

## 3. Global crisis and domestic financial deepening

In this section, we analyze financial deepening in Thailand in the context of scale and quality effects. Although financial liberalization and financial deepening tend to be related, they are not equivalent. Therefore, this study treats financial liberalization as a process that helps to induce financial deepening, improve the functioning of financial markets, and enhance macro-financial linkages.

### 3.1. Financial liberalization

Thailand has moved in a similar direction to other developing countries as the country has adopted development strategies to modernize its financial system by implementing a series of financial liberalization measures. After adopting Article VIII of the IMF Agreement in May 1990, the Thai monetary authority lifted foreign exchange controls on current account transactions. This marked the beginning of a series of financial liberalization measures, such as the lifting of most restrictions on capital account transactions in April 1991, establishment of the Bangkok International Banking Facilities in March 1993 as a means to developing an international financial center, and provision of additional channels for cross-border payments in February 1994. On the interest rate front, the authorities gradually removed interest rate ceilings in order to encourage savings mobilization and make the financial system more dynamic. More specifically, interest rate ceilings on long-term and short-term time deposits were abolished in June 1989 and in June 1992, respectively. In addition, the central bank gave commercial banks more flexibility by loosening the requirement to hold government bonds as a prerequisite for opening new branches. Other moves included establishment of new frameworks and organizations such as the Securities and Exchange Act, the Securities and Exchange Commission, and Thai Rating and Information Services.

The above-mentioned series of financial liberalization measures was undertaken with a view to strengthening competition in the domestic financial system, giving more resilience to financial institutions in preparation for the global-based liberalization of trade and services, and expanding Thailand's capability to serve as a regional financial center. Evidently, those measures led to a flood of external capital into the Thai market during 1990–6, which fueled investment spending, speculation, and current account deficits. Net capital inflows between 1990 and 1996 averaged 10 percent of GDP in each year, expanding the outstanding external debt from US$29 billion in 1990 to US$108.7 billion in 1996, or from 34 percent of GDP to 59 percent of GDP.

On the one hand, deregulation of domestic financial markets and liberalization of capital accounts help strengthen financial development and lead to financial deepening while also contributing to rapid economic growth. On the other hand, both processes increase the incidence of financial crises as they induce excessive risk-taking and increase macroeconomic uncertainties. In the early stage, we can observe large capital inflows into Thailand, which spurred investment, a real estate bubble, and import spending. Domestic financial institutions were also pressured by intense competition to extend excessive and imprudent credits, engendering too much risk and reducing asset quality. Concerned about possible financial panics or bank runs, the central bank could not resist extending financial aid packages to ailing commercial banks and finance companies. Unsurprisingly, these financial aid packages exacerbated macroeconomic imbalances.

After a long period of defending the value of the currency, the central bank had used up almost all of the country's reserves. Eventually, by mid-1997, the country was basically insolvent as a result of a lack of usable foreign currencies to meet all of its foreign currency obligations, either for trade payments or for repayment of foreign debt. This led to the floating of the baht. The lessons learned from this economic crisis experience are that, before financial liberalization is pursued, (a) the central authority should assess whether or not domestic financial institutions are prepared in several respects; (b) supervision of financial institutions should be even more prudent, as bad lending decisions by financial institutions can easily generate a bubble and create systemic risk to the overall economy; (c) the government should aim for ongoing consistency between financial liberalization and other domestic discretionary economic policies; and (d) keen attention should be paid to the development of a well-functioning long-term capital market as an alternative financing source for bank lending. Particularly if the country has a savings gap or current account deficit to be filled using foreign borrowings, and if the borrowings are mainly from bank lending, most of these borrowings tend to be short-term and more likely to engender risks. Therefore, policies that build up the capabilities of domestic companies to raise long-term capital are crucial in order to avert another similar crisis.

## 3.2. Financial depth

To assess the monetary effects of financial liberalization on the Thai economy, this study employs the ratio of the money supply to GDP and that of private sector credit to GDP as indicators that reflect the level of financial deepening. The more liquid money is available in the economy, the more opportunities exist for further growth. In addition, increased financial deepening also plays an important role in reducing risks and vulnerability for disadvantaged groups and increasing access by individuals and households to basic services such as education and healthcare.

Table 4.6 indicates that there has been some improvement in the level of financial deepening. Following the 1997 Asian financial crisis, the ratio of broad money to GDP tended to rise, indicating an improvement in access to banking and alternative financial instruments. In other words, an increase in this indicator signifies a larger financial sector and an expansion in the financial intermediary sector. However, the ratio of broad money to GDP was declining from 2001, implying that other financial instruments not included in broad money were being developed and became increasingly available. There is evidence that the stock and bond markets are growing in size as there have been new issues of bonds and equities. On average, the economy seems to rely less on the banking system and is financed to a greater extent via the capital market.

With regard to root causes, there were some explanatory factors common to both the 1997–8 Asian financial crisis and the 2008 global financial crisis: excessive borrowing and non-productive use of large sums of money, asset bubbles and subsequent deterioration of credit quality. Generally, an important consequence of these financial and economic crises was a steep decline in investor confidence. Such loss of confidence severely amplified the problems. For instance, it caused massive problems with regard to financing for monetary and financial institutions in money markets. Investors in both countries with sound financial standing and those affected by the crisis typically reacted by withdrawing their investments, usually through fire sales of real and financial assets, which brought about falls in asset prices. Several multinational enterprises based in crisis-hit countries began deleveraging by selling off some of their less attractive assets at hugely discounted prices in order to raise and bring back money. Deleveraging took place on a global scale, leading to capital outflows from emerging economies. Furthermore, financial institutions became more prudent and cautious in granting loans in order to improve the quality of loan portfolios, which otherwise could give rise to higher risk exposure and threaten the financial standing of the banks going forward. As the real and financial sectors were closely linked, the negative impact from the crisis would be exacerbated to a greater extent through feedback loops between the real and financial sectors of the economy.

Based on the experience of Thailand during the 1997–8 Asian financial crisis, a similar consequence of the crisis could be observed elsewhere, i.e., loss of investor confidence. However, the nature of the Asian crisis was far different from that of the current global financial crisis. Thailand's economic crisis could be characterized as a retail banking crisis coupled with a currency crisis, whereas

*Table 4.6* Financial deepening indicators (as ratios to GDP)

| | 1997 | 1998 | 1999 | 2000 | 2001 | 2002 | 2003 | 2004 | 2005 | 2006 | 2007 | 2008 | 2009 |
|---|---|---|---|---|---|---|---|---|---|---|---|---|---|
| Broad money | 1.11 | 1.24 | 1.26 | 1.23 | 1.25 | 1.19 | 1.19 | 1.15 | 1.12 | 1.09 | 1.07 | 1.10 | 1.17 |
| Broad money[a] | 1.00 | 1.12 | 1.13 | 1.11 | 1.12 | 1.07 | 1.07 | 1.03 | 1.00 | 0.98 | 0.96 | 0.99 | 1.05 |
| Private sector credit | 1.66 | 1.56 | 1.32 | 1.08 | 0.97 | 1.03 | 1.00 | 1.02 | 1.01 | 0.95 | 0.92 | 0.93 | 0.99 |
| Private sector credit[a] | 1.00 | 0.94 | 0.8 | 0.65 | 0.58 | 0.62 | 0.61 | 0.62 | 0.61 | 0.57 | 0.55 | 0.57 | 0.58 |
| Stock market capitalization | 0.23 | 0.27 | 0.47 | 0.26 | 0.31 | 0.37 | 0.81 | 0.70 | 0.72 | 0.65 | 0.78 | 0.40 | 0.65 |
| Stock market capitalization[a] | 1.00 | 1.16 | 2.02 | 1.13 | 1.35 | 1.57 | 3.50 | 3.01 | 3.11 | 2.80 | 3.37 | 1.70 | 2.81 |
| Private bond market capitalization | 0.03 | 0.03 | 0.04 | 0.05 | 0.05 | 0.05 | 0.08 | 0.07 | 0.08 | 0.11 | 0.11 | 0.11 | 0.13 |
| Private bond market capitalization[a] | 1.00 | 1.09 | 1.34 | 1.52 | 1.64 | 1.72 | 2.59 | 2.46 | 2.72 | 3.71 | 3.67 | 3.70 | 4.41 |

Source: Author's calculations based on data from Bank of Thailand, *Financial Market Statistics, Economic and Financial Statistics*.

Note: GDP stands for gross domestic product.

[a] Base in 1997.

the latest event was a wholesale banking crisis with huge derivative amplification effects. In terms of network effects, the latest global financial crisis was more far-reaching because its amplification effect covered two dominant economic powers, the United States and Europe, and was significantly larger and deeper. However, the impact was quite limited in Thailand.

### 3.3. Financial soundness of the banking sector

The recent global financial crisis was likely to affect Thailand and other Asian countries through international financial channels to a lesser extent than the United States and EU countries. This was because the Thai banking sector had a relatively strong initial position with low direct exposure to financial transactions associated with subprime mortgage instruments, partly because of significant developments in risk management and the regulatory framework after the 1997–8 crisis. The data in Figures 4.12 and 4.13 reveal the following facts:

- Thai banks relied more on deposits than external funding, which thus helped to cushion the banks against the effects of the global financial crisis. The loan-to-deposit ratio remained low after the 1997 Asian financial crisis but increased slightly in the latest crisis. The aggregate deposit base for all banks was much higher than the lending base during the period 2000–7, keeping their balance sheets very liquid in the run-up to the latest crisis.
- Following recovery from the global financial crisis, bank lending did not grow aggressively, as had happened before 1997, because the banks had become more prudent with respect to credit appraisal and approval, as well as risk management activities, and were reluctant to grant new loans or even to extend outstanding loans. According to the Bank of Thailand's business sentiment survey conducted during 2008, most firms found that banks had tightened their credit standards, demanding higher collateral value, limiting loan sizes, and imposing more stringent terms in order to protect the quality of their portfolios.
- The balance sheet situations of Thai banks were also strong enough to weather the impact of the global financial crisis. The central Bank of Thailand also strengthened its regulatory and supervisory frameworks, which significantly improved the economic fundamentals of the banking sector. The statistics show that the amount of non-performing loans relative to total loans during 2008–9 was not as threatening as had been the case during the 1997 Asian financial crisis.
- The Thai banking sector was able to weather the current crisis efficiently as a result of the presence of a large capital buffer. The average capital adequacy ratio stood at close to 15 percent, which was very high compared with the rule-of-thumb threshold for the capital adequacy ratio, at 8 percent.

Overall, the global financial crisis was likely to cause financial instability, which would delay financial deepening and also impede the development process. Meanwhile, the Thai government and other governments provided massive liquidity support, injected capital, and improved deposit insurance protections.

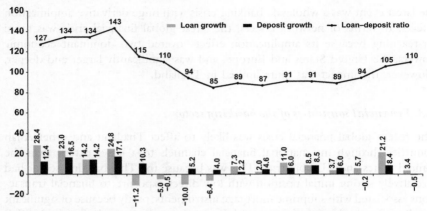

*Figure 4.12* Credit and deposit expansion (in %)

Source: Author's calculations based on data from Bank of Thailand, *Economic and Financial Statistics.*

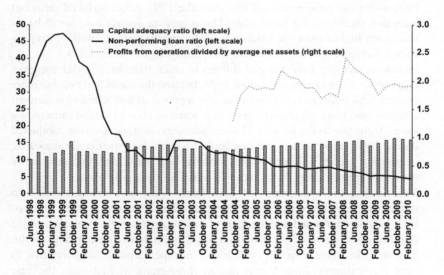

*Figure 4.13* The financial strength of Thai banks (in %)

Source: Bank of Thailand, *Financial Institutions Statistics.*

Since the lack of financial deepening in the financial system could harm economic growth, the recent crisis has accentuated the urgent need for reforms in various areas to increase market and institutional resilience. Further financial development in such countries as Thailand and other developing countries in the region should be accelerated in order to enhance domestic financial deepening and more efficient mobilization of resources, and to strengthen the international financial system while further developing the regional financial system. In this respect, stronger trans-national cooperation among countries in the same region can play an important part in making financial institutions stronger and more efficient and in promoting financial system development more vigorously. This will help strengthen those countries' economic resilience to shocks.

## 4. The role of regional financial cooperation

During the last two years, the economic crisis that broke out in major advanced economies has been a source of great concern for developing countries. As discussed thus far, the situation this time was quite different from the earlier Asian financial crisis of 1997–8, during which Thailand and other crisis-hit developing countries were still able to export. In the latest global financial crisis situation, the export option was no longer feasible owing to the sluggish domestic consumption and investment in the crisis-hit industrial countries that had long been major export destinations for various developing countries. To help alleviate the impacts, the governments have relied on monetary easing measures, together with substantial fiscal spending pumped into the economy. However, to make these measures more effective, there should be trans-national cooperation at the regional level to complement country-specific measures.

The painful lessons learned from the East Asian financial crisis served to stimulate economic cooperation within the region. Formation of the ASEAN+3 group (ASEAN members plus China, Japan, and Korea) was a good example of this. There have also been a number of financial cooperation schemes initiated in the region, including surveillance mechanisms, the Chiang Mai Initiative, the Asian Bond Market Initiative, currency coordination and integration, and management of foreign reserves to influence the direction of the global financial system. All of these modes of cooperation are aimed at preventing recurrence of a crisis, strengthening the capability to better manage any crisis that might arise, shaping the financial environment in the region, and supporting regional economic integration (Sussangkarn and Vichyanond, 2007).

Now is a good time to discuss and strengthen the role of regional financial cooperation in order to equip the region with more effective regional surveillance mechanisms and adequate financial resources for use as needed. Why is regional cooperation important? There are two underlying factors that illustrate the increasing importance, today, of regional cooperation: (a) the volume of international trade within the region is growing significantly, influenced by the lifting of trade barriers and integration of production networks of multinational corporations across Asian economies, for instance, in the electronics and automotive industries (Table 4.7); and (b) while trade integration has developed significant momentum during the past decade, we can also observe more interconnection among the intra-regional economies on the financial side. In particular, there have been notable increases in FDI flows within the region (Table 4.8). This is a consequence of more integrated regional production networks.

For Thailand, intra-ASEAN trade has increased substantially during the past 14 years. When we examined the currency profiles of actual trade and financial flows, we found that the U.S. dollar has been utilized predominantly (Table 4.9).

*Table 4.7* Intra-ASEAN trade, extra-ASEAN trade, and total ASEAN trade (US$ billions)

| Country | Billions of US$ | | | | | | | | % of total trade | | | | | | | |
|---|---|---|---|---|---|---|---|---|---|---|---|---|---|---|---|---|
| | 1996 | 1998 | 2000 | 2002 | 2004 | 2006 | 2008 | 1996–2008 | 1996 | 1998 | 2000 | 2002 | 2004 | 2006 | 2008 | 1996–2008 |
| **Intra-ASEAN:** | | | | | | | | | | | | | | | | |
| Brunei Darussalam | 3.3 | 0.8 | 1.2 | 1.3 | 1.5 | 2.6 | 3.5 | 26.6 | 47.6 | 25.4 | 36.3 | 30.6 | 23.0 | 28.9 | 29.9 | 30.9 |
| Cambodia | – | – | 0.6 | 0.7 | 0.8 | 1.2 | 1.8 | 10.8 | – | – | 22.6 | 19.3 | 16.7 | 19.1 | 21.0 | 22.7 |
| Indonesia | 13.9 | 13.9 | 17.7 | 16.9 | 24.7 | 37.9 | 68.2 | 344.3 | 13.8 | 18.3 | 18.5 | 19.1 | 20.9 | 23.4 | 25.6 | 20.6 |
| Lao PDR | – | – | – | – | 0.5 | 0.8 | 2.1 | 5.2 | – | – | – | – | 74.4 | 79.8 | 84.2 | 77.2 |
| Malaysia | 37.4 | 34.6 | 40.3 | 39.4 | 57.9 | 73.3 | 85.1 | 703.0 | 25.0 | 25.0 | 22.7 | 22.9 | 25.0 | 25.7 | 25.1 | 24.6 |
| Myanmar | – | – | 1.5 | 2.4 | 1.9 | 3.3 | 5.6 | 29.6 | – | – | 44.1 | 52.8 | 49.7 | 59.1 | 53.6 | 53.4 |
| Philippines | 7.0 | 8.2 | 10.9 | 11.1 | 15.2 | 18.4 | 21.4 | 174.4 | 14.6 | 14.0 | 15.1 | 15.7 | 18.2 | 18.6 | 20.3 | 16.8 |
| Singapore | 61.8 | 49.6 | 71.1 | 64.4 | 109.7 | 146.1 | 171.4 | 1,290.2 | 25.7 | 23.5 | 26.0 | 26.7 | 29.5 | 28.6 | 36.3 | 28.4 |
| Thailand | 21.9 | 13.8 | 23.5 | 23.7 | 37.0 | 50.5 | 69.4 | 453.8 | 17.0 | 15.6 | 18.0 | 18.4 | 19.2 | 20.3 | 19.7 | 18.7 |
| Vietnam | – | – | – | – | 11.5 | 18.7 | 29.5 | 96.9 | – | – | – | – | 20.0 | 24.2 | 20.9 | 21.6 |
| Total | 145.2 | 120.9 | 166.8 | 159.9 | 260.7 | 352.8 | 458.0 | 3,134.7 | 21.5 | 21.0 | 22.0 | 22.4 | 24.3 | 25.1 | 26.8 | 23.8 |
| **Extra-ASEAN:** | | | | | | | | | | | | | | | | |
| Brunei Darussalam | 3.6 | 2.4 | 2.1 | 3.0 | 5.1 | 6.5 | 8.3 | 59.6 | 52.4 | 74.6 | 63.7 | 69.4 | 77.1 | 71.1 | 70.1 | 69.2 |
| Cambodia | – | – | 2.1 | 2.9 | 3.8 | 5.2 | 6.9 | 36.7 | – | – | 77.5 | 80.7 | 83.3 | 81.0 | 79.0 | 77.3 |
| Indonesia | 86.6 | 62.3 | 78.0 | 71.5 | 93.4 | 124.0 | 198.1 | 1,327.1 | 86.2 | 81.8 | 81.5 | 80.9 | 79.1 | 76.6 | 74.4 | 79.4 |

| | | | | | | | | | | | | | | | | |
|---|---|---|---|---|---|---|---|---|---|---|---|---|---|---|---|---|
| Lao PDR | – | – | – | 0.2 | 0.2 | 0.4 | 1.5 | 75.0 | – | – | – | – | 25.6 | 20.2 | 15.8 | 22.8 |
| Malaysia | 112.2 | 103.5 | 137.5 | 132.7 | 173.9 | 212.3 | 253.7 | 2,159.1 | 75.0 | 75.0 | 77.3 | 77.1 | 75.0 | 74.3 | 74.9 | 75.4 |
| Myanmar | – | – | 1.9 | 2.2 | 2.0 | 2.3 | 4.8 | 25.8 | – | – | 55.9 | 47.2 | 50.3 | 41.0 | 46.4 | 46.6 |
| Philippines | 40.9 | 50.9 | 61.6 | 59.6 | 68.5 | 80.8 | 84.3 | 864.0 | 85.4 | 86.1 | 84.9 | 84.3 | 81.9 | 81.4 | 79.8 | 83.2 |
| Singapore | 179.0 | 161.7 | 202.0 | 177.0 | 262.4 | 364.0 | 300.8 | 3,261.3 | 74.3 | 76.5 | 74.0 | 73.3 | 70.5 | 71.4 | 63.7 | 71.7 |
| Thailand | 106.5 | 74.4 | 107.1 | 105.1 | 155.7 | 198.2 | 283.2 | 1,977.6 | 83.0 | 84.4 | 82.0 | 81.6 | 80.8 | 79.7 | 80.3 | 81.3 |
| Vietnam | – | – | – | – | 46.3 | 58.6 | 111.9 | 350.8 | – | – | – | – | 80.0 | 75.8 | 79.1 | 78.4 |
| Total | 528.8 | 455.2 | 592.3 | 553.9 | 811.2 | 1,052.0 | 1,252.3 | 10,063.6 | 78.5 | 79.0 | 78.0 | 77.6 | 75.7 | 74.9 | 73.2 | 76.3 |
| Total trade: | | | | | | | | | | | | | | | | |
| Brunei Darussalam | 6.9 | 3.2 | 3.2 | 4.3 | 6.6 | 9.1 | 11.9 | 86.2 | 100.0 | 100.0 | 100.0 | 100.0 | 100.0 | 100.0 | 100.0 | 100.0 |
| Cambodia | – | – | 2.8 | 3.6 | 4.5 | 6.4 | 8.7 | 47.5 | – | – | 100.0 | 100.0 | 100.0 | 100.0 | 100.0 | 100.0 |
| Indonesia | 100.5 | 76.2 | 95.6 | 88.4 | 118.1 | 161.9 | 266.2 | 1,671.4 | 100.0 | 100.0 | 100.0 | 100.0 | 100.0 | 100.0 | 100.0 | 100.0 |
| Lao PDR | – | – | – | – | 0.6 | 1.0 | 2.6 | 6.7 | – | – | – | – | 100.0 | 100.0 | 100.0 | 100.0 |
| Malaysia | 149.5 | 138.1 | 177.8 | 172.1 | 231.8 | 285.5 | 338.8 | 2,862.1 | 100.0 | 100.0 | 100.0 | 100.0 | 100.0 | 100.0 | 100.0 | 100.0 |
| Myanmar | – | – | 3.4 | 4.6 | 3.9 | 5.6 | 10.4 | 55.4 | – | – | 100.0 | 100.0 | 100.0 | 100.0 | 100.0 | 100.0 |
| Philippines | 47.9 | 59.2 | 72.6 | 70.6 | 83.7 | 99.2 | 105.7 | 1,038.4 | 100.0 | 100.0 | 100.0 | 100.0 | 100.0 | 100.0 | 100.0 | 100.0 |
| Singapore | 240.8 | 211.3 | 273.0 | 241.4 | 372.1 | 510.1 | 472.2 | 4,551.5 | 100.0 | 100.0 | 100.0 | 100.0 | 100.0 | 100.0 | 100.0 | 100.0 |
| Thailand | 128.3 | 88.2 | 130.6 | 128.8 | 192.7 | 248.7 | 352.5 | 2,431.4 | 100.0 | 100.0 | 100.0 | 100.0 | 100.0 | 100.0 | 100.0 | 100.0 |
| Vietnam | – | – | – | – | 57.8 | 77.3 | 141.4 | 447.6 | – | – | – | – | 100.0 | 100.0 | 100.0 | 100.0 |
| Total | 674.0 | 576.1 | 759.1 | 713.8 | 1,071.8 | 1,404.8 | 1,710.4 | 13,198.3 | 100.00 | 100.00 | 100.00 | 100.00 | 100.00 | 100.00 | 100.00 | 100.00 |

Source: Association of Southeast Asian Nations (ASEAN), *ASEAN Trade Statistics.*

*Table 4.8* Foreign direct investment inflows into ASEAN by source country (US$ millions)

| | 2001 | 2002 | 2003 | 2004 | 2005 | 2006 | 2007 | 2008 | 2009 | 2001–9 |
|---|---|---|---|---|---|---|---|---|---|---|
| a) ASEAN | 2,269 | 4,048 | 2,870 | 3,100 | 4,733 | 9,353 | 10,649 | 10,771 | 4,571 | 52,363 |
| b) Rest of the world: | 18,104 | 13,975 | 21,365 | 32,242 | 35,980 | 47,002 | 63,746 | 38,729 | 35,052 | 306,196 |
| • Asian NIEs: | 2,052 | 1,111 | 1,348 | 1,639 | 889 | 3,249 | 4,996 | 4,776 | 3,692 | 23,751 |
| - Hong Kong | -411 | 487 | 225 | 433 | 558 | 1,230 | 1,496 | 1,447 | 1,582 | 7,048 |
| - South Korea | -240 | 177 | 550 | 828 | 515 | 1,246 | 2,716 | 1,584 | 1,422 | 8,796 |
| - Taiwan (ROC) | 2,703 | 447 | 573 | 377 | -184 | 773 | 785 | 1,745 | 688 | 7,907 |
| • China | 144 | -72 | 187 | 735 | 608 | 1,046 | 1,684 | 2,110 | 1,510 | 7,951 |
| • India | 29 | 95 | 102 | 82 | 418 | -282 | 1,466 | 699 | 984 | 3,592 |
| • Japan | 2,204 | 3,026 | 3,908 | 5,667 | 6,645 | 10,440 | 8,829 | 4,658 | 5,308 | 50,686 |
| • European Union | 6,946 | 3,744 | 6,679 | 11,270 | 11,290 | 13,159 | 17,766 | 9,520 | 7,297 | 87,670 |
| • Other Europe[a] | 189 | 836 | 1,863 | 1,642 | 4,895 | 5,348 | 3,182 | 1,743 | -465 | 19,233 |
| • Canada | -80 | 377 | 101 | 853 | 741 | 255 | 394 | 799 | 311 | 3,750 |
| • United States | 4,817 | -213 | 1,495 | 4,384 | 3,216 | 3,018 | 8,068 | 5,133 | 3,358 | 33,276 |
| • Australia | -130 | 81 | 157 | 490 | 212 | 317 | 1,492 | 920 | 701 | 4,239 |
| • New Zealand | 15 | 102 | 88 | -21 | 512 | -209 | 101 | -165 | 240 | 662 |
| • All others[b] | 1,917 | 4,889 | 5,437 | 5,501 | 6,555 | 10,662 | 15,769 | 8,537 | 12,118 | 71,386 |
| Total | 20,630 | 17,788 | 24,067 | 35,201 | 40,041 | 54,758 | 73,428 | 49,191 | 39,481 | 354,584 |

Source: Association of Southeast Asian Nations (ASEAN), *ASEAN Trade Statistics*.

Note: NIEs refer to newly industrializing economies.

[a] Refers to the rest of Europe

[b] Includes Pakistan and the rest of Asia, Central and South America, and others, consisting of the rest of the world, unclassified sources, joint countries, and international organizations.

*Table 4.9* Currency composition of Thailand's exports and imports by economic community (%)

(a) Exports

| | 1995 | 1996 | 1997 | 1998 | 1999 | 2000 | 2001 | 2002 | 2003 | 2004 | 2005 | 2006 | 2007 | 2008 |
|---|---|---|---|---|---|---|---|---|---|---|---|---|---|---|
| **ASEAN** | | | | | | | | | | | | | | |
| US$ | 93.3 | 90.5 | 91.0 | 88.3 | 91.3 | 90.5 | 89.3 | 89.0 | 89.6 | 84.2 | 83.9 | 84.3 | 84.1 | 82.6 |
| Yen | 1.0 | 0.8 | 0.8 | 1.3 | 1.5 | 1.9 | 1.7 | 1.9 | 1.7 | 1.4 | 1.4 | 1.2 | 1.4 | 1.5 |
| Baht | 2.1 | 5.9 | 5.6 | 6.5 | 5.7 | 5.3 | 5.9 | 6.1 | 6.3 | 10.8 | 11.8 | 11.7 | 11.6 | 12.2 |
| Others | 3.6 | 2.8 | 2.6 | 3.9 | 1.5 | 2.3 | 3.1 | 3.0 | 2.4 | 3.6 | 2.9 | 2.8 | 2.9 | 3.7 |
| **NAFTA** | | | | | | | | | | | | | | |
| US$ | 99.6 | 99.6 | 99.7 | 99.4 | 97.3 | 96.8 | 97.1 | 96.4 | 95.8 | 96.6 | 96.3 | 96.0 | 95.9 | 95.6 |
| Yen | 0.1 | 0.1 | 0.1 | 0.1 | 0.2 | 0.2 | 0.3 | 0.4 | 0.3 | 0.6 | 0.8 | 0.8 | 0.8 | 0.9 |
| Baht | 0.0 | 0.0 | 0.1 | 0.3 | 2.3 | 2.9 | 2.5 | 3.0 | 3.6 | 2.4 | 2.5 | 2.9 | 2.8 | 3.1 |
| Others | 0.3 | 0.3 | 0.1 | 0.2 | 0.2 | 0.1 | 0.1 | 0.2 | 0.3 | 0.4 | 0.4 | 0.3 | 0.5 | 0.4 |
| **EU** | | | | | | | | | | | | | | |
| US$ | 90.4 | 91.2 | 91.2 | 89.0 | 81.0 | 80.8 | 75.7 | 73.0 | 73.8 | 71.4 | 71.9 | 70.8 | 70.4 | 69.3 |
| Euro | 0.0 | 0.0 | 0.0 | 0.0 | 1.2 | 3.5 | 13.8 | 22.9 | 20.1 | 17.8 | 16.2 | 17.7 | 18.8 | 18.9 |
| Baht | 1.2 | 1.0 | 1.0 | 0.9 | 1.2 | 1.5 | 1.4 | 1.3 | 1.8 | 6.2 | 6.5 | 6.9 | 5.6 | 6.7 |
| Others | 8.4 | 7.8 | 7.8 | 10.1 | 16.6 | 14.2 | 9.1 | 2.8 | 4.3 | 4.6 | 5.4 | 4.6 | 5.2 | 5.1 |
| **Japan** | | | | | | | | | | | | | | |
| US$ | 85.1 | 85.8 | 86.0 | 83.2 | 72.9 | 70.3 | 71.8 | 71.0 | 69.9 | 60.1 | 59.7 | 58.7 | 59.9 | 59.6 |
| Yen | 13.0 | 12.9 | 12.8 | 14.1 | 19.5 | 21.6 | 20.5 | 20.9 | 21.5 | 33.4 | 32.3 | 32.3 | 32.2 | 33.1 |
| Baht | 0.8 | 1.0 | 1.0 | 2.6 | 7.4 | 7.9 | 7.3 | 7.4 | 8.1 | 6.2 | 7.3 | 8.5 | 7.1 | 6.7 |
| Others | 1.1 | 0.3 | 0.2 | 0.1 | 0.2 | 0.1 | 0.4 | 0.7 | 0.5 | 0.3 | 0.7 | 0.5 | 0.8 | 0.6 |

(*Continued*)

*Table 4.9* (Continued)

**(b) Imports**

| | 1995 | 1996 | 1997 | 1998 | 1999 | 2000 | 2001 | 2002 | 2003 | 2004 | 2005 | 2006 | 2007 | 2008 |
|---|---|---|---|---|---|---|---|---|---|---|---|---|---|---|
| **ASEAN** | | | | | | | | | | | | | | |
| US$ | 84.9 | 85.1 | 86.6 | 88.3 | 88.5 | 88.6 | 89.5 | 87.2 | 85.2 | 86.7 | 88.0 | 88.0 | 88.0 | 88.7 |
| Yen | 2.2 | 1.8 | 2.1 | 2.2 | 3.2 | 3.8 | 2.6 | 1.9 | 1.4 | 1.6 | 1.2 | 1.2 | 1.5 | 1.6 |
| Baht | 1.7 | 2.9 | 2.9 | 3.0 | 3.8 | 3.7 | 4.0 | 5.5 | 7.3 | 5.5 | 5.6 | 5.9 | 6.0 | 4.6 |
| Others | 11.2 | 10.2 | 8.4 | 6.5 | 4.5 | 3.9 | 3.9 | 5.4 | 6.1 | 6.2 | 5.2 | 4.9 | 4.5 | 5.1 |
| **NAFTA** | | | | | | | | | | | | | | |
| US$ | 97.2 | 97.2 | 97.6 | 98.3 | 98.3 | 98.8 | 98.7 | 97.2 | 96.7 | 95.4 | 95.8 | 95.0 | 94.8 | 95.6 |
| Yen | 1.0 | 0.8 | 0.7 | 0.4 | 0.3 | 0.1 | 0.1 | 0.5 | 0.6 | 0.7 | 0.4 | 0.4 | 0.5 | 0.5 |
| Baht | 0.7 | 1.1 | 0.9 | 0.6 | 0.9 | 0.7 | 0.6 | 0.9 | 1.1 | 2.2 | 2.2 | 2.6 | 2.7 | 2.2 |
| Others | 1.1 | 0.9 | 0.8 | 0.7 | 0.5 | 0.4 | 0.6 | 1.4 | 1.6 | 1.7 | 1.6 | 2.0 | 2.0 | 1.7 |
| **EU** | | | | | | | | | | | | | | |
| US$ | 60.3 | 57.3 | 60.3 | 61.9 | 68.6 | 69.0 | 57.4 | 57.2 | 59.0 | 51.1 | 52.2 | 50.8 | 46.8 | 46.6 |
| Euro | 0.0 | 0.0 | 0.0 | 0.0 | 1.5 | 6.2 | 22.4 | 31.6 | 29.7 | 36.8 | 34.8 | 35.1 | 38.6 | 38.8 |
| Others | 39.7 | 42.7 | 39.7 | 38.1 | 29.9 | 24.8 | 20.2 | 11.2 | 11.3 | 12.1 | 13.0 | 14.1 | 14.6 | 14.6 |
| **Japan** | | | | | | | | | | | | | | |
| US$ | 67.4 | 64.4 | 66.7 | 65.8 | 54.4 | 51.1 | 51.8 | 52.9 | 49.8 | 43.0 | 47.1 | 46.8 | 51.0 | 49.5 |
| Yen | 31.6 | 34.1 | 31.7 | 32.5 | 41.4 | 42.9 | 38.5 | 36.5 | 40.3 | 44.5 | 44.1 | 44.1 | 41.8 | 43.1 |
| Baht | 0.7 | 1.2 | 1.4 | 1.5 | 2.1 | 2.8 | 5.9 | 6.8 | 8.4 | 9.5 | 7.6 | 8.4 | 6.5 | 6.8 |
| Others | 0.3 | 0.3 | 0.2 | 0.2 | 2.1 | 3.2 | 3.8 | 3.8 | 1.5 | 3.0 | 1.2 | 0.7 | 0.7 | 0.6 |

Source: Bank of Thailand, *Economic and Financial Statistics.*

Note: ASEAN stands for Association of Southeast Asian Nations; EU stands for European Union; and NAFTA stands for North American Free Trade Agreement.

This raises an important issue: whether or not further regional financial integration and cooperation will help to reduce currency exposure. Some discussion has taken place regarding the benefits of using local currency in intra-ASEAN trade, which would help to reduce cross-border foreign exchange settlement (for which most countries are currently using the U.S. dollar as a medium of international trade), lower transaction costs, and facilitate more intra-ASEAN trade.

However, there are three important issues that require further discussion with respect to enhancing the effectiveness of cooperation. These are the risk management capacity of the international financial system, the issue of procyclicality in the context of international regulatory and supervisory frameworks, and the management of cross-border spillover effects that can induce severe systemic risk. Since the impacts of any crises are tremendously costly and persist over a number of years, this presents an important opportunity for international bodies to be more dynamic and to encourage integration and cooperation.

However, the task of strengthening regional financial cooperation among ASEAN members is not an easy one for a number of different reasons, ranging from economic diversity, degree of trade openness, and level of economic development to different preferences with respect to the pace, extent, and direction of policy actions and of cooperation. Important steps toward bolstering regional financial cooperation include (a) ongoing promotion of regional trade liberalization and economic integration among ASEAN member countries because both factors help in shaping the depth and scope of financial cooperation needs; (b) strengthening of international economic cooperation to bridge the gaps in terms of economic disparities and diversity; (c) conclusion of the multilateral Chiang Mai Initiative, which requires cooperation among members in terms of a reserve pooling mechanism; (d) reinforcement of international coordination of financial, monetary, and economic policies among ASEAN countries; and (e) establishment of a regional monetary organization as an multinational surveillance body to supervise and coordinate the scheme for better flows of information among member countries and also to be responsible for providing both better regional and global surveillance in order to help prevent future crises and offer more balanced crisis resolution mechanisms (Sussangkarn, 2009).

In addition, the lessons learned from the recent debt crisis in Europe provided important experience for the countries in the East Asian region that are thinking of promoting closer ties through regional cooperation and integration. The problems experienced in EU countries spotlighted a design flaw that can lead to serious fiscal irresponsibility on the part of a few members. Hence, we should use this as a basis for developing a well-designed package for financial cooperation and integration, giving serious consideration to an economic governance system and coordinated fiscal plans among member countries.

## 5. Conclusions

A rising tide of delinquencies on subprime mortgages spread rapidly to other sectors and markets, triggering a credit crunch and market turmoil on a global scale. The spillover from the subprime mortgage turmoil was relatively extensive. Having an open economy and being linked with its trading partners through trade and investment, Thailand was consequently affected by the recent global financial crisis through trade and financial channels.

Overall, the U.S. subprime mortgage crisis that spread to Europe and Japan tended to affect the Thai economy more through trade channels than through financial channels because there was a fairly strong spillover effect on Thai exports from external demand shocks from the United States, Japan, and European countries. The export sector was hit hard, which adversely affected production, employment, and incomes. Expecting that the deterioration of domestic demand would hurt the economy, the government introduced a fiscal stimulus package as a key driver to ensure economic recovery and sustainable long-term growth.

However, having a relatively strong financial system in place before the onset of the crisis was a key factor in Thailand's ability to weather the impacts from the latest crisis. The financial sector had been in good health, and the banks, on average, had strong capital bases and low exposure to problem loans. There was not a great deal of concern about external vulnerability because Thailand had enjoyed a current account surplus for several years and had accumulated a large amount of international reserves, which led to an improved international investment position.

The findings in this study provide support for earlier studies such as those of Sethapramote (2010), Bank of Thailand (2009), and Berkmen et al. (2009). Sethapramote (2010) used the quarterly macroeconomic model to analyze the impacts of global crises on the Thai economy via both trade and financial channels. He found that the international trade channel had significant negative impacts on domestic economic activities, while the financial linkage had only marginal impacts on consumption and investment. Consistently, the latter two studies also identified substantial impacts of global crises resulting from trade contraction in Asian economies and developing countries, and further showed that countries were more vulnerable to financial shocks if they held large stocks of external debt from advanced countries and could not roll over their debt.

Looking ahead, it can be expected that there will be an increase in the complexity and international linkages of financial systems, along with closer cooperation among countries in the wake of the recent crisis with a view to helping reduce the impact and scale of any unforeseeable future crisis. As the linkages through financial activities become increasingly complex, there will certainly be a need for better development in terms of global regulatory and supervisory frameworks to handle cross-border implications. We also need better information flows and cooperation among regulators and government authorities. Otherwise, it will be very difficult to effectively handle and prevent spillovers from possible future financial crises. The potential solution to ensure macroeconomic and financial stability is to promote greater regional financial cooperation and integration. This is a long-term challenge confronting all of the countries in the region because it needs to be worked out not only at a national level but also at regional and global levels. The most recent important lessons learned from Europe's debt crisis should motivate all nations in this region to place the highest priority on promotion of well-designed and efficiently functioning financial cooperation and governance among ASEAN member countries.

## Notes

1 The subprime crisis made the situation different from that of the 1997–8 crisis, during which Thailand was still able to export, aided by the sharp depreciation of Thai baht. In contrast, during the recent crisis, there was a substantial decline in exports owing to lack of external demand. Moreover, the ongoing appreciation of the baht has made matters worse because it puts pressure on some manufacturers, particularly those in industries that have low import content and are labor intensive. These manufacturers are likely to lose competitiveness and close down because they have limited room for adjustment.
2 Based on the statistics for 2002, *Akyuz (2010)* stated that approximately 42 percent of all imported intermediate inputs, which were used to produce goods in China for export to various destination markets, including the United States and Europe, came from East Asian developing countries. Thus, if the composition remained as it was in 2002, one may conjecture that the recent crisis was likely to affect the export performance of Asian countries substantially because Asian countries' exports relied heavily on the economic conditions of the crisis-hit developed countries.

## References and Further Readings

Akyuz, Y. 2010. Other Asian Countries Face Deeper Problems – and Need to Rethink Their Growth Strategy. *South Views* 11. July 2. Available at http://www.southcentre.int/category/publications/southviews/.
Bank of Thailand. 2009. The Impact of the Global Financial Crisis on Asia and Other Emerging Market Economies. In *Inflation Report*, 61–2. April.
Berkmen, P., Gelos, G., Rennhack, R., and Walsh, J.P. 2009. The Global Financial Crisis: Explaining Cross-Country Differences in the Output Impact. International Monetary Fund Working Paper No. 09/280. International Monetary Fund. Available at http://www.imf.org/external/pubs/ft/wp/2009/wp09280.pdf.
Bernanke, B.S., Gertler, M., and Gilchrist, S.G. 1999. The Financial Accelerator in a Quantitative Business Cycle Framework. In J.B. Taylor and M. Woodford (Eds.), *Handbook of Macroeconomics*, 1st ed., Vol. 1, pp. 1341–93. Amsterdam: Elsevier North-Holland
International Monetary Fund. 2010. World Economic Outlook, Rebalancing Growth, World Economic and Financial Surveys, Washington DC: International Monetary Fund.
Poonpatpibul, C., Vorasangasil, N., Junetrakool, M., and Prasitdechsakul, P. 2009. Is There an Alternative to Export-Led Growth for Thailand? Discussion Paper

08/2009. Bank of Thailand. Available at http://www.bot.or.th/Thai/Economic-Conditions/Publication/Discussion_2552/dp082009.eng.pdf.

Reinhart, C.M., and Rogoff, K.S. 2008. Is the 2007 U.S. Subprime Crisis So Different? An International Historical Comparison. *American Economic Review* 98(2), 339–44.

Sethapramote, Y. 2010. The Impact of the Global Financial Crisis on Thailand: Transmission Channels and Policy Responses. A paper presented at the International Conference on "Tackling the Financial Crisis in East and Southeast Asia: Assessing Policies and Impacts" organized by the University of Hong Kong and the Institute of Southeast Asian Studies (Singapore) on 24–25 February 2010, Hong Kong.

Sussangkarn, C., and Vichyanond, P. 2007. Directions of East Asian Regional Financial Cooperation. *Asian Economic Papers* 5(3), 25–55.

Sussangkarn, C. 2009. New Impetus for Institution Building for East Asian Financial Cooperation. A paper presented at the International Workshop on "Global Economic Crisis and Institutional Building in East Asia for Peace and Development" organized by JICA RI and RIETI on 29 August 2009, Tokyo.

Tanboon, S., Piamchol, S., Ruenbanterng, T., and Pongpaichet, P. 2009. Impacts of Financial Factors on Thailand's Business Cycle Fluctuations. Discussion Paper 07/2009. Monetary Policy Group, Bank of Thailand. Available at http://www.bot.or.th/Thai/EconomicConditions/Publication/Discussion_2552/dp072009_eng.pdf.

Tinakorn, P. 2006. Indicators and Analysis of Vulnerability to Currency Crisis: Thailand. In Lawrence R. Klein and Tayyeb Shabbir (Eds.), *Recent Financial Crises: Analysis, Challenges and Implications* (pp. 69–117). Northampton (Massachusetts): Edward Elgar.

# 5 Macro-financial linkage and financial deepening in Chinese Taipei

## Sheng-Cheng Hu

## 1. Introduction

The U.S. subprime mortgage crisis became apparent in the summer of 2007 and soon developed into a global financial crisis and severe economic downturn. The world economic growth rate declined sharply from 3.02 percent in 2008 to –0.60 percent in 2009, and the average growth rate for advanced economies declined from 0.48 percent to –3.16 percent over the same two-year period (International Monetary Fund [IMF], 2010b).

During the global financial crisis, the U.S.A. and other countries attempted to stabilize financial markets by injecting liquidity and by repeatedly reducing interest rates to historically low levels. They further pursued aggressive fiscal stimulus policies by cutting taxes, raising subsidies for the poor or for affected industries, and increasing public infrastructure expenditures. These concerted stimulus efforts helped to bring about recovery of the global economy, with Asian growth being more robust than growth in advanced economies (IMF, 2009b).

However, the resulting increases in government budget deficits and debt levels led to fiscal crises in several European countries. According to IMF estimates, the fiscal deficits in G20 countries worsened relative to the pre-crisis level in 2007 by 6.9 percent and 5.9 percent of the gross domestic product (GDP, purchasing power parity-weighted) in 2009 and 2010, respectively. Government debts in advanced G20 countries could reach 118 percent of GDP by 2014. Greece and Ireland requested and received substantial international assistance, and some other countries required very large fiscal adjustments in order to return to fiscal stability (IMF, 2009a).

There are a number of causes for the global financial crisis. The easy monetary policy in the U.S.A. and global imbalances (a global savings glut) led to the subprime mortgage problem and the housing bubble in the U.S.A., while securitization and rapid capital flows sped the contagion throughout the world. (See, for example, Greenspan, 2010; Chari, Christiano, and Kehoe, 2008; Caprio, Demirgüç-Kunt, and Kane, 2008; Taylor, 2009.) Although the world economy has recovered from the financial crisis, with Asia leading the way, dealing with global imbalances, hot money, and fiscal deficits continues to be a challenge. There also remains the question of whether or not the financial reform efforts undertaken by the U.S.A. and European countries are sufficient to prevent another crisis.

As a mid-sized open economy, Chinese Taipei's economic performance is highly affected by the performance in the export sector. (See Figure 5.1.) There was no way that Chinese Taipei could be immune to the crisis. Its economic growth rate fell from 5.98 percent in 2007 to 0.73 percent in 2008 and further, to –1.81 percent, in 2009. The economy suffered the worst economic downturn in postwar history in the first quarter of 2009, when the growth rate declined to –8.12 percent year-on-year (yoy). The unemployment rate (the gray dashed line in Figure 5.1) rose from 3.91 percent in 2007 to 4.14 percent in 2008 and further to 5.85 percent in 2009. Total employment declined in 2009 for the first time since 2001.

Weakening of the labor market exacerbated wage stagnation and income inequality. The mean level of wages and salaries for both industrial and service sectors stayed static in 2008 and suffered a decline of 4.9 percent in 2009. The decline in the mean level of wages and salaries in the financial sector was even more telling: 5.7 percent in 2008 and 5.3 percent in 2009.

As in other economies, in order to counter the sharp downturn in the economy, the government of Chinese Taipei had to take extraordinary expansionary fiscal policy measures, incurring a budget deficit amounting to 6.2 percent of GDP in 2009. There were numerous calls by academics for the government to attend to the adverse effect of its policies on the economy's fiscal stability. The Central Bank of Chinese Taipei also had to repeatedly lower the rediscount rate.

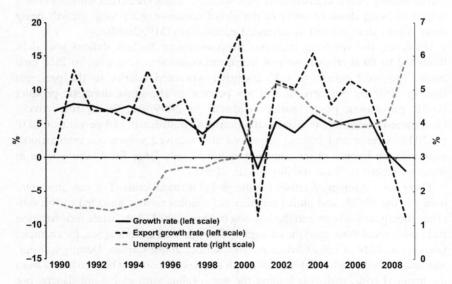

*Figure 5.1* Economic growth and unemployment (%)

Source: Director-General of Budget, Accounting and Statistics (DGBAS), Executive Yuan, Chinese Taipei (2010).

Chinese Taipei's infection with the financial crisis came via both financial and non-financial channels, but it appears that the latter were the primary source for transmission of the crisis. The Chinese Taipei financial sector was healthy at the onset of, and remained relatively stable during, the global financial crisis. The main effect of the crisis on the financial sector was a decline in stock prices and losses in the value of holdings of overseas assets.

However, as mentioned above, Chinese Taipei is heavily dependent on trade for economic growth. Total commodity trade (exports plus imports) as a percentage of GDP rose from 74.2 percent in 1990 to 124.0 percent in 2008 but declined to 100.1 percent in 2009 as a result of the global financial crisis. Chinese Taipei's largest export markets are China, members of the Association of Southeast Asian Nations (ASEAN), and the U.S.A. These three markets accounted for 41.8 percent, 15.1 percent, and 11.5 percent, respectively, of total exports in 2010. As part of the trend toward regionalization of trade, the U.S.A., which for a long time was Chinese Taipei's largest trading partner, has now become only its distant third largest export market, although part of its exports to China actually comprise indirect exports to the U.S.A. Chinese Taipei's exports are also concentrated in the highly capital-intensive and cyclical sector of information and communications technology. According to Ministry of Finance statistics, electronic, optical, and information and communications products accounted for 41.4 percent of its total exports in 2010. In this financial crisis, Chinese Taipei and other economies such as Japan and Korea with large proportions of their GDPs dependent on advanced manufacturing activities such as production of information technology and automotive products experienced sharper output declines than their peers (Sommer, 2009). In 2009 Chinese Taipei's exports to China fell by 15.9 percent (–40.5 percent yoy in the first quarter), and its exports to the U.S.A. declined by 23.5 percent (–24.4 percent yoy in the first quarter), while its total exports declined by 20.32 percent.

The next section describes Chinese Taipei's financial deepening process and its impacts on key macro-financial variables. The third section sheds light on the channels through which the contagion of the crisis took place and thereby on the nature of the macro-financial linkage. Section 4 briefly discusses how international cooperation can help in preventing and managing a possible financial crisis. The concluding section follows.

## 2. Financial deepening in Chinese Taipei

Chinese Taipei's financial deepening has taken the form of financial liberalization, improvement in asset quality, and expansion and globalization of securities markets.

### *2.1. Financial liberalization and asset quality*

For a long time, Chinese Taipei's financial sector was strictly regulated by the government, which also owned and managed almost all commercial banks. The first stage of financial liberalization was undertaken before the 1990s and took the form of liberalization of interest and exchange rates. There is evidence that the reforms increased financial efficiency by encouraging competition, improving asset allocation, and lowering transaction costs (Wu and Hu, 2000; Romer and Chou, 2001). The second stage of financial liberalization began at an accelerated pace in 1991, when private institutions and citizens were allowed to enter the banking sector. Within a span of one year or so, the government issued a total of 16 permits to allow the establishment of commercial banks by private-sector interests. As a result, the total number of domestic banks doubled from 16 in 1990 to 32 in 1992.

Although the market share of non-government banks after the entry of the new banks was still small, their entry did result in excessive competition and a decline in banking asset quality. The burst of the asset bubble in 1995; the Asian financial crisis in 1997; the major earthquake in central Chinese Taipei in 1999, in which more than 2,000 people perished; and the internet bubble in 2001 all contributed to further deterioration of asset quality and greatly weakened the banking sector. The non-performing loan (NPL) ratio of domestic banks peaked at 11.27 percent at the end of March 2002, forcing the government to implement restructuring measures at a cost of roughly 20 percent of GDP. The NPL ratio subsequently declined to 1.84 percent in 2007 (year end). The capital-adequacy ratio (the Bank for International Settlements) also rose, from 10.4 percent in 2001 to 10.81 percent in 2007. A lower NPL ratio and a higher capital-adequacy ratio have helped to improve the financial intermediation function of the banking sector.

## 2.2. Globalization

In the financial reforms undertaken since 2000, Chinese Taipei has greatly expanded globalization of its financial sector and encouraged entry into the market by foreign financial institutions. A number of local banks, of which a majority were financially weak, have since been acquired by international banks, and the market share of branches and subsidiaries of foreign banks rose from 2.48 percent in 2001 to 10.73 percent in 2008.[1] However, despite the entry of foreign and private banks, the banking sector is still dominated by government-controlled banks (including government-owned banks and those in which the government is a major shareholder and appoints a majority of the board of directors), which today still hold a market share of around 50 percent and account for 8 of the 10 largest banks.

In 2003 the government abolished the QFII (qualified foreign institutional investor) requirement for foreign portfolio investment and relaxed other restrictions on it. As a result, the foreign ownership of stocks listed on the Taiwan Stock Exchange (TWSE) rose from 19.8 percent in 2001 (year end) to 32.9 percent in 2007.

Taiwan's manufacturing sector is dominated by the ICT industries, which are highly capital-intensive and cyclical. The presence of foreign portfolio investors allows diversification of the accompanying financial risks through the stock markets. Because ICT stocks are one of its most important components, accounting for more than 50 percent of market value, the TWSE index is highly correlated with but more volatile than the NASDAQ index. The volatility of the TWSE index is also due to the dominance in stock trading of individual investors, who frequently display herd behavior. The increased foreign portfolio investment helps to reduce volatility in stock prices since foreign investors do not trade as frequently as the domestic individual investors who dominate stock trading. For example, in 2009, although foreigners owned 31.9 percent of stocks, they accounted for only 16.3 percent of stock trading. Trading by domestic individuals as a percentage of all trading fell from 77.8 percent in 2003 to 72.0 percent in 2009.

Restrictions on cross-border capital flows were also gradually relaxed over the last decade. Freer capital flows have helped to reduce the pressure on capital markets of Chinese Taipei's excess savings, which averaged 7.1 percent of GDP per year for the decade 2000–9. According to Central Bank statistics (see Table 5.1), total overseas assets held by Chinese Taipei rose by 211 percent, from US$274.1 billion in 2000 to US$852.3 billion in 2007. Meanwhile, total foreign holdings of assets in Chinese Taipei rose by 376.6 percent, from US$81.6 billion to US$388.7 billion. The net international asset position held by Chinese Taipei thus rose by 140.8 percent, from US$192.5 billion to US$463.6 billion over the same period. The increased net international investment position largely reflected the persistent excess savings situation described above.

Freer portfolio investment and capital flows allow substitution of portfolio investment for foreign direct investment. Foreign investment in Chinese Taipei can now take the form of acquisition of an existing firm instead of having to set up a factory or enterprise from scratch. Consequently, although cumulative inward foreign direct investment rose from US$19.5 billion in 2000 to US$55.7 billion in 2009, its value as a percentage of total cumulative foreign investment fell from 39.3 percent to 21.5 percent in that period. Likewise, cumulative outward direct investment rose from US$66.7 billion in 2000 (year end) to US$170.0 billion in 2009; its value as a percentage of total foreign investment declined from 69.9 percent to 41.2 percent.

Holdings of overseas financial derivatives have grown rapidly in the last decade, but they still account for only a small fraction of overseas portfolio investment (1.57 percent in 2008 and less than 1 percent in previous years).

A study by Goswami, Jobst, and Xin (2009) finds that financial innovations such as securitized products affect macro-financial linkages by reducing the interest-rate elasticity of real activity while increasing the interest-rate pass-through effect. However, because securitized products and related derivatives, despite rapid growth in recent years, still make up only a small fraction of Chinese Taipei's financial markets, their linkage effect is likely to be small, if it is present at all.

As a consequence of their increased exposure to foreign assets, financial institutions and individual investors suffered larger losses in the current crisis than they otherwise would have. Similarly, foreigners now also hold a larger share of TWSE stocks, and thus they were hurt more by a declining TWSE index than was previously the case. Foreign investors, in particular, tend to

*Table 5.1* International investment position (end-period stocks) (year end 2008)

| | 2000 | 2005 | 2006 | 2007 | 2008 | 2009 | 2010 | 2011 | 2012 |
|---|---|---|---|---|---|---|---|---|---|
| **Assets** | | | | | | | | | |
| Direct investment abroad (US$ billions) | 66.7 | 103.3 | 122.7 | 151.2 | 163.5 | 170.0 | 190.8 | 213.1 | 231.5 |
| Portfolio investment (US$ billions) | 28.7 | 147.3 | 197.8 | 249.0 | 188.9 | 242.9 | 304.8 | 307.0 | 391.0 |
| Equity securities (US$ billions) | 12.5 | 46.4 | 89.3 | 138.6 | 70.3 | 109.2 | 139.9 | 128.1 | 164.2 |
| Debt securities (US$ billions) | 16.2 | 101.0 | 108.5 | 110.4 | 118.6 | 133.7 | 165.0 | 178.9 | 226.8 |
| Financial derivatives (US$ billions) | 0 | 2.5 | 1.9 | 3.6 | 13.6 | 10.1 | 11.4 | 9.1 | 8.4 |
| Other investment (US$ billions) | 67.3 | 124.2 | 142.9 | 173.6 | 185.1 | 197.2 | 218.5 | 250.9 | 255.0 |
| Reserve assets (US$ billions) | 111.4 | 258.0 | 270.8 | 275.0 | 296.4 | 353.0 | 387.2 | 390.6 | 408.5 |
| Total assets (US$ billions) | 274.1 | 635.3 | 736.2 | 852.3 | 847.6 | 973.1 | 1,112.7 | 1,170.6 | 1,294.3 |
| **Annual rate of change (%)** | | 12.3 | 15.9 | 15.8 | -0.6 | 14.8 | 14.3 | 5.2 | 10.6 |
| **Rate of change since 2000 (%)** | | 131.8 | 168.6 | 211 | 209.3 | 255.1 | 306 | 327.1 | 372.3 |
| **Liabilities** | | | | | | | | | |
| Direct inward investment (US$ billions) | 19.5 | 43.2 | 50.2 | 48.6 | 45.5 | 55.7 | 63.0 | 55.1 | 59.8 |
| Portfolio investment (US$ billions) | 30.1 | 141.6 | 189.7 | 215.2 | 110.1 | 203.1 | 254.7 | 196.9 | 234.1 |
| Equity securities (US$ billions) | 25.7 | 134.1 | 183.2 | 209.4 | 104.4 | 197.6 | 244.6 | 187.5 | 224.4 |
| Debt securities (US$ billions) | 4.3 | 7.5 | 6.6 | 5.8 | 5.7 | 5.5 | 10.0 | 9.4 | 9.7 |
| Financial derivatives (US$ billions) | 0 | – | – | – | 15.3 | 9.9 | 10.1 | 10.0 | 8.3 |
| Other investment (US$ billions) | 32.0 | 104.8 | 112.5 | 121.0 | 118.1 | 120.6 | 152.2 | 182.6 | 190.5 |
| Total liabilities (US$ billions) | 81.6 | 292.7 | 355.0 | 388.7 | 288.9 | 389.2 | 480.0 | 444.6 | 492.6 |
| **Annual rate of change (%)** | | 29.0 | 21.3 | 9.5 | -25.7 | 34.7 | 23.3 | -7.4 | 10.8 |
| **Rate of change since 2000 (%)** | | 258.9 | 335.2 | 376.6 | 254.2 | 377.2 | 488.5 | 445.1 | 504.0 |
| Net international investment position (US$ billions) | 192.5 | 342.6 | 381.2 | 463.6 | 558.7 | 583.9 | 632.6 | 726 | 801.7 |
| **Annual rate of change (%)** | | 1.0 | 11.3 | 21.6 | 20.5 | 4.5 | 8.3 | 14.8 | 10.4 |
| **Rate of change since 2000 (%)** | | 78.0 | 98.0 | 140.8 | 190.2 | 203.4 | 228.7 | 277.2 | 316.5 |

Source: Databank of the Central Bank of Chinese Taipei: http://www.cbc.gov.tw/public/Data/46131619117l.pdf.

concentrate portfolio investment on financial institutions and ICT firms, which were the most badly hurt victims of the financial crisis. Without foreign ownership of one-third of TWSE stocks, domestic investors might have felt even more pain from the downturn in the economy. In this sense, financial globalization helps to bring about financial risk diversification and risk sharing.

### 2.3. Interest and exchange rates

The relaxation of capital flows does not seem to have made the exchange rate significantly more volatile. The standard deviation of the monthly rate of change in the value of the NT dollar was 1.24 percent for 2000–9, compared to 1.39 percent for 1990–9, the period in which capital flows were more tightly regulated.

Figure 5.2 provides some evidence that volatility of the exchange rate was influenced by the Central Bank's policy. From the figure, we see that the growth rate of broad money (M2) had a declining trend. The mean growth rate was 12.33 percent per annum in the decade 1990–9, but declined to an average 5.22 percent in the decade 2000–9. The standard deviation of the monetary growth rate also declined from 4.49 percent for 1990–9 to 2.05 percent for 2000–9. While the annual growth rate of M2 was lower in the latter decade, the ratio of M2 to GDP rose from an average 168.07 percent for 1990–9 to an average 205.95 percent for 2000–9. Moreover, changes in the net holdings

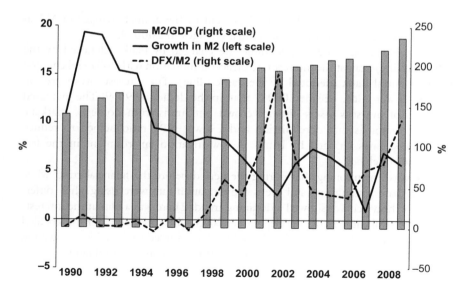

*Figure 5.2* Growth rate of the money supply (M2) (%)
Source: DGBAS (2010).
Note: DFX = Change in foreign exchange.

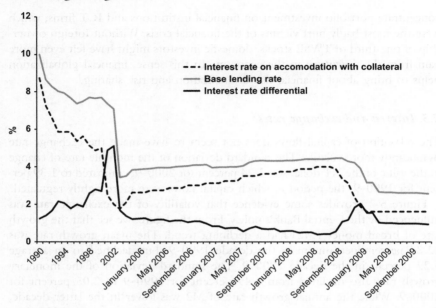

*Figure 5.3* Interest rates (%)

Source: Databank of the Central Bank of Chinese Taipei: http://www.cbc.gov.tw/ct.asp?xIte
m=995&ctNode=523&mp=1.

of foreign assets accounted for 11.43 percent of the annual changes in M2 in
1990–9 but 82.78 percent of the annual changes in 2000–9.

Figure 5.3 depicts the base lending rate charged by banks (denoted by the
solid gray line) against the interest rate on accommodation with collateral charged
by the Central Bank (denoted by the dashed line). The interest rates were, on
average, lower in the decade 2000–9 than in the decade 1990–9. The increased
holdings of overseas assets did not crowd out funds from domestic markets.
Another reason is that deregulation and a lower NPL ratio helped to reduce
the interest rates charged by banks. A low inflation environment in the last
decade also helped.

It is worth mentioning that during the period before the financial crisis, while
both the base lending rate and the accommodation rate were rising, their differential (the heavy curve) showed a declining trend. There was a blip in the interest-
rate-differential curve right after September 2008, when the Lehman Brothers filed
for bankruptcy protection and the Central Bank responded to the crisis by lowering
the accommodation rate. The blip reflects a riskier lending environment.

### 2.4. Private-sector financing

Overall, financial deepening can be measured by total private-sector financing,
through both bank loans (including investments) and securities markets as a
percentage of GDP. As shown by the dashed line in Figure 5.4, the percentage

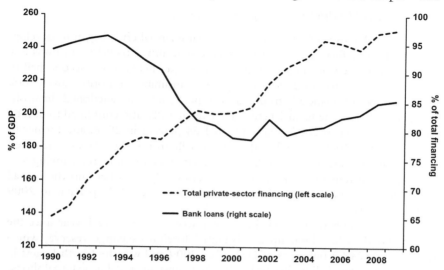

*Figure 5.4* Private-sector financing

Source: Databank of the Central Bank of Chinese Taipei: http://www.cbc.gov.tw/ct.asp?xIte m=1077&CtNode=524&mp=1.

showed a rising trend over the last two decades as a consequence of easier access to financial markets made possible by financial liberalization. Note that there is a dip in the curve in 2005. That year, the economy suffered a credit card crisis in which losses by financial institutions were between 2.4 and 3.4 percent of GDP. The crisis resulted in a decline in total private-sector financing relative to GDP.

The ratio of bank financing to total financing (through bank financing and securities markets), denoted by the solid line in Figure 5.4, showed a declining trend before surging in 2001. The rise in the proportion of financing through bank loans between 2001 and 2002 reflects the debt issues made by the government to finance fiscal stimulus measures in order to accelerate economic recovery from the internet bubble. The rise in the percentage of financing through bank loans in the first decade of the 2000s, amid the development of securities markets, was partly the consequence of a continued decline in NPLs.

In sum, Chinese Taipei's financial deepening has helped to enhance the functioning of financial intermediation, particularly in the areas of risk diversification and credit availability.

## 3. Financial crisis and macro-financial linkage

The contagion of a global financial crisis can be transmitted through both financial and non-financial channels. On the financial side, Chinese Taipei's financial sector was relatively stable throughout the latest crisis, although there were losses in stock markets and in its holdings of overseas assets.

126    *Sheng-Cheng Hu*

### 3.1. *Financial health before the financial crisis*

As mentioned above, when the current global financial crisis began to develop, Chinese Taipei's financial system was relatively healthy.[2] Its NPL ratio was low and its capital-adequacy ratio was in the safe range. Between the second half of 2007 and the first half of 2008, the depository insurance authority actively took over a number of financially troubled "zombie" banks and auctioned them off. As a result, despite the financial crisis, the overall NPL ratio continued to decline from 1.84 percent in 2007 (year end) to 1.54 percent in 2008, and further to 1.15 percent in 2009. Several of these financially troubled banks were acquired by international institutions, facilitating the latter's entry into the banking sector. Their injection of capital into these banks helped to beef up the overall capital-adequacy ratio from 10.81 percent in 2007 to 11.86 percent in 2009 despite the crisis.

Chinese Taipei had maintained a current account surplus each year since the 1980s and thus had built up a substantial foreign exchange reserve, which stood at US$348.2 billion as of December 2009 and was the fourth largest in the world, to provide liquidity and to buffer against any possible external shocks to the economy and financial markets. Although on an annual basis, there has been a net accumulation in foreign exchange reserves each year since the 1980s, Figure 5.5 shows that during the financial crisis period, there were months in which rapid outflows of capital caused declines in foreign exchange reserves.

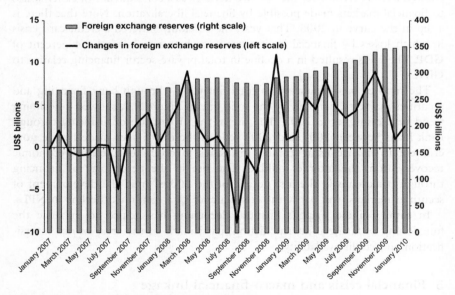

*Figure 5.5* Changes in foreign exchange reserves

Source: Databank of the Central Bank of Chinese Taipei: http://www.cbc.gov.tw/ct.asp?xItem=995&ctNode=523&mp=1.

## 3.2. Banking sector

There were no bank runs during the crisis. However, as a precautionary measure, the government declared a "three supports" policy; namely, the government would support banks, but banks should support businesses, and businesses should support labor. Under this policy, the government engaged in moral suasion to the effect that banks should provide businesses with liquidity. More importantly, the government announced a policy of guaranteeing all deposits in the full amount rather than up to the normal limit of NT$1.5 million (or around US$46,900) per account, in order to maintain public confidence in the banking system. At the end of 2010, the government terminated the full insurance policy but raised the normal insurance limit from NT$1.5 million to NT$3 million.

As part of the three supports policy, the Financial Supervisory Commission provided incentives for cooperation by banks in providing liquidity to businesses, particularly small and medium-sized enterprises. In addition, the Central Bank expanded liquidity facility and lowered the rediscount rate seven times, from 3.625 percent in June 2008 to 1.25 percent in February 2009. In September 2008 the accommodation rate began to fall as the Central Bank took action to protect the economy against the effects of the Lehman Brothers collapse. However, the base bank lending rate continued to rise because of a riskier market environment for lending. The base lending interest rate began to fall in March 2009 when the financial crisis appeared to have been brought under control (see Figure 5.3).

The dominance of government-controlled banks turned out to be a stabilizing factor for the banking sector during the global financial crisis since these banks were considered by depositors to be safe havens for their money. There was a shift in deposits from non-government banks to government-controlled banks, raising the deposits in the government-controlled banks from 55.74 percent of total deposits in domestic banks in 2007 (year end) to 56.96 percent in 2008, but they then dropped to 54.69 percent in 2009. The shift of deposits came to an end when the full depository insurance policy was implemented.

## 3.3. Capital flows

During the global financial crisis, there were greater fluctuations in capital flows as foreign financial institutions had to help their financially troubled parent companies with capital injections and as capital looked for arbitrage opportunities and safe havens (Figure 5.5). At times, the Central Bank had to intervene vigorously. As can be seen from Figure 5.2, the annual changes in M2 attributable to net international asset positions increased from 72 percent in 2007 to 79 percent in 2008, and further to 134 percent in 2009.

Together with more rapid capital flows, there was increased volatility in the value of the New Taiwan dollar (NT$) against the U.S. dollar (US$). In particular, from July 2008 through February 2009, the value of the NT$ against the US$ declined by 11.6 percent, reflecting a deteriorating economy and increasing net capital outflows (Figure 5.6). This trend was in line with what happened in

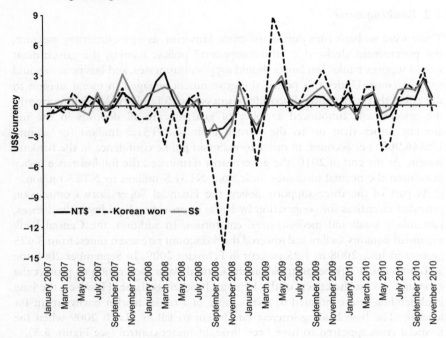

*Figure 5.6* Monthly rates of change in currency values (US$/currency)

Source: Data Bank of the Central Bank of Chinese Taipei: http://www.cbc.gov.tw/content.
asp?mp=1&CuItem=36599.

Note: NT$: New Taiwan dollar; S$: Singapore dollar.

neighboring economies, but Chinese Taipei's exchange rate was less volatile than
theirs. The standard deviation of monthly rates of change in the value of the NT
dollar rose from 0.67 percent in 2007 to 1.83 percent in 2008, compared to a
rise from 1.10 percent to 4.67 percent for the Korean won, and a rise from 1.09
percent to 1.93 percent for the Singapore dollar. In sum, the Central Bank was
able to maintain a relatively stable foreign exchange rate regime during the crisis
despite increased globalization and freer capital flows. (See Wang [2005] for
analysis of how the changes in the exchange rate affected Chinese Taipei's exports.)

### 3.4. Private-sector financing

As can be seen from Figure 5.4, the ratio of total private-sector financing through
bank loans and securities markets continued to rise during the crisis period of 2008–9.
The growth of private-sector financing was positive, albeit lower, while the growth
rate in real activity turned negative. This trend provides some evidence that the
economy did not have a liquidity problem, even at the height of the crisis. The
monetary policy was relaxed, and there was plenty of liquidity in the market as the
growth rate of M2 was 7 percent in 2008 and 5.74 percent in 2009, higher than
the mean growth rate of 5.22 percent for 2000–9. And, as noted above, the rediscount rate declined from 3.375 percent to 2 percent during the same time span.

However, the financial crisis exacerbated the increasing trend of financing through the banking sector. There are two possible reasons. First, during the financial crisis, there were sharp drops in stock prices, making it more costly to finance investment through both domestic and international stock markets. Second, the sharp rise in government debt-financing of stimulus expenditures crowded out business financing of fixed investments through debt issuance. Third, owing to the government's three supports policy, banks (at least the government-controlled ones) were more forthcoming with respect to approving loans.

### 3.5. Stock markets

As in other economies, Chinese Taipei's stock markets were badly hurt by the crisis. In 2008 the decline in the TWSE index was 46.0 percent, better only than those for Singapore (49.41 percent) and Shanghai (65.4 percent). The fall in the TWSE index resulted in a decline in the market value of stocks by NT$9.51 trillion (US$289.4 billion), although those losses were almost fully recovered in 2009 when the TWSE index jumped by 78 percent. Despite the capital losses financial institutions incurred from the financial crisis, the TWSE financial stock index declined by only 36.5 percent between 2007 and 2008, compared to the decline of 46.0 percent for the overall TWSE index (Figure 5.7).

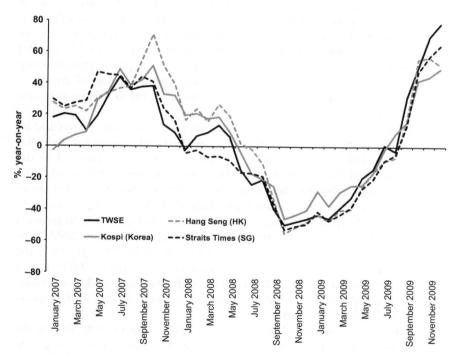

*Figure 5.7* Fluctuations in stock prices: newly industrialized Asian economies (%, year-on-year)

Source: DGBAS (2010).

In addition, Chinese Taipei's total holdings of overseas financial assets fell from US$249.0 billion in 2007 (year end) to US$188.9 billion in 2008 before climbing back to US$242.9 billion in 2009 and US$304.8 billion in 2010. The fall in value in 2008 was partly a result of capital losses in the securities markets during the crisis. The direct losses in toxic assets, including subprime mortgages, Lehman Brothers' structured products, and others, were estimated to be NT$265.1 billion (US$8.07 billion), or 1.96 percent of Chinese Taipei's GDP of US$412.6 billion in 2008 (Yen, 2009). Foreign holdings of financial assets also fell, from US$215.2 billion in 2007 to US$110.1 billion in 2008. The decline in foreign ownership of stocks brought about a fall in the ratio of foreign ownership of TWSE stocks from 32.9 percent in 2007 to 30.4 percent in 2008, but the ratio returned to 31.9 percent at the end of 2009.

### 3.6. Private consumption and investment

Because of the losses in asset value, a sharp rise in the unemployment rate, and the resulting collapse of consumer confidence, there was a decline in private consumption. To stimulate private consumption, the government took a number of measures, including, among others, (i) distribution of a consumption coupon worth around US$120 per citizen and (ii) reduction of the commodity tax on small vehicles by around US$1,000 per vehicle. Studies find that the effect of these measures fell short of government expectations.[3] In the first quarter of 2009, although these measures were in place, private consumption still fell at the real rate of −2.12 percent yoy. For the entire year, the real growth rate of private consumption was only a modest 1.08 percent, compared to 2.91 percent per annum in the pre-crisis period (2003–7). Overall, it appears that the sharp rise in the unemployment rate and the accompanying collapse of consumer confidence were the most important factors underlying the slowdown in private consumption.

Private investment also declined by 35.88 percent in the first quarter and by 31.06 percent in the second quarter (yoy), and by 17.91 percent for the entire year in 2009. This occurred despite the easy monetary policy pursued by the Central Bank and the government's exhortation that banks (particularly government-controlled banks) should support businesses. Specifically, the mean interest rate on capital-expenditure loans charged by the five largest (and government-controlled) banks, which held a 41 percent market share of loans made by all (domestic) banks as of 2009, declined from 3.05 percent in 2008Q4 to 2.20 percent in 2009Q1, and further to 2.10 percent in 2009Q2, while the loans they made declined by 7.5 percent quarter-on-quarter in 2009Q1, and another 2.09 percent in 2009Q2. In other words, the sharp decline in private investment in this period should be explained primarily by the fall in exports rather than by the financial conditions.

Exports account for around 60 percent of Chinese Taipei's GDP. During the crisis, exports fell sharply while the value of the NT dollar was declining. The growth rate of exports (in U.S. dollars) was 3.63 percent in 2008 but fell to

–20.32 percent in 2009 before resurging to 34.8 percent in 2010. The sharp drop in exports, in turn, brought about a deep recession and a drastic fall in private investment. The ICT sector, which accounted for 13.5 percent of Chinese Taipei's GDP and 31.1 percent of industrial fixed investment as of 2007, experienced a decline in investment by 22.7 percent in 2008 and by 29.5 percent in 2009. During the same period, the decline in total private investment was –15.6 percent and –17.9 percent in 2008 and 2009, respectively.

In sum, Chinese Taipei's infection with the financial crisis occurred mainly through the non-financial channel, particularly through declines in exports. The preliminary evidence suggests that the effect of the decline in asset value on private consumption and investment was not significant. This is in contrast to how the U.S. financial crisis was transmitted directly through the financial channels to a number of countries. For example, the three largest banks in Iceland and the bank Northern Rock in the United Kingdom were among the first casualties of the crisis and required government rescue assistance before other segments of the respective economies suffered from the contagion.

The deep recession was also in stark contrast with what happened to the economy in the 1997 Asian financial crisis. At that time, Chinese Taipei suffered only a relatively minor economic downturn. Its growth rate declined from 5.48 percent in 1997 to 3.47 percent in 1998 but quickly returned to 5.97 percent in 1999. The main reason was that, unlike the situation in the current crisis, the 1997 crisis-hit countries, such as Korea, Thailand, and Indonesia, were not major export markets for Chinese Taipei. Together, they accounted for only 5.7 percent of Chinese Taipei's exports in 1997, and Korea was one of its major competitors in export markets. Meanwhile, the U.S.A., Chinese Taipei's most important export market, was still maintaining a respectable 4.47 percent growth rate in 1998. Although Hong Kong, Chinese Taipei's second largest trading partner, had a growth rate of –6.0 percent, most exports to Hong Kong at that time were indirect exports ultimately destined for China, which was enjoying a growth rate of 7.8 percent in 1998.

Some possible explanations for why Chinese Taipei's infection with the global financial crisis occurred primarily through the non-financial channel follow: First, while securitized products played an important role in the spread of the financial crisis to other advanced countries, they still represented only a small fraction of Chinese Taipei's financial markets (see Table 5.1).[4] Second, its banks had not been highly leveraged. Third, the Central Bank was able to effectively counter the attacks of capital flows, thanks to its holdings of large foreign exchange reserves.

## 4. Aftermath of the financial crisis

As the world recovers from the financial crisis, some basic problems remain to be tackled. First, the rapid increases in fiscal deficits have already caused problems for some European countries and will continue to be a source of instability for other economies. Second, the global savings glut and hot money are still flooding financial markets, both globally and particularly in East Asia, which has enjoyed a more robust recovery from the crisis than have the advanced countries (Strauss-Kahn, 2010). Since the fourth quarter of 2009, the inflow of capital has fueled increases in both stock and housing prices in Chinese Taipei. Overall, the rise in housing prices (in Taipei City) was 23.6 percent (yoy) in 2009Q4 and 17.1 percent in 2010Q4, following a fall of −0.88 percent in 2008Q4. While the rise in housing prices is still limited to certain localities in metropolitan Taipei, it did exacerbate public sentiment regarding increasing income inequality and prompted the Central Bank to take selective credit control measures to prevent its spread to other regions of Chinese Taipei.

Thus, unavoidably, there will be debates about how to protect Asian countries against another attack of hot money and the eruption of another asset bubble. Some available policy alternatives recommended by the IMF (Strauss-Kahn, 2010) include appreciating the currency value, lowering interest rates, accumulating reserves, and tightening fiscal policy. In cases where the flood of capital is expected to be temporary, or when there is a real danger of the exchange rate overshooting, the IMF even recommends capital controls. Asian countries have already adopted capital control measures in one form or another. Some have imposed, while others are contemplating, a Tobin tax on short-term capital flows. In deciding on an appropriate policy mix, each economy must consider its own circumstances, the seriousness of floods of hot money, the possibility of overshooting, the adequacy of foreign exchange reserves, the stage of recovery, and the size of the country, among other considerations.

However, it would be difficult for any country to deal with floods of hot money, a fiscal imbalance, or even the contagion of a financial crisis all by itself, especially if the country is small. In certain cases, the individual-country approach may even spark friction with its trading partners. As long as hot money is there, capital control to prevent its invasion into a single economy would intensify its attack on neighboring economies. Thus, the IMF has proposed strong international policy collaboration within the IMF structure to respond to hot money and economic crises (Strauss-Kahn, 2010). The Central Bank of Chinese Taipei similarly called for international cooperation on capital control as a means of containing rapid flows of capital (Perng, 2009, 2010). However, Bernanke (2010) observed that in the process of recovery from the global financial crisis, the sense of common purpose had waned and tensions over economic policies had emerged and intensified.

Recent experience in dealing with the fiscal crises in Greece, Portugal, Italy, Ireland, and Spain suggests that when a country is in crisis, neighboring countries or regional organizations would have greater impetus and incentive to help solve the problem. Hence, it would be worthwhile to consider a regional cooperative approach parallel to or supplementary to the IMF's global approach to crisis prevention and management (see Chen, Hu, and Wu 2000).

Duan (2009) and others have proposed the establishment of an Asian currency unit as a measurement instrument for trade and finance. The concept of an Asian monetary unit is similar to that of the European Monetary Union

(EMU). The performance of the EMU during this crisis provides an insight into how well this approach to international cooperation can work. Basically, in such a monetary union, each country gives up its monetary policy power to a regional central bank. A regional central bank may be more effective in coping with shocks that are regional or global in nature, but it may not be effective in dealing with country-specific shocks or country-specific impacts of regional or global shocks. Each country is thus left with only fiscal policy instruments to cope with country-specific shocks or country-specific impacts of regional or global shocks.

When a country has to rely too heavily on fiscal policy instruments, as is the case for Ireland and Spain in the current financial crisis, the ultimate outcome will be excessive fiscal deficits and fiscal instability. Thus, there is a tradeoff between monetary stability and fiscal stability. Moreover, a monetary union without substantial reserves would not be in a position to deal effectively with a regional or global shock. Another problem with the idea of an Asian currency unit is that given the diversity of Asian countries in terms of development stages, cultural backgrounds, and past political histories, it could take a long time to identify an Asian currency unit that is acceptable to all major participants.

A softer approach would be to foster regional cooperation through the establishment of an arrangement similar to European Financial Stability Facility, which was created in 2010 to preserve financial stability in Europe by providing financial assistance to eurozone states in difficulty. The facility raises funds by issuing bonds or other debt instruments. The Chiang Mai Initiative (CMI) Multi-lateralization established in 2010 by members of the Association of Southeast Asian Nations plus China, Japan, and Korea represents a financial arrangement of policy cooperation among However, its facility of US$240 billion is only around 1.5 percent of the region's GDP. By comparison, the European Financial Stability Facility's €750 billion as of 2011 amounts to 8 percent of the region's GDP. It remains to be seen whether CMI is adequate if the need arises. In any case, China, Japan, Chinese Taipei, and Korea together hold a substantial proportion of the world's foreign exchange reserves (US$3.9 trillion as of 2009). Pooling their resources in a regional framework could provide liquidity in addition to the CMI and enhance the ability of the region to cope with hot money and other problems facing the region, as well as future crises, in pursuit of financial stability.

## 5. Conclusions

In this global financial crisis, Chinese Taipei suffered its worst downturn since World War II, as a result of the steep decline in exports due to the global economic downturn. Although Chinese Taipei has expanded liberalization and globalization of its financial sector in recent years, the financial channel did not appear to be the primary channel through which the contagion of the crisis was transmitted. The financial sector was healthy at the onset of, and remained relatively stable during, the global financial crisis. The main effect of the crisis on

Chinese Taipei's financial sector was the losses in asset value, while the decline in output resulted primarily from a fall in exports.

Even as the global economy has recovered from the crisis, the macroeconomic causes of the crisis have not been eliminated. The problem of the global savings glut persists, and a number of countries still suffer from serious fiscal imbalances. Solutions must be found to these problems in order to prevent another asset bubble or financial crisis. While each country must solve its own fiscal problems and contain hot money, an international cooperative approach, at both global and regional levels, may be necessary to prevent the contagion of crises or the sparking of friction among countries.

## Notes

1 Subsidiaries wholly owned by foreign institutions are considered foreign institutions in this calculation but are considered domestic banks in government statistics.
2 See Chung (2009) for a stress test of Taiwan's financial system. According to this report, Chinese Taipei's ability to withstand outside shocks similar to those that arose during the global financial crisis was relatively strong.
3 Empirical evidence suggests that around 60–70 percent of personal consumption in Taiwan is determined by lifetime wealth and is thus affected by permanent changes in the value of stocks, while 30 percent is determined by current income. See Chan and Hu (1997), Wu, Chen, and Fu (2010), and Kan (2010).
4 Taiwan's financial institutions are allowed to invest only in investment-grade government and corporate bonds. Thus, to some extent, they were insulated from the subprime mortgage problems.

## References and Further Readings

Bernanke, Ben S. 2010. Rebalancing the Global Recovery. Keynote speech delivered at the Sixth ECB Central Banking Conference, November 19.
Blanchard, Oliver, Giovanni Dell'Ariccia, and Paolo Mauro. 2010. Rethinking Macroeconomic Policy. International Monetary Fund Staff Position Note SPN/10/03, February. Washington, DC: International Monetary Fund.
Caprio, Gerard, Jr., Asli Demirgüç-Kunt, and Edward J. Kane. 2008. The 2007 Meltdown in Structured Securitization: Searching for Lessons Not Scapegoats. World Bank Policy Working Paper 4756, September. Washington, DC: World Bank.
Chan, Vei-lin and Sheng-Cheng Hu. 1997. Financial Liberalization and Aggregate Consumption: Evidence from Taiwan. *Applied Economics*, 29: 1525–35.
Chari, V.V., Lawrence Christiano, and Patrick Kehoe. 2008. Facts and Myths about the Financial Crisis of 2008. Federal Research Bank of Minneapolis Working Paper 666, October. Minneapolis: Federal Reserve Bank of Minneapolis.
Chen, Lii-Tan, Sheng-Cheng Hu, and Chung-Shu Wu. 2000. Financial Crisis and Economic Friction among Asian and Pacific Countries. In *Economic Friction and Dispute Resolution in Asia-Pacific: Dreams and Dilemma*, edited by Koichi Hamada, Mitsuo Matsushita, and Chikara Komura, chap. 3. Singapore: Institute of South East Asian Studies.

Chung, Ching-Fan, 2009. A Stress Test of Taiwan's Financial System. Research Report 97CBC-F-1, January. Taipei: The Central Bank.

Cottarelli, Carlo. 2009. Crisis-Hit Countries to See Sharp Rise in Government Debt. *IMF Survey Magazine*, March. http://www.imf.org/external/pubs/ft/survey/so/2009/res030609a.htm.

Coulibaly, Brahima and Jonathan Millar. 2008. The Asian Financial Crisis, Uphill Flow of Capital and Global Imbalance: Evidence from a Micro Study. Finance and Economics Discussion Series 942, August. Washington, DC: Board of Governors of the Federal Reserve System.

Director-General of Budget, Accounting and Statistics (DGBAS), Executive Yuan, Chinese Taipei. 2010. Data Bank. http://ebas1.ebas.gov.tw/pxweb/Dialog/statfile1L.asp?lang=1&strList=L.

Duan, Jin-Cuan. 2009. Asian Currency Unit without Monetary Union – a Practical Unit of Measurement for Trade and Finance. Paper presented at Dr. Sam-Chung Hsieh Memorial Conference: The Impact of the Current Financial Crisis on the East Asian Economy, held at Chung-Hua Institution for Economic Research, Taipei, July.

Freeman, Charles, Michael Kumhof, Douglas Laxton, and Jaewoo Lee. 2009. The Case for Fiscal Stimulus. International Monetary Fund Position Paper, Note SPN/09/03, March. Washington, DC: International Monetary Fund.

Goswami, Mangal, Andreas Jobst, and Xin Long. 2009. An Investigation of Some Macro-financial Linkages of Securitization. International Monetary Fund Working Paper WP/09/06, February. Washington, DC: International Monetary Fund.

Greenspan, Alan. 2009. The Fed Didn't Cause the Housing Bubble. *Wall Street Journal*, March 12.

Greenspan, Alan. 2010. The Crisis. *Brooking Papers on Economic Activity*, Spring 2010, 201–61.

Hu, Sheng-Cheng. 2011. Global Financial Crisis: Lessons for Taiwan. In *The Impact of the Economic Crisis on East Asia Policy Responses from Four Economies*, edited by Daigee Shaw and Bih Jane Liu, 3–28. Cheltenham, UK: Edward Elgar.

International Monetary Fund (IMF). 2009a. The State of Public Finances Cross Country Fiscal Monitor. Prepared by the Staff of the Fiscal Affairs Department, November 3. Washington, DC: International Monetary Fund.

International Monetary Fund (IMF). 2009b. World Economic Outlook (October, updated January 2010). Washington, DC: International Monetary Fund.

International Monetary Fund (IMF). 2010a. Fiscal Monitor: Navigating the Fiscal Challenges Ahead. Prepared by the Staff of the Fiscal Affairs Department, May 14. Washington, DC: International Monetary Fund.

International Monetary Fund (IMF). 2010b. World Economic Outlook (April). Washington, DC: International Monetary Fund.

Kan, Kamon. 2010. Economic Analysis of Taiwan's Consumption Coupon. Paper presented at the Consumption-Coupon Policy Conference, held in the Institute of Economics, Academia Sinica, Taipei, January 15.

Miline, Alistair and Geoffrey Wood. 2008. Banking Crisis Solutions New and Old. *Federal Reserve Bank of St. Louis Review* 90(5): 517–30.

Mizen, Paul. 2008. The Credit Crunch of 2007–2008: A Discussion of the Background, Market Reaction, and Policy Responses. *Federal Reserve Bank of St. Louis Review* 90(5): 531–67.

Perng, Fai-Nan. 2009. Preface. *Special Issue on the Global Financial Crisis*, December. Taipei: Central Bank.

Perng, Fai-Nan. 2010. Management of International Capital Movement. *The Banker*, September: 116–17.

Romer, Michael, and Ji Chou. 2001. Macroeconomic Policy. In *Industrialization and the State: The Changing Role of the Taiwan Government in the Economy, 1945–1998*, edited by Li-Min Hsueh, Chen-Kuo Hsu, and Dwight H. Perkins, chap. 4. Cambridge, MA: Harvard University Press.

Sommer, Martin. 2009. Why Has Japan Been Hit So Hard by the Global Recession? International Monetary Fund Staff Position Note, SPN/09/05, March. Washington, DC: International Monetary Fund.

Strauss-Kahn, Dominique. 2010. 2010 – a Year of Transformation for the World and for Asia. Address at the Asian Financial Forum, International Monetary Fund, Hong Kong, January 20.

Taylor, John. 2009. The Financial Crisis and Policy Responses: An Empirical Analysis of What Went Wrong. National Bureau of Economic Research Working Paper 14631, January. Cambridge, MA: National Bureau of Economic Research.

Wang, Hong J. 2005. The Effect of NT Exchange Rate on Taiwan's Economic and Financial Activity. Commissioned Research Report, 93CBC – Economics 1, January. Taipei: The Central Bank.

Wu, Chung-Shu and Sheng-Cheng Hu. 2000. Interest Rates, Credit Rationing and Banking Deregulation in Taiwan. In *Deregulation and Interdependence in the Asia Pacific Region*, edited by Takatoshi Ito and Anne O. Krueger, chap. 8. National Bureau of Economic Research East Asia Seminar on Economics Vol. 8. Chicago: University of Chicago Press, 2000.

Wu, Chung-Shu, Cheng-Fu Chen and Tsu-Tan Fu. 2010. The Short-Run Macroeconomic Effect of the Consumption Coupon. Paper presented at the Consumption-Coupon Policy Conference, Institute of Economics, Academia Sinica, Taipei, January 15.

Yen, Ching-Chang. 2009. A Reflection on the Anniversary of Financial Tsunami. *Global Industry and Commerce*, No. 619, October. Taipei: Chinese National Association of Commerce and Industry.

# Part II
# Monetary policy regimes

# 6 Monetary policy regimes

## An overview

*Akira Kohsaka*

## Introduction and summary

In the Asian financial crisis (AFC) in 1997–8, because of *sudden stops* and/or reversals of foreign capital inflows, emerging economies in the Pacific region experienced nightmarish economic downturns for the first time in two decades. Their *virtual dollar peg* system of exchange rates collapsed, and their domestic financial systems were forced to implement structural reforms. In contrast, in the global financial crisis (GFC) in 2008–9, these economies were mostly immune from those sudden stops of foreign capital flows and were able to sustain handsome economic growth compared to advanced economies, which suffered from sudden stops of capital flows and prolonged economic downturns thereafter.

Why these differences occurred and what causes the *resilience* of emerging economies concern many economists, including those at the International Monetary Fund (IMF, 2012). Focusing on AFC-hit emerging economies in the Pacific region, we examine where the difference in economic performance between the two crises in these economies comes from, by looking at their monetary policy regimes before and after the AFC. We observe increased *financial deepening* (accumulation and diversification of financial assets) and expanded *financial globalization* (increases in cross-border assets and liabilities) as backgrounds for these regimes to deal with financial business cycles.

We consider how we can more effectively set macroeconomic policy instruments, and in what kinds of institutional settings. Many emerging and developing economies abandoned the virtual dollar peg system of exchange rates and adopted, as another nominal anchor, inflation targeting with *flexible exchange rates and freer capital movement*. But they are now confronted with volatile international financial flows and exchange rate risks, which may impact their long-term growth paths to a significant degree.

In light of the current global turmoil, the *macroeconomic policy trilemma* among the three policy goals, i.e., exchange rate stability, free capital mobility and monetary autonomy, has been reexamined. Recently, even the IMF admitted, albeit reluctantly, that *capital controls* and monetary policy discretion could be useful in some circumstances. We are not sure, however, precisely in what circumstances, to what extent and exactly where in the trilemma we should attain a balance among the three goals. As a first step, we review our diverse experiences in the region since the 1990s and then pursue a new perspective on monetary policy regimes by liberating ourselves from the mantra of "the freer and the more flexible, the better". Again, we need to take into account the new realities that we found under the name of *financial deepening and globalization*.

The above observations lead us to discuss the following questions: The current crisis has seriously affected domestic financial systems and macroeconomic developments in the region. How have the policy authorities coped with these, and how can we assess their efforts to date? Then, does the above examination suggest that we should change the framework of monetary policy management or monetary policy regimes in terms of monetary policy independence, exchange rate stability and capital mobility? If so, how? If not, why?

Reviewing our diverse experiences in the region, we confirmed the diverse monetary policy regimes and their developments; we also identified a few common facets that are worthwhile to learn for more robust monetary policy regimes as follows:

1.  Policy objectives: Faced with financial globalization, emerging market economies need to cope with increasing volatile foreign capital flows. Meanwhile, prudential policies regarding the financial sector need to be better coordinated with macroeconomic stabilization policy under the name of *macro-prudential policy* in advanced economies. Through the series of financial crises in the 1990s, emerging economies in the Pacific region continued to resort to unorthodox but traditional instruments, i.e. a combination of foreign exchange market intervention and capital controls. Conventional wisdom, such as corner solutions within the macroeconomic policy trilemma, was challenged, and the emerging economies settled on non-corner solutions to address the new global economic environment.

2.  Policy transmission: The region consists of surplus economies that have expanded their linkages with the global financial market on a "gross" basis, i.e., both hosting foreign investment and investing abroad themselves. Moreover, the composition of capital inflows has been dominated by foreign direct investment (FDI), not by restless portfolio and other flows. Nevertheless, domestic financial deepening appears to have stagnated. In the 2000s the non-financial corporate sector came to rely less and less on financial intermediation (bank credits) and more on self-financing as well as on FDI (*financial internalization*).

3.  Assessments of policy outcomes: Emerging economies in the Pacific region have successfully coped with the destructive force of volatile foreign financial flows, using unorthodox policy tools. *This time is very different* from 1997. These economies have minimized reliance on foreign financial resources and diversified across categories toward less volatile flows. Remarkably, their private sectors have also done the same through their financial internalization. Their domestic financial systems are not as deep as those of advanced economies, but neither are they as shallow as those of emerging economies in other regions, which enables their policy mix.

4.  Sustainability from a global perspective: It is often argued that emerging economies have appeared to be far more resilient during the GFC, but we

must note that they are far from immune to some new types of risks. Under the prolonged recession in advanced economies, emerging economies may have to confront more destabilizing capital flows in the short run and trend currency appreciation along with accelerated income convergence in the long run, if ever. These risks are inevitable anyway. The real concerns over the long run are macroeconomic rebalancing in domestic demand and financial development in these economies. Significant declining trends in domestic investment, persistently high savings, and persistently low household consumption are notable. Whether or not they are sustainable and appropriate for long-run growth remains to be seen.

In the following, we discuss monetary policy regimes in emerging economies in the Pacific region in the context of a macroeconomic policy trilemma (Section 1). Their positions in the trilemma are not corner solutions. We examine motivations and outcomes of their non-corner solutions. In Section 2, we look into policy transmission channels, i.e., international capital flows and domestic financial systems. We examine, as to the former, changes in the composition of foreign capital inflows and then, as to the latter, changes in the structure of domestic financial intermediation. We also discuss the general orientation of these structural changes in macroeconomic transmission.

Then, we assess the macroeconomic outcomes of these monetary policy regimes in Section 3. Recognizing the potentially destructive forces of international capital flows, we reappraise attainments in stability and growth and the roles played by monetary policy regimes and the private sector's responses. Finally, in Section 4, we touch on a few issues related to the sustainability of the concurrent monetary policy regimes from a global perspective. In addition to the intrinsic volatility of international financial flows, we might need to consider long-run implications of these regimes.

## 1. Policy objectives: challenges to the conventional wisdom

Policymakers in an open economy must confront a *trilemma* in choosing their monetary regimes, where they cannot attain more than two goals among the following three: exchange rate stability, independent monetary policy and free movement of international capital flows. In fact, the collapse of the Bretton Woods system of international finance in 1973 meant that all advanced economies decided to give up the first goal, exchange rate stability, for the other two goals, opting for floating exchange rates.

Many developing economies have long been left behind, wondering whether to stick to the old fixed exchange rate regime or to follow the lead of advanced economies. In practice, emerging markets compromised by more or less liberalizing capital accounts under stable exchange rates. The series of currency crises in emerging market economies in the 1980s and the 1990s were often characterized by huge foreign capital inflows and resulting currency overvaluation in advance of the crises.

Observing the crises, some economists advocated "corner solutions" among the three trilemma goals, i.e., completely abandoning one of the goals, sticking to a clean fixed exchange rate or a completely open capital account, or both (then, inevitably, forgoing monetary independence). Actually, in the Pacific region, Hong Kong has chosen the third course since 1983, while China chose the first course until 2008.

Many other emerging economies, however, have behaved differently from what they officially claim, which is to have flexible exchange rates and free capital movements. In practice, they are more or less away from the corners in terms of exchange rate stability and free capital mobility. Emerging economies in the Pacific region are no exception. Figure 6.1 shows one example estimate where the policy combination of a flexible exchange rate and free capital mobility, as in Japan, is in the top corner and that of a fixed exchange rate and capital controls, as in China, is in the bottom-left corner.[1] While we see some shifts in position during the 1990s, the figure demonstrates that even in the late 2000s, Indonesia, Korea, Malaysia and Thailand were remote from the top corner of flexible exchange rates and free capital mobility.[2]

An increasing number of countries have been adopting inflation targeting as monetary policy. Under inflation targeting, flexible exchange rates are presumed

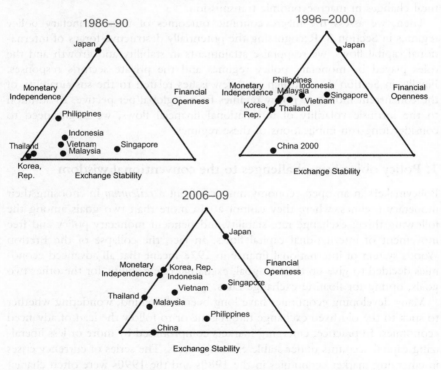

*Figure 6.1* Macroeconomic policy trilemma: ASEAN+3 economies

Source: Ito and Kawai (2011).

Note: ASEAN+3: members of the Association of Southeast Asian Nations plus China, Japan, and Korea.

because inflation rates are regarded as a substitute for fixed exchange rates as a nominal anchor for macroeconomic stabilization. Some emerging economies have become inflation targeters, including the above-mentioned four economies in the Pacific region. As Figure 6.2 shows, however, the resulting exchange rates in East Asia (*Other Asia*) appear relatively stable compared to those of other regions such as *LAC* (Latin America and the Caribbean) along with an accelerated pace of foreign exchange reserves.

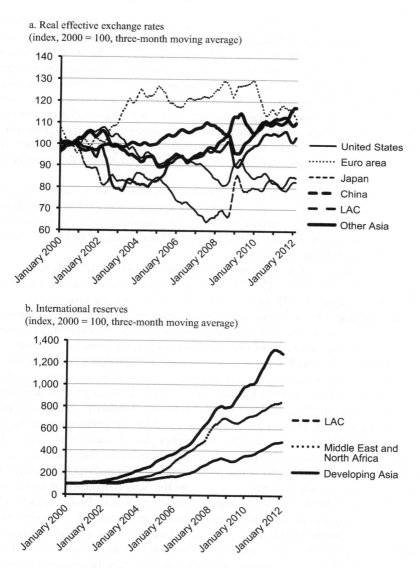

*Figure 6.2* Exchange rates and international reserves

Source: International Monetary Fund, *World Economic Outlook*, April 2012, Figure 1.11.

Note: LAC: Latin America and the Caribbean.

In fact, there is evidence that not only the inflation and output gap, as in the *Taylor rule*,[3] but also exchange rate stability have been pursued by the policy authorities in emerging inflation targeters. Specifically, there is reasonable conjecture that some authorities have sought to maintain some desirable exchange rate levels, when at least part of the accumulated foreign exchange reserves was unintended. This observation seems to be consistent with apparent non-corner solutions in the triangle of the monetary policy trilemma in emerging economies in the Pacific region.

For example, estimating the monetary policy responses of these inflation targeters in emerging economies, Ostry et al. (2012) found that they are concerned with not only the inflation and output gap, as in the Taylor rule, but also with (real effective) exchange rate stability. For this additional policy target, they seem to be equipped with an additional policy tool, i.e., foreign exchange market intervention. Indeed, it is well known that emerging market economies, particularly in the Pacific region, have accumulated foreign exchange reserves against huge foreign capital inflows so as to prevent currency appreciation through intervention in the foreign exchange market. Their interventions are asymmetrical, i.e., mostly against currency appreciation except for some occasional capital reversals.

Figure 6.3 illustrates the cases of Thailand and Korea. After a desperate currency defense in 1997, foreign exchange market intervention has been almost exclusively on the side of dollar purchasing, i.e., against currency appreciation.[4] The same holds true for other emerging economies such as Indonesia, Korea and Malaysia, not reported here.

The ultimate goals of macroeconomic policy have been both internal and external balances in the short run. The former includes price stability and full capacity utilization (minimized GDP gap), and the latter includes some sustainable current account balance. The macroeconomic policy trilemma is about the combination of policy arrangements needed to attain these ultimate goals. Even under flexible exchange rates, the external balance remains valid because markets, especially the international capital market, do not always adjust and stabilize it automatically.

In sum, under financial globalization, emerging market economies need to be equipped with more safety policy measures in order to cope with increasing volatile foreign capital flows. Their initial conditions are relatively shallow domestic financial markets, including credit markets and foreign exchange markets and almost negligible securities markets. Meanwhile, in advanced economies with relatively deeper financial systems, prudential policies in the financial sector need to be better coordinated with macroeconomic stabilization policy under the name of macro-prudential policy. Through the series of financial crises and capital reversals in the 1990s, emerging economies in the Pacific region continued resorting to unorthodox but traditional instruments, i.e., a combination of foreign exchange market intervention and capital controls, under whatever names they applied. Conventional wisdom, such as the macroeconomic trilemma and/or corner solutions within it, was challenged and settled through non-corner solutions to address the new global economic environment.

a. Thailand

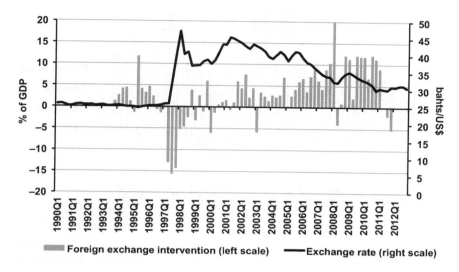

b. Korea

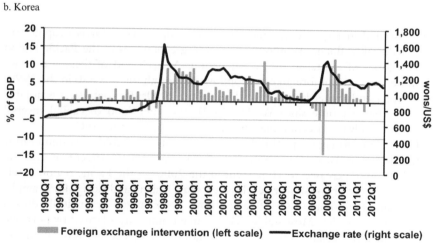

*Figure 6.3* Exchange rate and foreign exchange market intervention

Source: Adapted from International Monetary Fund, *International Financial Statistics*, CD-ROM.

## 2. Policy transmission: global financial linkages and domestic financial deepening

As discussed extensively in Chapter 1, financial linkages of emerging economies in the Pacific region to the international capital market have experienced two large waves – in the 1990s up to 1997, and in the 2000s up to 2008 – as

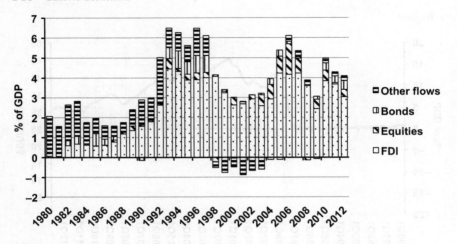

*Figure 6.4* Financial inflows: Asia and the Pacific region

Source: Adapted from World Bank, *World Development Indicators*, http://databank.worldbank.
org/data/views/variableSelection/selectvariables.aspx?source=world-development-indicators,
accessed in 2014.

demonstrated in Figure 6.4, which shows developments of foreign capital (or, interchangeably, financial) inflows to emerging economies in the Pacific region by categories of capital in the recent period. At each end of these waves, we witnessed reversals of foreign capital inflows, although the reversals in the 1990s were larger and longer-lasting than those in the 2000s. By contrast, it is notable that for the first time since World War II, the same kind of capital reversal occurred in advanced economies in the late 2000s, i.e., the GFC.

The scale of foreign capital inflows as a percentage of GDP was significantly expanded in the two waves. Namely, inflows peaked at 6 percent of GDP in the 1990s and increased to 10 percent in the 2000s in the Pacific region, while we can see more or less similar developments in Thailand and Korea, for example. Meanwhile, the composition of capital flows has changed dramatically during the past two decades. Most stable FDI became dominant, followed by portfolio flows, and most volatile other flows, including loans, became less dominant. After 2008, even FDI shrank.[5]

These developments in capital inflows in emerging economies in the region were documented in Chapter 1. We should note, moreover, that we need to watch not only the inflows but also the outflows of these economies in order to understand their financial linkages to the international capital market. On average across the region, outflows peaked at 10 percent of GDP in 2007, excluding foreign exchange market interventions, and exceeded 20 percent if interventions are included.

In discussing the financial linkages of these emerging economies, we need to do so not on a net basis but on a gross basis, just as in the case of advanced economies. Note that we are not suggesting that they are at the stage of advanced economies in terms of financial development, as we will discuss later. This is important because we need to be careful about how these financial linkages relate to their monetary policy regimes with non-corner solutions.

In light of the financial linkages of East Asian emerging economies to the international capital market, we should note, in addition to foreign financial flows, the movements of official foreign exchange reserves. There has been much debate on the huge accumulation of these reserves by East Asian emerging economies. While many emerging economies have accumulated reserves since the late 1990s, East Asia is distinguished from other regions by being both the earliest and the fastest. Moreover, various combinations of economies concluded foreign exchange swap agreements in East Asia, which shows that they paid meticulous attention to liquidity in foreign exchanges.

The changes in the financial linkages of East Asian emerging economies to the international capital market since the Asian crisis can be summarized as follows.

1.  With respect to foreign capital inflows, non-debt FDI has become dominant in composition, and intra-regional investors have played more important roles. This probably reflects financial account liberalization policies and robust industrialization in the region.
2.  Debt capital inflows such as loans and bonds are sensitive to capital market sentiments, and their volatile movements tend to magnify rather than dampen business cycles. This suggests the presence of imperfections inherent in capital markets, which are likely to be lessened by the increasing presence of intra-regional investments.
3.  The accumulation of official foreign exchange reserves, which themselves might be by-products of stabilizing exchange rates, is particularly remarkable in emerging economies in the Pacific region. These reserves have played the role of buffers against capital market stresses. Whether they are in excess or not remains to be seen, however.

In other words, parallel with the case of trade flows, we have witnessed increasing intra-regional dependence in capital flows. In the case of FDI, as well as equity investment, old emerging economies such as Hong Kong, Korea, Singapore and Chinese Taipei have become important investors in new emerging economies such as ASEAN4 (i.e. Indonesia, Malaysia, Philippines and Thailand) and China.[6] These are rational behaviors that compensate for capital market flaws in information asymmetry and would moderate the volatile effects of investment flows from old advanced economies. These new developments suggest that it is no longer sufficient to look only at capital flows from North (advanced economies) to South (developing economies).

Now, we turn to the interaction between these foreign financial flows and domestic financial systems. How are these foreign capital inflows linked to domestic finance?

Chapter 1 summarized the linkages to the international capital market and the contrast between emerging economies in the Pacific region and those in other regions, as follows:

1.   Reliance on foreign capital flows in emerging economies in East Asia is significantly lower than in other developing countries.
2.   The scale of financial intermediation is not only far larger than in other regions but has expanded in a sustained manner, resulting in more financial deepening.

These observations may not necessarily imply that the financial systems in emerging economies in the region are now sufficiently resilient to cope with a headwind coming from globalized financial flows. Figure 6.5 shows outstanding amounts of financial assets as a ratio to GDP in Thailand (and Indonesia) as examples of these economies. The figure illustrates the degree of financial intermediation in the private sector as measured by private bonds and private credits.[7] Apparently, domestic credits to the private sector did not recover to the previous peak level relative to GDP, and this decline was not compensated for by substituting growth of private bond markets, resulting in continued overall financial disintermediation in the private sector since 1997. Note that Thailand is not an exception but is atypical among the crisis-hit economies in the Pacific region.

Our assessment of the domestic financial systems in emerging economies in the region is as follows:

1.   Recovery of domestic financial systems in the wake of the Asian crisis is far from complete. In fact, these economies have not attained pre-crisis levels yet, in contrast to the recovery and dynamism of their real economies.
2.   Particularly notable are the retrenchment of private credits on one hand and the slow growth of private bond markets on the other.
3.   Probably because of the above, the growth of the real economies appears to be underpinned less by external financing through the domestic financial system and more by FDI (foreign savings) and own finance (corporate savings),[8] both of which can be regarded as internal financing.

In sum, in the Pacific region, global financial linkages are no longer on a "net" basis. In fact, emerging markets in the region have expanded their linkages with the global financial market on a "gross" basis, both hosting foreign investment and investing abroad themselves. Moreover, the composition of capital flows has been dominated by FDI, not by restless portfolio and other flows.

Nevertheless, domestic financial deepening appears to have stagnated. The non-financial corporate sector has relied less and less on financial intermediation (bank credits), which is far from compensated for by the development of private bond markets. In other words, the corporate sector financed itself through its own resources as well as through FDI in the 2000s. We are concerned with whether this trend of financial internalization is temporary and/or sustainable for the future.

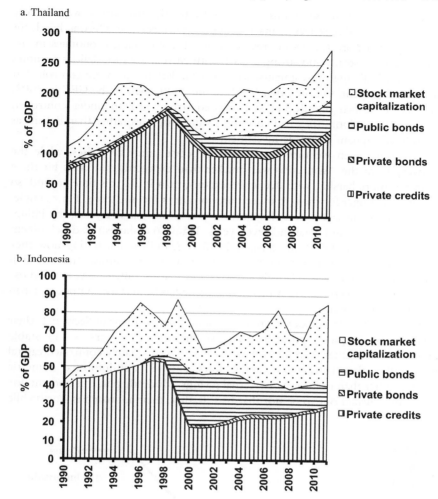

*Figure 6.5* Financial (dis)intermediation to the private sector

Source: Adapted from World Bank, *A New Database on Financial Development and Structure*, http://econ.worldbank.org/WBSITE/EXTERNAL/EXTDEC/EXTRESEARCH/0,,contentM DK:20696167~pagePK:64214825~piPK:64214943~theSitePK:469382,00.html, accessed in 2014.

## 3. Assessments of policy outcomes: this time is very different

To date, the macroeconomic performances of emerging markets in the Pacific region have generally been superior to those of emerging markets in other regions. Relatively low inflation, high income growth, stable exchange rates and current account surpluses have been attained. Their fiscal balances are in relatively good shape, and their interest rates are very positive. Hence, no one can argue that the resulting non-corner solutions of monetary regimes in the regions are unsuccessful.

If we compare the situations before and after the two crises, we can note some important differences in macroeconomic performance. On one hand, for several years before the Asian crisis in 1997, the emerging economies in the region enjoyed steady and strong growth with current account deficits resulting from historically high investments, while their inflation rates were controlled at around ±5 percent. On the other hand, in the 2000s, before the GFC in 2008, they slowed down slightly but still enjoyed strong growth under controlled inflation. In addition, they had current account surpluses rather than deficits as a result of stagnant domestic investment.

Moreover, when we turn to recovery processes after the crises, while the recovery from the Asian crisis was quicker than expected, that crisis hit these countries more harshly, with deeper recessions, than it did this time around, so that it took longer for them to exceed previous peak income levels. For example, it took Indonesia seven years, Korea three years, Malaysia five years, the Philippines three years and Thailand seven years. Figure 6.6 shows the development of their per capita GDPs in constant 2005 U.S. dollars, illustrating how they witnessed sharp downturns during the Asian crisis. In contrast, the recession following the GFC was relatively shallow, and it took only one year for those economies to regain their previous peak income levels, in stark contrast to Japan and the United States.

Referring back to the observations on policy management in Section 1, their experiences, in fact, appear to suggest that what matters is (1) stable exchange rates rather than freely flexible rates, (2) adequately controlled capital flows rather than laissez-faire capital flows, and (3) well-informed domestic savings rather than ill-informed external savings. Modestly put, this unorthodox policy mix turned out to be not that bad. Rather, their approach is worthwhile

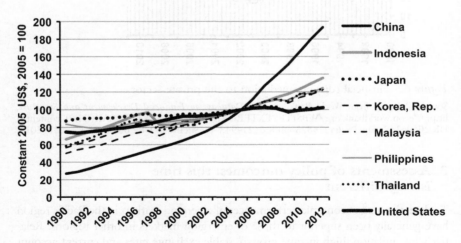

*Figure 6.6* Per capita GDP growth

Source: Adapted from World Bank, *World Development Indicators*, ibid.

to examine further in pursuit of optimal monetary regimes for emerging markets under financial globalization.

Emerging economies in the Pacific region learned a lot from their painful experiences of the Asian currency and economic crisis during 1997–8. First, they learned and felt to their bones that unconditional global financial integration or capital account liberalization is very risky. Indeed, they realized 15 years ago that these global financial linkages could be "a destructive force, increasing volatility and setting off devastating crises rather than promoting growth or helping diversify risk by increasing investment opportunities" (Prasad, 2011, p. 8). Second, there is no reliable international safety net when rescue is acutely needed. International organizations and their supporters (international bankers) could have helped, but they sometimes do not know or care much about Asia, imposing ready-made tight policy prescriptions designed for some lax, stereotypical emerging economies, which was far from the reality in East Asia (or elsewhere).

Since the Asian crisis, emerging economies in the Pacific region have formally converted to inflation targeters under flexible exchange rates, opening up financial accounts and strengthening prudential controls. In practice, however, they have continued to pursue exchange rate stability through foreign exchange market intervention and sterilization on one hand and to control capital flows with various deliberate prudential measures on the other. Policy goals are stability and growth under monetary independence,[9] for which complete financial openness is not a practical intermediate target. And they were right. Emerging economies in general, and particularly those in the Pacific region, have recovered quickly from the GFC as compared to advanced economies. Furthermore, they look more resilient with regard to ever more volatile international financial flows in the following years.[10]

We observe from Figure 6.6 that emerging economies in the Pacific region have kept realizing income convergence to advanced economies throughout the past two decades, except during the AFC period. It is really remarkable that they have attained this income convergence in a continuous way with very few setbacks, which is exceptional compared to emerging economies in the other regions. Both stability and growth appear to have been attained so far under the post-AFC monetary regimes in the Pacific region.

In sum, emerging economies in the Pacific region have successfully coped with the destructive force of volatile foreign financial flows, using foreign exchange market intervention and capital controls as additional policy tools. They have minimized reliance on foreign financial resources and diversified them across categories toward less volatile flows. Remarkably, their private sectors have also done the same through financial internalization. Their domestic financial systems are not so deep as in advanced economies but not so shallow as in emerging economies in other regions. Resulting changes in domestic demand may need to be reexamined, though. Significant trends of declines in domestic investment, persistently high savings and persistently low household consumption are notable. Whether or not they are sustainable and appropriate for growth in the long run remains to be seen.

## 4. Sustainability from a global perspective

For emerging economies in the Pacific region, the days of heavy reliance on foreign capital inflows and *fear of float* are long gone since the Asian crisis. Today, they live with somewhat flexible exchange rates and somewhat open financial accounts, using large foreign exchange reserves as buffers or insurance against the volatility inherent in the international capital market. They could still be exposed to some new types of risks, however.

As long as advanced economies remain in deep and prolonged recessions, emerging economies in the region could be good targets for international investors seeking promising investment opportunities and/or for flights to quality. Emerging economies' huge foreign exchange reserves could be exposed to major currency realignments and capital losses. Or it could be argued that the resilience and/or savings gluts of those emerging markets are the ultimate cause of the GFC and the prolonged global recessions.

It is indeed possible that a surge of capital inflows ignites domestic credit booms and asset bubbles, currency appreciation and/or domestic inflation in emerging economies, damaging their export-led industrialization, which eventually leads to a series of boom-and-bust cycles, sudden stops of capital inflows/ capital reversals and then long and deep recessions. In fact, we can ascertain a series of ins and outs of foreign capital flows to and from emerging economies since the GFC, as shown in Figure 6.7.

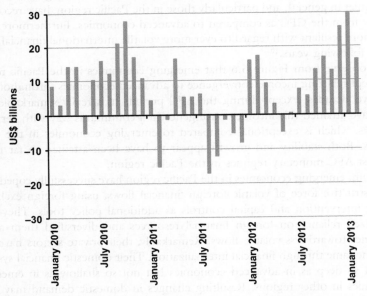

*Figure 6.7* Net capital flows to emerging economies (US$ billions, monthly flows)

Source: International Monetary Fund, *World Economic Outlook*, April 2013, Figure 1.3.

Note: Greek crisis, April 2010; Irish crisis, November 2010; 1st ECB LTROs (European Central Bank's Longer-Term Refinancing Operations), November 2011; and the turbulence, June 2012.

The upper panel of the figure shows interest spreads that reflect investors' risk perception. We can observe a few hiccups in 2010 and 2011, which coincide with some capital reversals. From Figure 6.7, we can find at least three capital flow reversals during the years from 2010 to 2012. But it seems that, at least thus far, they have fared well, one way or another, successfully avoiding the above-mentioned traps. No substantial currency appreciation or uncontrollable domestic inflation resulted there.

Also, it is possible that as long as the United States and other advanced economies continue their current low productivity growth due to public debt burdens, emerging economies with higher productivity growth cannot avoid currency appreciation in the medium term, which implies significant wealth transfer to advanced economies. But, again, it is inevitable, with or without the Great Recession, when we expect long-run income convergence between emerging economies and advanced economies. Figure 6.6 above appears to suggest that this could happen for at least a few more years. Income convergence with advanced economies is, without doubt, a blessing, not a curse.

Rather than worrying about these new risks, which are inevitable anyway, we may need to consider the long-term issues of macroeconomic rebalancing and financial development in these emerging economies, even beyond the current recession.

Figure 6.8, from IMF (2013), shows that global imbalances in current accounts have significantly narrowed because external deficit economies cut

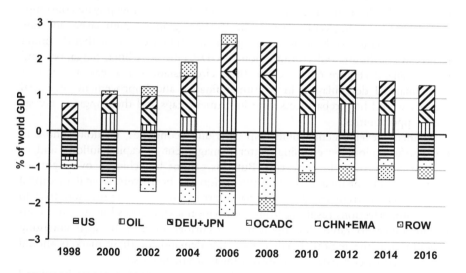

*Figure 6.8* Global imbalances

Source: International Monetary Fund, *World Economic Outlook*, April 2013.

Note: OIL: oil exporters; DEU+JPN: Germany and Japan; OCADC: Bulgaria, Croatia, Czech Republic, Estonia, Greece, Hungary, Ireland, Latvia, Lithuania, Poland, Portugal, Romania, Slovak Republic, Slovenia, Spain, Turkey, and the United Kingdom; CHN+EMA: China and emerging Asia; and ROW: rest of the world.

back their domestic demand during the Great Recession. Emerging economies in the Pacific region, as external *surplus* economies, have not contributed much in this process, however. Crisis-hit economies witnessed a significant trend of decline in their investment-to-GDP ratios during the Asian crisis and have never recovered to pre-crisis levels, while they have more or less maintained their national savings-to-GDP ratios throughout the post-crisis period. The resulting gaps between savings and investment are equivalent to current account balances. Moreover, China is well known in that her very high investment has been more than financed by higher national savings, consisting of ample saving by households, corporate and non-corporate firms, and the public sector.

These investment slowdowns in emerging economies in the Pacific region do not mean that their investment levels are lower than those in other regions. In fact, they have stayed significantly higher than those of Latin American and European emerging economies throughout the past couple of decades. We are not certain, therefore, whether or not the current investment levels are to be corrected upward. Note that these investments have been financed internally, as pointed out earlier, rather than through financial intermediation and/or capital markets. Since there is no evidence that their investments have been constrained by fund availability, these financial internalization trends have little to do with the investment slowdowns.

Rather, high savings-to-GDP ratios may have room for reduction. It is also well known that both domestic financial liberalization and strengthened social security will help reduce these high private savings and the low private consumption. While emerging economies in the Pacific region are high savers and low consumers relative to those in other regions, we still have seen further declining trends in the household consumption-to-GDP ratio in China, Singapore and even Thailand (Figure 6.9).[11] Given these circumstances, it is easy to see that both financial deregulation in consumer finance and improvements in social security would help rebalance saving-investment gaps and then upgrade investment opportunities.

Financial development would help emerging economies, including those in the Pacific region, by enabling better management of capital inflows and of their volatility over the long run. But this cannot be achieved overnight, or without strong financing needs. Information on borrowers is vital in capital markets. The current trend of financial internalization may be one way to help reduce imperfections resulting from information asymmetries but may not contribute much to rapid development of securities markets in such emerging economies in the region. Furthermore, the demand for these markets should come ahead of construction of institutional arrangements.[12]

One other possible reason why household consumption is low may be related to income distribution. As higher corporate savings reflect a lower income share for labor, the resulting cheap labor or low real wages could hamper

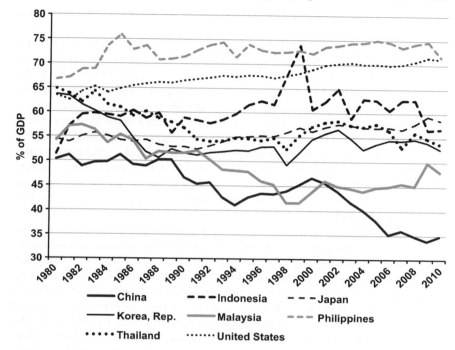

*Figure 6.9* Household consumption
Source: Author's calculation from World Bank, *World Development Indicators 2012.*

domestic household consumption growth. In this connection, these economies may be more ready for real exchange rate appreciation in the medium and/ or long run, too. Sustained economic growth accompanies changes in industrial structure, which needs labor and other resources to be shifted to sectors with higher productivity growth. Wage increases in those sectors motivate these resource shifts. To upgrade these economies or for them to exit from *middle income traps,* they may need a higher labor share as well as gradual currency appreciation.

It is possible, anyway, that as long as the United States and other advanced economies continue their current low productivity growth as a result of public debt burdens, emerging economies with higher productivity growth cannot avoid currency appreciation in the medium term, which implies significant wealth transfers from emerging to advanced economies through capital losses accruing to the former's accumulated foreign exchange reserves. But, again, it is inevitable, with or without the Great Recession, when we expect long-run income convergence between some emerging economies and advanced economies. Figure 6.5 appears to suggest that this could happen for at least a few more years. Income convergence with advanced economies is, without doubt, a blessing, not a curse.

In sum, it is often argued that emerging economies have appeared to be far more *resilient* during the GFC than during the AFC. But they are far from immune to risks associated with volatile international capital flows. Under the prolonged recession in advanced economies, emerging economies may have to confront more destabilizing capital flows in the short run and currency appreciation trends along with accelerated income convergence in the long run. These risks are inevitable. The real concerns over the longer run are macroeconomic rebalancing in domestic demand and financial development in these economies (see Prasad, 2009, for example). Significant declining trends in domestic investment, persistently high savings and persistently low household consumption are notable. Whether or not they are sustainable and appropriate for long-run growth remains to be seen.

With internal and external financial liberalization as well as freely flexible exchange rates, emerging economies could possibly invest more among themselves rather than financing debt buildups in advanced economies. If they see that it is in their interests, they should do so. In fact, until recently, advanced economies found it in their interests to borrow heavily from whomever abroad, while emerging economies found it in their interests to lean against capital inflows through exchange rate manipulation or, equivalently, to unintentionally lend to whomever abroad through foreign exchange reserve accumulation. Now that advanced economies realize that their *Great Moderation* is unsustainable, they have no choice but to behave themselves. What about emerging economies? They know what they should do. Fortunately, they have choices as to how fast to go.

## Notes

1  From Ito and Kawai (2011). In the literature on measuring the trilemma, measures of exchange rate stability (ES), monetary independence (MI), and financial openness (FO) are defined as follows: ES = volatility of or deviation between home and reference exchange rates, MI = correlation or co-movement between home and reference interest rates, and FO = de jure or de facto index of financial openness, respectively. These are then normalized as $0 < ES, MI, FO < 1$. Then, $ES + MI + FO \leq 2$ holds, and each trio can be located somewhere in the triangle where a distance from each target stands for a deviation from 1 for the respective measure.

2  Note that the degrees of ES, FO and MI depend on definitions, and alternative measures produce varying and/or diverse results in trends, movements and levels of these variables. Also note that the trilemma between MI, ES and FO does exist, but the trio is not goals but rather intermediate targets used to attain some other goals such as short-run macroeconomic stability and long-run growth. We cannot discuss the optimal mix of the trio without specifying how they are related to policy goals.

3  The rule proposed by John B. Taylor (1993) is a formula for how to control the policy interest rate in order to minimize some combination of gaps from

two policy targets: the gross domestic product (GDP) gap from the natural unemployment level and the gap from the inflation target.

4 We simply proxied changes in foreign exchange reserves as foreign exchange market intervention here. These changes may understate the scale of intervention such as in the case of Thailand in 1997.

5 As to the composition of financial inflows, in Korea other flows were replaced not by FDI but by portfolio flows after the AFC. As shown in the figure, Korea again experienced a sudden stop of inflows as well as sharp currency depreciation in the GFC.

6 A geographical distribution of FDI shows that, as of the end of 2009, the share of East Asia in total FDI in the region is 39 percent, which is larger than the shares of the European Union (31 percent) and the United States (24 percent; Kohsaka, 2011).

7 Note that stock market capitalization does not stand for financial intermediation because it represents mostly capital gains.

8 In fact, we can detect upward trends in corporate savings as a percentage of GDP in China, Korea and the Philippines and downward trends in household savings there in the 2000s (Kohsaka, 2011).

9 It has become well known that longer and stronger expansions and shorter and shallower downturns go hand in hand with long-run steady economic growth, which is rare in the case of developing economies.

10 Defining resilience as represented by shorter and shallower downturns and more rapid recoveries, the IMF (2012, chap. 4) argues that the resilience of emerging market and developing economies has increased markedly during the past two decades except for in Europe. Undertaking a multivariate analysis on a panel dataset of about 75 developing economies, they identify two reasons for the increased resilience: relatively small shocks to these economies, and good policies and policy frameworks with policy space. The latter includes inflation targeting and flexible exchange rates, but not necessarily financial openness, and the composition of capital flows.

11 It may be partly due to the increasing trend of corporate saving. Yet we observe that some emerging economies, including China, show an increasing trend of household saving as compared to their disposable income rather than to the GDP.

12 The same holds true for capital controls. They sometimes tend to distort capital inflows and outflows. But we know that capital markets themselves sometimes add economic distortions, particularly when absorptive capacities are lacking in recipient economies. We have learned that an oversupply of financial resources could be worse than nothing and that it could also distort exchange rates if they are left freely floating, destabilizing the aggregate economy.

## References and Further Readings

International Monetary Fund. 2012. *World Economic Outlook*, Chapter 4, October, Washington, D.C.

International Monetary Fund. 2013. *World Economic Outlook*, April, International Monetary Fund, Washington, DC.

Ito, Hiro, and Masahiro Kawai. 2011. "The Trilemma Challenge for SEACEN Member Economies: New Measures of the Trilemma Hypothesis and Their Implications on Asia," paper presented at the annual conference of the Asian Development Bank Institute, Tokyo, November.

Kohsaka, Akira, ed. 2011. *Macrofinancial Linkages and Financial Deepening in the Pacific Region*, Japan Committee for Pacific Economic Outlook, Osaka.

158    *Akira Kohsaka*

Ostry, Jonathan D., Atish R. Ghosh, and Marcos Chamon. 2012. "Two Targets, Two Instruments: Monetary and Exchange Rate Policies in Emerging Market Economies," International Monetary Fund Staff Discussion Note, SDN/12/01, February, International Monetary Fund, Washington, DC.

Prasad, Eswar S. 2009 "Rebalancing Growth in Asia," *NBER Working Paper* 15169, NBER, Cambridge, Massachusetts.

Prasad, Eswar S. 2011. "Role Reversal," *Finance and Development*, December, International Monetary Fund, Washington, DC.

Taylor, John B., "Discretion Versus Policy Rules in Practice," *Carnegie-Rochester Conference Series on Public Policy* 39.

# 7 Monetary policy frameworks in Asia

*Peter J. Morgan*

## 1. Introduction

East Asian monetary policy frameworks have evolved substantially over the past two decades, chiefly in response to shocks from the Asian financial crisis of 1997–1998 and the global financial crisis of 2007–2009. The Asian financial crisis showed the importance of exchange rate flexibility and credible policy frameworks, leading to increased central bank independence, greater focus on inflation policy, and more flexible exchange rates. A key lesson of the 2007–2009 global financial crisis was the importance of containing systemic financial risk and the need for a "macroprudential" approach to surveillance and regulation that can identify system-wide risks and take appropriate actions to maintain financial stability. Emerging economies face particular challenges because of their underdeveloped financial systems and vulnerability to volatile international capital flows, especially sudden stops or reversals of capital inflows.

The chapter is organized as follows. Section 2 reviews the history of monetary policy frameworks since 1990.[1] Section 3 describes current monetary policy frameworks, including issues of price versus financial stability for a central bank and the policies a central bank can use to manage financial stability. Section 4 examines the monetary policy transmission mechanism based on financial linkages and financial deepening. Section 5 provides assessments of policy outcomes including inflation targeting and responses to the "Impossible Trinity", and Section 6 concludes the chapter.

## 2. History of policy frameworks since 1990

Monetary policy is to a large extent constrained by the exchange rate regime. Before the Asian financial crisis of 1997–1998, most East Asian economies aside from Japan had their exchange rates relatively fixed relative to the US dollar and tended to focus on controlling monetary aggregates. In the absence of foreign exchange controls, this implied little independence of monetary policy, and, indeed, the easing of capital controls during the period created the conditions leading up to the Asian financial crisis. Table 7.1 shows the classification of Asian monetary policy regimes by Stone and Bhundia (2004) for the

*Table 7.1* Monetary regime classification in East Asia

| Country | 1995 | 1996 | 1997 | 1998 | 1999 | 2000 | 2001 | 2002 | 2003 |
|---|---|---|---|---|---|---|---|---|---|
| People's Republic of China | XRP | XRP | XRP | XRP | XRP | XRP | XRP | XRP | XRP |
| Indonesia | ITL | ITL | ITL | ITL | ITL | ITL | ITL | ITL | ITL |
| Japan | IIT | IIT | IIT | IIT | IIT | IIT | IIT | IIT | IIT |
| Republic of Korea | MoA | MoA | ITL | ITL | ITL | ITL | FFIT | FFIT | FFIT |
| Malaysia | ITL | ITL | ITL | XRP | XRP | XRP | XRP | XRP | XRP |
| Philippines | XRP | XRP | ITL | ITL | ITL | ITL | ITL | FFIT | FFIT |
| Singapore | IIT | IIT | IIT | IIT | IIT | IIT | IIT | IIT | IIT |
| Thailand | XRP | XRP | ITL | ITL | ITL | FFIT | FFIT | FFIT | FFIT |

Source: Stone and Bhundia (2004).

Note: XRP: exchange rate peg; MoA: monetary aggregate anchor; ITL: inflation targeting lite; FFIT: fully fledged inflation targeting; IIT: implicit inflation targeting (implicit price stability anchor).

pre-Asian-crisis and post-crisis periods. In the pre-crisis period, only the People's Republic of China (PRC), the Philippines, and Thailand were classified as having fixed exchange rates, but those of Indonesia, Korea, and Malaysia were not far off. The monetary regime of Hong Kong, China, although not included in the table, clearly remained an exchange rate peg over the period. The monetary regime of Taiwan (Taipei, China) is not included either but may be regarded as being a monetary aggregate anchor.

Singapore managed the exchange rate as an intermediate target, a monetary policy framework that had been in place since the early 1980s. Singapore's high share of imports in gross domestic product (GDP) and its role as a price-taker in international markets made the country highly susceptible to imported inflation. Thus, Singapore considers the exchange rate to be a more effective tool than the interest rate for stabilizing inflation. Its monetary policy framework, however, can be considered a variant of inflation targeting (IT).

As most emerging Asian economies moved toward more flexible exchange rate regimes after the crisis, most monetary policy frameworks in the region have changed accordingly to allow more monetary autonomy, with IT policies becoming a popular option. Table 7.1 shows that, after the crisis, the number of East Asian countries using fixed exchange rate regimes decreased while the number of countries using the IT monetary policy frameworks increased. The PRC also moved away from the exchange rate peg beginning in 2005, although it was temporarily reinstated during the global financial crisis, so its regime probably can be regarded as implicit inflation targeting. The Bank of Japan has made the link of policy with inflation more explicit over time and adopted an official inflation target of 2 percent for the consumer price index (CPI) in 2013 as part of the "Abe-nomics" policies.

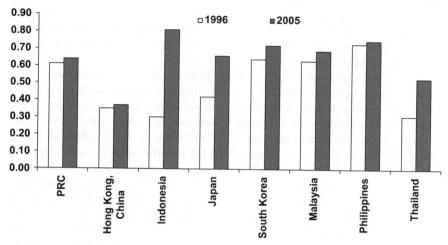

*Figure 7.1* Increase in central bank independence, 1996 to 2005
Source: Adapted from Ahsan, Skully, and Wickramanayake (2008).
Note: PRC: People's Republic of China.

Along with this development, many central banks in the region gained increased independence so that they could focus on controlling inflation. Ahsan, Skully, and Wickramanayake (2008) constructed indices of central bank governance and independence (CBGI) using 27 variables to capture different aspects of governance and independence, including legal independence, political independence, independence to focus on price stability, independence of exchange rate policy, freedom from requirements to finance government debt, and transparency and accountability. Figure 7.1 shows the overall indices in 1996 and 2005. The indices in 2005 increased in all East Asian countries, especially in Indonesia, Japan, and Thailand.

## 3. Policy objectives and frameworks

### 3.1. Price stability

As mentioned in the previous section, most central banks in the East Asian region have chosen to pursue price stability as at least one principal objective of monetary policy. Based on information contained on their websites, the monetary authorities of Japan, Korea, the Philippines, Singapore, and Thailand currently aim for price stability as an overarching objective. Three central banks – the People's Bank of China, Bank Indonesia, and Bank Negara Malaysia – state their goal as maintaining the stability of the value of the currency, which could mean either the internal value in terms of goods and services (i.e., the price level), the external value (the exchange rate) or some combination of the two. Bank Indonesia, for example, makes it explicit that the term refers to both aspects. The Bank Negara Malaysia states that an adequate supply of credit to the economy is also an explicit goal of the central bank. The Hong Kong Monetary Authority puts exclusive emphasis on exchange rate stability (vis-à-vis the US dollar) and pursues this goal by means of a currency board arrangement.

The strategies adopted to achieve the objectives are quite diverse. Five central banks are self-proclaimed inflation targeters – Bank Indonesia, the Bank of Japan, the Bank of Korea, Bangko Sentral ng Pilipinas, and the Bank of Thailand. These central banks are relative new-comers to inflation targeting, with the Republic of Korea (hereafter Korea) starting in 1999, Indonesia and Thailand in 2000, the Philippines in 2002, and Japan in 2013. The other central banks employ a range of eclectic strategies generally reflecting a set of policy tradeoffs, not least being those associated with IT, sustainable growth, and exchange rate stability.

With respect to policy instruments, the majority of the institutions carry out their policy by means of targeting a short-term interest rate (Table 7.2). The principal exceptions are the Monetary Authority of Singapore, which, as already noted, uses the nominal effective exchange rate as an intermediate target; the Hong Kong Monetary Authority, which intervenes in the foreign exchange market to keep the exchange rate vis-à-vis the US dollar within a pre-specified constant target zone; and the People's Bank of China. The People's Bank has adopted the growth rates of monetary aggregates as intermediate targets and typically employs several instruments in the implementation of its monetary policy – the exchange rate, the required reserve ratio, interest rates, and open market operations. Existing controls on the domestic financial system and on international capital flows arguably make it possible for the People's Bank to use several instruments somewhat independently of each other, an option less feasible in jurisdictions with more liberalized and efficient domestic financial markets and with more open capital accounts.

### 3.2. Financial stability and systemic risk

The global financial crisis raised questions about the adequacy of IT policy frameworks in particular and the focus on price stability in general, and heightened the awareness of financial stability and the need for a macroprudential dimension to financial surveillance and regulation. The International Monetary Fund's (IMF) analysis (2009) found that macroeconomic policies did not take into account building systemic risks and that a key failure during the boom was the inability to spot the big picture threat of a growing asset price bubble. It is widely believed the US Federal Reserve underestimated the buildup of financial imbalances coming from housing price bubbles, high leverage of financial institutions, and interconnections among different segments of the financial market. In addition, Taylor (2009) argued that the Federal Reserve's monetary policy stance was too easy, in that it kept the federal funds rate too low for too long, fueling the housing boom and other economic imbalances, although Bernanke (2010) disputed this view.

Several excellent reviews of what went wrong in financial regulation (Group of Thirty 2009; Brunnermeier et al. 2009; de Larosiere Group 2009) point to

Table 7.2 Institutional frameworks for monetary policy in East Asia

| Economy | Targeting arrangement | Formal policy rate | Formal operating target |
|---|---|---|---|
| PRC | Reference to money growth targets | 1-year deposit and loan reference rates | Excess reserves |
| Hong Kong | Currency board: target range centered on HKD 7.8 = US$1 | | USD/HKD spot rate |
| Indonesia | IT: target range of 4.5 ± 1% (2012–2014) for year-on-year CPI inflation | BI rate (= target rate for 1-month SBI) | 1-month SBI rate |
| Japan | IT: target of 2% in terms of the year-on-year rate of change in the CPI, to be achieved at the earliest possible time | Uncollateralized O/N call rate target (in normal times) | Increase in monetary base of about 60–70 trillion yen per year |
| Korea | IT: target range of 3 ± 0.5% in terms of annual headline CPI inflation (2013–2015) | O/N call rate target | O/N call rate |
| Malaysia | Not disclosed | O/N policy rate | Average O/N interbank rate |
| Philippines | IT: target range of 4 ± 1% (2011–2014) for the average year-on-year change in the CPI over the calendar year | O/N repo and reverse repo rates | No formal target |
| Singapore | Since mid-2012, modest and gradual appreciation of the undisclosed Singapore dollar NEER policy band | Policy band for Singapore dollar NEER | Singapore dollar NEER |
| Taiwan | Intermediate target for M2 growth: 2.5%–6.5% | Rediscount rate | Rediscount rate |
| Thailand | IT: target range of 0%–3.5% for quarterly average of core inflation | 1-day repo rate | 1-day repo rate |

Source: BIS (2009b); http://www.bi.go.id/en/moneter/inflasi/bi-dan-inflasi/Contents/Default.aspx, http://www.boj.or.jp/en/mopo/outline/qqe.htm/, http://eng.bok.or.kr/broadcast.action?menuNavild=1612, http://www.bsp.gov.ph/monetary/targeting.asp, http://www.mas.gov.sg/News-and-Publications/Speeches-and-Monetary-Policy-Statements/Monetary-Policy-Statements/2014/Monetary-Policy-Statement-14-Oct-14.aspx, http://www.cbc.gov.tw/ct.asp?xItem=43516&ctNode=448&mp=2, and http://www.bot.or.th/English/MonetaryPolicy/Target/Pages/Target.aspx.

Note: BI = Bank Indonesia; CPI = consumer price index; HKD = Hong Kong, China, dollar; IT = inflation targeting; NEER = nominal effective exchange rate, O/N = overnight; PRC = People's Republic of China; repo = repurchase, i.e., an agreement to sell a security to investors, usually on an overnight basis, and buy them back the following day; SBI = Bank Indonesia promissory notes.

regulatory and supervisory deficiencies, including inadequate macroprudential supervision. Owing to the propensity to focus on individual institutions (the traditional "microprudential" approach), supervisors around the world failed to recognize interconnections and links across financial firms, sectors, and markets because of the lack of a macroprudential approach. Supervisors focused only on their piece of the puzzle, overlooking the larger problem. Shin (2009) pointed out that "mis-educated" supervisors and examiners were focused on individual institutions, without regard to the impact on the system.

Nonetheless, there is no generally agreed definition of financial stability because financial systems are complex with multiple dimensions, institutions, products, and markets. Indeed, it is perhaps easier to describe financial instability than stability. The European Central Bank website defines financial stability as

a condition in which the financial system – comprising of financial inter-mediaries, markets and market infrastructures – is capable of withstanding shocks, thereby reducing the likelihood of disruptions in the financial intermediation process which are severe enough to significantly impair the allocation of savings to profitable investment opportunities.

(European Central Bank 2012)

Further, the ECB defines three conditions associated with financial stability:

1. The financial system should be able to efficiently and smoothly transfer resources from savers to investors.
2. Financial risks should be assessed and priced reasonably accurately and should also be relatively well managed.
3. The financial system should be in such a condition that it can comfortably absorb financial and real economic surprises and shocks.

(European Central Bank 2012)

Perhaps the third condition is the most important because the inability to absorb shocks can lead to a downward spiral whereby they are propagated through the system and become self-reinforcing, leading to a general financial crisis and broadly disrupting the financial intermediation mechanism.

In a similar vein, threats to financial stability are considered to pose systemic risks. The Committee on the Global Financial System (CGFS 2010: 2) defines systemic risk as "a risk of disruption to financial services that is caused by an impairment of all or parts of the financial system and has the potential to have serious negative consequences for the real economy".

### 3.3. Macroprudential policy

In turn, the aim of macroprudential supervision and regulation is to reduce systemic risk and preserve systemic financial stability by identifying vulnerabilities in a country's financial system and implementing policy actions to address those vulnerabilities in a timely manner to prevent a crisis. In contrast to macroprudential supervision, which takes a bottom-up approach that focuses on the health and stability of individual financial firms, macroprudential supervision takes a top-down approach that focuses on the economy-wide system in which financial market players operate and helps assess sources of risks and incentives. It requires the integration of detailed information on banks, nonbank financial firms, corporations, households, governments, and financial markets.

CGFS (2010: 2) notes more specifically: "Preventative in its orientation, macroprudential policy is distinct from financial crisis management policy". Commentaries on macroprudential policy acknowledge that prevention of crises or economic boom-and-bust cycles may be too ambitious a goal. For example, CGFS (2010: 15) concludes that "[i]t is uncertain whether a more activist approach to operating the instruments would actually be effective in moderating the financial cycle". The key point is to increase the resilience of the financial system so that it can absorb losses from economic and other shocks while remaining viable. Nonetheless, a second and related aim of macroprudential policy is to limit the buildup of systemic risk by leaning against the financial cycle and thereby dampening its volatility (CGFS 2010). As part of this, it should work to reduce the procyclicality of the financial system and the regulatory framework.

### 3.4. Need for stronger macroprudential policy in Asia

In Europe and the United Sates, undetected systemic risks before the global financial crisis arose for several reasons, including widespread use of sophisticated derivative financial products to move risks around the system, the development of the unregulated shadow-banking system, excessive reliance on wholesale funding by banks, under-capitalization of banks, and lack of understanding of the riskiness of innovative financial products. These factors on the whole did not apply to Asian financial systems during the crisis, and this helps to explain why those economies did not suffer financial crises and recovered relatively quickly. Moreover, in the aftermath of the 1997–1998 Asian financial crisis, Asian economies greatly strengthened their financial systems, reduced foreign debt, improved their monetary policy and financial regulatory frameworks, and moved toward greater currency flexibility.

Nonetheless, Asian economies need to strengthen their macroprudential policy frameworks for several reasons. First, although emerging Asia does not have much of the shadow-banking system that plagued the financial stability in developed economies, many financial institutions exist outside the formal banking system, including real estate finance companies and credit card companies. Finance companies triggered the Thai financial crisis, and merchant banks were behind the Korean financial crisis, both in 1997. Asian financial systems also show signs of procyclicality, most notably in the close relation between bank lending, real estate cycles, and overall economic growth.

Perhaps most importantly, Asian economies are subject to large and volatile international capital flows. Capital inflows provide emerging market economies with valuable benefits in pursuing economic development and growth as they enable them to finance needed investment, smooth consumption, diversify risks, and expand economic opportunities. However, large capital flows, if not managed properly, can expose capital-recipient countries to at least three types of risks (Kawai and Takagi 2010):

1. Macroeconomic risk. Capital inflows could accelerate the growth of domestic credit; create economic overheating, including inflation; and cause the real exchange rate to appreciate, thus threatening sustainable economic growth and price stability.
2. Risk of financial instability. Capital inflows could create maturity and currency mismatches in the balance sheets of private sector debtors (particularly banks and corporations), push up equity and other asset prices, and potentially reduce the quality of assets, thereby contributing to greater financial fragility.
3. Sudden stops and/or reversals of capital flows. Capital inflows could stop suddenly or even reverse themselves within a short period, resulting in rapid reserve decumulation or sharp currency depreciation.

The Asian financial crisis, as well as other emerging economy crises, highlighted the systemic risks associated with so-called double mismatches associated with borrowing short term in foreign currencies and lending longer term in domestic currencies. It is noteworthy that about 15 percent of the large capital inflow episodes over the past 20 years ended in crisis, with emerging Asia experiencing proportionately more episodes of hard landings (Schadler 2010).

Asian economies are also exposed to the activities of large global banks, which could become an issue if one or several such banks needed to be resolved. Finally, Asian financial systems are likely to increase in complexity as they develop, so that issues of market transparency and interconnectedness of financial firms are likely to become more relevant.

### 3.5. The role of a central bank in financial stability

A country's central bank is well qualified to play a key role in monitoring and regulating financial stability from the point of view of its surveillance capacity and the policy tools at its disposal. This reflects its routine work of monitoring the macroeconomic developments and financial system conditions and its responsibility for overseeing payments and settlement systems. As described in more detail below in this section, central banks have a number of policy tools that can affect financial stability, including monetary policy instruments and, in some cases, exchange rate and capital flow management tools and macroprudential policy tools. These tools can be used both to prevent crises and to mitigate crises when they occur. Nonetheless, there is wide debate about the consistency of an objective of financial stability with the more traditional and well-established central bank objective of price stability. More broadly, the current debate focuses on the appropriate role of a central bank within a broad architecture of financial stability and macroprudential policy responsibility.

### 3.6. Financial stability mandate versus price stability mandate

The debate has been lively about whether a central bank mandate for financial stability would potentially conflict with the more traditional mandate for price stability. Some studies concluded that targeting asset prices directly, as part of an augmented Taylor Rule, could be potentially destabilizing. For example, Bernanke and Gertler (2000: 46) argue:

> Given a strong commitment to stabilizing expected inflation, it is neither necessary nor desirable for monetary policy to respond to changes in asset prices, except to the extent that they help to forecast inflationary or deflationary pressures.

However, few proponents of a financial stability mandate actually propose targeting asset prices; instead, they merely support taking asset price movements into account as a risk factor in setting monetary policy over a longer period of time. Cecchetti et al. (2000: xix) conclude:

> A central bank concerned with stabilizing inflation about a specific target level is likely to achieve superior performance by adjusting its policy instruments not only in response to its forecasts of future inflation and the output gap, but also to asset prices.

Similarly, Borio and Lowe (2002: 20) argue that

> a slightly modified policy regime, under which the central bank responds not only to short-term inflation pressures but also, at least occasionally, to financial imbalances, may ultimately deliver a better combination of monetary and financial stability.

The crux of the matter is that an environment of low and stable inflation may be conducive to the development of financial imbalances, as low interest rates and profitable investment opportunities contribute to an increasing appetite for risk. This pattern was described by Minsky (1986) and has been emphasized by Borio and Lowe (2002), Borio and White (2004), and others. This implies that in a period of low inflation, systemic imbalances are likely to appear first in the financial sector and later in the real sector with a significant lag. This also highlights the need for a longer-term time horizon for monetary policymaking.

This debate is closely related to the "lean versus clean" debate of whether it is preferable for the monetary authority to "prick" bubbles before they burst by "leaning against the wind," or to wait until after the bubble bursts and then clean up the mess via aggressive monetary policy easing. However, the huge costs and lengthy recovery period following the global financial crisis as a result of the deleveraging process have severely undermined the argument in favor of the "clean" approach. This experience highlights the potential risks of a credit-driven bubble and supports argument in favor of leaning to prevent such bubbles, rather than cleaning up after them. As a result, the consensus has swung strongly in favor of a central bank paying close attention to financial stability and leaning against the wind, even if it is not an official part of its mandate.

### 3.7. The current situation of central bank financial stability mandates

The specific responsibilities for financial stability vary widely across central banks. Figure 7.2 provides a good summary of the financial stability mandates of a large number of central banks of advanced and emerging economies as of 2009, based on a survey of central banks by the Bank for International Settlements (BIS 2011). A darker shade is associated with a stronger mandate. The survey divides mandates into three major areas: banking sector, payments system, and financial system. The mandate for the banking sector varies widely across

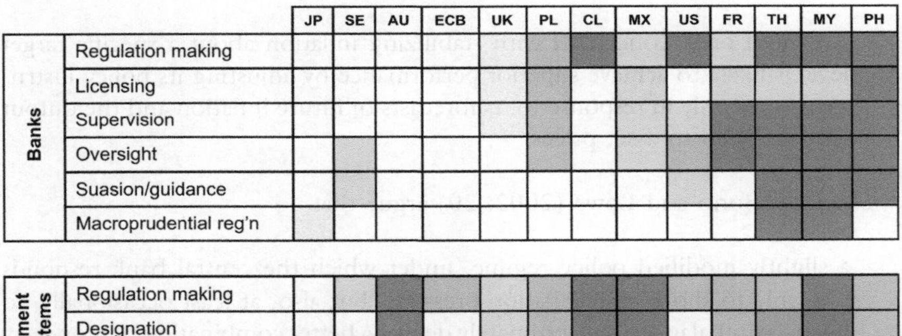

| | | JP | SE | AU | ECB | UK | PL | CL | MX | US | FR | TH | MY | PH |
|---|---|---|---|---|---|---|---|---|---|---|---|---|---|---|
| **Banks** | Regulation making | | | | | | | | | | | | | |
| | Licensing | | | | | | | | | | | | | |
| | Supervision | | | | | | | | | | | | | |
| | Oversight | | | | | | | | | | | | | |
| | Suasion/guidance | | | | | | | | | | | | | |
| | Macroprudential reg'n | | | | | | | | | | | | | |
| **Payment systems** | Regulation making | | | | | | | | | | | | | |
| | Designation | | | | | | | | | | | | | |
| | Oversight | | | | | | | | | | | | | |
| **Financial systems** | Oversight | | | | | | | | | | | | | |
| | Suasion/guidance | | | | | | | | | | | | | |
| | MP with finstab objective | | | | | | | | | | | | | |

| None or very minor | Intermediate | Major or full |
|---|---|---|

*Figure 7.2* Financial stability–related mandates of central banks in 2009

Source: Adapted from Bank for International Settlements (2011).

Note: AU = Australia; CL = Chile; ECB = European Central Bank; FR = France; JP = Japan; MX = Mexico; MY = Malaysia; PH = Philippines; PL = Poland; SE = Sweden; TH = Thailand; UK = United Kingdom; US = United States. In the left columns, reg'n = regulation; MP = monetary policy; finstab = financial stability.

countries. European central banks are generally very light in their banking sector responsibilities, while emerging economy central banks in Latin America and Asia have the strongest mandates, and Japan and the United States fall in between. For the financial system as a whole, relatively strong mandates are recognized for oversight, suasion, and guidance, but few central banks have an explicit monetary policy mandate for financial stability. Interestingly, all central banks with such mandates are in Asia. It seems likely that the relative emphasis placed by Asian central banks on financial stability contributed to their good performance during the global financial crisis.

### 3.8. Tools for a central bank can help achieve financial stability

A central bank has a number of policy tools that can affect financial stability, including monetary policy instruments and, in some cases, exchange rate and capital flow management tools and macroprudential policy tools. These tools can be used to help prevent and mitigate crises. Monetary policy tools are ordinarily aimed at affecting the demand for and supply of money, primarily open market operations and reserve ratio requirements. In a crisis, the function of the central bank as the lender of last resort can simply be seen as an extreme version of open market operations. Macroprudential policy tools are aimed at reducing systemic financial risk, most typically by restraining bank credit growth.

There has been a good deal of debate about whether capital flow management tools should be classified as macroprudential tools, or whether they belong in a separate category. Ostry et al. (2010) represented a sharp break from previous thinking at the IMF by arguing that emerging economies could and should adopt capital flow management tools in some cases. However, they argued that capital control measures should be considered separately from domestic prudential measures, partly because long-lasting and widespread adoption of capital control measures could distort capital flows and exchange rates, thereby worsening international imbalances, and therefore should be used only as a last resort when other policy options are exhausted. However, in the presence of large and destabilizing capital flows, many observers in emerging economies believe that this position is too extreme and that capital control measures could be used on a more regularized basis. It may be helpful to distinguish them by arguing that macroprudential measures are aimed primarily at domestic balance while capital control measures are aimed mainly at international balance, but this distinction clearly blurs in practice.

It should also be emphasized that the prime justification for capital flow controls is to shield shallow and unsophisticated financial sectors from the damaging effects of capital flow volatility. As financial sectors deepen and become more sophisticated in line with economic development, their resilience to capital flow volatility should increase, thereby gradually lessening and eventually ending the need for capital control measures. In this regard, the openness of capital markets in Hong Kong, Japan, and Singapore provides an endpoint toward which other Asian economies may expect to evolve.

There is also a fair degree of confusion about the distinction between micro-prudential and macroprudential policy tools. For example, loan-to-value ratios were originally developed as microprudential tools to ensure viability at the level of an individual bank. But they have been employed as macroprudential tools to control the real estate cycle in several economies, including the PRC, Hong Kong, and Korea. Therefore, whether or not a policy tool is regarded as micro-prudential or macroprudential has to be judged in terms of its broad objective, that is, whether it is used to promote the health of individual financial firms or to contain financial vulnerabilities in certain sectors such as the real estate sector. It should be clear that if loan-to-value ratios are modified in response to the regulator's perception of the risks of the credit cycle, they should be regarded as macroprudential policy tools.

### 3.9. Monetary policy tools

In normal times, open market operations are typically conducted with sales of short-term government paper (a virtually riskless asset) for cash with the aim of raising the level of short-term money market rates. If the economy falls into a liquidity trap with zero nominal short-term interest rates and/or suffers seize-ups in particular markets that disrupt the normal financial intermediation process, then the central bank can resort to so-called unconventional measures.[2] Open market operations can become unconventional ones if they broaden the types and maturities of assets to be purchased, the credit rating or equivalent metric of the assets, and the time horizon of the purchases. The objectives of such purchases can range from lowering long-term bond yields to easing freeze-ups of specific markets, such as those for interbank borrowing or asset-backed securities. Lender of last resort operations are just one example of this.

Descriptions of central bank balance sheet operations typically distinguish between quantitative easing and credit (or qualitative) easing – see, for example, Bernanke and Reinhart (2004) and Borio and Disyatat (2009) – although the distinction in practice is not so clear-cut.[3] The aim of quantitative easing is to expand the size of the central bank's balance sheet by increasing the size of reserve deposits – current account balances – beyond the level that is required to bring the overnight funds rate to zero. Possible channels of impact for such a policy include (i) the permanent positive effect on base money and the money supply, (ii) the signaling effect of the central bank's commitment to keep the policy interest rate low, and (iii) the portfolio balance effect of money supply increase, that is, the effect of inducing investors to shift toward other assets because of the imperfect substitutability of money for other financial assets, thereby raising their value and stimulating final demand (Morgan 2012).

Credit (or qualitative) easing is aimed at changing the shares of various kinds of assets held by the private sector, with the expectation that this will lead to changes in their relative prices and thereby stimulate real economic activity. For example, a central bank's outright (permanent) purchases of long-term government bonds could be expected to reduce long-term bond yields, stimulate long-term investment, and boost overall economic activity. A central bank's direct lending to market participants could reduce credit market spreads and improve the functioning of private credit markets more generally, when the normal transmission mechanism breaks down. Like quantitative easing, credit (or qualitative) easing generally involves an increase in the size of a central bank's balance sheet but attempts to change the mix of assets, not the level of bank reserves (liabilities). Bernanke (2009) provides a detailed description of the US Federal Reserve's credit easing measures.[4]

In Asian emerging economies, unconventional measures were adopted by the Bank of Korea, the Monetary Authority of Singapore, the Reserve Bank of India, and the Central Bank of Taiwan. Perhaps the most significant unconventional policy measures in the region outside Japan have been those involving provision of foreign currency liquidity by central banks via the Federal Reserve swap arrangements to offset the shortage of US dollars arising from capital outflows.[5]

For example, the Federal Reserve and the Bank of Korea announced the implementation of a US$30 billion swap agreement on October 29, 2008. This appears to have been effective in easing the shortage of dollar funds in the Korean market. The spread between the Korean one-year interbank rate and the one-year Treasury bill rate, a measure of banking sector credit risk, spiked upward from mid-2008, when the Bank of Korea's foreign exchange reserve holdings (mainly US Treasuries) dropped sharply. However, once the foreign reserve holdings began to rise again in December, as a result of the loan by the Fed, the spread shrank rapidly again. The Bank of Korea drew roughly half of the Fed's swap line, and total foreign exchange reserve holdings rose by 40.8 trillion won (roughly US$29 billion) during that period. The Bank of Korea also expanded its won–yen swap agreement with the Bank of Japan from US$3 billion equivalent to $20 billion equivalent and established a won–yuan swap with the People's Bank of China of up to 180 billion yuan, although it did not make use of these.

The Central Bank of Taiwan also adopted a number of unconventional measures in September and October 2008, including expanding the eligible counterparties for its repurchase operations, extending the term of such operations from 30 days to 180 days, expanding eligible collateral to include certificates of deposit, and linking the interest rates on central bank reserve deposits to market rates (Central Bank of Taiwan 2008a, 2008b). These operations seem to have been effective in reducing interbank spreads relative to policy rates by about 30–40 basis points during that period.

Central banks can also attempt to influence market expectations by making announcements about the expected trend of future monetary policy. A large volume of literature has developed around what generally is referred to as the "commitment" or "policy duration" effect. The basic idea is simple – even though a central bank may set the very short-term rate, normally the overnight interbank rate, at zero, the market still has considerable uncertainty about the future development of monetary policy. Therefore, if a central bank can persuade the market that it will keep the policy rate lower than the market would otherwise expect, this should cause longer-term rates to fall, thereby stimulating the economy. This type of policy has been analyzed theoretically by a number of authors, including Svensson (2001) and Eggertsson and Woodford (2003).

### 3.10. Currency and capital flow management

Capital inflows provide emerging market economies with substantial potential benefits in pursuing economic development but, if not managed properly, can expose recipient countries to macroeconomic risks, financial instability, and sudden stops and/or reversals of capital flows. A central bank's management of the exchange rate and capital flows can play a key role in reducing such volatile and potentially destabilizing capital flows.

Sterilized intervention has been the favorite tool applied by many emerging Asian economies to prevent nominal exchange rate appreciation and economic overheating. Between 2000 and 2007, intervention in the foreign exchange market was unidirectional, that is, purchasing US dollars to prevent domestic currency appreciation against the dollar, leading to large buildups of foreign exchange reserves across the region. Such interventions had to be sterilized to prevent overheating of the economy.

In addition to sterilized intervention aimed at stabilizing exchange rates, capital controls are a common tool for limiting capital inflows in emerging market economies.[6] In countries that have substantially liberalized their capital accounts, market-based controls – such as the Chilean unremunerated reserve requirement imposed on capital inflows – have been the predominant option in recent years.[7] However, designing and implementing capital inflow controls is not easy. Administering capital controls requires highly competent country regulatory authorities as they must constantly watch for unwanted flows – often disguised – entering through various channels. For these economies, returning to draconian capital controls or recreating a system of extensive administrative controls is no longer a viable option.

### 3.11. Macroprudential policy tools

Some central banks also have macroprudential powers to promote financial stability by virtue of having responsibility for supervising the banking sector. This enables them to restrain the buildup of financial imbalances by using tools such as loan-to-value ratios, debt-service-to-income ratios, credit exposure limits on specific sectors (especially real estate), and limits on loan growth, among others. Some of these tools tend to be time-invariant, while others can be altered in a discretionary way according to the authorities' assessment of the economic and financial situation. Many macroprudential tools have been developed for use as microprudential tools (loan-to-value ratios and exposure limits, among others) at a bank level but can be adapted to macroprudential use by calibrating them in relation to the macro-financial cycle. If central banks do not have such powers, they must try to work with the supervisory agencies having those powers if they believe it is necessary to have them implemented.

Sector-targeted macroprudential tools are used to restrict bank lending and other financial activity during boom periods. They generally aim to limit the tendency for a self-perpetuating cycle between asset values and credit growth to lead to an unsustainable asset bubble. Measures include loan and underwriting standards, loan-to-value ratios, debt-service-to-income ratios, caps on credit growth, and exposure limits. Table 7.3 provides a summary of macroprudential measures in Asia.

*Table 7.3* Asian experience with macroprudential tools

| Objective | Tools | Examples |
|---|---|---|
| Manage aggregate risk over time (procyclicality) | Countercyclical provisioning | PRC, India |
| | Loan-to-value ratios | PRC, Hong Kong, Indonesia, Japan, Korea, Malaysia, Philippines, Singapore, Thailand |
| | Debt-service-to-income ratios | PRC, Hong Kong, Korea |
| | Tighter lending criteria | PRC, Hong Kong, Korea, Malaysia, Philippines, Singapore, Thailand |
| | Credit limits | PRC, Hong Kong, India |
| | Tighter supervision | PRC, Hong Kong, India, Korea, Malaysia, Singapore |
| | Capital requirements | India, Malaysia |
| | Exposure limits on lending to specific sectors | Korea, Malaysia, Philippines, Singapore |
| Manage aggregate risk at every point in time (systemic oversight) | Capital surcharges for systemically important banks | PRC, India, Philippines, Singapore |
| | Liquidity and funding requirements | PRC, India, Korea, Malaysia, Philippines, Singapore, Thailand |
| | Loan-to-deposit requirements | PRC, Korea |
| | Foreign exchange exposure limits | Korea, Philippines |
| | Limits on currency mismatches | India, Malaysia, Philippines |

Sources: CGFC (2010); Lamberte, Manlagñit, and Prativedwannakij (2010); Sheng (2010).

Note: PRC = People's Republic of China.

### 3.12. Architecture for financial stability

The experience of the global financial crisis shows the need for a strong systemic stability regulator that can make objective assessments of the financial situation and take pre-emptive actions where needed (Kawai and Pomerleano 2012). However, responsibilities for financial stability are frequently divided among multiple entities, mainly central banks and financial regulators. Moreover, other policymakers need to be involved in decision-making as well, especially the finance ministry, since it is responsible for committing public funds in the case of resolution, and the deposit insurance agency, which often has responsibility for bank resolution. An effective structure for systemic stability regulation must ensure adequate sharing of information and good coordination of decision-making and policy implementation.

The relationship between such a systemic stability regulator in charge of macroprudential policy and a central bank charged with traditional monetary policy is an important issue. To achieve both price stability and financial stability, there have to be at least two policy instruments, that is, monetary policy and macroprudential policy. However, in practice it is often questionable to what extent macroprudential policy tools can be wielded independently of monetary policy. If monetary conditions are easy and investments attractive, market participants may try to evade specific macroprudential regulations and make investments by alternative means, and their ability to evade such regulations tends to increase over time. This suggests that both monetary and macroprudential policies should aim in the same direction.

A cooperative effort to regulate financial stability requires that financial system information be shared fully. However, experience shows that there is a natural tendency for individual regulators not to share information to the extent needed. Therefore, there is a strong argument in favor of the central bank having some direct oversight responsibility for the financial sector so that it can obtain needed information about financial market conditions directly rather than having to request it from another agency.

### 3.13. Regional cooperation

The discussion so far has dealt with macroprudential policy in a single country, but the experiences of the Asian financial crisis, the global financial crisis, and the eurozone financial crisis show that such crises can be contagious, transmitted by volatile capital flows within a region. Therefore, regional perspectives on systemic risk regulation are needed as well. This is particularly so when global systemically important financial institutions are involved.

Within Asia, existing policy dialogue processes include the ASEAN+3[8] meeting for finance ministers and the Executives' Meeting of East Asia-Pacific Central Banks for central bank governors. From 2012 central bank governors joined the ASEAN+3 finance ministers' meeting for the Economic Review and Policy Dialogue, whereas only deputy governors had attended previously. However, the development of an Asian Financial Stability Dialogue (AFSD), as proposed by Kuroda (2008), could enhance communication about common risk factors and possibly lead to coordinated actions to reduce systemic risks. The AFSD would include finance ministries, central banks, financial supervisors, and deposit insurance companies.

At the global level, the IMF and Financial Stability Board can assist in assessing risk, while the newly formed ASEAN+3 Macroeconomic Research Office, which is the surveillance arm of the Chiang Mai Initiative Multilateralization (CMIM) and the Economic Review and Policy Dialogue, could be a counterpart of the IMF, and the AFSD could become the regional counterpart to the Financial Stability Board.

There is no doubt that Asia needs an effective mechanism of intensive policy dialogue and cooperation. The existing policy dialogue processes among the region's finance ministers described above can play a critical role in fostering the establishment of such a mechanism, but the development of an AFSD could provide a more complete platform for such cooperation.

The CMIM has the responsibility to act as a regional financial safety net for its members (ASEAN+3), i.e., to provide foreign exchange if a member country faces a balance of payments crisis. A reliable safety net could limit the need for an individual country to acquire foreign exchange reserves and thereby reduce the potential impact of such reserve accumulation on the worsening of global current account imbalances. However, there are many practical issues that need to be resolved to achieve such reliability. The biggest stumbling block is IMF conditionality, which is required if a country needs to draw more than 30 percent of its quota. However, making the provision of reserves automatic without conditionality invites the risk of moral hazard. Adding pre-approved credit lines can help, but until such issues are solved, Asian countries are likely to continue to rely on their own foreign exchange reserves as the first line of defense against capital outflows.

## 4. Policy transmission mechanism based on financial linkages and deepening

This section discusses the policy transmission mechanism based on financial linkages and deepening, including global financial linkages and domestic financial deepening. The former focuses on developments in the size and composition of capital flows, while the latter includes credits, private bonds, government bonds, equities, corporate savings, household savings, and household balance sheets. It is not possible to go into detail on every economy, so we focus on sketching the broad outlines.

### 4.1. Financial openness in Asian emerging economies

Financial systems tend to become more open as economies develop and restrictions in areas such as capital accounts ease. However, capital account regimes can also become more restrictive, particularly in countries that experience shocks and crises from rapid capital inflows or outflows. The Asian financial crisis was a watershed in Asia in terms of the perceived risks associated with open capital accounts. Financial openness is not easy to measure. There are two broad approaches – *de jure* and *de facto*. *De jure* measures assess the restrictiveness of published laws and regulations regarding foreign exchange and capital account transactions. These are typically based on the IMF's *Annual Report on Exchange Arrangements and Exchange Restrictions* (IMF 2008). Examples of this approach include Quinn (2003) and the Chinn-Ito Index[9] (Chinn and Ito 2008).

The degree of openness has ranged widely and has changed substantially in major Asian emerging economies, according to the Chinn–Ito Index for 1996 and 2011 (Figure 7.3). Hong Kong and Singapore are rated as fully open, consistent with their status as regional financial centers. Both the PRC and India have maintained relatively low ratings of –1.17, suggesting they are relatively closed. Viet Nam has become significantly more open, while Indonesia, Malaysia, the Philippines, and Thailand have become less open, primarily as a result of their experiences during the Asian financial crisis.

However, it is widely recognized that *de jure* measures may not reliably capture the effective degree of capital market openness. The alternative approach is to measure *de facto* capital market openness based on estimates of actual capital flows. One of the main sources in this regard is Lane, P. R. and Milesi-Ferretti, G. M. (2006). The essential idea was that a higher level of external assets and liabilities (relative to GDP or some other measure) indicated the effective openness of capital markets. The series was updated to 2009 by Kawai, Lamberte, and Takagi (2012). The external assets and liabilities ratios generally rose for all Asian economies from 1990 to 2009. Despite the region's relatively low overall *de jure* openness scores, the ratios were close to or exceeded 100 percent for all but

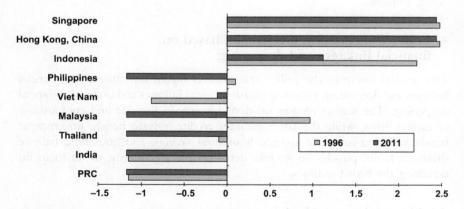

*Figure 7.3* Chinn–Ito Indices for major Asian emerging economies
Source: Chinn and Ito (2008).
Note: PRC: People's Republic of China.

one economy in 2009. The capital accounts of many Asian economies therefore in fact appear to have been quite open on this measure.

### 4.2. Capital flow composition

Gross capital inflows to emerging Asia[10] have risen rapidly over the past two decades, although the share of GDP peaked in 2007 (see Figure 7.4). Direct investment flows have been relatively stable, with persistent positive inflows. Portfolio flows have been somewhat more volatile, although there were only two years of actual outflows, which corresponded to the two crisis years of 1998 and 2008. Other inflows, mainly loans, have shown by far the greatest volatility, underlining the persistent concern about the risks to financial stability emanating from this category. Nonetheless, the outflow of "others" in 2008 was much smaller than in 1998, pointing to the improved fundamentals of emerging Asian economies at the time.

The picture for net inflows is similar but shows little sign of an upward trend as a percentage of GDP over time, as the peak in 1996 was never exceeded (Figure 7.5). The pattern of relative stability of direct investment flows is maintained, but both portfolio and other flows show greater volatility on a net basis, with more episodes of net outflows for both. The large net portfolio outflows seen in 2006 and 2007 appear to reflect the increasing role of Hong Kong and Singapore as investment intermediary centers.

There is a continuing debate about whether gross or net capital flows are a better indicator of currency and financial stability risks. Net inflows are probably more relevant for currencies, but gross inflows may be more directly related to financial stability risks, since they are a function of total transaction volumes.

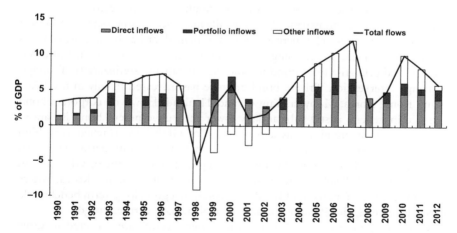

*Figure 7.4* Gross capital inflows in emerging Asia
Source: CEIC Data (http://www.ceicdata.com/).

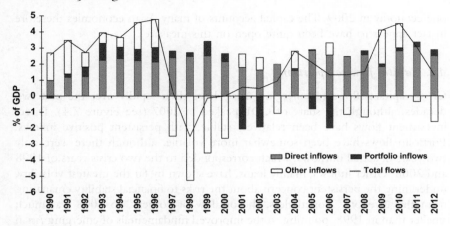

*Figure 7.5* Net capital inflows in emerging Asia

Source: CEIC Data (http://www.ceicdata.com/).

### 4.3. Domestic financial development

All East Asian emerging economies showed substantial increases in total private liabilities relative to GDP from 2000 to 2009, especially the PRC and Viet Nam. As Table 7.4 shows, however, there were some differences when it comes to types of liability. Private bank credit fell relative to GDP in Indonesia in the aftermath of the Asian financial crisis of 1997–1998. Stock market capitalization relative to GDP rose in all Asian emerging economies, while private bond market capitalization fell only in Singapore. However, among other Asian emerging economies, private bond market capitalization is high only in Korea and Malaysia, which underlines the scope for further development of this sector.

Local currency bond issuance has generally increased substantially in Asia over the past two decades. The increase in government debt has been most obvious in the PRC, Japan, Korea, Singapore, Taiwan, and Thailand. In many cases, this resulted primarily from bond issuance accompanying sterilization of foreign exchange intervention. Private bond issuance has increased mainly in the PRC, Hong Kong, Korea, Malaysia, Taiwan, and Thailand. However, corporate bond issuance in general is still substantially lower than government bond issuance.

Life insurance premiums as a percentage of GDP have reached very high levels in Hong Kong and Singapore, befitting their status as international financial centers.[11] Malaysia's level is also relatively high, at 6.3 percent of GDP. Levels in the PRC and Thailand are relatively close to that of South Korea, where premiums equal 4.5 percent of GDP and represent a good long-term benchmark. India, Indonesia, the Philippines, and Viet Nam have further to go.

Asian emerging economies' asset management sectors are expected to grow rapidly as a result of rising incomes, high savings rates, and the aging of populations in most economies. Again, however, there is wide variation in the region.

*Table 7.4* Sources of private sector funding (% of GDP)

| | Private credit by deposit money banks | | Stock market capitalization | | Private bond market capitalization | | Total | |
|---|---|---|---|---|---|---|---|---|
| | 1990 | 2011 | 1990 | 2011 | 1990 | 2011 | 1990 | 2011 |
| PRC | 74.3 | 121.5 | — | 58.8 | 2.9 | 23.1 | 77.3 | 203.3 |
| Hong Kong | — | 186.2 | 108.5 | 396.8 | 0.2 | 15.3 | 108.7 | 598.4 |
| India | 24.2 | 47.1 | 12.2 | 69.7 | 0.3 | 4.9 | 36.6 | 121.7 |
| Indonesia | 38.1 | 28.2 | 7.1 | 45.1 | — | 1.4 | 45.1 | 74.7 |
| Japan | 168.2 | 174.9 | 95.5 | 68.8 | 39.8 | 37.2 | 303.4 | 280.8 |
| Korea | 47.2 | 98.4 | 42.1 | 96.2 | 28.3 | 59.3 | 117.5 | 253.9 |
| Malaysia | 77.0 | 106.4 | 110.4 | 144.1 | 18.8 | 58.1 | 206.2 | 308.6 |
| Philippines | 17.0 | 29.8 | 13.4 | 73.9 | — | 1.0 | 30.4 | 104.7 |
| Singapore | 78.2 | 106.9 | 93.1 | 148.1 | 14.6 | 10.0 | 185.9 | 265.1 |
| Taiwan | 97.8 | 141.8 | 60.5 | 140.5 | 1.2 | 9.9 | 61.7 | 292.2 |
| Thailand | 72.3 | 130.9 | 28.0 | 81.7 | 6.5 | 12.7 | 106.8 | 225.3 |
| Viet Nam | — | 107.7 | — | 15.4 | — | 1.7 | — | 123.1 |

Sources: International Monetary Fund, *International Financial Statistics* (http://elibrary-data.imf.org/QueryBuilder.aspx?key=19784651&s=322); CEIC Data (http://www.ceicdata.com/); *Bank for International Settlements Quarterly Review*, June 2013; World Bank, *World Development Indicators* (http://databank.worldbank.org/data/views/variableSelection/selectvariables.aspx?source=world-development-indicators).

Hong Kong and Singapore have very high shares of assets under management relative to GDP, followed by Thailand. Using Korea as a benchmark, where such assets equal around 20 percent of GDP, countries such as the PRC and India seem likely to develop further.

## 5. Assessments of policy outcomes

Assessments of monetary policy performance in Asian emerging economies have generally been favorable. Filardo and Genberg (2012) argue that monetary policy frameworks in Asia and the Pacific region have performed well since the late 1990s in terms of inflation outcomes. They cite three main reasons: central banks have focused on price stability as the main objective of monetary policy, institutional arrangements have facilitated the successful pursuit of this objective, and other economic policies, mainly fiscal policy, have supported this pursuit by reducing concerns about fiscal dominance. We may add to this the availability of a large number of policy tools, including unconventional policies, macroprudential measures, and capital flow measures that help to deliver financial and economic stability.

## 5.1. Effectiveness of IT

Trying to assess the effectiveness of IT has been difficult. Figure 7.6 shows that CPI inflation rates fell substantially in both Asian IT economies (those adopting IT frameworks after the Asian financial crisis – Indonesia, Korea, the Philippines, and Thailand) and non-IT economies (PRC, Japan, Malaysia, Singapore, and Taiwan) in the decade after the Asian financial crisis. The degree of improvement in 2000–2013 relative to the pre-crisis period was about the same for both groups, about 3 percentage points. Therefore, this improvement in inflation cannot necessarily be attributed to the implementation of IT policies. At the same time, central banks in the region generally gained greater independence, their management was strengthened, exchange rates became more flexible, and, in a number of cases, trend growth slowed, which would lead to lower inflation by itself.

More sophisticated studies using econometric techniques have not reached firm conclusions regarding the impacts of IT on macroeconomic performance, including inflation rates, inflation persistence, and output gaps. Optimistic studies (e.g., Mishkin and Posen 1997; Neumann and Hagen 2002; Bernanke et al. 1999) marshaled evidence that IT is associated with lower rates of inflation, lower volatility of inflation and output, better-anchored inflation expectations, and reduced inflation persistence. However, others reached more skeptical conclusions, including Cecchetti and Ehrmann (1999) and Ball and Sheridan (2003), pointing to other factors such as the general downward trend in inflation before the adoption of IT policies and the period of the "great moderation".

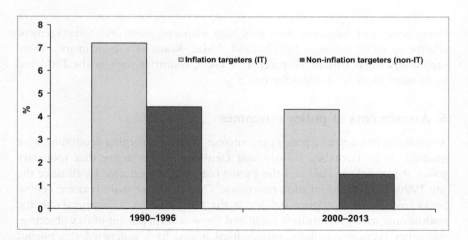

*Figure 7.6* Inflation rates of Asian IT and non-IT countries

Source: CEIC Data (http://www.ceicdata.com/).

Note: IT countries are Indonesia, Korea, the Philippines, and Thailand. Non-IT countries are the People's Republic of China, Japan, Malaysia, Singapore, and Taiwan.

Most of these studies focused on the experience of developed economies and hence may be less relevant for emerging economies. Following the methodology of Ball and Sheridan, Batini and Laxton (2007) and Gonçalves and Salles (2008) compared the economic performance of inflation targeters versus non-targeters in emerging economies. Gonçalves and Salles found that those emerging economies that adopted an IT framework experienced greater reduction in inflation and GDP growth variability, even after controlling for mean reversion. Batini and Laxton reported similar results by saying that IT appears to have been associated with lower inflation, lower inflation expectations, and lower inflation volatility.

Naqvi and Rizvi (2009) focused on the experience of IT in Asia, analyzing the performance of four IT economies (Indonesia, the Philippines, South Korea, and Thailand) against six Asian non-IT economies (PRC, Hong Kong, India, Malaysia, Singapore, and Pakistan). They conclude that economic performance has improved in all Asian economies in the post-targeting period, but IT does not seem to have played any significant role in this improvement on the part of targeting countries. They also find strong evidence that all variables showed strong reversion to the mean, suggesting that the improved performance of variables today is simply relative to poor economic performance in the past. On the other hand, a more recent study by Gerlach and Tillman (2011) finds a significant improvement in inflation persistence attributable to IT in a sample of nine Asian economies, four of which are using IT. On the whole, it seems difficult to attribute significant improvement in inflation and output performance to IT policy in particular, but the general improvement in currency and monetary policy frameworks and management during the period should accept a good deal of the credit for this improved inflation performance.

Ito and Hayashi (2004) note that there are a number of issues specific to the implementation of IT in emerging market economies. First, economic statistics are not as reliable as in advanced countries. Second, structural changes tend to be larger, especially in Asian economies, and therefore price bias may be more serious. Also, modeling the monetary transmission mechanism for use in inflation forecasting is much more difficult. Fourth, the inflation target needs to take into account, on the one hand, possible Balassa-Samuelson effects in economies that are fast-growing and therefore have a rising price level and, on the other, the Japanese experience of deflation. Taking into account all of these factors, they recommend that emerging market countries set their inflation targets at a higher central rate than in advanced economies and with a wider band of fluctuation. They also emphasize the need to achieve a certain degree of currency stability as well.

Inoue, Toyoshima, and Hamori (2012) took a somewhat different approach by analyzing the effect of adopting IT on the correlation of a country's economy with the global economic cycle. They applied the methodology of dynamic conditional correlation to analyze the degree of synchronization of the four Asian IT countries – Indonesia, Korea, the Philippines, and Thailand. They found some signs of increasing synchronicity in these countries after the adoption of IT. However, they did not compare this with the results for a control group of non-IT countries, so it is difficult to interpret the results.

## 5.2. Policy frameworks have multiple tools

One important point that perhaps has not received sufficient attention is that Asian monetary policy frameworks have become increasingly sophisticated and make use of a number of different policy tools, including both macroeconomic and macroprudential ones. Management of capital flows provides another instrument for such control. Unlike central banks in advanced economies, Asian central banks have shown themselves willing and able to use such tools regularly and aggressively. This means that the standard characterizations of monetary policy frameworks focusing on the use or non-use of explicit IT are probably too simplistic. In some cases, they have also developed more explicit cooperation frameworks with financial regulators and finance ministers to monitor and manage systemic financial risk. This multiplicity of instruments should make it easier for central banks and financial regulators to achieve both price and financial stability, even when the requirements of these objectives may appear to differ in the short run.

## 5.3. Monetary policy and the trilemma

The well-known "Impossible Trinity" or trilemma hypothesis states that an economy cannot enjoy monetary policy independence, free capital flows, and a fixed exchange rate simultaneously. Although some economists concluded from this that policy frameworks under this constraint would tend to gravitate to "corner solutions" – either fixed exchange rates or fully floating exchange rates – this generally has not happened in East Asia. Instead, most economies in the region have moved to an "interior solution" characterized by independent monetary policy, some restrictions on capital movements, and some degree of currency flexibility coupled with active intervention. The main exceptions to this are Hong Kong, whose exchange rate is pegged to the US dollar, and Japan, which, with rare exceptions, maintains a free-floating exchange rate.[12]

There have been various attempts to categorize exchange rate regimes. These have been complicated by the fact that a country's officially announced regime is not necessarily an accurate reflection of that currency's behavior. One recent empirical attempt to quantify currency flexibility in East Asia is that of Patnaik and Shah (2012), who apply the methodology of Frankel and Wei (1994) to identify the extent of correlation of 11 Asian currencies with major reserve currencies. Figure 7.7 shows the mean and median trend of flexibility of these currencies since 1991. The vertical axis shows the amount of currency movement explained by movements of key currencies, i.e., the $R^2$ from the Frankel-Wei equation. Although currency flexibility in recent years is higher than that it was before the Asian crisis, correlations with key currencies are still high, suggesting that these currencies are far from freely floating.

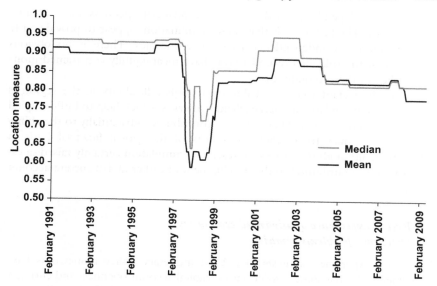

*Figure 7.7* Evolution of exchange rate flexibility in Asia
Source: Patnaik and Shah (2012).

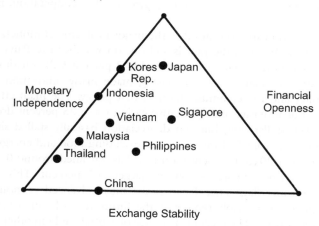

*Figure 7.8* Trilemma values for ASEAN+3 economies in 2009
Source: Ito and Kawai (2012).

Note: ASEAN+3: members of the Association of Southeast Asian Nations plus China, Japan, and Korea.

There have also been various attempts to quantify the three aspects of the trilemma – monetary policy independence, freedom of capital flows, and exchange rate flexibility. Ito and Kawai (2012) developed estimates of these values to place East Asian economies on the trilemma triangle, as shown in Figure 7.8. These results clearly show a wide range of values but skewed in the direction of monetary independence, with only partial financial openness and exchange rate flexibility. The key point is that these combinations appear to provide fairly complete monetary independence to these economies. There is no obvious evidence that the trilemma-related factors have meaningfully constrained monetary policy in these economies.

Another important factor contributing to policy flexibility in the region is the accumulation of large foreign exchange reserves, which help to buffer capital outflows when they occur. These reserves contributed substantially to the ability of Asian economies to weather the shocks of the global financial crisis in 2007–2009, although the process of reserve accumulation certainly raised questions about its contribution to the development of earlier global current account imbalances.

## 5.4. Recent experience of advanced economies shows that problems remain

The above experience suggests that Asian monetary policy frameworks have performed well, that some restrictions on capital account openness and currency flexibility are useful and that no major changes are needed. Perhaps the main suggestions would be to make financial stability an explicit objective of monetary policy and to strengthen institutions for regional policy cooperation, including the CMIM.

However, it is too early to claim that the major problems of monetary policy have been solved. Notably, the jury is still out on whether the Bank of Japan will be able to achieve its target of sustainable 2 percent CPI inflation despite having a floating exchange rate and having made many innovations in both monetary policy and the communication of that policy. The main effect of its latest round of quantitative and qualitative easing was a 25 percent drop in the value of the yen–dollar rate, but yen depreciation basically stalled since June 2013. Although the core CPI inflation rate (excluding food and energy) turned positive in October 2013, in recent months it has remained around 0.7 percent in year-on-year terms, still well below the target of 2 percent. This exception should raise warning flags since Japan is the most advanced economy in the region and therefore arguably represents the future toward which other Asian economies are evolving. The recent experience of central banks in other advanced economies, especially the United States, the United Kingdom, and the eurozone, should give pause for thought as well, in view of their recent struggles to achieve their policy objectives. Most worrisomely, the ballooning of government debt and increasing calls on central banks to act as lenders of last resort to governments in those countries suggest that that the demon of fiscal dominance may not be securely chained.

It is beyond the scope of this chapter to analyze the reasons for these shortfalls in monetary policy performance, as they touch on the fundamental limits of monetary policy. As noted by Morgan (2012) the experience of using unconventional monetary policy measures when the policy rate falls to zero suggests that they are effective in relieving specific bottlenecks in financial markets and raising asset prices but less effective in stimulating aggregate demand.

In other words, most Asian economies may simply have been lucky in that they still have relatively high trend growth rates and low government debt ratios and were able to pick "low-hanging fruit" by improving their monetary policy frameworks. Also, the lack of exposure to sophisticated financial instruments in the run-up to the global financial crisis meant that central banks in the region mainly faced garden-variety drops in aggregate demand rather than more challenging financial sector disruptions. Their risks in this regard are likely to increase in line with rising financial development. In that sense, monetary policy frameworks in the region have not yet been adequately tested.

## 6. Conclusions

Monetary policy frameworks in East Asia have evolved substantially in the past two decades, mainly in response to the shocks of the Asian financial crisis of 1997–1998 and the global financial crisis of 2007–2009. The Asian financial crisis showed the importance of exchange rate flexibility and credible policy frameworks, leading to increased central bank independence, greater focus on inflation policy, and more flexible exchange rates. A number of Asian central banks adopted explicit IT frameworks, and even those that did not have evidently placed greater emphasis on controlling inflation than previously. Both groups achieved similar degrees of success in reducing inflation.

The global financial crisis highlighted the problems that surveillance and regulation of system-wide financial stability were inadequate in many countries in the pre-crisis period and that central banks may not have focused sufficiently on financial stability risks. The dimensions of systemic risk in both the procyclicality of the financial system and the interconnectedness of various financial institutions and markets were not adequately appreciated, nor was the need for a macroprudential perspective on such risks. Moreover, when responsibility for financial supervision was divided among central banks and financial supervisors, most countries lacked an adequate architecture to ensure coordinated surveillance, analysis, information sharing, and policy actions.

Defining financial stability is not an easy task because it has multiple dimensions and is related to complex financial systems. But this should not lessen the need to do so. Central banks' overview of the macroeconomic developments and financial system conditions, together with their oversight of payment and settlement systems, gives them a unique perspective on system-wide financial stability. The case is strong for central banks to have an explicit mandate for financial stability. Although there may be short-term conflicts between the traditional central bank objective of price stability and that of financial stability, in the medium and long term these objectives should be largely consistent with each other because the development of a financial crisis during periods of price stability will eventually lead to deflation and economic downturn.

Central banks have various tools to support financial stability, including standard and unconventional monetary policy tools, currency market intervention tools, and, in some cases, supervisory authority, macroprudential tools, and capital flow management tools. These can be used to help prevent crises by dampening the credit cycle and strengthening banks and other financial firms to ensure that they are adequately capitalized and reserved to be able to ride out systemic shocks. Asian central banks have in fact frequently resorted to such tools to safeguard financial stability and reduce the volatility of capital flows. There is no guarantee that macroprudential and capital flow management tools will always be effective, but a multiplicity of tools makes it easier to achieve both price stability and financial stability. This also implies that central bank policy frameworks are more complex than simply being characterized by the presence or absence of explicit IT.

Monetary policy frameworks in the region have evolved to deal with greater financial openness and depth. The ratio of gross capital inflows to GDP is still showing an upward trend, although that of net capital inflows appears to be stabilizing or declining. Domestic financial markets have also deepened substantially, which should contribute to strengthening the monetary transmission mechanism. Aside from Japan, there is no evidence of major failures of the policy transmission mechanism in the region.

Overall, monetary policy frameworks in the region appear to have worked well in achieving low and stable inflation coupled with economic growth. This mainly reflects three factors: central banks have focused on price stability as the main objective of monetary policy, institutional arrangements have facilitated the successful pursuit of this objective, and other economic policies, mainly fiscal policy, have supported this pursuit by reducing concerns about fiscal dominance. We may add to this the availability of a large number of policy tools, including unconventional policies, macroprudential measures, and capital flow measures that help to deliver financial and economic stability. East Asian central banks also appear to have coped well with the constraints of the trilemma hypothesis and for the most part have gravitated toward an "interior solution" with an independent monetary policy, partial financial openness, and partly managed currencies. On the whole, this positive experience does not suggest the need for any major changes in policy frameworks. Perhaps the most important suggestion at this stage is to give greater weight to financial stability as a policy objective and to strengthen institutions for regional policy coordination, including the CMIM.

However, the difficulties faced by the Bank of Japan in achieving its inflation target, and the struggles of advanced-economy central banks in the United States and Europe to achieve full recoveries after the global financial crisis, point to problems that may confront other Asian economies in the future as they achieve higher levels of economic and financial development. Therefore, their recent positive experience to some extent reflects luck as well as improved policy frameworks. In that sense, monetary policy frameworks in the region have not yet been adequately tested.

## Notes

1 This chapter covers the monetary policy frameworks of the People's Republic of China; Hong Kong, Indonesia, Japan, Korea, Malaysia, the Philippines, Singapore, Taiwan, and Thailand. I am grateful for helpful comments from the participants of the Pacific Economic Outlook Seminars on March 17–18, 2012, and September 21–22, 2012. This work was done in the personal capacity of author and is not related to the Asian Development Bank Institute's work, and the views expressed in this chapter are those of the author and do not necessarily reflect the views or policies of the Asian Development Bank Institute or the Asian Development Bank, its Board of Directors, or the governments they represent.
2 Such measures are regarded as unconventional mainly relative to the standard practice during normal times of central banks in developed economies, which is almost exclusively to target the short-term money market interest rate by open market operations. Emerging-market economies tend to use a broader range of operations much more regularly, as did developed-economy central banks in earlier periods.
3 See Morgan (2012) for a more detailed discussion.
4 Although the Federal Reserve's large-scale outright purchasing operations of Treasury bonds, agency bonds, and mortgage-backed securities in 2009 and 2010 were widely referred to as quantitative easing (QE1 and QE2, respectively), the Federal Reserve has not described them as such, instead referring to them as credit easing measures.
5 There is some debate about whether such measures can be regarded as unconventional or not.
6 For Ostry et al. (2010), however, tools aimed at controlling large capital inflows that may fuel domestic credit booms are not seen as macroprudential tools per se but rather as measures that can buttress prudential regulations.
7 Brazil imposed a tax on fixed-income and equity inflows in October 2009 in response to surges in capital inflows and, in the following month, imposed another tax on certain trades to prevent circumvention.
8 The 10 member nations of the Association of Southeast Asian Nations plus the PRC, Japan, and Korea.
9 The Chinn-Ito Index is compiled by evaluating four major categories of restrictions on external accounts: (i) the presence of a multiple exchange rate regime, (ii) the presence of restrictions on current account transactions, (iii) the presence of restrictions on capital account transactions, and (iv) the presence of a requirement of the surrender of export proceeds. The index score ranges from –1.84, which indicates that they are fully closed, to +2.48, meaning they are fully open.
10 Total for PRC, Hong Kong, India, Indonesia, Korea, Malaysia, the Philippines, Singapore, Taiwan, and Thailand.
11 Data on assets are not available for most economies.
12 Brunei Darussalam's currency is linked to the Singapore dollar.

## References and Further Readings

Ahsan, W., M. Skully, and J. Wickramanayake. 2008. Does Central Bank Independence and Governance Matter in Asia Pacific? Paolo Baffi Centre Research Paper Series, 2008-27. Milan: Baffi Centre, Universita Bocconi. http://papers.ssrn.com/sol3/papers.cfm?abstract_id=1263908.

Ball, L. and N. Sheridan. 2003. Does Inflation Targeting Matter? National Bureau of Economic Research Working Paper Series 9577. Cambridge, MA: National Bureau of Economic Research.

Bank for International Settlements (BIS). 2009a. *BIS Quarterly Review*. June. Basel: Bank for International Settlements.

———. 2009b. MC Compendium: Monetary Policy Frameworks and Central Bank Market Operations. Basel: Bank for International Settlements. http://www.bis.org/publ/mktc04.pdf.

———. 2011. Central Bank Governance and Financial Stability: A Report by a Study Group. Basel: Bank for International Settlements.

Basel Committee on Banking Supervision (BCBS). 2010. The Basel Committee's Response to the Financial Crisis: Report to the G20. October. Basel: Bank for International Settlements.

Batini, N. and D. Laxton. 2007. Under What Conditions Can Inflation Targeting Be Adopted? The Experience of Emerging Markets. In F. Mishkin and K. Schmidt-Hebbel, eds., *Monetary Policy under Inflation Targeting*, 467–506. Santiago: Central Bank of Chile.

Bernanke, B. 2009. Federal Reserve Policies to Ease Credit and Their Implications for the Fed's Balance Sheet. Speech to the National Press Club, Washington, DC, February 18. http://www.federalreserve.gov/newsevents/speech/bernanke20090218a.htm.

———. 2010. Monetary Policy and the Housing Bubble. Speech at the Annual Meeting of the American Economic Association, Atlanta, Georgia, January 3. http://www.federalreserve.gov/newsevents/speech/bernanke20100103a.htm.

Bernanke, B. and M. Gertler. 2000. Monetary Policy and Asset Price Volatility. National Bureau of Economic Research Working Paper 7559. Cambridge, MA: National Bureau of Economic Research.

Bernanke, B., T. Laubach, F.S. Mishkin, and A. Posen. 1999. *Inflation Targeting: Lessons from the International Experience*. Princeton, NJ: Princeton University Press.

Bernanke, B. and V.R. Reinhart. 2004. Conducting Monetary Policy at Very Low Short-Term Interest Rates. *American Economic Review* 94(2): 85–90.

Borio, C. and P. Disyatat. 2009. Unconventional Monetary Policies: An Appraisal. Bank for International Settlements Working Papers 292. Basel: Bank for International Settlements.

Borio, C., and P. Lowe. 2002. Asset Prices Financial and Monetary Stability: Exploring the Nexus. Bank for International Settlements Working Papers 114. Basel: Bank for International Settlements.

Borio, C. and W. White. 2004. Whither Monetary and Financial Stability? The Implications of Evolving Policy Regimes. Bank for International Settlements Working Papers 147. Basel: Bank for International Settlements.

British Bankers' Association (BBA). 2010. A Possible Macro-prudential Approach. London: British Bankers' Association.

Brunnermeier, M., A. Crockett, C. Goodhart, A. Persaud, and H.S. Shin. 2009. *The Fundamental Principles of Financial Regulation*. Geneva: International Center for Monetary and Banking Studies; London: Centre for Economic Policy Research.

Carmichael, J. and M. Pomerleano. 2002. *The Development and Regulation of Non-bank Financial Institutions*. Washington, DC: World Bank.

Cecchetti, S.G. and M. Ehrmann. 1999. Does Inflation Targeting Increase Output Volatility? An International Comparison of Policymakers' Preferences and Outcomes. National Bureau of Economic Research Working Paper 7426. Cambridge, MA: National Bureau of Economic Research.

Cecchetti, S., H. Genberg, J. Lipsky, and S. Wadhwani. 2000. *Asset Prices and Central Bank Policy. Geneva Report on the World Economy 2.* London: Centre for Economic Policy Research; Geneva: International Center for Monetary and Banking Studies.

Central Bank of Taiwan. 2008a. Monetary Policy Decisions of the Executive Directors Meeting. September 25. http://www.cbc.gov.tw/ct.asp?xItem=32637&ctNode=448&mp=2.

———. 2008b. Monetary Policy Decisions of the Executive Directors Meeting. October 30. http://www.cbc.gov.tw/ct.asp?xItem=33012&ctNode=448&mp=2.

Chinn, M. and H. Ito (2008). "A New Measure of Financial Openness". Journal of Comparative Policy Analysis, Volume 10, Issue 3, p. 309–322 (September).

Committee on the Global Financial System (CGFS). 2010. Macroprudential Instruments and Frameworks: A Stocktaking of Issues and Experiences. Committee on the Global Financial System Papers 38. Basel: Bank for International Settlements.

de Larosiere Group. 2009. Report on Financial Supervision: High-Level Group on Financial Supervision in the EU. February. http://www.ec.europa.eu/internal_market/finances/docs/de_larosiere_report_en.pdf.

Eggertsson, G. B. and M. Woodford. 2003. The Zero Bound on Interest Rates and Optimal Monetary Policy. *Brookings Papers on Economic Activity* 1: 139–233.

European Central Bank (ECB). 2012. "What Is Financial Stability?" *Financial Stability Review.* Frankfurt: European Central Bank. http://www.ecb.int/pub/fsr/html/index.en.html.

Filardo, A. and H. Genberg. 2012. Monetary Policy Strategies in the Asia and Pacific Region: Which Way Forward? In M. Kawai, P. Morgan, and S. Takagi, eds., *Monetary and Currency Policy in Asia,* 64–96. Cheltenham, UK: Edward Elgar.

Frankel, J. and S. J. Wei. 1994. Yen Bloc or Dollar Bloc? Exchange Rate Policies of the East Asian Countries. In T. Ito and A. Krueger, eds., *Macroeconomic Linkage: Savings, Exchange Rates and Capital Flows,* 295–333. Chicago: University of Chicago Press.

Genberg, H. and A. Filardo. 2009. Monetary Policy Strategies in the Asia and Pacific Region: Which Way Forward? Presentation at Asia Development Bank Institute Conference on Implications of the Global Financial Crisis for Financial Reform and Regulation in Asia, Tokyo, Japan, July 28–29.

Gerlach, S. and P. Tillman. 2011. Inflation Targeting and Inflation Persistence in Asia-Pacific. Hong Kong Institute for Monetary Research Working Paper 25. Hong Kong: Hong Kong Institute for Monetary Research.

Gonçalves, C. and J. Salles. 2008. Inflation Targeting in Emerging Economies: What Do the Data Say? *Journal of Development Economics* 85: 312–318.

Group of Thirty. 2009. Financial Reform: A Framework for Financial Stability. Washington, DC: The Group of Thirty. http://www.group30/pubs/reformreport.pdf.

Inoue, T., Y. Toyoshima, and S. Hamori. 2012. Inflation Targeting in Korea, Indonesia, the Philippines and Thailand: The Impact on Business Cycle Synchronization between Each Country and the World. Institute for Development Economics Discussion Paper 328. Tokyo: Institute for Development Economics. http://www.ide.go.jp/English/Publish/Download/Dp/pdf/328.pdf.

International Monetary Fund. 2008. *Annual Report on Exchange Arrangements and Exchange Restrictions.* Washington, DC: International Monetary Fund.

International Monetary Fund (IMF). 2009. Initial Lessons of the Crisis for the Global Architecture and the IMF. Prepared by the Strategy, Policy, and Review

Department. Washington, DC: International Monetary Fund. http://www.imf. org/external/np/pp/eng/2009/021809.pdf.

Ito, H. and M. Kawai. 2012. New Measures of the Trilemma Hypothesis and Their Implications for Asia. Asian Development Bank Institute Working Paper 381. Tokyo: Asian Development Bank Institute. http://www.adbi.org/working-paper/2012/09/21/5236.new.measures.trilemma.hypothesis.asia/.

Ito, T. and T. Hayashi. 2004. Inflation Targeting in Asia. Hong Kong Institute for Monetary Research Occasional Paper 1. Hong Kong: Hong Kong Institute for Monetary Research.

Kawai, M., M. Lamberte, and S. Takagi. 2012. Managing Capital Flows: Lessons from the Recent Experiences of Emerging Asian Economies. Unpublished ms.

Kawai, M. and M. Pomerleano. 2012. Strengthening Systemic Financial Regulation. In M. Kawai, D. Mayes, and P. Morgan, eds., *The Implications of the Global Financial Crisis for Financial Reform and Regulation in Asia*, 29–49. Cheltenham, UK: Edward Elgar.

Kawai, M. and S. Takagi. 2010. A Survey of the Literature on Managing Capital Inflows. In M. Kawai and M.B. Lamberte, eds., *Managing Capital Flows: The Search for a Framework*, 46–72. Cheltenham, UK: Edward Elgar.

Kuroda, H. 2008. Asia's Contribution to Global Development and Stability. Speech at the Asian Development Bank Institute Annual Conference, Tokyo, Japan, December 5. http://www.adbi.org/files/speech.2008.12.05.closing.remarks. kuruda.adbi.annual.meeting.2008.pdf.

Lamberte, M., M. Manlagnit, and K. Prativedwannakij. 2010. Financial Supervision and Regulation for Postcrisis Asia. Presented at the Pacific Economic Cooperation Council, Singapore National Committee for Pacific Economic Cooperation and Asian Development Bank Institute Conference towards Balanced and Sustainable Growth Strategies for Post-crisis Asia: A Shifting Paradigm and Challenges, Singapore, August 16.

Lane, P. R. and Milesi-Ferretti, G. M. 2006. "The External Wealth of Nations Mark II: Revised and Extended Estimates of Foreign Assets and Liabilities, 1970–2004," IMF Working Paper 06/69.

Minsky, H. 1986. *Stabilizing an Unstable Economy*. New Haven, CT: Yale University Press.

Mishkin, F.S. and A.S. Posen. 1997. Inflation Targeting Lessons from Four Countries. *Federal Reserve Bank of New York Economic Policy Review* 3(1): 79–110.

Morgan, P. 2012. The Role and Effectiveness of Unconventional Monetary Policy. In M. Kawai, P. Morgan, and S. Takagi, eds., *Monetary and Currency Policy Management in Asia*, 27–63. Cheltenham, UK: Edward Elgar.

Naqvi, B. and S. Rizvi. 2009. Inflation Targeting Framework: Is the Story Different for Asian Economies? Munich Personal Research Papers in Economics (RePEc) Archive Paper 19546, posted December 23. http://mpra.ub.uni-muenchen. de/19546/1/MPRA_paper_19546.pdf.

Neumann, J.M. and J. von Hagen. 2002. Does Inflation Targeting Matter. *Federal Reserve Bank of St. Louis Review* 84(4): 127–148.

Ostry, J., M. Chamon, A. Ghosh, K. Habermeier, M. Qureshi, and D. Reinhardt. 2010. Capital Inflows: The Role of Controls. International Monetary Fund Staff Position Notes SPN/10/04. Washington, DC: International Monetary Fund.

Patnaik, I. and A. Shah. 2012. Asia Confronts the Impossible Trinity. In M. Kawai, P. Morgan, and S. Takagi, eds., *Monetary and Currency Policy Management in Asia*, 193–216. Cheltenham, UK: Edward Elgar.

Quinn, D. 2003. "Capital Account Liberalization and Financial Globalization, 1890–1999: A Synoptic View," *International Journal of Finance and Economics, Vol. 8, No. 3*, pp. 189–204.

Reserve Bank of India. 2009. Third Quarter Review of RBI Monetary Policy 2008–09, Press Statement by Dr. D. Subbarao, Governor, January 27. http://www.banknetindia.com/banking/3qreview09_press.htm.

Schadler, S. 2010. Managing Large Capital Inflows: Taking Stock of International Experiences. In M. Kawai and M. B. Lamberte, eds., *Managing Capital Flows: The Search for a Framework*, 105–128. Cheltenham, UK: Edward Elgar.

Sheng, A. 2010. Procyclicality in Advanced and Emerging Economies. Asia Development Bank Institute Distinguished Speaker Seminar, November 29. Tokyo: Asia Development Bank Institute.

Shin, H. S. 2009. It Is Time for a Reappraisal of the Basic Principles of Financial Regulation. 31 January. Available: http://www.voxeu.com/index.php?q=node/2949

Stone, M. R., and A. J. Bhundia. 2004. A New Taxonomy of Monetary Regimes. International Monetary Fund Working Paper WP/04/191. Washington, DC: International Monetary Fund.

Svensson, L. E. O. 2001. The Zero Bound in an Open Economy: A Foolproof Way of Escaping from a Liquidity Trap. *Monetary and Economic Studies* 19(S1): 277–312.

Taylor, J. B. 2009. *Getting Off Track: How Government Actions and Interventions Caused, Prolonged, and Worsened the Financial Crisis*. Stanford, CA: Hoover Institution Press.

# 8 Monetary policy regime in China

*Dongmin Liu and Zhenxin Zhu*

## 1. Brief history of China's monetary policy regime

### 1.1. Exploration stage: 1978–1992

The People's Bank of China (PBOC) was split off from the Ministry of Finance (MOF) in 1978. However, from 1978 through 1983, China's monetary policy regime effectively operated as an integrated system, which acted more like a "cashier" for the MOF. In fact, the PBOC was not a real central bank but a combination of central bank and commercial bank; in other words, it was functioning simultaneously as both the "referee" and the "contestant", which prevented it from carrying out the function of managing the money supply. More importantly, regardless of the objectives or the tools of monetary policy, the PBOC operated virtually as an instrument for the MOF's fiscal plans.

It was not until 1984 that the PBOC began functioning as a true central bank and set up the required reserve system. It was only subsequent to that move that China developed a monetary policy in any meaningful sense. And the centralized planning system was replaced by a macro-management system. At this stage, the PBOC began using indirect monetary policy tools, but direct credit management remained its primary policy mechanism. Moreover, it was notable that credit scale management was not decided by the PBOC, which served only as an adviser rather than a decider. The State Council called the shots.

### 1.2. Development stage: 1992–1997

Following Deng Xiaoping's Southern Tour Speech in 1992, China stepped up market-oriented reform activity. The pent-up domestic demands for consumption and investment were unleashed. The money supply was out of control and inflation rose sharply to nearly 20 percent, seriously threatening financial stability. Faced with this ominous risk, Premier Zhu acted decisively to restore financial order and improve the monetary policy system. A number of measures were taken to strengthen the PBOC's macro-management capability. However, because the socialist market economy system had only just been established, monetary policy was constrained by various political factors, which underscored numerous structural flaws.

## *Strengthened indirect management of money supply*

In November 1993, the Communist Party of China (CPC) Central Committee issued "Decisions on Several Issues Concerning the Establishment of a Socialist Market Economy", which explicitly noted that the "PBOC, as China's central bank, implements monetary policies under the leadership of the State Council. It is committed to switching the management model from credit scale management to use of indirect tools, including a required reserve ratio, benchmark interest rates and open market operation, in order to control the money supply and thereby maintain exchange rate stability." At that time, China defined the functions of the central bank and the objectives and tools of monetary policy.

However, direct intervention based on credit scale management is still the primary method of implementing monetary policy. In the third quarter of 1994, the PBOC began publishing money supply indicators. In 1995 appropriate legislation was passed to set the money supply as the most important objective. In 1996 the PBOC began publishing M0, M1 and M2 on a monthly basis. A liquidity management system was basically taking shape.

## *Attempts at interest rate liberalization*

In 1996 experimentation with interest rate liberalization was initiated. At this point, the PBOC focused on interest rates in the money markets and the bond markets, leaving deposit and lending rates untouched. China has typically espoused this kind of incremental approach to reform rather than "big bangs" or "shock therapy"; this is consistent with China's cultural traditions and has applied to all Chinese reform activity.

In June 1996 China established a money market and liberalized the interbank offered rates. A year later, in June 1997, an interbank bond market was set up, and the interbank bond repurchase rate was liberalized. However, it transpired that the policies were more symbolic than practical, given that the infrastructure was still underdeveloped. China's monetary policy still relied on direct intervention through quantity channels instead of indirect management through price channels.

## *Reform of RMB exchange rate regime*

With the development of the opening-up strategy, reform of the RMB exchange rate regime was put on the agenda. From 1978 through 1993, China actually maintained a fixed exchange rate. And because a dual exchange rate system (official price and market price) also existed, this frequently led to market turmoil. In 1994 the PBOC started reforming the old two-track system and

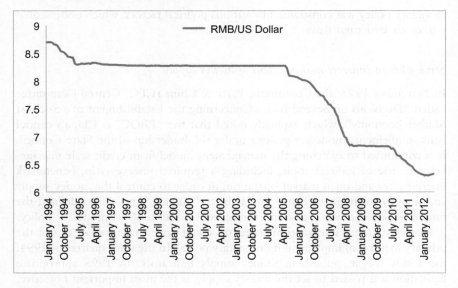

*Figure 8.1* RMB exchange rate
Source: CEIC Data.

announced the establishment of a unitary and well-managed floating exchange rate system based on market supply and demand. In principle, the PBOC set a target range for RMB exchange rates and kept the currency value stable through market operation. Following the 1994 reform, foreign exchange reserves became the primary channels of money supply. China's foreign exchange reserves increased rapidly between 1994 and 1997. Then, during the Asian financial crisis, the pace of growth began to slow down.

Despite having announced the establishment of a well-managed floating exchange rate system, China's policymakers actually preferred to keep the value of the RMB artificially low and thereby enhance the country's export competitiveness. Furthermore, with no capital account in place, the PBOC was able to manipulate the value of the currency through direct intervention in the foreign exchange market. From 1994 through the second reform of the exchange rate system in 2005, the RMB appreciated by only 4 percent despite a large current account surplus. Particularly after the end of the Asian financial crisis, China kept the RMB exchange rate virtually fixed (Figure 8.1). In this context, the PBOC found it difficult to manage the foreign exchange reserves, which were an important source of money supply.

## 1.3. Reform stage: 1998–2001

After the emergence of the Asian financial crisis, China dramatically accelerated reform of its monetary policy regime.

*Abolition of limits on the credit scale*

In 1998 the PBOC abolished the limits on the credit scale and stopped giving lending instructions to banks, indicating that China's monetary policy had almost completed the transition from direct intervention to indirect management. A number of researchers have argued that this transition was the most significant development in the history of China's monetary policy because it meant that China was jettisoning the primary policy tools that had been used for over half a century. However, the transition was not fully complete because interest rate liberalization was not finalized and quantity tools were still regarded as more important than price tools.

*Attempts to reform the interest rate system*

Although interest rates are not completely liberalized, some progress was made on reform of the interest rate system. First, the PBOC began macro-managing interest rates in a more flexible manner. In just one year after the end of the Asian financial crisis, the PBOC cut the rates four times. Second, the floating range for interest rates was extended. Third, discount and rediscount mechanisms were reformed, and the discount rate was liberalized. Fourth, the PBOC promoted liberalization of the money market and the bond market. In September 1998 the policy-type financial bond rate was liberalized.

*Development of money market and open market operation*

The PBOC began developing open market operation. The most important step was to develop money markets, especially a bond market.

It began by strengthening the infrastructure. Chief measures included unifying the interbank market, absorbing qualified security companies and fund management companies into the interbank market and seeking to cultivate market demand. Furthermore, the government stopped apportioning to policy banks and allowed them to issue policy-type financial bonds in a market-type manner. It also sought to lower the cost of bond issues, thereby providing the conditions for the PBOC's open market operation.

Driven by these supportive measures, the interbank bond market developed rapidly, more than doubling in size in 1999. With the development of the money market, an open market operation, which had been virtually non-existent up to 1998, generally took shape in 1999. The money supplied through the PBOC's open market operation accounted for 52 percent of the base money in 1999.

However, foreign exchange purchasing made up most of the open market operation. Worse, because the state-owned banks were reluctant to sell treasury bonds, leading to a lack of transactions in the interbank market, PBOC's open market operation had a negligible effect on the money supply.

*Imposition of "window guidance" on commercial banks*

In China, the "Big Four", including the Industrial and Commercial Bank of China, Agriculture Bank of China, Construction Bank of China and Bank of China, accounted for more than 80 percent of the gross assets of China's banking sector. Until the dawn of the 21st century, nearly 70 percent of loans were controlled by the Big Four. Thus, whether or not the PBOC's monetary policy could exert any effect on the economy depended to a large extent on the behavior of the Big Four. Unfortunately, the Big Four had not established advanced governance structures and incentive systems. Hence, they were not particularly motivated to look for new borrowers while they had ample deposits, especially given the high credit risks due to the financial crisis. In some sense, China's non-market-based environment gave rise to non-market-based policy tools. In order to solve the above-mentioned problems, the government attempted to find a more balanced approach that would stave off bureaucratic fiat but still keep the banks in control. Against this backdrop, "window guidance" came into being.

In March 1998 the PBOC started holding regular analysis meetings on the economic and financial situations, through which the PBOC provided guidance to the banks. On one hand, the PBOC would make monetary policy according to feedback from the banks. On the other hand, window guidance was actually mandatory even though it had not been written into law. So it played an important role in China's monetary policy regime.

### 1.4. Relatively mature stage: 2001–2009

Following China's admission to membership of the World Trade Organization (WTO) in 2001, new economic opportunities opened up and China stepped up integration of its industrial activity with the global production system. This presented new requirements and conditions for reform of the monetary policy regime.

*New channel of money supply: foreign exchange purchasing*

Before 2001 the PBOC conducted an open market operation through reverse purchasing of treasury bonds on the interbank market. The objects of the money supply were the banks rather than enterprises. Commercial banks were reluctant to lend in light of the capital requirements and limits on non-performing loans. Hence, the base money supplied by the PBOC tended to become the excess reserves of commercial banks, and the real economy was at risk of suffering liquidity shortfalls.

In 2001 the PBOC began increasing the money supply through foreign exchange purchasing; this marked a turning point in the history of China's monetary policy regime. Through this approach, the PBOC could easily provide liquidity to the economic entity, which could directly increase money supply. It transpired that China's policymakers were underprepared for the transition. Over subsequent years, China's inflation rate fluctuated to a significant degree.

*New policy tool: central bank bills*

With the shifting model of money supply, China's policymakers sought to identify new tools for managing liquidity. In April 2003 they even created a new financial instrument: the "central bank bill" (or *yangpiao*), the maturity of which differed from those of common treasury bonds and could be as short as three months.

Before 2007 the PBOC used the central bank bill to take back excess liquidity. After 2007 its function changed significantly. The PBOC started using it to guide market sentiment.

*Further progress on interest rate liberalization*

The government drafted a clear roadmap for market liberalization: liberalize rates in the money market and the bond market first, then the lending rate and eventually the deposit rate. At this stage, reform activity was focused on the lending rate and the deposit rate.

In January 2004 the PBOC simultaneously raised both the ceiling and the floor for the lending rate. In October 2004 it abolished the lending rate ceiling and deposit rate floor in order to enable banks to price according to the market. However, the lending rate floor and deposit rate ceiling were maintained.

Despite the significant progress made, it was still a long haul to enable China's interest rates to reflect the real financing cost. With stagnation of interest rate reform since 2004, the inconsistency between official and market rates has been increasingly pronounced, underscoring the need for further reforms.

*Restarting reform of exchange rate regime*

China's exchange rate regime transitioned into a fixed exchange rate system after the first reform of the exchange rate regime in 1994. The value of the RMB was kept stable due to strict capital control and market intervention by the PBOC. While the undervalued RMB played an important role in promoting economic growth, it significantly undermined the effectiveness of monetary policy. With the further opening of China's markets, it was inevitable that there should be a switch from a fixed to a floating exchange rate regime.

Against this backdrop, China initiated the second reform of its exchange rate regime in 2005. The new goal was to establish a managed floating exchange rate regime based on market supply and demand with reference to a basket of currencies. Subsequently, the RMB entered an appreciation cycle, which played an important role in the rapid foreign exchange accumulation.

### 1.5. Reform extension stage: 2009–present

In 2008 the biggest financial crisis since the Great Depression hit the global economy, significantly accelerating the rise of emerging market economies. In 2010 China replaced Japan as the world's second largest economy. But China's financial and monetary systems were still underdeveloped and relatively closed, which was inconsistent with China's rising strength. Most importantly, the RMB was not an international currency, which meant that China's economy was still enslaved to the US dollar. In order to solve this problem, China's policymakers felt it necessary to promote liberalization of the financial system and internationalization of the monetary system.

## Liberalization of the interest rate

Given the potential risk, the government took a relatively conservative position toward liberalization of the financial system, which largely centered on liberalization of the interest rate. On the one hand, the PBOC cut bank loan and deposit rates several times during the crisis. Interest rates were increasingly used for macro-management, and the benchmark interest rate was increasingly rational. On the other hand, the PBOC seized the opportunity to reform the interest rate system. In June 2012 the PBOC adjusted the upper limit for the deposit rate to 1.1 times the benchmark rate and the lower limit for the lending rate to 0.8 times the benchmark rate, which gave the commercial banks more room to price funds. Previously, the deposit rate was exclusively determined by the PBOC, and the commercial banks were not permitted to adjust the deposit rate, which was widely seen as blocking rational pricing of private capital. Subsequently, both the lending rate and the deposit rate were allowed to float, and a new era had begun.

## Internationalization of the RMB

As discussed above, the time seemed ripe for internationalization of the RMB as demand for the currency had increased sharply during the major fluctuations in the values of leading currencies generated by the crisis. For this reason, the government took more measures for RMB internationalization. (Interestingly, mention of RMB internationalization has never appeared in any official Chinese documents, but all of the government's actions pointed to such a strategy.)

It is widely acknowledged that an open capital account is the premise for currency internationalization. Under capital control conditions, the Chinese government could rely only on indirect means.

PROMOTION OF CROSS-BORDER RMB TRADE SETTLEMENT

In order to facilitate international trade for and investment in China's enterprises, the government began experimenting with cross-border RMB trade settlement in five cities (e.g., Shanghai) in 2009, then extended the concept to 20 provinces in 2010. At the same time, the scope of partner countries was extended beyond the members of the Association of Southeast Asian Nations to encompass all countries. In 2011 the experiment was extended to all provinces in China.

DEVELOPMENT OF BILATERAL CURRENCY SWAPPING

China began promoting bilateral currency cooperation with neighboring countries in 2008. To date, China has signed bilateral currency swap arrangements with 18 countries, amounting to 1.67 trillion yuan (Table 8.1). Through currency swap arrangements, the RMB is able to enter these partner countries' financial systems, helping to enhance efficiency in yuan settlement.

DEVELOPMENT OF RMB SETTLEMENT BUSINESS UNDER CAPITAL ACCOUNTS

The PBOC began experimenting with RMB settlement business relating to overseas direct investment in 2010. In 2011 domestic private investors were allowed to use RMB to make overseas direct investments, and foreign investors

*Table 8.1* Bilateral currency swap arrangements between China and other countries

| Date | Partner | Swap value (RMB billion) |
| --- | --- | --- |
| December 12, 2008 | Korea | 180.0 |
| February 8, 2009 | Malaysia | 80.0 |
| March 11, 2009 | Belarus | 20.0 |
| March 23, 2009 | Indonesia | 100.0 |
| April 2, 2009 | Argentina | 70.0 |
| June 9, 2010 | Iceland | 3.5 |
| July 23, 2010 | Singapore | 150.0 |
| April 18, 2011 | New Zealand | 25.0 |
| April 19, 2011 | Uzbekistan | 0.7 |
| May 6, 2011 | Mongolia | 5.0 |
| June 13, 2011 | Kazakhstan | 7.0 |
| January 20, 2009 | Hong Kong | 200.0 |
| October 26, 2011 | Korea | 360.0 |
| November 22, 2011 | Hong Kong | 400.0 |
| December 22, 2011 | Thailand | 70.0 |
| December 23, 2011 | Pakistan | 10.0 |
| January 17, 2012 | United Arab Emirates | 35.0 |
| February 8, 2012 | Malaysia | 180.0 |
| February 21, 2012 | Turkey | 10.0 |
| March 20, 2012 | Mongolia | 10.0 |
| March 22, 2012 | Australia | 200.0 |
| June 26, 2012 | Ukraine | 15.0 |

Source: PBOC website.

were allowed to use RMB to make foreign direct investments. RMB settlement amounts in overseas direct investments and foreign direct investments reached 20.15 billion and 90.72 billion, respectively.

DEVELOPMENT OF THE HONG KONG OFFSHORE RMB MARKET

The value of RMB held in the Hong Kong market increased sharply from less than 56 billion yuan in 2008 to more than 650 billion in 2011; most of this increase resulted from the cross-border yuan trade settlement activities of domestic enterprises. As of 2011 RMB deposits accounted for 10 percent of total deposits in Hong Kong banks, behind only the Hong Kong dollar and US dollar deposit totals. Meanwhile, the number of financial institutions conducting RMB business also increased, from 40 to 132.

FURTHER REFORM OF THE EXCHANGE RATE REGIME

The global financial crisis underscored the flaws in China's exchange rate regime. Several academics argued for liberalization of the exchange rate regime. In June 2010 the PBOC announced its decision to improve the exchange rate system and make the exchange rate more flexible.

Measures included further developing the currency market, introducing over-the-counter transactions and a market maker system; developing an interbank market for RMB forward, swap and option; introducing new hedge tools; promoting overseas investment; and relaxing restrictions on foreign exchange holdings.

FINANCIAL OPENING AND INNOVATION IN THE QIANHAI
SPECIAL FINANCIAL DISTRICT

The Shenzhen Qianhai government has worked hard to create the Qianhai Special Financial District, which has become the bridgehead for RMB internationalization and capital account opening. To date, two reform measures that can be revealed are (a) permitting bi-directional RMB loans between Mainland China and Hong Kong, whereby Hong Kong RMB holders can invest on the mainland by means of bank loans; and (b) cooperating with Hong Kong to develop a capital market, including development of bi-directional RMB cross-border Exchange Traded Fund (ETF) transactions. Through these vehicles, RMB holders in Hong Kong are able to invest in the mainland derivative market, and mainland-based investors have a way to buy ETFs on the Hong Kong market. These measures have been conducive to RMB internationalization and capital account opening.

## 2. Monetary policy targets in China

Since the conferring of the functions of a true central bank on the PBOC in 1984, multi-target decision-making has been a typical model for China's monetary policy regime. As stated by a PBOC official in 2000, "It is rare for a central bank anywhere in the world to undertake so many tasks, such as inflation control, employment incentivization, economic growth, collaboration with fiscal policy to expand domestic demand, guaranteeing of increases in foreign reserves,[1] stabilizing the exchange rate. But China's central government does ask its central bank to achieve all of these goals" (Xie 2000).

In 1995 China enacted the Law on the People's Bank of China, declaring that the target of monetary policy is to maintain stability of the value of the RMB, thereby promoting economic growth. This was the first time the PBOC had set up a single-target model. But there has always been robust debate about single-target models in China. This law could be passed in 1995 because China had experienced high inflation during 1993–1994. In fact, the central bank promptly switched from inflation targeting to growth targeting after 1997 because inflation had gone into negative territory in that year. Up to that point, the central bank had actually been making multi-target decisions.

Although several economists, both Chinese and foreign, believe that monetary policy can never achieve multiple targets, China's central bank has pursued this model over a long period. One reason is that the PBOC is not an independent agency. Another is that, as an emerging economy, China has experienced such rapid economic growth during the last three decades that its government has had to deal with numerous unforeseen issues during a time when the monetary policy regime was still largely in the planning stages. Perhaps there is a third reason. China's traditional culture sets high store by adoption of a comprehensive perspective in order to deal with multiple issues. Many Chinese officials and economists do not believe that a central bank, operating as a large agency, should undertake only a single task. They argue that the central government should carry out multiple policies (e.g., should integrate fiscal policy, monetary policy and other policies) to achieve multiple targets.

The US financial crisis and the eurozone crisis clearly demonstrated that a central bank has to serve as the lender of last resort in the event of a serious crisis. Even under normal financial market conditions, most national governments now hold the view that a central bank should be responsible for financial stability, which means that the bank has at least two targets. In an era of financial deepening and globalization, a central bank cannot meet the requirement of good economic governance solely through inflation targeting. Without doubt, monetary policy will have to play a key role going forward despite the difficulties entailed in meeting those demands.

Consequently, the PBOC will stick with the multi-target decision-making model. In fact, in the wake of the global financial crisis, the responsibilities of the PBOC could be generalized as four tasks: economic growth, inflation control, financial stability and internationalization of the RMB. The fourth target is a new one, last but not least. Some people regard stability of the exchange rate as a key target for China's central bank. They are right, but the PBOC's real concern with respect to the exchange rate is economic growth.

Almost everyone at the PBOC would admit that a central bank cannot achieve so many goals at once. For the PBOC, the key task is to formulate a discretionary policy so that it can meet whatever may be the most important or most urgent need of the central government. At certain times, the PBOC may be required to spur domestic demand in order to combat depression, as happened in 1997–1998 and 2008–2009. At other times the PBOC may be occupied with controlling inflation, as was the case in 2011. So the real implication of the multi-target decision-making model is that the PBOC must be ready to switch to a different core target as the situation requires. If some targets conflict with one or more other targets at a particular point, such as inflation control and economic growth, the PBOC will always choose to target growth. To a large extent, growth targeting was appropriate for China in the past, while it was a developing country.

Besides the four targets mentioned above, the PBOC is also engaged in a very important mission: financial reform and opening. China had a real monetary policy until 1984; since then, the PBOC has done its best to transition the former planned system into a marketing system. So, compared to its counterparts in advanced economies, China's central bank has had to deal with many more issues. Over the last three decades, China has succeeded in reforming and opening its real economy. But in the financial market area, there is still a lot of work to be done. Recently, interest rate liberalization, entry of private capital into the financial industry and capital account opening have begun to accelerate. Given the unhealthy global economic situation and the fact that the transition of domestic development patterns is at a difficult stage, the PBOC is definitely facing major challenges. Without doubt, the PBOC will stick with the multi-target decision-making model. But how can PBOC make a trade-off if the growth objective conflicts with other targets? We don't exactly know. In the authors' view, the most important goal for the PBOC is to firmly and comprehensively realize financial marketization reform and opening, which will at least ensure sustainable economic development. In other words, reform targeting should be a priority for the PBOC.

## 3. The monetary policy transmission mechanism

With today's financial deepening and globalization, monetary policy transmission mechanisms are becoming more effective and widespread in China. Open market operation, deposit reserve ratio, rediscounting, the RMB counterpart of foreign exchange reserves, the interest rate and the PBOC's proposals constitute the nation's main transmission mechanism.

Since interest rate controls are in place, the most effective methods for adjusting the money supply in China are open market operation and the deposit reserve ratio. In recent years, under the crawling peg exchange rate system, an excessive current account surplus with capital inflow forced the PBOC to generate a large amount of RMB counterparts of foreign exchange reserves. The PBOC had to employ sterilized intervention, including open market operation and a deposit reserve ratio, to stabilize the monetary base. Many years' practice shows that sterilized intervention is effective, indicating that the above transmission mechanism works well.

The PBOC's proposals are also an effective tool in implementing China's monetary policy. At the PBOC's suggestion, Chinese commercial banks are actively engaged in the business of cross-border RMB trade settlement, which is making an excellent contribution to rapid development of internationalization of the RMB. Another PBOC suggestion, that all commercial banks set a quota of loans for small and very small companies, significantly improved availability of loans for such companies in 2011. A number of foreign economists and bankers argue that government suggestions and guidance to commercial banks are a non-market approach, which is very risky because the ratio of non-performing loans will rise. But the situation in China is special. Most Chinese commercial banks are state controlled, and they are strongly motivated to issue loans to state-owned companies because it is the "politically correct" thing to do. Although many small companies (clearly private companies) are running very well, they would previously have struggled to get loans from banks. Thanks to the suggestion made by the PBOC, well-performing private companies get loans, and the banks profit from these arrangements.

But planning-style monetary tools are not an appropriate way to encourage sustainable economic development over the long term. With financial deepening, the PBOC will steadily move away from employing planning approaches.

## 4. Achievements of China's monetary policy

### 4.1. Policy achievements before the 2008–2009 crisis

#### Increasing capacity to cope with inflation

In the late 1980s, China's monetary policy underwent its first test as inflation soared. After the second half of 1989, the PBOC began to tighten monetary policy significantly. In order to control credit growth, the PBOC even returned to mandatory plans on credit scale and created some special deposits. It was not surprising that the suddenly tightened policy produced immediate effects. China saw a period of low inflation from 1990 through 1992. However, this policy brake turned out to be palliative, and the overheating of economic fundamentals continued. Without the support of structural reforms and improvement of economic fundamentals, the inflation risk could flare up again (Figure 8.2).

Developments in subsequent years confirmed our worst fears. After 1992 the inflation rate increased sharply to hit a record high of nearly 30 percent. There were many reasons for this, most important of which was the turmoil in the financial system. Market liquidity was out of control owing to an imperfect monitoring system, resulting in over-investment in real estate and the stock market. Against that backdrop, the PBOC continued to adhere to a tight policy, but this proved to be ineffective because high inflation persisted for nearly three years.

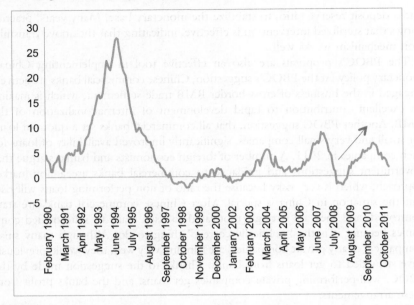

*Figure 8.2* Consumer price index: 1990–2013 (%, year-on-year)
Source: CEIC Data.

The policymakers came to realize that it was much more important to reform macro-management of liquidity than to take measures under the old framework. Thanks to the accelerating reforms, inflation started falling in 1994 and returned to normal in 1996.

This experience helped to significantly enhance the government's ability to manage inflation, and the inflation level has been kept moderate over a lengthy period, with China strongly outperforming other emerging market economies, such as India and Russia, in this respect.

### Successful responses to the Asian financial crisis

When the Asian financial crisis struck, the government had two important tasks to accomplish. First, as export and domestic demand began to decline sharply in 1998, the policymakers needed to expand the money supply, a mission that was heavily reliant on increasing bank lending, in order to promote economic recovery. However, because of the requirement imposed by the central government that banks must keep a low non-performing loans ratio, most commercial banks were reluctant to lend. So the government had to take measures to increase banks' willingness to lend money to private sector businesses.

Second, the competitive currency devaluations in some Asian countries exerted strong pressure on the RMB exchange rate and on China's exports. If not properly managed, the RMB exchange rate could have fallen sharply and led to significant chaos in the monetary system and the financial market.

Given the domestic and foreign environment, China's government took various measures to loosen the money supply and maintain stringent control of the capital account in order to maintain a fixed exchange rate for the RMB. These actions enabled China to successfully weather the storm and bring both inflation and economic growth back to normal levels. Most notably, economic growth was maintained at a high level even during the crisis (7.6 percent in 1998 and 1999).

## 4.2. Policy achievements since the 2008–2009 crisis

### Ensuring adequate liquidity to spur economic growth

When Lehman Brothers went bankrupt on September 18, 2008, and the financial crisis rapidly escalated, China immediately switched its monetary policy from "prudent" to "moderately loose". Then the PBOC implemented a series of actions designed to provide sufficient liquidity.

*Providing liquidity through open market operation.* In July 2008 the PBOC began to slow the pace of bond and bill issues in order to ensure adequate liquidity in the market. At the same time, the PBOC increasingly used short-term bills rather than long-term bonds because the bills were more flexible and could help enhance the flexibility of monetary policy and the resilience of China's financial system against liquidity shocks. As economic conditions improved, the PBOC restarted issuing bonds with maturities of more than one year in order to keep the money supply under control. In addition, the PBOC created a Term Auction Facility to provide adequate resources to troubled financial institutions.

*Cutting benchmark lending and deposit rates.* The PBOC cut the benchmark lending and deposit rates on September 16, one day after the Lehman Shock. Over subsequent months, the interest rates were cut five times, reaching historic lows of 2.25 percent for deposits and 5.4 percent for loans; this helped to lower financing costs and increase the money supply. In October 2010 the PBOC started to raise the rates again out of concern about an over-supply of money.

*Cutting the required reserve ratio.* The PBOC cut the required reserve ratio for commercial banks four times, from 17.5 percent on September 25, 2008, to 13.5 percent at the end of 2009. Then, with the money supply rapidly increasing again, the PBOC started raising the required reserve ratio in January 2010.

*Abolishing the credit limit on commercial banks.* The PBOC intended to increase the flexibility of the credit market and thereby provide the private sector with sufficient funds. However, due to the waning risk appetite during the crisis, banks' unwillingness to lend still significantly hampered the credit market.

All of these measures contributed toward ensuring provision of sufficient liquidity. After several cuts in benchmark interest rates and the required reserve ratio, M2 grew by 17.8 percent in 2008, 29.7 percent in 2009 and 19.7 percent in 2010. So there can be no doubt that China's monetary policy was quite

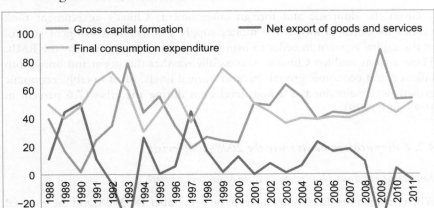

*Figure 8.3* Contribution to GDP growth (%)
Source: CEIC Data.

aggressive following the crisis, especially its credit market policy, which certainly had a significant impact in terms of supporting economic growth.

Thanks to the positive monetary policy and fiscal policy, China's economy maintained strong growth during the crisis. In November 2008 the State Council put forward a stimulus package amounting to 4 trillion yuan. At the same time, the PBOC reduced financing costs and encouraged banks to lend through window guidance. None of these projects could have worked without the support of monetary policy.

Driven by the rapid growth in bank loans, investment in infrastructure projects such as transportation facilities increased sharply, stimulating demand for manufacturing materials such as iron and steel. The contribution to gross domestic product (GDP) growth by gross capital formation increased from 46.9 percent in 2009 to hit a record high level. As shown in Figure 8.3, when the export market deteriorated sharply and private consumption remained weak, the only path to economic recovery was to rely on investment demand.

The strong demand for investment led to a strong rebound in China's economic growth. The four-season decline in the GDP growth rate, from 11.3 percent in the first quarter of 2008 to 6.5 percent in the first quarter of 2009, came to an end in the second quarter of 2009. And the economy grew by 8.9 percent in 2009, surpassing the government's target of 8 percent. Economic growth in the following four years reached 10.4 percent (2010), 9.4 percent (2011), 7.7 percent (2012) and 7.7 percent (2013). As shown in Figure 8.4, China's economic growth did best during the crisis, while both other developing countries and developed countries all experienced sharp declines in 2009 and 2010.

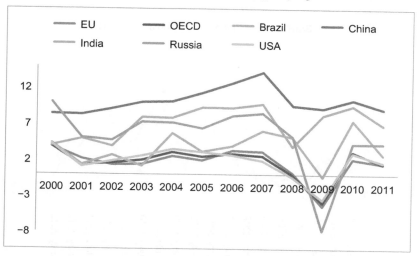

*Figure 8.4* GDP growth for major countries (%, year-on-year)
Source: CEIC Data.

Note: EU: European Union; OECD: Organisation for Economic Co-operation and Development.

## Controlling inflation

Compared to the other emerging market countries, China's management of inflation during the crisis seemed to be more successful.

In 2007, as the subprime mortgage crisis worsened, China's external environment changed significantly. However, domestic economic fundamentals seemed to be very strong, even showing some upward movement. After the rapid growth of the previous seven years, inflation was poised to go high again. In light of the difference between internal and external conditions, the government made the risk of inflation its top priority and took timely and effective containment measures. The prudent policy that had been followed for the preceding seven years was replaced by a tight policy in the second half of 2007, which immediately worked to lower the inflation rate over the subsequent months.

In the wake of the Lehman Shock, further deterioration in global demand gave rise to a significant deflation risk. The PBOC immediately switched its monetary policy to "accommodative", which not only averted the deflation risk but also avoided a high inflation rate, as was experienced by the other emerging market countries. Compared to the situations in other BRIC countries (Brazil, Russia, India and China), and Brazil in particular, China's inflation rate appeared to be much more stable (Figure 8.5). Although China's inflation rate was significantly affected by global market conditions, as were those of the other emerging countries, the PBOC's hand was not weakened to the same extent, and it succeeded in containing the external shock.

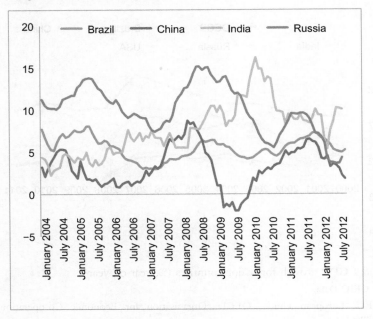

*Figure 8.5* Inflation rates for BRIC nations (%)
Source: CEIC Data.
Note: The BRIC nations are Brazil, Russia, India and China.

## Limiting real estate prices

The mind-boggling magnitude of banking loans not only stimulated the real economy but also caused upward pressure on real estate prices. The real estate price average fell sharply in 2008 and in the first half of 2009, then began to boom under the expansionary monetary policy in late 2009, reaching a high point in 2010.

Against that backdrop, the government began pushing down prices through direct interventions. The major step was to increase the financing cost for home purchases and tighten credit in the real estate market. Moreover, the government imposed a number of purchasing restrictions on residential real estate. Together, these measures contributed to preventing excessive price increases.

From the real estate price index in 70 major cities, it is easy to observe the significant reversal in price after the highest point in 2010 (Figure 8.6). Overall, the timely policy responses had a positive impact on the real estate market. However, the real estate price in 70 major cities boomed again at the beginning of 2013.

## Improving the national welfare

The special monetary policy regime with unique Chinese characteristics showed its superiority during the global financial crisis. Through extensive intervention, the PBOC made a significant contribution to the national welfare.

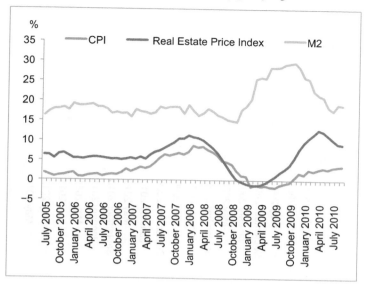

*Figure 8.6* Real estate price index in 70 major cities and M2
Source: Wind Data.

*Livelihood projects.* The PBOC instructed the banks to lend to some important livelihood projects such as health care, education and social security. For example, 12.6 billion yuan of new bank loans were channeled into financing affordable housing projects, which contributed to alleviating housing shortage problems.

*Support for small and very small firms.* The PBOC also focused on increasing lending to small and very small firms and thereby stimulating employment. Under the PBOC's guidance, the commercial banks did lend more to small and very small firms than they normally would have. However, owing to risk aversion on the part of the banks, some 73 percent of the loans went to large state-owned enterprises, which meant that a significant number of small businesses got into financial trouble and many went bankrupt.

*Employment.* The rapid economic recovery had a positive impact on employment and the national average income. Although China's official data may be less than precise, the trend revealed in the data was still noteworthy. In this case, a significant decline in the registered unemployment rate (Figure 8.7) and a rebound in disposable income (Figure 8.8) would seem to support our contention that both employment and the national average income improved as a result of the growth-friendly monetary policy.

### Significant progress on RMB internationalization

The international standing of the RMB improved significantly as a result of the measures mentioned below. First, cross-border yuan trade settlement experienced rapid development. Settlement amounts were 3.58 billion yuan in 2009, 506.31

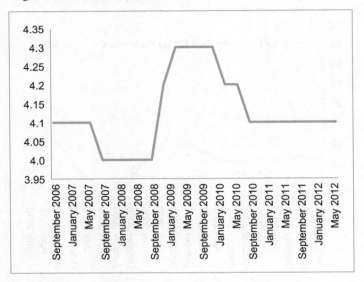

*Figure 8.7* The registered unemployment rate (%)
Source: CEIC Data.

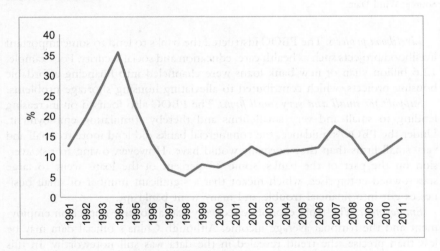

*Figure 8.8* Growth of disposable income per capita for urban households
Source: CEIC Data.

billion yuan in 2010, 2.08 trillion yuan in 2011, 2.94 trillion yuan in 2012 and 4.63 trillion yuan in 2013 (Figure 8.9).

Driven by the supportive policies and strong market demand, the RMB became one of the most important settlement currencies in China's cross-border trade. The proportion of RMB settlement in international trade increased from 0.04 percent in 2009 to about 10 percent in 2011 (Figure 8.10).

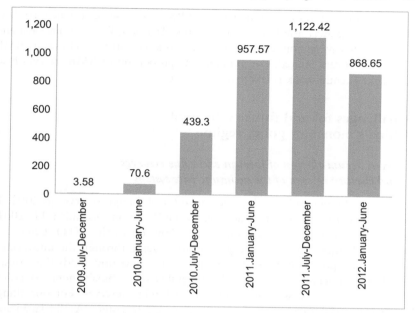

*Figure 8.9* Cross-border yuan trade settlement amounts
Source: People's Bank of China website.

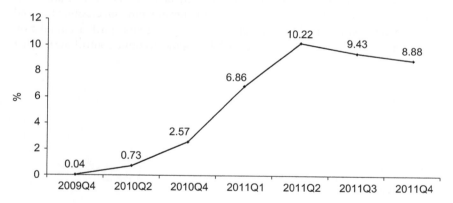

*Figure 8.10* Proportion of RMB settlement in China's international trade
Source: PBOC website.

Second, the RMB was more widely used in neighboring countries, especially those closely linked to China through bilateral trade.

Third, an exchange system between the RMB and several foreign currencies was established. As of 2011, there were nine foreign currencies, including US dollars, euros, yen, Hong Kong dollars, pounds and other major currencies, that could be directly exchanged for RMB in China's currency market.

Fourth, some countries began to adopt the RMB as a reserve currency. To date, South Korea, Malaysia, the Republic of Belarus, Thailand, Russia, Cambodia and the Philippines have announced the RMB as a reserve currency. However, RMB reserves remain very limited. For example, the proportion of RMB reserves held by Thailand's central bank is less than 1 percent.

## 5. Challenges for and future reform of China's monetary policy regime

### 5.1. Excess accumulation of foreign exchange reserves and further reform of the exchange rate system

China initiated rapid and ongoing accumulation of foreign reserves in 2002. It should be noted that China formally joined the WTO on December 11, 2001. This was no coincidence. As a result of its admission to the WTO, China has become the biggest winner in the globalization game through the unexpected growth of its export industries. As a by-product, China now holds the world's largest foreign reserves. Besides its WTO membership, China's monetary policy contributed to the excessive accumulation of foreign reserves. For one thing, China has not established a free-floating exchange rate system. As did Japan and Korea in their respective economic take-off phases, China encourages export-oriented development by means of a pegged exchange rate system. Although the PBOC declared the adoption of a managed floating system in 2005, it is clear that export industries and related departments in China successfully blocked rapid appreciation of the RMB, thereby sustaining ongoing quick accumulation of foreign reserves (Figure 8.11). Meanwhile, capital account control meant that

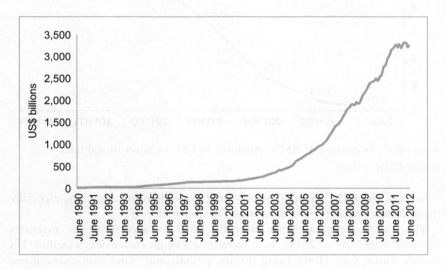

*Figure 8.11* China's foreign exchange reserves
Source: Wind Data.

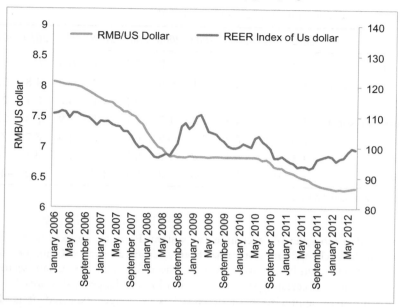

*Figure 8.12* RMB exchange rate LHS for RMB/US Dollar, and the RHS for REER Index of Us dollar

Source: CEIC Data.

the private sector and residuals in China could not easily invest abroad; consequently, foreign reserves were concentrated in the hands of the PBOC.

From July 2007, when the PBOC announced the launch of a managed floating system, to the end of 2011, appreciation of the RMB against the US dollar amounted to 31.5 percent (Figure 8.12). Because of the appreciation of the currency and falling external demand, China's current account surplus quickly dropped from 10.1 percent in 2007 to 2.8 percent in 2011, which was already much lower than those of Germany and Russia (Table 8.2). As a result, annualized growth of foreign reserves was only 3.7 percent in the first half of 2012, compared to 31.1 percent from 2001 through 2011.

From the end of 2011, the RMB showed a slight depreciation trend against the US dollar. From December 30, 2011, through September 14, 2012, the RMB declined by 0.3 percent against the greenback. Three factors account for this depreciation. First, the euro crisis forced large-scale deleveraging by Western financial institutions. Second, there was popular expectation of a slowdown of China's economic growth. Third, the RMB has actually achieved a clear appreciation. Some economists even argue that the RMB is already overvalued. In other words, unilateral appreciation of the RMB has been broken, which means that significant progress has been made on reforming China's exchange rate system.

However, the reform is far from a total success. According to the International Monetary Fund's classification of exchange rate regimes, China is still using a crawling peg-like arrangement. Whether the RMB is undervalued or overvalued,

*Table 8.2* Current account surplus to GDP ratio (%)

|  | 2002 | 2003 | 2004 | 2005 | 2006 | 2007 | 2008 | 2009 | 2010 | 2011 |
|---|---|---|---|---|---|---|---|---|---|---|
| Germany | 2.0 | 1.9 | 4.7 | 5.1 | 6.3 | 7.5 | 6.2 | 6.0 | 6.2 | 5.7 |
| Russian Federation | 8.4 | 8.2 | 10.1 | 11.1 | 9.6 | 6.0 | 6.2 | 4.0 | 4.8 | 5.3 |
| China | 2.4 | 2.8 | 3.6 | 5.9 | 8.6 | 10.1 | 9.1 | 5.2 | 5.1 | 2.8 |
| Republic of Korea | 1.3 | 2.4 | 4.5 | 2.2 | 1.5 | 2.1 | 0.3 | 3.9 | 2.8 | 2.4 |
| Japan | 2.8 | 3.2 | 3.7 | 3.6 | 3.9 | 4.9 | 3.3 | 2.9 | 3.7 | 2.0 |
| India | 1.4 | 1.4 | 0.1 | −1.2 | −1.0 | −0.7 | −2.5 | −1.9 | −3.1 | — |
| Brazil | −1.5 | 0.8 | 1.8 | 1.6 | 1.3 | 0.1 | −1.7 | −1.5 | −2.2 | −2.1 |

Source: World Bank Website.

China needs a more flexible exchange rate system. From the outset, liberalizing reform of the exchange rate system has been a sensitive issue for China because it would affect a number of areas, in both the public and the private sectors. Thus, the PBOC is certainly still faced with a big challenge in this area.

Since unilateral appreciation of the RMB is no longer expected, it is also doubtful whether PBOC intervention in currency valuation is still necessary. In fact, some economists believe that the RMB now has a relatively firm basis for becoming a floating currency. During the last seven years, the PBOC has pursued a gradual reform of the exchange rate system and recorded considerable achievements. It is very likely that the PBOC will continue its prudent and gradual approach to reform. In April 2012 the PBOC announced a widening of the floating band of RMB trading prices against the US dollar on the interbank spot foreign exchange market, from 0.5 percent to 1 percent, which definitely enhanced the flexibility of the RMB exchange rate in both directions. The next step of the reform is to further widen the floating band of the RMB rate. The RMB still has a relatively long way to go before it becomes a fully floating currency.

### 5.2. Opening of the capital account

Faced with a macroeconomic policy trilemma in an open economy, China's government has maintained a combination of independent monetary policy, a fixed exchange rate system (the "crawling peg" adjustment method used since 2005 was similar to a fixed exchange rate) and capital account controls, which strongly supported rapid economic growth. However, capital control has resulted in over-accumulation of official foreign reserves and, to some extent, has impaired the independence of China's monetary policy. Moreover, in the context of RMB internationalization, capital control also made the RMB less attractive to foreign investors. In short, it is imperative to step up the opening of the capital account.

*Potential risk: significant but manageable*

Undeniably, opening of the capital account would create significant risk. However, given the special case of China, most of the potential risks can be managed.

First, the risk of currency mismatches resulting from capital account liberalization is relatively low. According to PBOC statistics, about 98 percent of deposits in and 95 percent of loans by commercial banks are denominated in RMB.

Second, most of China's foreign exchange reserves assets are in the form of bonds, and exchange rate volatility would not affect repayments of principal and interest.

Third, as of 2011, China's foreign exchange reserves had reached a record high of 3.18 trillion dollars, enough to withstand the capital outflows after opening of the capital account. Furthermore, given China's economic fundamentals and growth prospects, which are much better than those of other emerging market countries, it is doubtful that a large-scale capital outflow would have occurred.

Fourth, the proportion of short-term external debt in China's total debt is relatively low. As of 2011, the short-term external debt was US$507.6 billion, or about 15.9 percent of official foreign exchange reserves. China's government has plenty of money to handle any potential risk due to short-term capital outflows.

Fifth, risk in the real estate market and capital market appears to be manageable. In 2010 the amounts of foreign direct investment in real estate and business services were US$24 billion and US$7.1 billion, respectively, or just 6.6 percent of the international payments surplus for that year. Foreign investment in the capital market was much lower. As of 2012, the quotas for 117 Qualified Foreign Institutional Investors (QFII) and 17 RMB Qualified Foreign Institutional Investors (RQFII) were US$22.24 billion and 20 billion yuan.

For all of the above reasons, opening of the capital account need not be conditional on liberalization of the interest rate and the exchange rate. In fact, one of the main reasons why the PBOC is dedicated to promotion of RMB internationalization is its desire to strengthen capital account opening, which would also stimulate liberalization of the exchange rate and the interest rate at the same time. This is a piece of political wisdom known as a "reverse transmission mechanism". In a sense, China's joining the WTO is a typical successful case of a reverse transmission mechanism.

*Roadmap*

In February 2012 the PBOC released a roadmap for opening of the capital account. Generally, the principle is "inflow before outflow, long-term before short-term, agencies before individuals".

(A) SHORT-TERM STRATEGY (1–3 YEARS)

Loosen restrictions on investment based on real deals and encourage firms to venture offshore.

Foreign direct investment is less vulnerable to the business cycle, so loosening restrictions on it is less risky. Given the excessive domestic investment and foreign exchange reserves, it is imperative and valuable for China to increase investment abroad. Moreover, the appreciation of the RMB has lowered the cost of investment, and the financial crisis has increased demand for RMB investment.

### (B) MEDIUM-TERM STRATEGY (3–5 YEARS)

Loosen restrictions on commercial loans based on real deals and promote RMB internationalization.

Commercial loans based on real deals are mostly related to the current account. China's exports and imports accounted for 10 percent of global trade, and China's commercial loans accounted for more than 25 percent of the world's commercial loans. Loosening restrictions on commercial loans would be conducive to promotion of growth in international trade and would provide circumfluence channels for the RMB in the Hong Kong offshore market. It would also be conducive to reinforcement of competition among domestic banks.

### (C) LONG-TERM STRATEGY (5–10 YEARS)

Strengthen financial markets; liberalize capital inflows first, then outflows; and replace the quantitative limit with price management.

Transactions in real estate, stocks and the bond market are linked to both investment demand and speculative demand. It is always difficult for us to distinguish between the two kinds of demand. So, given the potential risk, we should open the more developed markets first. As a general rule, the principle is to open "the primary market before the secondary market" and "nonresidential domestic transactions before residential foreign transactions", which could help to reduce the risks associated with the reform.

### 5.3. Liberalization of interest rates

#### Potential challenges

China extended the floating ranges of lending and deposit rates and revived promotion of liberalization of the interest rate in June 2012, demonstrating both determination and confidence in the reform. However, there are quite a few challenges ahead on the road to reform.

First, the reform could impair the stability of commercial banks. China's commercial banks used to rely on the spreads between deposit rates and lending rates, which accounted for 80 percent of the banks' profits. Intermediary business was a fairly weak point. If the interest rate were to be fully liberalized, the deposit rate would rise, and the spreads would be narrowed. For example, following the adjustment in June, the spreads decreased, which reduced the profits of some banks. Worse, the commercial banks lent a lot of money during the 2008–2009 crisis, and the number of non-performing loans increased, impairing their resilience against losses. All of these would make it more difficult to further liberalize the interest rate in the near future.

Second, the reform is not conducive to improving the market structure of the banking system, which could lead to reinforcement of the monopoly held by state-owned big banks. Small banks' profitability could be significantly impaired because they rely heavily on traditional business, which would shrink as the spread between deposit and lending rates narrowed. Competition in the banking system would become increasingly fierce. In order to attract more depositors and borrowers, the banks have to cut lending rates and raise deposit rates, which would increase their costs and reduce revenues. Compared to small banks, the state-owned banks enjoy significant advantages. They not only possess more capital and resources but also enjoy government guarantees. So a number of small banks could go bankrupt, making it harder for small and very small companies to secure financing.

## Policy priority

(A) IMPROVE THE INTEREST RATE SYSTEM AND TRANSMISSION MECHANISM

The principle for interest rate reform is to let the market determine interest rates. China will step up construction of the transmission mechanism on the basis of Shibor (the Shanghai interbank offer rate). Then, the PBOC will use monetary policy tools to indirectly manage market interest rates, which will affect the interest rate behavior of financial institutions. Firms and individuals will respond to the rates through adjustments to consumption and investment. First, the government should link the prices of marketized products to Shibor. Specifically, short-term financial products and financial bonds should come first, and then long-term financial products and corporate bonds would follow. Then, deposit and lending rates should be linked to Shibor.

(B) PROMOTE TRANSITIONS BY COMMERCIAL BANKS

With the interest rate liberalized, the commercial banks will have to focus on a market orientation, which will require the banks to reform their internal management systems and keep abreast of customer needs. It is also imperative for the banks to develop a new profit model centered on intermediary business.

(C) PROVIDE SUPPORT MEASURES

The government should also attach major importance to support measures such as a deposit insurance system, which would help to protect depositors' interests and prevent potential financial risks.

In sum, we have confidence in liberalization of the interest rate in China. The financial institutions will become more competitive under the pressure, just as our people have. There were similar concerns that foreign firms would outpace our companies when China joined the WTO in 2001; however, China succeeded in surmounting all of the difficulties and became the "world factory" over the last 10 years. In addition, Chinese companies learned a great deal through buying foreign enterprises, and we will continue to act modestly and keep learning from other countries.

## 6. Brief conclusion

Some economists believe that China has already missed its best chance for financial marketization reform and opening. In our view, such a judgment is not easily justified. Economic reform is by no means a theoretical calculation. It is almost impossible to find an optimal solution for a country's reforms. We only need to find a satisfactory solution. As long as the Chinese central government and the PBOC steadfastly pursue financial reform and opening over the near term, China will build a well-performing monetary policy regime and accomplish its economic transformation, thereby becoming a powerful player on the world financial stage, just as it previously did in the manufacturing sphere.

## Note

1 In the 1990s China did not accumulate sufficient foreign reserves, so it was important for the PBOC to ensure an increase in such reserves.

## References and Further Readings

Becker, S. 2007. *Global Liquidity "Glut" and Asset Price Inflation: Fact or Fiction?* May 29. Deutsche Bank Research, Frankfurt am Main, http://www.docin.com/p-232912717.html.
Communist Party of China Central Committee. 1993. Decisions on Several Issues Concerning the Establishment of a Socialist Market Economy. November (Article 19).
Cui, Jian Jun. 2008. Historical Evolution of China's Financial and Fiscal Policy. *Economist (China)*, No.3, Pages 106–112.
Dai, Gen You. 2000. Theoretical and Practical Issues of China's Monetary Policy. *Journal of Financial Research*, No.9, Pages 1–12.
Xie, Ping. 2000. Challenge of China's Monetary Policy in the New Century. *Journal of Financial Research*, No.1, Pages 1–4.
Yu, Yong Ding. 2007. Understand the Liquidity Glut. *International Economic Review*, No.4, Pages 5–7.
Zhang, Bin. 2012. Why to Increase the Elasticity of China's Foreign Exchange Rate. *CEEM Review*, June 2. Working Paper, Institute of World Economics and Politics.

# 9 Monetary policy regime in Indonesia

*Solikin M. Juhro and Miranda S. Goeltom*

## 1. Introduction

The monetary policy regime in Indonesia has been significantly affected by rapid changes in the macroeconomic environment, structural adjustments, and a dynamic political climate over the last four decades. As we know, Indonesia has undergone a number of far-reaching structural adjustments in all economic sectors since the early 1970s. These adjustments, which were fostered by accelerating globalization and two major financial crises in 1997–8 and 2008–9, have had major implications for monetary management. Before the financial crisis of 1997–8, monetary policy in Indonesia was characterized by a shift from one regime to another. It started with the credit and interest rate control policy, coupled with the exchange rate and capital flow management, which were relatively restrained in the 1970s. Monetary targeting was sequentially implemented in the era of financial sector deregulation, with a more market mechanism-based monetary management approach in operation from the early 1980s through the first half of the 1990s. During this period, the Indonesian economy was in a boom phase with ample foreign capital flows.

The aftermath of the financial crisis of 1997–8 was a period in which the monetary policy regime was directed at implementation of the inflation targeting framework (ITF) with a strong emphasis on institutional and governance development aspects. In the early 2000s, despite the substantial progress made following the process of recovery from the crisis, the economy was still burdened by various constraints and problems. The main challenges confronting the Indonesian economy were to maintain stability amid rising global uncertainty and to accelerate growth. In the second half of the 2000s, amid the struggle to reinforce macroeconomic performance, monetary management was confronted with a series of fundamental challenges associated with occurrence of the global financial crisis (GFC) of 2008–9. In a climate of high global uncertainty, the GFC significantly affected not only the domestic financial system and macroeconomic developments in the region but also how monetary policy should be implemented.

Related to the above background, one important policy issue that needs to be addressed is the "impossible trinity" (the monetary policy trilemma). In practice, in line with the increase in global financial market integration and large capital flows that impose pressures and complications on implementation of monetary policy, there is a tendency for monetary authorities to prefer to shift from a "corner solution" to a "middle solution", particularly in developing countries. It is widely argued that there should be a more accommodative response that takes into account the concept of managing exchange rate movements within a certain range (not fully flexible) and restricts movements of foreign capital.

In the case of Indonesia, the orientation of monetary policy in the midst of high global uncertainty is tactically directed not only toward controlling inflation but also toward managing the exchange rate in a specified range, in line with macroeconomic fundamentals, through quite active interventions in the foreign exchange market. In addition, the monetary policy regime simultaneously manages international reserves at safe levels. This condition has a logical consequence whereby the exchange rate dynamic will not be completely influenced by market forces but will also be strongly influenced by domestic monetary policy (Juhro, 2010b). Quantitatively, this is reflected in the decomposition of co-movement between exchange rate and capital flows, which decreased significantly, from 86 percent during the financial crisis of 1997–8 to 53 percent during the post-GFC period (Table 9.1). Meanwhile, the decomposition of co-movement between the exchange rate and the interest rate differential increased significantly, from 14 percent to 47 percent.

Table 9.2 provides strong empirical evidence that there is a tendency for monetary policy strategy to move away from that which is hypothesized by the monetary policy trilemma. With regard to the trilemma index developed by Aizenman et al. (2008), it can also be seen that over the last 15 years, along with the high degree of integration between Indonesian financial markets and global financial markets and improvement in domestic monetary policy autonomy, exchange rate developments have tended to be more stable.

These facts trigger additional complications in the implementation of ITF-based monetary policy in the context of a small open economy such as that of

*Table 9.1* Co-movement of exchange rate with capital inflows and interest rate differential

|  | 1997–2000 1997–8 crisis | 2001–5 Trend of ITF | 2006–8 ITF pre-GFC | 2009–13 GFC to post-GFC |
|---|---|---|---|---|
| Capital inflows (net foreign assets) | 0.86 | 0.74 | 0.56 | 0.53 |
| Interest rate differential | 0.14 | 0.26 | 0.44 | 0.47 |

Source: Juhro (2010b), updated.

Note: GFC: global financial crisis; ITF: inflation targeting framework.

*Table 9.2* Indonesian monetary policy trilemma index

|  | 1997–2000 | 2001–5 | 2006–8 | 2009–13 |
|---|---|---|---|---|
|  | 1997–8 crisis | Trend of ITF | ITF pre-GFC | GFC to post-GFC |
| Exchange rate stability | 0.11 | 0.27 | 0.25 | 0.28 |
| Monetary policy autonomy | 0.45 | 0.30 | 0.50 | 0.57 |
| Financial market integration | 0.74 | 0.69 | 0.69 | 0.71 |

Source: Juhro (2010b), updated.

Note: GFC: global financial crisis; ITF: inflation targeting framework.

Indonesia. This is because the hypothesized role of the exchange rate as a shock absorber is not completely fulfilled, and, on the other hand, there is a tendency for the monetary authority to steer monetary policy, directly or indirectly, toward managing the exchange rate. Amid a deluge of foreign capital inflows, a policy orientation toward managing external balances can become counterproductive to central bank liquidity management in the money market.

This chapter focuses on two questions. First, how has the monetary policy authority coped with these challenges? Second, does the assessment suggest a need for changes in the monetary policy framework or monetary policy regimes in terms of monetary policy autonomy, exchange rate stability, and capital mobility, i.e., the impossible trinity? Thus, it explores rational arguments for the monetary authority to confront these issues, specifically, how to optimally transform the impossible trinity into a possible trinity.

It can be shown that in a small open economy such as that of Indonesia, the multiple challenges faced by monetary policy as a result of capital flow dynamics, amid inflationary pressures, imply that the monetary authority should apply unconventional wisdom to monetary policy and employ multiple instruments. This chapter shows that coordinated implementation of a policy instrument mix is a key part of an important strategy of optimally managing the monetary policy trilemma in the current climate, which is fraught with widespread uncertainty. The chapter also shows that the post-GFC monetary policy framework in Indonesia is, as a general rule, characterized by "enhanced" ITF. In "enhanced" ITF, the monetary policy framework continues to adhere to an inflation target as the overriding objective. The main characteristics of ITF remain: the inflation target is announced publicly, and the monetary policy is forward-looking, transparent, and clearly accountable. However, ITF is implemented in a more flexible manner, in the sense that Bank Indonesia must not only look at the inflation target merely in terms of policy formulation but also consider a number of other factors, including the financial sector stability and the dynamics of capital flows and the exchange rate.

The next section presents the monetary policy framework that was operative before the GFC, touching on policy instruments, targets, and objectives, which are inherent in the strategy for building policy credibility. The third section elaborates on the impacts of the recent GFC and changes in the financial environment with regard to the monetary policy transmission mechanism. The fourth section offers arguments regarding a strategy for enhancing the monetary policy framework from an unconventional wisdom perspective. It details a preliminary design for a post-GFC monetary policy framework for Indonesia, i.e., "enhanced" ITF. The final section of this chapter presents our conclusion.

## 2. Monetary policy framework

### 2.1. *Monetary policy framework before the Asian financial crisis of 1997–8*

The types of monetary policy frameworks adopted by Indonesia over time have been highly influenced by the stage of financial sector development. Before the 1983 financial deregulation, Indonesia's system was less developed and was characterized by financial repression. The essential policy ingredients were a credit ceiling policy and an administered interest rate regime. Bank lending was also allocated directly through selective credit control whereby the government determined lending priorities for economic sectors, activities, and beneficiaries.[1]

In June 1983 the Indonesian government announced the removal of credit ceilings for all banks and the lifting of most interest rate controls previously imposed on state banks. The financial deregulation was launched primarily in response to the decline in oil revenues, which compelled the government to act to promote domestic savings as a means of financing development. Furthermore, removal of financial repression would improve financial sector efficiency and attract offshore deposits. Finally, abolishing credit allocations was expected to improve efficiency in the use of capital.[2]

In October 1988 the government launched a more aggressive financial sector deregulation, whereby the reserve requirement was substantially reduced, from 15 percent to 2 percent. Reintroduction of the reserve requirement as an instrument of monetary policy was indirectly intended to control bank credit in light of the surge in capital inflows. The new provisions also reinforced the ability of monetary policy to influence bank balance sheets.[3] Bank Indonesia also made use of banking regulations to support monetary policy objectives, for example, by requiring foreign exchange banks to comply with a specified capital adequacy ratio.

Despite substantial changes in monetary operation, the monetary policy objectives remained the same: price stability (low inflation), sustainable economic growth, and a sound balance of payments (BOP). To achieve these multiple objectives, Bank Indonesia adopted an indirect monetary policy management approach, utilizing several key instruments such as open market operation (OMO), discount facilities, and a reserve requirement. The monetary operational target was defined in terms of base money (M0). Monetary policy transmission was seen as originating from base money, through monetary aggregates as intermediate

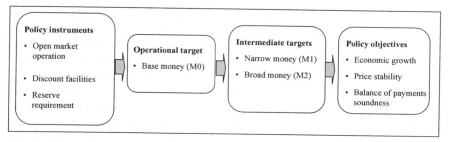

*Figure 9.1* Monetary policy framework before the Asian financial crisis of 1997–8
Source: Warjiyo and Juhro (2003), modified.

targets, such as narrow money (M1), consisting of currency and demand deposits, and broad money (M2), consisting of M1 and time deposits, to output and inflation (Figure 9.1). This set of targets became an important but not exclusive guide in implementing monetary policy. Close watch was also kept on other economic variables, such as interest rates (especially interbank rates), exchange rates, and bank credit expansion, in order to monitor the M0 direction.[4]

Despite the apparent effectiveness of the monetary policy framework in the 1990s, when M0 was used as the policy target, in the subsequent period this approach faced a number of serious challenges.[5] Some concerns arose over the difficulties confronting policymakers in controlling M0 growth. These are attributed to three important factors (Budiono, 1994; Sarwono and Warjiyo, 1998; Goeltom, 2008): First, the money markets for the instruments were relatively thin and fragmented. The central banking certificates (Sertifikat Bank Indonesia [SBIs]) were mostly held by state banks, and Bank Indonesia experienced difficulty in controlling economic liquidity through indirect use of these instruments.[6] Second, at certain times, M0 is *endogenous* toward output. During periods of upswing in the economy, M0 growth is driven mainly by aggregate demand reflected as growth in foreign borrowings and drawing of funds from SBIs. Third, there was growing instability in the relationship between nominal income and money. With the rapid development of Indonesian financial markets, banking operations and products have varied in terms of different forms of money market instruments. On the other hand, the capital market developed so rapidly, both in transaction volume and the types of securities traded, that there was a tendency to decouple the financial sector from the real sector, leading to a weakening of the relationship of money with inflation and real output.

## 2.2. Monetary policy framework during the Asian financial crisis of 1997–8

The economic and financial crisis that began in mid-1997 proved to be more severe, prolonged, and difficult for Indonesia than for other countries in the region. Triggered by sharp depreciation of the rupiah, the crisis led to an unprecedented economic collapse. In 1998 the economy shrank by 13.68 percent while inflation soared. Banks and businesses failed in rapid succession, leaving behind large numbers of newly unemployed. In the early days of the crisis, the government attempted to shore up the battered rupiah by widening the intervention band and intervening on both the forward and spot markets. However, as efforts to defend the currency against overwhelming pressure became increasingly futile, the government finally allowed the exchange rate to float freely in mid-August 1997. Soon after floating the currency, the government instituted an extremely tight money policy through sharp and dramatic increases in interest rates while also suspending activity in expansionary instruments.

Soaring interest rates and steep depreciation dealt severe blows to banks and the real sector. Already in a fragile condition, banks saw rapid deterioration in asset quality, and many companies were forced to close. To prevent runs on banks and a collapse of the entire banking system, Bank Indonesia extended massive liquidity support to commercial banks. As the public quickly lost confidence in the rupiah, a cycle of currency depreciation, soaring prices, and expanding money supply threatened to spiral into hyperinflation. Bank Indonesia's principal objective, therefore, was to restore confidence in the national currency. To achieve this aim, monetary expansion first had to be halted. Bank Indonesia also needed to regain control over its own balance sheet. All sources of money creation by the central bank needed to be brought under control and excess liquidity reabsorbed from the banking system.[7]

Because of various factors hampering the effectiveness of money market instruments, such as the thin market for SBIs, the excess liquidity in the economy could not be fully absorbed through OMOs.[8] Another innovation in enhancing monetary policy operations was "rupiah intervention". This was introduced as a means of monetary restraint and as a fine-tuning instrument to counteract interest rate volatility in the interbank money market. Rupiah intervention thus not only served as a contractionary instrument but also as a way to promote monetary expansion. Attempts to control the monetary expansion arising out of liquidity support originating in government expenditures were also supported by sterilization in the foreign exchange market, which simultaneously increased the supply of foreign exchange, thereby helping to stabilize the domestic currency.

To summarize, Bank Indonesia adopted base money targeting following the crisis as a temporary framework that was aimed primarily at absorbing the monetary expansion originating out of liquidity support, rather than for more fundamental considerations such as maintaining a stable relationship between inflation and base money (Iljas, 1999).

## 2.3. ITF in the period after the 1997–8 Asian financial crisis

In the aftermath of the crisis, a groundbreaking change in the conduct of monetary policy came with a new Bank Indonesia establishment law prescribing full independence for the central bank with regard to policy formulation and implementation (Bank Indonesia Law of 1999). The most important provision in the law, other than that legally establishing Bank Indonesia as an autonomous state institution free from government intervention, was the provision setting forth a single monetary policy objective of *achieving and maintaining stability of the rupiah*. Toward this end, the law empowered Bank Indonesia to execute monetary policy by setting monetary targets – with due consideration given to the inflation target – and managing monetary aggregates. In other words, Bank Indonesia was vested with both *goal independence* and *instrument independence*. Another important change instituted by the new law was to prohibit the central bank from financing government deficit spending and from purchasing government bonds on the primary market. However, the central bank was permitted to buy bonds on the secondary market for monetary policy purposes.

Following an ITF transition period between 2000 and 2005, Bank Indonesia formally adopted the ITF in July 2005, with a more transparent communications strategy aimed at strengthening monetary signals through the use of interest rates, in particular, through the Bank Indonesia Rate (BI Rate) as the policy rate and the short-term money market rate as the operational target (see Figure 9.2).[9] Under this new framework, Bank Indonesia envisages strengthening of the policymaking and implementation mechanisms through a forward-looking strategy for pursuing the inflation target. This, as expected, will alleviate inflation expectations. Because the monetary instruments must be easily understood by the public, interest rates are the preferred choice. This choice stems from the greater clarity in the interest rate policy signal, which makes it easier to shape public expectations. Furthermore, because inflation in Indonesia is driven to a significant extent by supply factors, bringing inflation down by influencing expectations will have minimal impact on overall demand.

The decision to use interest rates as the operational target under the ITF was not based solely on the need to influence expectations. Interest rates also have the advantage of measurability. In this sense, they offer greater accuracy, urgency, and clarity compared to base money. Interest rates are also easier to control than monetary aggregates, which often appear somewhat unstable. This control

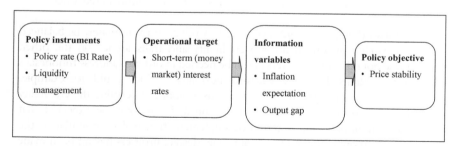

*Figure 9.2* Inflation targeting policy framework in the period after the 1997–8 Asian financial crisis

Source: Warjiyo and Juhro (2003), modified.

can operate through liquidity adjustments and direct signaling to guide public expectations. A further advantage is the ability of interest rates to affect the ultimate target. Several studies show that interest rates contain strong information on inflation and have the capability to curb inflation through various transmission channels. That said, interest rates can produce optimum results in policy signals only if public expectations are forward-looking.

To this end, the main priority for Bank Indonesia is to build credibility through the following actions (Goeltom, 2008):

1. Bank Indonesia has taken extensive steps to communicate the policy framework to the public through seminars and round-table discussions with bankers, academics, government officials, Bank Indonesia regional office officials, and the media.
2. Communication is reinforced by quarterly policy announcements in order to establish consistency, a key prerequisite for communication of the inflation targeting policy. Success in building credibility will ensue only if the policy is clearly and consistently implemented in line with deviations of expected inflation from the target.
3. Decision-making processes within Bank Indonesia are strengthened as required by the forward-looking strategy for determining monetary policy responses for achieving the inflation target. Overall macroeconomic conditions, the inflation forecast, and monetary policy responses are assessed in each quarterly board meeting as the basis for deciding the BI Rate for achievement of the inflation target.[10]
4. Regular press releases and press conferences are held to announce the decisions of the board meeting. These are supplemented by a quarterly Monetary Policy Report presenting an overall assessment of macroeconomic, inflation, and monetary conditions; the inflation forecast; and the monetary policy responses necessary to keep inflation on track with the target.
5. Policy coordination with the fiscal authorities is being strengthened. The magnitude of influence from hikes in administered prices on inflation means that inflationary pressures can potentially be mitigated through regular consultation on proper timing for adjustments in administered prices.[11]

Going forward, implementation of monetary policy must ultimately be balanced between flexibility on one hand and credibility and transparency on the other. Within these bounds, some discretion will be needed in order to address Indonesia's short-term problems. However, excessive flexibility – which could, for example, give rise to unclear changes in policy decisions – would undermine the credibility and policies of the central bank. Looking ahead, it can only be expected that consistent commitment and determined implementation will be essential to the realization of a more credible ITF. Meanwhile, despite progress having been made since the crisis, the economy is still burdened by various constraints and problems. The main challenges confronting the Indonesian economy are maintaining stability amid rising global uncertainty and reducing unemployment and poverty through accelerated growth. In this regard, the challenge in monetary policy is to contain rising inflationary pressures without impeding economic growth.

## 3. Changes in the financial environment and monetary policy transmission

No one could have foreseen that the impact of the GFC would propagate so rapidly and deeply. The crisis – triggered by the subprime mortgage debacle in July 2007, which quickly brought about the bankruptcy of a number of international financial institutions, such as Lehman Brothers in September 2008 – has seriously undermined the global economy in a short period of time. A number of policies were implemented in order to stabilize the financial sector and to reduce adverse impacts on the real sector. While some of these policies were conventional, other measures taken showed more initiative in comparison to those introduced during the Great Depression and the Japanese recession in the 1990s (Reinhart and Rogoff, 2009). Numerous fiscal policy stimulus packages were implemented, although they were also overshadowed by increasing future debt risk.[12] A loose monetary policy was implemented in the form of reducing central banks' policy rates to extremely low levels. This was followed by a quantitative easing policy.[13] Meanwhile, fund insurance policies to maintain financial system stability were implemented, not only through expanding the insurance cover but also through fully guaranteeing funds and injecting capital into troubled financial institutions (bailouts).

Unlike many others, the Indonesian economy was able to navigate a challenging 2009 with remarkable success. Despite having slowed compared to 2008, economic growth reached 4.5 percent in 2009, the third highest in the world after China and India. Further slowing of economic growth amid global economic contraction was avoided owing to the predominantly demand-driven structure of the economy. After the daunting pressures sustained in the first quarter of 2009, financial markets and macroeconomic stability also improved toward the end of 2009. These positive achievements were closely linked to a number of policies, both conventional and unconventional, adopted by Bank Indonesia and the government to safeguard macroeconomic and financial stability and prevent a further decline in economic growth through monetary and fiscal stimulus.

However, despite these positive achievements, the Indonesian economy is still confronted with some major policy challenges that have significant implications for monetary policy management. Some of these challenges are related to the dynamics of capital flows and the exchange rate, or to changes in financial sector behavior amid persistent excessive banking liquidity.

### 3.1. Dynamics of foreign capital flows and exchange rate

As a small open economy, Indonesia faces a number of challenges in its implementation of monetary policy relating to its recent and persistent inundation by foreign capital flows. First, the deluge of foreign capital inflows has

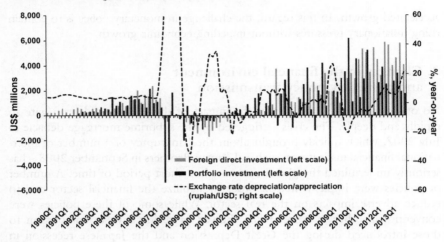

*Figure 9.3* Capital flows and exchange rate depreciation/appreciation

Source: Bank Indonesia, Indonesia Financial Statistics.

encouraged rupiah appreciation, which could potentially undermine purchasing power and the current account. An open capital account, coupled with an influx of capital flows, ensures that capital flows, rather than the current account, tend to predominantly affect exchange rate behavior. Accordingly, capital inflows drove nominal rupiah appreciation up by 15.9 percent in 2009 and by 4.5 percent in 2010 (Figure 9.3). Risk of the exchange rate overshooting has been mitigated by Bank Indonesia through foreign exchange market intervention. In real terms, the value of the rupiah appreciated by 17.8 percent in 2009 and by 11.4 percent in 2010, even though the currency remained relatively competitive compared to those of a number of other Asian countries.

Second, capital flow volatility creates financial system vulnerability. Capital flows that fluctuate widely compared to the capital account, amid ubiquitous herd behavior, encourage excess flows that can reverse suddenly in the event of a change in market sentiment. Moreover, an increase in capital flows, especially over the short term, can amplify financial market volatility and, in turn, act as a shock amplifier. These consequences could be further exacerbated by weak infrastructure and a lack of financial deepening, as is often found in developing countries like Indonesia. This can be reflected by some indicators, such as a low credit to gross domestic product (GDP) ratio and shallow markets in non-banking instruments (Table 9.3). Amid that lack of financial deepening and investment opportunities, a significant portion of capital inflows tends to be directed toward short-term financial instruments, such as SBIs, government bonds (Surat Utang Negara [SUNs]), and stocks, which are particularly vulnerable to any sudden reversal.

Third, a surge in foreign capital inflows compounds the complexity of challenges faced in terms of domestic monetary management. Persistent foreign capital inflows undermine the efficacy of monetary management, given that a

Table 9.3 Indicators of financial deepening and foreign ownership

| Rupiah, billions | Banking credit | | Government bonds | | | Central bank certificates | | | Stocks | | |
|---|---|---|---|---|---|---|---|---|---|---|---|
| | Level | % of GDP | Level | % of GDP | % of foreign ownership | Level | % of GDP | % of foreign ownership | Level | % of GDP | % of foreign ownership |
| 1990 | 95,704 | 0.5 | – | – | – | – | – | – | – | – | – |
| 1995 | 234,611 | 51.6 | – | – | – | – | – | – | – | – | – |
| 2000 | 269,000 | 19.4 | – | – | – | – | – | – | – | – | – |
| 2004 | 555,236 | 24.2 | 402,099 | 17.5 | 2.7 | 102,731 | 4.5 | 7.7 | 291,393 | 12.7 | 73.0 |
| 2005 | 698,695 | 25.2 | 399,839 | 14.4 | 7.8 | 72,237 | 2.6 | 20.5 | 342,034 | 12.3 | 73.0 |
| 2006 | 796,767 | 23.9 | 418,751 | 12.5 | 13.1 | 207,400 | 6.2 | 8.7 | 522,341 | 15.6 | 73.4 |
| 2007 | 1,004,178 | 25.4 | 477,750 | 12.1 | 16.4 | 267,710 | 6.8 | 10.9 | 790,839 | 20.0 | 66.4 |
| 2008 | 1,313,873 | 26.5 | 525,690 | 10.6 | 16.7 | 166,714 | 3.4 | 3.9 | 446,178 | 9.0 | 67.8 |
| 2009 | 1,446,808 | 25.8 | 581,750 | 10.4 | 18.6 | 255,520 | 4.6 | 17.3 | 772,572 | 13.8 | 67.1 |
| 2010 | 1,783,601 | 27.7 | 641,220 | 9.9 | 30.5 | 200,110 | 3.1 | 27.4 | 1,184,282 | 18.4 | 62.8 |
| 2011 | 2,223,685 | 30.0 | 723,620 | 9.8 | 30.8 | 119,780 | 1.6 | 6.5 | 1,251,886 | 16.9 | 60.0 |
| 2012 | 2,738,054 | 33.3 | 820,260 | 10.0 | 33.0 | 78,870 | 1.0 | 0.5 | 1,484,385 | 18.0 | 58.8 |
| 2013 | 3,322,683 | 36.6 | 995,250 | 11.0 | 32.5 | 91,390 | 1.0 | 4.1 | 1,475,474 | 16.2 | 62.9 |

Source: Bank Indonesia, Indonesia Financial Statistics.

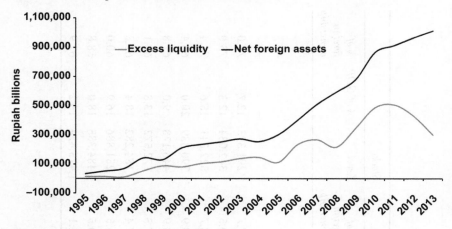

*Figure 9.4* Net foreign assets and excess liquidity
Source: Bank Indonesia, Indonesia Financial Statistics.

measure for managing liquidity in the economy, such as an interest rate increase, can ultimately be offset by the sheer magnitude of the capital inflows. On the other hand, in order to manage exchange rate appreciation pressures, high capital inflows should be responded to through intensive interventions, which cause the amount of excess liquidity in the banking system to increase significantly (Figure 9.4).[14] These capital flow dynamics can reduce the degree of monetary policy autonomy to respond to external forces (Juhro, 2010b) and consequently shift the orientation of monetary policy, which not only works to control inflation but also mitigates rupiah appreciation through intensive intervention.

### 3.2. Changes in financial sector behavior and procyclicality

Financial sector procyclicality also becomes more prevalent when driven by foreign capital inflows. Capital will flow into an economy when the outlook is favorable and will flow out of an economy during a contractionary phase (Ocampo, 2008). Consequently, the financial sector tends to exacerbate economic fluctuations. In Indonesia procyclicality is reflected in the performance of bank credit during expansionary and contractionary phases. Observing credit growth during periods of expansion and contraction reveals the magnitude of procyclicality in the Indonesian banking system. Figure 9.5 shows that real credit moves procyclically and outpaces GDP growth during expansionary periods but that the opposite is true during a contractionary phase. As an example, following the crisis of 1997–8, the ongoing credit crunch, namely, risk aversion by banks in terms of extending credit, undermined the already sluggish economic recovery process in Indonesia. Subsequently, from the beginning of 2002, credit expanded gradually before ultimately contracting sharply in line with the economic slowdown in the wake of fuel price hikes in 2005. After plummeting to its trough in 2006, credit steadily rebounded to peak at 38 percent in the third quarter

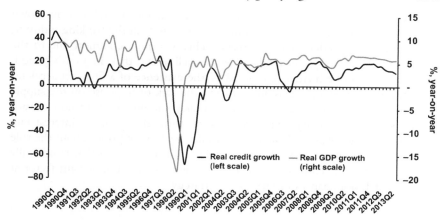

*Figure 9.5* Growth of real GDP and credit
Source: Bank Indonesia, Indonesia Financial Statistics.

of 2008. That period perfectly illustrates a cyclical upswing on the back of rising international commodity prices and confidence among economic players in both the banking sector and the real sector.

Risk behavior also contributes to procyclicality in the financial sector. Similar to the findings proposed by Borio et al. (2001), a disproportionate response by market players in terms of risk evaluation will heighten procyclicality. Market players and banks generally tend to be overly optimistic during a propitious economic cycle and overly pessimistic during an unfavorable cycle. In the case of Indonesia, a study conducted by Satria and Juhro (2011) found that the risk perception of market participants and the level of risk in the banking sector played significant roles in inducing procyclicality and monetary policy transmission.

### 3.3. Workings of the monetary policy transmission mechanism

Theoretically, the monetary policy response is transmitted through a number of channels such as interest rates, money, credit, asset values, and the exchange rate. In normal circumstances, monetary policy is expected to be capable of directing economic activities effectively. In the case of the Indonesian economy, some observations show that monetary policy transmission in Indonesia has performed well in the financial market and the real sector (Warjiyo and Agung, 2002). During the ITF implementation era, when monetary policy prioritized the interest rate as its operational target, a policy signal would be transmitted through policy interest rate setting, namely, the BI Rate. Given this signal, through use of various monetary instruments to manage liquidity in the money market, the Bank Indonesia's monetary policy would be transmitted through various channels, which in turn would affect domestic demand and inflation.

However, the global economic downturn and changes in financial sector behavior forced the monetary policy transmission process to grapple with some challenges. The spreading effects of the crisis were strong enough to drive down the economy, and they pushed economic actors, mainly in the banking industry, to become more prudent and risk averse. This was quite common due to the fact that the financial system tends to be procyclical and that, in a crisis period, such behavior can be further reinforced by the existence of a financial accelerator. Amid the persistent excess liquidity and the lack of response on the supply side – which reduced the effectiveness of policy stimulus transmission toward the real sector – monetary policy transmission through use of the interest rate and credit channels was weakened. Meanwhile, weak assumptions about the role of the exchange rate as a shock absorber, in a financial system that is not fully efficient, created a need to position the exchange rate as an important factor at the heart of Indonesian monetary policy strategy.

### Interest rate and expectation channels

The ability of Bank Indonesia to steer the BI Rate so as to influence interest rates in the money market and the banking sector has improved over time. Initial assessment of the hypothesis of the *term structure of interest rates* during the ITF implementation era shows that, generally, monetary policy transmission via the interest rate channel is effective.[15] However, during a crisis period, the lending rate response to a BI Rate decline tends to be rigid. In this regard, the magnitude of a decline in the lending rate turned out to be smaller than that of the decline of the BI Rate and the deposit rate. Observation also shows that the gap between the lending rate and the deposit rate widened. The same can be seen with respect to the gap between the base lending rate and the BI Rate (Figure 9.6).

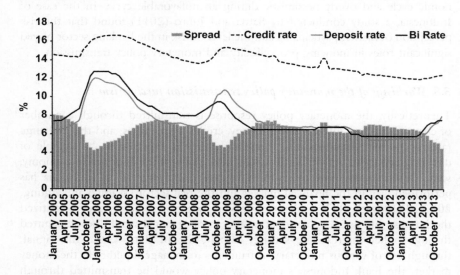

*Figure 9.6* BI Rate and market interest rates

Source: Bank Indonesia, Indonesia Financial Statistics.

From a micro-banking perspective, there are some factors contributing to the rigidity of lending rate movement: namely, the cost of funds and risk premiums that tend to rise, and a relatively higher profit margin set by the banks. An initial observation indicates that the decrease in the aggregate banking cost of funds throughout 2009 tended to be slower than the BI Rate decline. Furthermore, as risk premiums in the economy were still perceivably high in 2009, there was an indication that the banking industry preferred to maintain its profit margins. Efforts to strengthen the internal conditions of banks by competing to attract public funds, charging greater business risk premiums (*risk aversion*), and also accumulating profit seemed contradictive to macroeconomic developments, as the real sector was still going through a recovery process. This condition could be perceived as banking prudential efforts given the still nascent improvement in global financial markets.

Banking excess liquidity, which tends to be persistent, is another factor that could explain the unusual response of interest rates. Persistent and structural excess liquidity is deemed to be a burdensome challenge to implementation of a monetary operation. Such a challenge, if not well managed, will take a toll on high volatility of the money market interest rate, which in turn will undermine exchange rate stability and the effectiveness of monetary policy transmission. Some observations show that if banking excess liquidity fails to be absorbed by the authority, this could exert pressure on monetary stability, inflation, and the exchange rate.

Amid the policy transmission impairments, an initial observation shows that during the ITF implementation era, Bank Indonesia's monetary policy predictability was quite good. During the period of December 2005 to February 2012, the degree to which financial market participants correctly predicted the monetary policy stance was 83 percent. This is comparable to the prediction accuracy levels for other Asian countries that were implementing ITF, which varied between around 70 percent and 85 percent. Meanwhile, amid uncertainties in the global economy, which escalated in the second half of 2012, the monetary policy stance became less predictable. A recent observation also suggests that the existence of the BI Rate is sufficiently feasible as an anchor for future inflation expectations. Changes in the BI Rate have a positive impact on changes in inflation expectations. Meanwhile, if market perception of the monetary policy stance goes in the wrong direction, market participants can make appropriate and immediate adjustments, within around one to two months.

*The exchange rate channel*

In the early stage of ITF implementation, the exchange rate was regarded only as an information variable in the implementation of monetary policy. However, taking into account the increasing integration of global financial markets, exchange rate management is directed toward accommodating the dynamics of the exchange rate, which is not allowed to float freely and follow the market mechanism. In this regard, the exchange rate should be geared so as to align with the economic fundamentals through measurable interventions in the foreign exchange market. This is a reasonable strategy in that it takes into consideration the role of the exchange rate, which tends to serve as a shock amplifier rather than as a shock absorber, while its passthrough effect on inflation is also expected to remain significant.

Previous observations for the period before the GFC showed a substantial passthrough effect of the exchange rate on inflation. Kurniati and Permata (2008) argued that the passthrough would matter at a certain threshold of exchange rate depreciation, which was 4.2 percent (monthly). If the exchange rate changes were above that threshold, then the effect on inflation would be quite significant. Meanwhile, the estimation of the passthrough coefficient in general conditions, below the threshold, is relatively small. Machmud (2008) disaggregated the general price into tradable and non-tradable prices and suggested that, in the long run, 1 percent depreciation in the exchange rate would lead to a 0.3 percent increase in the tradable price. For non-tradable prices, 1 percent depreciation in the exchange rate would lead to only a 0.18 percent increase. Meanwhile, a recent assessment incorporating the post-GFC period showed that 1 percent depreciation in the exchange rate could lead to an inflation increase of only 0.15 percent (Juhro and Affandi, 2012). This result most likely stems from the declining trend in global commodity prices, together with an exchange rate management strategy implemented by Bank Indonesia that has allowed the rupiah to stabilize in recent years, thereby neutralizing the effects of external shocks, via the exchange rate, on inflation (Figure 9.7).[16]

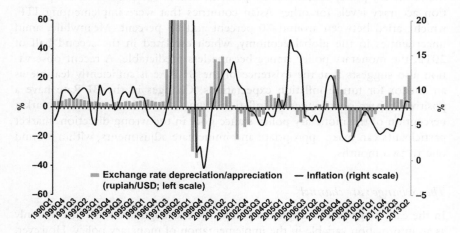

*Figure 9.7* Exchange rate depreciation/appreciation and inflation

Source: Bank Indonesia, Indonesia Financial Statistics.

*Money and credit channels*

Monetary aggregates (e.g., money and credit) play a pivotal role in the monetary management regime in Indonesia. Although there has been no monetary targeting framework formally in place since the early 2000s, empirical observations indicate that money and credit mattered in the period following the crisis of 1997–8, which is reflected in the behavior of credit and M1 growth (gap) preceding that of inflation (Figure 9.8).[17] In this case, the average lead time of M1 growth to inflation was around five to six quarters, while the average lead time of credit growth to inflation was about three months (Juhro, 2010a). This finding is in line with that of a previous study (Anglingkusumo et al., 2009), which illustrated the significant role played by monetary aggregates, in this case the non-cash component of M1 (demand deposits), in predicting future inflationary pressures. Using business cycle analysis, the study concluded that the lag effect of demand deposits against the turning point of the consumer price index inflation rate is about four to six quarters.

Related to the important role of money, one can observe another important aspect from the asset side of the central bank balance sheet. A preliminary observation concluded that Bank Indonesia's policy strategy to foster foreign reserves contributed to the increase of liquidity in the banking system and disrupted the effectiveness of monetary policy in the period of ITF implementation (Mochtar and Kolopaking, 2010). The problem might have become more severe because the policy strategy could not reduce inflation to a lower level, whereas, on the other hand, it could induce the exchange rate to act as a shock amplifier for the economy.

The above empirical facts provide a strong argument as to why the monetary authority needs to properly monitor monetary developments, including credit.

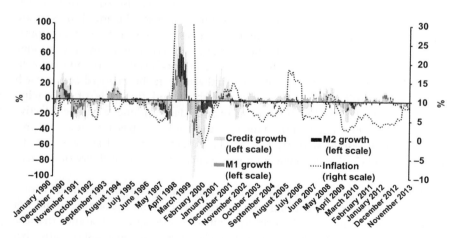

*Figure 9.8* Growth of monetary aggregates and inflation
Source: Bank Indonesia, Indonesia Financial Statistics.

In this case, management of liquidity should be aimed at working toward a level of monetary aggregate growth that is in line with the economic capacity. Meanwhile, despite the tendency of the behavior of M2, which is less stable, the information value of overall money growth remains noteworthy, given its influence on the formation of expectations.

## 4. Post-GFC monetary policy framework

Post-GFC challenges have revealed some valuable lessons for monetary policy implementation in Indonesia. First, the multiple challenges facing monetary policy as a result of a deluge of capital inflows suggest that Bank Indonesia should employ multiple instruments. Such an instrument mix would allow Bank Indonesia to address multiple dilemmas. In the face of capital flows, while the exchange rate should remain flexible, it should be maintained in such a way that the exchange rate is not misaligned with its fundamentals. Concomitantly, measures are required for accumulation of foreign exchange reserves as self-insurance, given that short-term capital flows are particularly vulnerable to sudden halts. In terms of capital flow management, a variety of policy options are available to deal with the excessive procyclicality of capital flows, especially short-term and volatile capital. Regarding monetary management, the dilemmas have been partially resolved through application of quantitative-based monetary policy to support the standard interest rate policy instrument. In addition, macroprudential policies aimed at maintaining financial system stability should also be adopted in order to mitigate the risk of asset bubbles in the economy.

Second, while price stability should remain the primary goal of Bank Indonesia, the GFC demonstrated that maintaining low inflation alone, without preserving financial stability, is insufficient to achieve macroeconomic stability. A number of crises that have occurred in recent decades also show that macroeconomic instability is primarily rooted in financial crises. Financial markets are inherently imperfect and can potentially generate excessive macroeconomic fluctuations if not well regulated. Therefore, the key to managing macroeconomic stability is managing not only the imbalance of goods (inflation) and externalities (balance of payments) but also any imbalance in the financial sector, such as excessive credit growth, asset price bubbles, and the cycle of risk-taking behavior in the financial sector. In this regard, Bank Indonesia will be effective in maintaining macroeconomic stability if the bank also has a mandate to promote financial system stability. Hence, the monetary policy framework of the ITF needs to be enhanced by including the substantial responsibility of financial sector control.

Third, exchange rate policy should play an important role in the ITF of a small open economy. According to a standard ITF, Bank Indonesia should not be attempting to manage the exchange rate. This benign view argues that the exchange rate should be allowed to float freely, thereby acting as a shock absorber for the economy. However, in a small open economy with open capital movement, exchange rate dynamics are largely influenced by investor risk perception, which triggers capital movements. In this environment, there is a case for managing the exchange rate in order to avoid excess volatility that could push the exchange rate beyond its inflation target band.

### 4.1. The relevance of the ITF

Many agree that the overarching goal of monetary policy should continue to be achieving price stability or low inflation. However, the problem is that, when confronted by the challenges summarized in the previous section, the standard ITF cannot be applied effectively. As an example, under the standard ITF, the interest rate is used as the sole monetary policy instrument, which subsequently affects aggregate demand and the output gap, with inflation expectations guided toward the inflation target. However, in an open economy, raising the interest rate is frequently ineffective because of the subsequent surge in capital inflows that add liquidity into the economy. Without sterilization, the additional liquidity will drive up inflation and trigger an asset bubble, which will affect financial system stability.

The crisis taught us that monetary policy must remain focused on price stability as the primary goal. The failures of advanced countries' central banks to avoid the worst effects of the global crisis were often reflected in the failure of monetary policies, which were narrowly focused on price stability. It cannot be denied that in the era known as the "great moderation", the global economy was able to maintain low inflation with sustained economic growth over quite a long period. However, the nascent consensus seems to indicate that achieving price stability is insufficient to guarantee macroeconomic stability overall because macroeconomic instability frequently stems from instability in the financial sector, even when inflation is maintained at a low level (Bean et al., 2010). The question is whether or not a monetary policy framework aimed at achieving price stability, e.g., ITF, is still relevant. The answer is a resounding "yes".[18]

Empirically, evaluations of ITF implementation in Indonesia over the past five years have yielded a number of noteworthy outcomes: (i) institutional strengthening of the monetary policy decision-making process; (ii) clear monetary policy signals that affect inflation expectations; and (iii) increased policy credibility (Juhro et al., 2009). Referring to the institutional strengthening of monetary policy, implementation of ITF has institutionally improved Bank Indonesia in terms of its systematic implementation of monetary policy, in a structured manner and based on principles of good governance. This is evidenced by the policy-making process and procedures that are more transparent and utilize independent decision-making as well as having public accountability. As a public institution, Bank Indonesia has also changed from a previously internally oriented organization to a more outward-oriented organization that conducts intensive communication with the general public concerning its monetary policymaking.

Regarding policy signal clarity, through a gradual and ongoing learning process, buttressed by intensive communication with the public, the ITF has successfully bolstered monetary policy transmission through expectations. The general public increasingly understands the background behind monetary poli-cymaking and more readily catch monetary policy signals, thereby strengthening and expediting monetary policy transmission. Such circumstances differ greatly from conditions before ITF implementation, when policy signals relied on base money, were not easily picked up by the market, and hence, under certain conditions, tended either not to alter expectations or, worse, to undermine expectations.

In harmony with the two successes detailed above, improved monetary policy credibility could slowly but surely be strived for. Several indicators support this conclusion. First, observations through surveys and empirical tests demonstrate that there is, or has been, a behavioral shift in public expectation formation, which previously tended to be backward-looking but is now more forward-looking. This has had a positive effect on reducing the degree of inflation persistence. Second, in line with nurturing sought-after credibility, Bank Indonesia regularly announces its policy stance, employing the BI Rate as a key economic indicator that is referred to by money market players and by the business community as a whole.

Nevertheless, achievement of the inflation target is not as straightforward as it may seem. A number of structural shocks on the supply side over the past eight years have pushed inflation beyond the target corridor set, more specifically in 2005 and 2008 (Table 9.4). In 2005 and 2008, inflation jumped to double digits as a result of government policy to raise fuel prices.[19] Meanwhile,

*Table 9.4* Inflation target and actual inflation

| Year | Inflation target | Actual inflation | Core inflation | BI Rate | Underlying factors |
|------|------------------|------------------|----------------|---------|--------------------|
| 2005 | 6 ± 1 | 17.1 | 9.7 | 9.2 | Global shocks, fuel price increases in March and October |
| 2006 | 8 ± 1 | 6.6 | 6.0 | 11.8 | |
| 2007 | 6 ± 1 | 6.6 | 6.3 | 8.6 | |
| 2008 | 5 ± 1 | 11.1 | 8.3 | 8.7 | Fuel price increase (May) |
| 2009 | 4.5 ± 1 | 2.8 | 4.3 | 6.5 | |
| 2010 | 4.5 ± 1 | 7.0 | 4.3 | 6.5 | Global commodity price increase, weather anomaly |
| 2011 | 4.5 ± 1 | 3.8 | 4.3 | 6.0 | |
| 2012 | 4.5 ± 1 | 4.3 | 4.4 | 5.8 | |
| 2013 | 4.5 ± 1 | 8.4 | 5.0 | 7.5 | Fuel price hike (June 2013), weather anomaly, and exchange rate depreciation |

Source: Bank Indonesia, Indonesia Financial Statistics

in the other years, inflation slightly exceeded the target also owing to the impact of soaring prices for internationally traded commodities and weather anomalies that disrupted agricultural production. Looking ahead at potential inflationary pressures, it seems unlikely that inflation will hit the long-term target of 3–4 percent in the near term. This situation closely parallels conditions in advanced countries and neighboring member countries of the Association of Southeast Asian Nations.

In addition to structural constraints on the supply side, difficulty in achieving the inflation target is also linked to the complexities faced by Bank Indonesia in the monetary sector. As experienced over the past three years, in order to overcome the inundation of capital flows, so that excessive appreciation pressures are not levied on the rupiah exchange rate, Bank Indonesia has intervened to purchase foreign currency, thereby increasing the liquidity in the domestic money market. This contributed to excess liquidity, which subsequently had to be reabsorbed by Bank Indonesia in order to avoid future inflationary pressures. Of course, these efforts undertaken by Bank Indonesia to maintain macroeconomic stability were not without their own consequences, considering the magnitude of the monetary operational costs expended, which will ultimately affect Bank Indonesia's balance sheet. On the other hand, the problems are also increasingly emanating from the financial system, which is characterized by procyclical behavior. Therefore, efforts to maintain macroeconomic stability are inseparable from endeavors to reduce immoderate procyclicality. To this end, synergy between monetary policy and macroprudential policy should be sought.

### 4.2. Enhancement under unconventional wisdom on monetary policy

Although Bank Indonesia still sees ITF as a reliable monetary policy strategy for Indonesia, it needs to be enhanced by refining the future ITF implementation strategy. There are two rationales underlying such enhancement. First, evaluations of ITF implementation in Indonesia have evidenced the need for a number of adjustments to and refinements in the ITF, which have been undertaken in line with conventional wisdom on monetary policy. In this case, there is justification for the need to implement a less rigid ITF as an ideal format for the Indonesian economy (Juhro et al., 2009). Second, Indonesian economic performance during the GFC inspires confidence as to the aptness of the ITF as a reliable monetary policy strategy for Indonesia. However, given the dynamics and complexity of the challenges we are facing, the framework needs to be further enhanced.

There are five principles of enhancement:

1.  Continuing adherence to the policy framework to inflation target as the overriding objective of monetary policy. The main characteristics of ITF will remain, e.g., preemptive, independent, transparent, and accountable policy implementation.

2.  Integrating monetary and macroprudential policy. Appropriate monetary and macroprudential policy integration is required in order to buttress monetary and financial system stability.
3.  Managing the dynamics of capital flows and exchange rates. To support macroeconomic stability, coordinated implementation of a policy instrument mix must ultimately be part of an important strategy for optimally managing the monetary policy trilemma.
4.  Strengthening policy communication strategy as part of the tool chest of policy instruments. Policy communication is no longer practiced purely for the sake of transparency and accountability; it is now regarded as a valuable monetary policy instrument.
5.  Strengthening Bank Indonesia and government policy coordination. Policy coordination is crucial given that inflation stemming from the supply side creates most inflation volatility.

Therefore, under the unconventional wisdom of "enhanced" ITF, to manage the monetary stability framework is indeed to manage the monetary policy trilemma and achieve the three intermediate goals of (1) maintaining monetary policy autonomy in achieving price stability by employing a monetary and macroprudential policy (instrument) mix; (2) stabilizing exchange rate movement in line with its fundamentals by employing exchange rate management; and (3) managing capital flow dynamics to support macroeconomic stability by implementing capital flow management.

Monetary policy complexity stemming from the interest rate can partially be resolved by quantitatively applying tighter monetary policy through raising the reserve requirement. In addition, macroprudential policy is aimed at avoiding financial risks such as asset bubbles and excessive credit growth, which could trigger financial system instability. This type of macroprudential policy is effective if banks can intermediate capital flows. However, if the capital flows emanate directly from unregulated sectors, as in direct loans from the private sector, measures to control capital inflows are another option, for example, limiting private loans.

In terms of the exchange rate, the rupiah should be managed so as to remain flexible and should be allowed room to appreciate/depreciate. But it is also necessary to avoid the currency becoming misaligned with economic fundamentals as this would endanger macroeconomic stability. Consequently, Bank Indonesia's presence is required in the foreign exchange market in order to ensure that the rupiah does not deviate with excessive volatility. Of course, this option will no longer be available if the rupiah becomes overvalued. Simultaneous efforts to accumulate foreign exchange reserves are vital as a form of self-insurance, given that short-term capital flows are particularly vulnerable to risk of sudden reversal.

Regarding capital flows, in continuing to adhere to a free foreign exchange regime, macroprudential measures also consist of policy options designed to reduce excessive short-term capital flows that could potentially lead to financial risks from the external side. Such measures have been introduced by Bank Indonesia through regulations that oblige investors to hold SBIs for a minimum period of one month. This policy has helped to diversify foreign portfolio capital flows and to extend the durations of SBIs, which consequently also promoted financial deepening, especially in the foreign exchange market.

Coordinated implementation of a policy instrument mix is ultimately part of an important strategy for managing the monetary policy trilemma in the current climate, which is blighted by widespread uncertainty. Coordination is critical, not only to address the sources of imbalances from external and internal sides, but also to optimally manage the impact of monetary policy while avoiding overkill and mutual exclusivity (Figure 9.9).

Within the above policy perspective, achievement of macroeconomic stability not only is tied to monetary stability (price stability) but also interacts with financial system stability. Therefore, the central bank's policy formulation should evaluate the strategic role of monetary policy and the financial system at the same time. In this regard, under "enhanced" ITF, flexibility in policy implementation can be achieved through, among other means, additional macroprudential

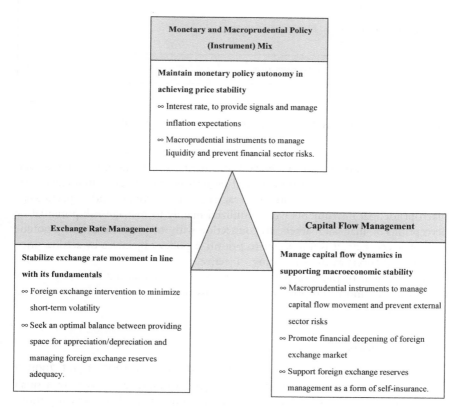

*Figure 9.9* Bank Indonesia monetary policy trilemma management

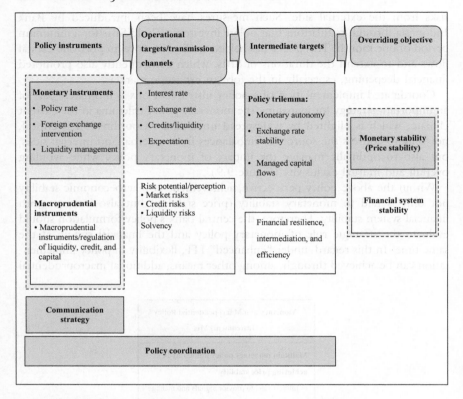

*Figure 9.10* Monetary policy framework under "enhanced" ITF

instruments in addition to monetary instruments, which should reinforce each other. While monetary instruments will be utilized to influence monetary variables, such as the interest rate, the exchange rate, credit, and expectations, macroprudential instruments will be utilized mainly to manage risk potential or perceptions in financial markets. In connection with measures for averting potential policy conflicts, it is important to prioritize policy objectives by setting price stability (inflation) as the overriding objective.

Improvement of the monetary framework under "enhanced" ITF, by means of a monetary and macroprudential policy instrument mix, can be described as shown in Figure 9.10.

## 5. Conclusions

The challenges encountered after the financial crises of 1997–8 and 2008–9 have revealed some valuable lessons with regard to monetary policy. In a small open economy, such as that of Indonesia, the multiple challenges facing monetary policy as a result of capital flow dynamics, amid inflationary pressures, suggest that the monetary authorities should employ multiple instruments. This chapter shows that coordinated implementation of a policy instrument mix should ultimately be part of an important strategy for optimally managing the monetary policy trilemma in the current climate, which is fraught with widespread uncertainty.

It also shows that a post-GFC monetary policy framework in Indonesia is, generally, characterized by "enhanced" ITF. In "enhanced" ITF, the policy framework continues to adhere to an inflation target as the overriding objective of monetary policy. The main characteristics of ITF will remain, namely, that the inflation target is announced publicly and that the monetary policy is forward-looking, transparent, and clearly accountable. However, the ITF is implemented in a more feasible manner, which means that Bank Indonesia must not only look at the inflation target merely in terms of policy formulation but also consider a number of other factors, including financial sector stability and the dynamics of capital flows and the exchange rate. Therefore, achievement of macroeconomic stability not only is tied to monetary stability (price stability) but also interacts with financial system stability.

A change in the framework will have a number of significant implications for the institutional mandate of Bank Indonesia. The paradigm that monetary policy requires the support of macroprudential policy has the consequence of an inability to separate monetary policy from macroprudential policy in order to ensure effective implementation. Therefore, strengthening Bank Indonesia and government policy coordination in maintaining monetary and financial system stability is essential.[20]

Policy coordination can also be carried out from a broader perspective, including during the process of handling a crisis. The 1997–8 financial crisis showed that any measures taken to handle a crisis without a clear authority and decision-making structure would only protract the process, potentially incur very high economic and social costs, and require a longer time for recovery. In a crisis management context, coordination or cooperation among central banks in the region can be established in order to formulate a kind of international financial safety net, for example, in the case of escalating external liquidity pressures that could destabilize the financial system in a particular country and potentially subsequently spread to other countries in the region. The moral is that strengthening the framework for maintenance of monetary and financial system stability is indeed necessary, but this must be underpinned by a crisis management framework that is clear, expeditious, and able to provide legal certainty.

## Notes

1 The credit ceilings were criticized in two respects. First, in regard to the banks themselves, the credit ceilings were set equally for efficient and non-efficient banks. The ceilings also hampered bank efficiency by smothering competition for deposit funds. Second, in the operation of monetary policy, the credit ceilings were ineffective in controlling the growth of the money supply and thus

inflation. McLeod (1994), for example, shows that the sustained positive balance of payments impact on base money was a major factor in feeding the growth of the domestic money supply. Similarly, Nasution (1982) also argued that the relationship between credit and money supply was unstable because international reserves, especially if not sterilized, were not under government control.

2 In the deregulated financial environment, capital would be allocated to the best projects with maximum returns. Bank Indonesia also wound down the liquidity credit facility for banks, as this had removed the incentive for banks to engage actively in funds mobilization. However, liquidity credit from Bank Indonesia was still available for high priority loans.

3 These more recent requirements applied a more restrictive definition in which fund components in bank liabilities subject to the reserve requirement include demand deposits, time deposits, savings deposits, and other liabilities irrespective of maturity. In comparison, the former provision extended only to liabilities with a maturity of less than 24 months.

4 Under this policy, Bank Indonesia established an annual monetary program based on a money demand function in which money was related to the ultimate targets of output and inflation, as well as to interest rates. The program also set out the operational targets (M0), intermediate targets (M1 and M2), and factors affecting the monetary base (M0) and M2 in line with the ultimate targets. For day-to-day monetary control operations, Bank Indonesia introduced two new money market instruments: Bank Indonesia certificates (Sertifikat Bank Indonesia [SBIs]) and money market securities (Surat Berharga Pasar Uang [SBPUs]) issued or endorsed by banks. SBIs were issued when the central bank wanted to squeeze liquidity, while SBPUs were purchased by the central bank to expand the available liquidity in the system. These instruments were necessary to indirect monetary operations since the government did not issue treasury bills, used in many countries for OMOs and repurchase transactions. SBIs were used not only in monetary operations but also in short-term management of liquidity for banks, companies, and individuals.

5 Another money market instrument employed by Bank Indonesia was the foreign exchange swap facility. A swap is essentially a spot transaction concluded simultaneously with a forward transaction. While swaps are used in hedging to encourage foreign investment in Indonesia, Bank Indonesia would also buy foreign exchange reserves from banks during times of monetary expansion, either in direct deals or through auction. When conditions called for monetary contraction, Bank Indonesia would sell foreign exchange reserves using swap transactions or by terminating the rollover of matured swaps. Monetary policy also operated through two types of discount window facility introduced in early 1984. Discount Window I was designed to provide funds for daily liquidity and operated as an indirect monetary policy instrument. Discount Window II was a facility for assisting banks faced with long-term mismatches. In practice, these instruments proved ineffective. Banks appeared reluctant to avail themselves of the facilities due to the perception that use of lender of last resort instruments would be harmful to their reputations.

6 For example, in September 1984 interbank overnight rates soared to 90 percent per annum during a period of liquidity squeezing. On other occasions, to counteract speculation over impending devaluation in the second quarter of 1987, the authorities took drastic measures to force banks to cut their reserves. State banks were required to repurchase SBPUs, and state enterprises were ordered to use their deposits to buy SBIs. A similar situation occurred in early 1991. This massive transfer of funds from state-owned banks to the central bank became

known as the Sumarlin Shock, after J.B. Sumarlin, the minister of finance at the time.

7 To curb expansion in liquidity support, Bank Indonesia acted in April 1998 to impose stiff penalties on the discount window facilities and negative balances held by commercial banks at Bank Indonesia. In May 1998 Bank Indonesia announced a ceiling on deposit rates and the interbank rate guaranteed by the government to prevent banks from adopting imprudent measures that would lead to self-reinforcing expansions of liquidity support.

8 The first attempts to achieve the quantitative target involved improvements to the OMO mechanism. On July 29, 1998, Bank Indonesia changed the SBI auction system from emphasis on interest rate targets to quantitative targets. The scope of auction participants, formerly restricted to primary dealers, was expanded to include bankers, money brokers, securities houses, and the general public. These changes were intended to promote competition among auction participants, enabling the SBI rate to better reflect the interaction between demand and supply.

9 For a comprehensive survey on the background to ITF implementation in Indonesia, see Alamsyah et al. (2001).

10 A number of methods, research tools, and economic models have been developed to assist with the board's analyses, forecasts, and policy recommendations. The analysis is also supported by a range of indicators and survey findings. Equally important are the regional economic analyses conducted by Bank Indonesia's regional offices throughout the country.

11 The Indonesian Government and Bank Indonesia have set up a team of senior officials from relevant government agencies and the central bank to set the inflation targets and monitor inflationary fluctuations.

12 Fiscal stimulus packages are evidenced by the value of fiscal deficits, which surged in many countries in 2009. The average fiscal deficit for member countries of the Organisation for Economic Co-operation and Development (OECD) is projected at 7.2 percent of GDP compared to 3.0 percent in 2008 (OECD, 2009, p. 13). This rise was driven by the U.S. fiscal deficit of 10.2 percent of GDP, a sharp increase from 5.8 percent in 2008.

13 As an illustration, the Fed Funds Rate in April 2009 was at the level of 0 to 0.25 percent, whereas the Euro Refinance Rate, European Central Bank (ECB), dropped to 1.25 percent.

14 Excess liquidity occurs where cash flows into the banking system *persistently* exceed withdrawals of liquidity from the market by the central bank. This is reflected in holdings of reserves in excess of the central bank's required reserves. In Indonesia excess liquidity is measured by the total amount of open market instruments owned by banks, consisting of SBIs, term deposits, reverse repo government bonds (SUNs), and deposit facility instruments.

15 Under an ITF regime with an interest rate as an operational target basis, the assumption applied is that through policy rate setting under a monetary operation (liquidity management), a central bank can affect current and expected money market overnight interest rates (shortest market interest rates), fund/credit market interest rates (longer-term interest rates), and thereby real economic activities.

16 An important role of the exchange rate in monetary policy strategy can also be seen from its significant impact in improving the performance of monetary policy responses, i.e., monetary policy rules. Estimation using a Taylor-type rule that takes into account the role of the exchange rate (a bending rule) outperforms a simple rule (Juhro and Mochtar, 2009). Empirical counterfactual exercises

showed that the bending rule can better explain the dynamics of the monetary policy response in Indonesia.

17 The growth (gap) of monetary aggregates is measured as the difference between its actual growth and medium-term growth (based on the Hodrick–Prescott Filter).

18 Theoretically, an ITF policy framework oriented toward achieving low inflation and implemented with greater transparency is surely still relevant when the objective of monetary policy is to achieve price stability. Mishkin (2011), who holistically evaluated nine principles of monetary policy, including ITF, which had become a kind of consensus prior to the crisis, concluded that "none of the lessons from the financial crisis in any way undermines the nine basic principles of the science of monetary policy" (p.31).

19 Fuel price hikes occurred twice in 2005, once in March by an average of 30 percent and then in October by an average of 96 percent. Furthermore, fuel prices were also raised in May 2008 by around 33 percent.

20 Starting in early 2014, banking regulatory and supervisory functions are under the Financial Services Authority (FSA; Otoritas Jasa Keuangan), no longer under Bank Indonesia. In this regard, Bank Indonesia still acts as the macro-prudential authority, while the FSA acts as the microprudential authority. Bank Indonesia has the ability to assess macroeconomic and financial stability risks as well as global financial market developments, while the FSA has the ability to assess individual financial institution risks. Therefore, the macroprudential policy framework will inevitably involve these two institutions. This is due to the fact that the implementation of macroprudential policy requires consistency in the use of microprudential instruments. In order for the system to function properly, there must be close coordination between Bank Indonesia and the FSA.

# References and Further Readings

Aizenman, Joshua, Menzie D. Chinn, and Hiro Ito. 2008. Assessing the Emerging Global Financial Architecture: Measuring the Trilemma's Configurations Overtime. National Bureau of Economic Research Working Paper 14533. December. Cambridge, MA: National Bureau of Economic Research.

Alamsyah, H., C. Joseph, J. Agung, and D. Zulverdy. 2001. Towards Implementing Inflation Targeting in Indonesia. *Bulletin of Indonesian Economic Studies* 37(3): 309–24. Canberra: Australian National University.

Anglingkusumo, Reza, Myrnawati Savitri, and Ina Nurmalia. 2009. Siklus Inflasi IHK dan Penggunaan Besaran Moneter sebagai Indikator Dini Penduga Arah Fase Siklikal Inflasi. Research Paper. Jakarta: Bank Indonesia.

Bean, Charles, Matthias Paustian, Adrian Penalver, and Tim Taylor. 2010. Monetary Policy after the Fall. Federal Reserve Bank of Kansas City Annual Conference, Jackson Hole, Wyoming, August 28.

Bernanke, Ben, T. Laubach, F. Mishkin, and A. Posen. 1999. *Inflation Targeting: Lessons from the International Experience*. Princeton, NJ: Princeton University Press.

Binhadi. 1995. *Financial Sector Deregulation and Monetary Policy: The Indonesian Experience*. Jakarta: Institut Bankir Indonesia.

Blinder, Allan S. 2010. How Central Should the Central Bank Be? Center for Economic and Policy Studies Working Paper 198. January. Princeton, NJ: Center for Economic and Policy Studies, Princeton University.

Borio, C., C. Furfine, and P. Lowe. 2001. Procyclicality of the Financial System and Financial Stability: Issues and Policy Options in Marrying the Macro- and Micro-prudential Dimensions of Financial Stability. Bank for International Settlements Papers 1. March. Basel: Bank for International Settlements.

Budiono. 1994. Revisiting Our Monetary Targets: M0, M1, or M2? Mimeo. Jakarta: Bank Indonesia.

Filardo, Andrew, and Hans Genberg. 2010. Monetary Policy Strategies in the Asia and Pacific Region: What Way Forward? Asian Develompment Bank Institute Working Paper Series 195. February. Manila: Asian Develompment Bank Institute.

Goeltom, Miranda S. 2008. *Essays in Macroeconomic Policy: The Indonesian Experience.* Jakarta: Gramedia.

Goeltom, Miranda S. 2009. Financial System and Monetary Policy Transmission Mechanism: How to Address the Increasing Risk Perception. Paper presented at Bank Indonesia's 7th International Seminar "Global Financial Tsunami: What Can We Do?," Bali, June.

Hannoun, Hervé. 2010. The Expanding Role of Central Banks since the Crisis: What Are the Limits? Speech at the 150th Anniversary of the Central Bank of the Russian Federation in. Moscow, June 18. http://www.bis.org/speeches/sp100622.htm. Basel: Bank for International Settelemnts.

Iljas, Achjar. 1999. Peranan Bank Indonesia Dalam Pengendalian Inflasi. Paper presented at Seminar on the Role of Bank Indonesia in Inflation Control, Jakarta, December 6.

International Monetary Fund. 2011. Recent Experiences in Managing Capital Inflows – Cross-Cutting Themes and Possible Guidelines. Washington, DC: International Monetary Fund.

Juhro, Solikin M. 2010a. Flexible ITF and the Role of Monetary Aggregates in Indonesian Monetary Management. Policy Research Note. Jakarta: Bank Indonesia.

Juhro, Solikin M. 2010b. The Vicious Circle of Rising Capital Inflows and Effectiveness of Monetary Control in Indonesia. Research Note. Jakarta: Bank Indonesia.

Juhro, Solikin M., and Yoga Affandi. 2012. Inflation Dynamic and Exchange Rate Pass-through in Indonesia. Policy Research Note. Jakarta: Bank Indonesia.

Juhro, Solikin M., Harmanta, Firman Mochtar, and Kiki N. Asih. 2009. Review of the Implementation of ITF in Indonesia. Jakarta: Bank Indonesia.

Juhro, Solikin M. and Firman Mochtar. 2009. The Role of Exchange Rate in Flexible ITF: Alternative Thoughts on the Policy Rules. Policy Research Note. Jakarta: Bank Indonesia.

Kurniati, Y. and M. Permata. 2008. Exchange Rate Pass-through in Indonesia. Bank Indonesia Working Paper No. 9. Jakarta: Bank Indonesia.

Machmud, T.M. Arief. 2008. Determinants of Inflation in Indonesia: An Econometric Analysis. PhD Thesis. Canberra: Australian National University.

McLeod, Ross H. (Ed.). 1994. Indonesia Assessment 1994: Finance as a Key Sector in Indonesia's Development. Canberra: Australian National University and Institute of Southeast Asian Studies.

Mishkin, Frederic S. 2011. Monetary Policy Strategy. National Bureau of Economic Research Working Paper 16755. February. Cambridge, MA: National Bureau of Economic Research.

Mochtar, Firman, and Erwindo Kolopaking. 2010. ITF, Cadangan Devisa, dan Stabilitas Moneter. Policy Research Note. Jakarta: Bank Indonesia.

Nasution, Anwar. 1982. *Financial Institutions and Policies in Indonesia*. Singapore: Institute of Southeast Asian Studies.

Ocampo, J.A. 2008. Macroeconomic Vulnerability: Managing Pro-cyclical Capital Flows. Bangkok: Bank of Thailand. http://www.bot.or.th/English/Economic-Conditions/Semina/Documents/09_Presentation_Ocampo.pdf

Organisation for Economic Co-operation and Development. 2009. OECD Economic Outlook, Vol. 2009/1. Paris: Organisation for Economic Co-operation and Development.

Palley, Thomas I. 2009. Rethinking the Economics of Capital Mobility and Capital Controls. *Brazilian Journal of Political Economy* 29(3): 15–34.

Reinhart, Carmen M., and Kenneth S. Rogoff. 2009. The Aftermath of Financial Crises. National Bureau of Economic Research Working Paper 14656. January. Cambridge: National Bureau of Economic Research.

Sarwono, Hartadi A., and Perry Warjiyo. 1998. The Search for a New Paradigm of Monetary Management within a Flexible Exchange Rate System: A Rationale for Its Implementation in Indonesia. *Bulletin of Monetary Economics and Banking* 1(1): 5–83. July. Jakarta: Bank Indonesia.

Satria, Doni, and Solikin M. Juhro. 2011. Risk Behaviour and Monetary Policy Transmission Mechanism in Indonesia. *Bulletin of Monetary Economics and Banking* 13(3): 251–80. January. Jakarta: Bank Indonesia.

Warjiyo, Perry, and Juda Agung (Eds.). 2002. *Transmission Mechanism of Monetary Policy in Indonesia*. Jakarta: Bank Indonesia.

Warjiyo, Perry, and Solikin M. Juhro. 2003. Monetary Policy in Indonesia. *Bank Indonesia Central Banking Series* 6. Jakarta: Bank Indonesia.

# 10 A macroprudential perspective in central banking

*Shigenori Shiratsuka*[1]

## 1. Introduction

In this chapter I explore a policy framework for central banks from a macroprudential perspective, to pursue price and financial system stability in a consistent and sustainable manner.[2] Here I emphasize the importance of a "macroprudential perspective", not just "macroprudential policy" itself, in a policy framework for central banks. That is because achieving the stability of the entire financial system needs to bring together contributions not only from financial regulation and supervision but also from macroeconomic policy, particularly monetary policy.[3]

Financial crises are generally preceded by a period of a benign economic and financial environment with a prevailing euphoric sentiment. Behind the scenes, financial imbalances are built up, typically seen as an asset-price and credit bubble,[4] and the subsequent unwinding of such imbalances produces significant adverse effects, potentially leading to prolonged economic stagnation.[5] Once the economy enters a downturn, the harmful effects of a bubble emerge, exerting stress on the real side of the economy and the financial system due to the unexpected correction of asset prices. Such financial crisis developments are fundamentally endogenous to the financial system, especially arising from exposure to common risks.

Before the recent crisis, the global economy enjoyed seemingly steady growth with low and stable inflation, which was referred to as the "great moderation". The prolonged boom in the global economy coexisted with low policy interest rates, elevated asset prices across broad asset classes, and unusually low short-term volatility in financial markets. In retrospect, under such circumstances, the financial system on the whole took excessive risk in the form of the expansion of leverage and the extension of maturity mismatches. Such a mechanism of amplifying risks is embedded in the process of financial intermediation that transfers funds and risks between financial market participants.

The recent crisis shed light on crucial deficiencies in the regulatory and supervisory framework in maintaining the stability of the financial system as a whole. Before the crisis, mainly from a microprudential perspective, it was thought that financial system stability could be achieved by assembling sound financial institutions with adequate capital and liquidity positions as well as proper risk management. Based on our experience under the recent crisis, however, the soundness of individual financial institutions does not necessarily assure the stability of the financial system as a whole. Crises are fundamentally endogenous to the financial system and arise from exposure to common risks among financial institutions, underpinned by complicated incentives at both the micro and macro levels.[6]

There are a lot of arguments calling for more stringent regulations, such as minimum regulatory requirements significantly stricter than the existing Basel rules to ensure the quality and quantity of overall capital in the global banking system.[7] Achieving higher stability just by more stringent microprudential regulations, however, tends to result in lower efficiency in financial intermediation as a basis for economic growth. In addition, the higher regulatory burden is likely to produce incentives for regulatory arbitrage. To harness the benefits from globalization and technological progress in the financial system, while limiting its inherent instability, we need additional and supplementary policy tools to balance the efficiency and stability of the financial system as a whole. Such measures need to be designed so as to serve as a shock absorber, instead of a transmitter of risk to the broader economy, thus functioning as an automatic stabilizer of boom-and-bust cycles.

In that context, macroprudential policy is often pointed out as a missing element in the current policy framework.[8] To enhance the robustness of the entire financial system, macroprudential policy needs to identify and dampen systemic risk, which is likely to disrupt the function of the financial system, thereby destabilizing the macroeconomy. Macroprudential policy thus focuses on two key externalities in the financial system: procyclicality in an intertemporal dimension as well as spillover effects in a cross-sectional dimension.[9] Procyclicality concerns an intertemporal amplification mechanism within the financial system as well as between the financial system and the macroeconomy. Spillover effects concern a cross-sectional amplification mechanism through a complex network of various types of financial institutions, comprising not only commercial banks but also other market-based financial intermediaries and institutional investors.[10]

The recent crisis fundamentally challenged the dichotomy between monetary and prudential policies. Before the crisis, monetary and prudential policies were deemed separable and better allocated to different policy authorities. Monetary policy focused primarily on the macroeconomic goal of low and stable inflation, while prudential policy put emphasis on maintaining the soundness of individual financial institutions, thereby reducing systemic risk. At the moment, however, there seem to be increasing arguments to support the view that pursuing the two objectives, price and financial system stability, in a consistent and sustainable manner requires the combination of monetary policy and microprudential and macroprudential policies with close cooperation among related policy authorities.[11] In addition, once financial distress materializes, the boundary between monetary and prudential policies becomes extremely ambiguous, as evidenced by the unconventional monetary policy responses at major central banks.[12]

Given the close interaction between monetary and macroprudential policies, it is crucial for central banks to consider an overall policy framework for central banking, encompassing both policies. In that regard, I propose a framework of constrained discretion for central banking to pursue price and financial system stability in a consistent and sustainable manner. Such a policy framework extends constrained discretion for monetary policy, proposed as the conceptual basis for flexible inflation targeting, to overall central banking, thereby providing central banks with a basis for implementing monetary and macroprudential policies in a compatible, systematic, flexible, and accountable manner.[13]

This chapter is structured as follows. Section 2 reviews the basic concept of an asset-price and credit bubble, as a symptom of financial imbalances in the run-up to a crisis. Section 3 presents a selective review of the current discussions on designing macroprudential policy tools in addressing two key externalities in the financial system: intertemporal procyclicality and cross-sectional spillover effects. Section 4 explores how to design a policy framework for central banks from a macroprudential perspective, with special emphasis on the interactions between monetary and macroprudential policies. Section 5 concludes the paper.

## 2. An asset-price and credit bubble

In this section I will discuss the nature of an asset-price and credit bubble, which plays a crucial role in amplifying the boom-and-bust cycle in asset prices and credit through macrofinancial linkages. As I mentioned earlier, financial imbalances, associated with an asset-price and credit bubble, are built up under benign financial and economic conditions, including low and stable inflation. The subsequent unwinding of such imbalances, after the burst of an asset-price and credit bubble, produces significant adverse effects, potentially leading to long-lasting economic stagnation and the risk of falling into a deflationary spiral.

### 2.1. The nature of an asset-price and credit bubble

While the term "bubble" is used differently among people, I follow Okina, Shirakawa, and Shiratsuka (2001) and define it by three symptoms for financial and macroeconomic variables: a marked increase in asset prices, an expansion of monetary aggregates and credit, and an over-heating of economic activity (Figure 10.1).

In that regard, it is important to note that an asset-price and credit bubble is generally a euphoric phenomenon, not a rational bubble. A rational bubble, as modeled by Blanchard and Watson (1982), assumes that economic agents correctly recognize the economic fundamentals. Euphoria, in contrast, corresponds to excessively optimistic expectations with respect to future economic fundamentals, which lasts for several years and then bursts.

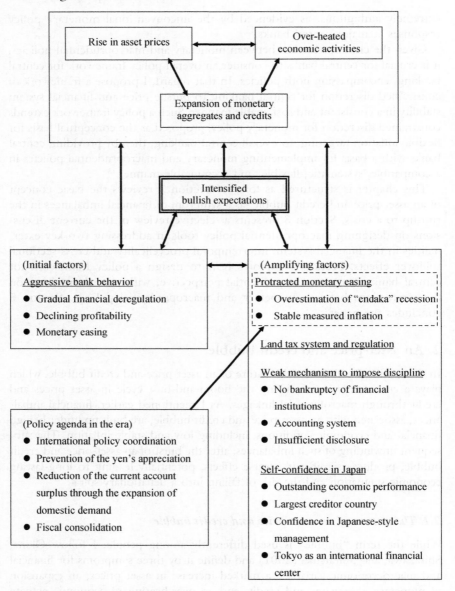

*Figure 10.1* Illustration of the bubble economy in Japan

Source: Figure 13 in Okina, Shirakawa, and Shiratsuka (2001).

When looking back at Japan's experience in the late 1980s, or the "bubble period", measured inflation was relatively moderate, and expectations that low interest rates would continue over time were generated, making economic agents' expectations extremely bullish with respect to the future (see Figure 10.2 for Japan's financial and economic environment).[14] During the bubble period Japan

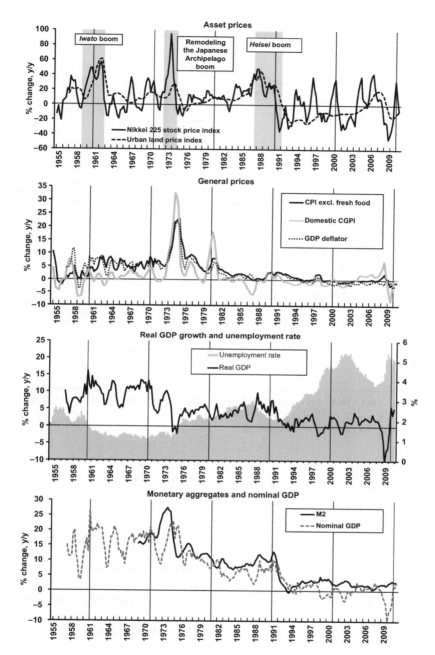

*Figure 10.2* The financial and economic environment

Sources: Bank of Japan, Financial and Economic Statistics Monthly, and other sources.

Notes: CGPI: corporate goods price index; CPI: consumer price index; GDP: gross domestic product; year on year: The urban land price index is figured for commercial land in six major cities. Regarding the CPI before 1970 and the domestic wholesale price index before 1960, the prewar base series is connected to the current series. The unemployment rate is seasonally adjusted.

(a) Ratio of debts to nominal GDP (private non-financial corporations)

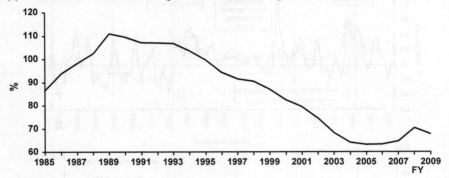

(b) Employment condition DI (all industries)

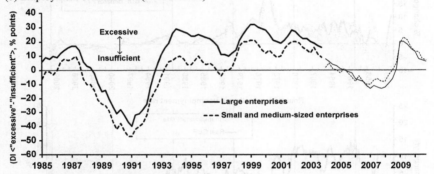

(c) Production capacity DI (manufacturing)

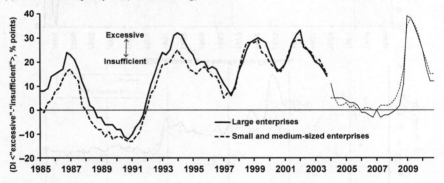

*Figure 10.3* The "three excesses" in the Japanese business sector

Sources: Cabinet Office, Annual Report on National Accounts; Bank of Japan, Bank of Japan, Tankan: Short-Term Economic Survey of Enterprises in Japan, Flow of Funds.

Notes: DI: diffusion index. The Tankan has been revised from the March 2004 survey. Figures up to the December 2003 survey are based on the previous data sets. Figures from the December 2003 survey are on a new basis. Debts are the sum of loans and securities (other than equities) in private non-financial corporations.

faced difficulty in evaluating *ex ante* whether it was the arrival of a new era or simply euphoria.[15] As described by Okina, Shirakawa, and Shiratsuka (2001), the intensified bullish expectations were certainly grounded in several intertwined factors: progress in financial liberalization, the aggressive behavior of financial institutions, the introduction of the capital accords, protracted monetary easing, taxation and regulations biased toward accelerating the rise in land prices, over-confidence and euphoria, and overconcentration of economic functions in Tokyo as an international financial center.[16]

If the intensified bullish expectations that previously supported a bubble are left unchecked, the expansion and subsequent burst of a bubble will become more intense, affecting the real economy directly or, by damaging the financial system, indirectly. Excessive optimism and self-confidence in the Japanese economy induced businesses to build up "three excesses": financial debt, employment, and production capacity (Figure 10.3). When the asset-price and credit bubble burst, the ensuing adjustments of such excesses were all the more painful and prolonged. Although mild deflation of less than 1 percent per annum attracted public attention, it was asset-price deflation, which con-tinued at an annual rate of close to 10 percent for more than 10 years, that exerted the most significant adverse pressure on the Japanese economy (Figure 10.4).[17] In retrospect, land prices were a common and significant risk factor for the financial sector and non-financial business sector during the bubble period in Japan.[18]

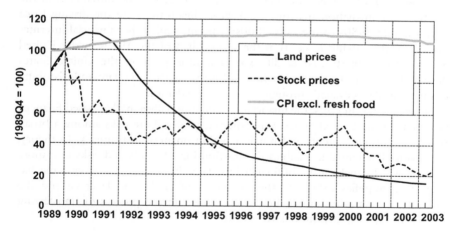

*Figure 10.4* Asset-price deflation

Sources: Bank of Japan, Financial and Economic Statistics Monthly; Ministry of Public Man-agement, Home Affairs, Posts and Telecommunications, Consumer Price Index; Japan Real Estate Institute, Urban Land Price Index.

Notes: CPI: consumer price index. The CPI excluding fresh food is seasonally adjusted by X-12-ARIMA with options of (0 1 2) (0 1 1) ARIMA model and level shifts in April 1989 and April 1997 when the consumption tax was introduced and subsequently hiked, respectively.

## 2.2. Financial structure and credit expansion

As noted earlier, an asset-price and credit bubble has three fundamental symptoms: a marked increase in asset prices, an expansion of monetary aggregates and credit, and an over-heating of economic activity. Among those three symptoms, an expansion of credit and monetary aggregates is directly linked with a build-up of financial imbalances.

In that context, Figure 10.5 plots the overall asset size of the private financial sector relative to nominal gross domestic product (GDP) in Japan and the United States. That figure illustrates two things. One is the delivery channel of credit in the financial intermediation process, and the other is the amount of credit.

First, focusing mainly on the composition of financial intermediaries, the figure clearly shows that Japan has a largely bank-centered financial system, while the United States has a primarily market-based financial system. In Japan the overall picture of the financial intermediation structure remains almost unchanged over time, with depository institutions still playing a leading role. In the United States, in contrast, other financial intermediaries have the largest share, and depository institutions have a much smaller share.[19] Other financial intermediaries include investment trusts, financial dealers and brokers, nonbanks, and funding companies, which are major players in the originate-and-distribute business.

Second, looking at the size of the financial sector relative to the nominal GDP, the asset size expands significantly in the run-up to a financial crisis in both Japan and the United States. Of course, reflecting the differences in the financial intermediation structure, depository institutions are the driving force from the mid-1980s to the early 2000s in Japan, while other financial intermediaries are the driving force from the second half of the 1990s in the United States. That suggests that credit expansion took place in the United States during the run-up to the recent financial crisis, as the originate-and-distribute business model prevailed through those intermediaries.

Before the recent crisis, the financial system, especially a market-based financial system as in the United States, was expected to distribute risks among a broad range of economic agents and not just within financial institutions. In theory, the financial system thus enables the distribution of funds and risks in a more efficient way by making use of financial markets. In practice, however, a mechanism that amplifies risks, i.e., the expansion of credit and leverage and the extension of maturity mismatches, is embedded in the process of transferring risks from financial institutions to investors.

## 2.3. The recent financial crisis as an asset-price and credit bubble

As described above, the recent financial crisis, starting from the U.S. subprime mortgage problem, can be seen as a typical example of an asset-price and credit bubble, as in the case of Japan's bubble in the second half of the 1980s. One difference between the two cases can be seen in the fact that the U.S. subprime

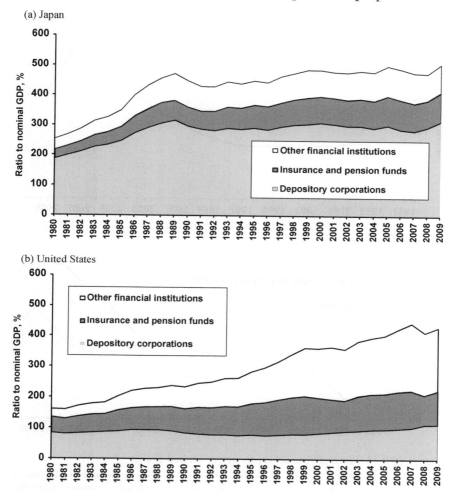

*Figure 10.5* Structure of financial intermediations

Sources: Cabinet Office, National Accounts; Bank of Japan, Flow of Funds Accounts; Bureau of Economic Analysis, National Economic Accounts; FRB, Flow of Funds Accounts of the United States.

Notes: Other financial institutions in Japan comprise securities investment trusts, nonbanks, and financial dealers and brokers. Those in the United States are the sum of investment trusts, financial dealers and brokers, nonbanks, and funding companies.

mortgage problem was associated with a sharp increase in credit in the household sector (Figure 10.6).

Before the recent crisis, the global economy enjoyed seemingly steady growth with low and stable inflation, which was referred to as the "great moderation." Under such circumstances, high optimism and ample liquidity undeniably

(a) Housing prices

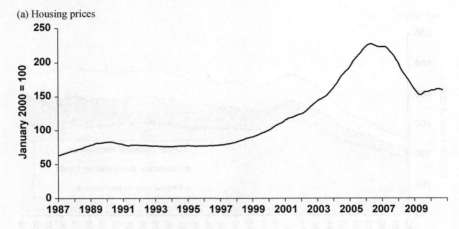

(b) Credit-to-GDP ratios

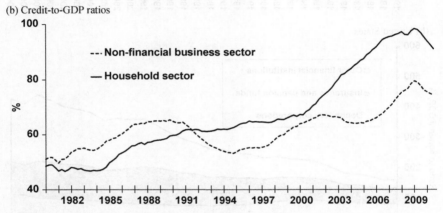

*Figure 10.6* Housing prices and credit in the United States

Sources: Standard & Poor's, S&P/Case-Shiller Home Price Indices; Board of Governors of the Federal Reserve System, Flow of Funds Accounts of the United States; Bureau of Economic Analysis, National Economic Accounts.

contributed to the U.S. credit boom and the associated housing price bubble. In the process, many financial institutions failed to properly evaluate and manage the risks related to structured credit products, and a number of investors and financial institutions also failed to evaluate the risks inherent in such complex financial transactions.

The structured credit products business related to mortgages has been regarded as a typical example of the originate-and-distribute business (Figure 10.7). Financial institutions converted mortgages into structured credit products, thereby removing credit and liquidity risks associated with mortgages from their balance sheets and transferring them to various financial institutions and

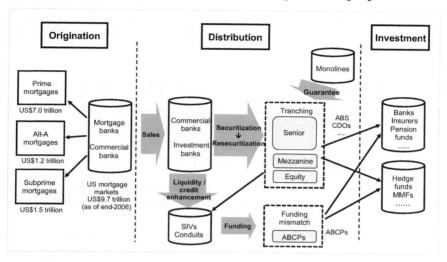

*Figure 10.7* Securitization markets related to U.S. subprime mortgages

Source: Bank of Japan, Financial System Report, March 2008.

Note: ABCPs: asset-backed commercial papers; ABS: asset backed securities; CDOs: collateralized debt obligations; MMFs: money market funds; SIVs: structured investment vehicles.

investors. In the process, financial institutions repackaged mortgages several times and split them into tranches such as senior, mezzanine, and equity to generate complex structured credit products. At the same time, they made wide use of an investment strategy to create a funding mismatch and raise leverage through off-balance sheet investment vehicles, such as conduits and structured investment vehicles.[20]

The above observation suggests that even in a market-based financial system like the United States, a network of various types of financial institutions plays a crucial role in channeling funds from savers to borrowers. That network is thus often called a "shadow banking system".[21] In the process of transferring risks from financial institutions to investors, the shadow banking system embedded a mechanism of amplifying risks, i.e., the expansion of credit and leverage as well as the extension of maturity mismatches. In addition, such amplified risks continued to remain within the shadow banking system, while those risks were initially considered as being separable from the system through the originate-and-distribute business.

The episodes of asset-price and credit bubbles examined so far suggest that incentives for a financial institution are underpinned not only by the framework for financial regulation and supervision at a micro level but also, importantly, by the financial and economic environment at a macro level. At the micro level, the risk perception and risk tolerance of economic agents change gradually but steadily under benign economic and financial conditions, thereby affecting their risk-taking behavior. That induces an expansion of credit and leverage at financial institutions and results in the accumulation of financial imbalances behind the scenes at the macro level.

## 3. Macroprudential orientation in the financial reform

In this section I will selectively review the issues related to recent debates on the design of macroprudential policy tools.

### 3.1. Overall direction of regulatory reform

Triggered by the recent financial crisis, fundamental reform of the financial system is advocated to establish more stable foundations for supporting sustainable growth in the global economy.

There are a lot of voices calling for more stringent regulations, such as raising minimum regulatory requirements significantly above the existing Basel rules to ensure the quality and quantity of overall capital in the global banking system.[22] The Basel Committee on Banking Supervision (2009) recommends four types of measures to influence the size, composition, and riskiness of the balance sheet at financial institutions by[23] (i) improving the quantity and quality of capital; (ii) limiting the extent of maturity transformation and the reliance on wholesale funding; (iii) improving risk coverage on counterparty credit exposures related to derivatives, repurchase agreements, securities lending, and complex securitizations; and (iv) introducing leverage ratios to supplement risk-weighted capital requirements.

Achieving higher stability purely by more stringent microprudential regulations, however, tends to result in lower efficiency in financial intermediation as a basis for economic growth.[24] In addition, it is crucial to understand that the higher regulatory burden is likely to produce incentives for regulatory arbitrage. At the same time, it has become widely recognized that the soundness of individual financial institutions does not necessarily assure the stability of the financial system as a whole. Financial crises are fundamentally endogenous to the financial system and arise from exposure to common risks among financial institutions. Incentives for a financial institution are underpinned not only by a framework for financial regulation and supervision at the micro level but also, importantly, by a financial and economic environment at the macro level. In that context, macroprudential policy is often pointed out as a missing element in the recent policy framework in order to strike a balance between the efficiency and the stability of the financial system as a whole.

It seems to have become a general consensus that macroprudential policy aims at reducing systemic risk, which is likely to disrupt the function of the financial system as a whole, thereby potentially destabilizing the macroeconomy.[25] Macroprudential policy thus needs to address two key externalities in the financial system: procyclicality in an intertemporal dimension as well as spillover effects in a cross-sectional dimension. Procyclicality concerns an intertemporal amplification mechanism within the financial system as well as between the financial system and the macroeconomy. Spillover effects concern a cross-sectional amplification mechanism through a complex network of various types of financial institutions, comprising not only commercial banks but also other market-based financial intermediaries and institutional investors.[26]

To address the key externalities, macroprudential policy tools are formulated as an extension of existing microprudential policy tools by incorporating a system-wide perspective in their implementation. It is thus crucially important to consider the fact that incentives for a financial institution are underpinned not only by a framework for financial regulation and supervision at the micro level but also, importantly, by the financial and economic environment at the macro level.[27] As experience with monetary policy suggests that policy actions can work best when they are fairly predictable and transparent, macroprudential policy is most likely to work well when implemented based on simple rules and guidelines, presumably linked to clear indicators of systemic risk.

In that context, central banks need to be closely involved in the formulation and implementation of macroprudential policy, based on close coordination among the related policy authorities.[28] That reflects the extensive experience of central banks in system-wide analysis and their role as a lender of last resort, as well as the close, two-way relationship between macroprudential policy and monetary policy. I will elaborate on that point later in Section 5.

Another important point in that regard lies in the fact that once financial distress materializes, the boundary between monetary and prudential policies becomes extremely ambiguous, as evidenced by the unconventional monetary policy responses at major central banks.[29] In a normal situation, once a policy interest rate is set at a desirable level from the perspective of monetary policy, a central bank expects the thus-determined policy interest rate to be transmitted to other longer-term interest rates through arbitrage in the financial markets. During financial crises, however, the above transmission mechanism is unlikely to work properly because the behavior of financial institutions is severely restricted by liquidity constraints. Financially stressed banks tend to have serious difficulties not only with lending but also with arbitraging and dealing in financial markets, thus hampering the transmission mechanism from a policy interest rate to longer-term rates, resulting in market segmentation among various financial markets.

### 3.2. Measures to dampen procyclicality

One mechanism of the so-called procyclicality of the financial system attracts increasing attention as an amplification mechanism for economic fluctuations. In particular, since the current framework for capital adequacy requirements (Basel II) is more risk-sensitive than Basel I, procyclicality has been discussed mainly from the viewpoint of whether regulatory and institutional factors have amplified economic fluctuations by inducing changes in the behavior of financial institutions.[30]

It should be noted, however, that the financial system is inherently procyclical, as emphasized by Borio and White (2003). The inherent procyclicality of the financial system also interacts with the real economy, thereby amplifying economic fluctuations and potentially leading to a persistent decline in a trend growth path. During booms, self-reinforcing processes of taking larger amounts of risks can develop, resulting in the build-up of financial imbalances. Those processes operate in a reverse direction during contractions.

The current regulatory and supervisory framework does not have the effective mechanisms and instruments necessary to control the inherent procyclicality of the financial system. Measures against procyclicality need to address the build-up of financial imbalances in upturns and their subsequent unwinding in downturns from a system-wide perspective. Such measures need to be considered to ensure financial system stability through serving as a shock absorber, instead of as a transmitter of risk to the broader economy, thus functioning as an automatic stabilizer of boom-and-bust cycles.[31]

Some measures are currently explored to encourage financial institutions to accumulate sufficient buffers in good times that can be drawn down in bad times. More precisely, two measures are actively explored: one is to promote more forward-looking provisions (dynamic provisioning), and the other is to conserve capital buffers (countercyclical capital buffers).[32] The provisioning measures focus on strengthening the banking system against expected losses, while the capital measures focus on unexpected losses.

In designing such countercyclical measures, one important element is the choice of conditioning variables that link financial and macroeconomic conditions with the build-up and release of buffers at individual financial institutions. With appropriate conditioning variables, countercyclical measures enable financial institutions to build up the margin to a sufficient level in good times and release it at the right speed and in the right amount in bad times.

The Basel Committee on Banking Supervision (2010d, e) proposes a scheme for a countercyclical capital buffer using the credit-to-GDP gap, computed as a deviation of the credit-to-GDP ratio from its Hodrick–Prescott filtered trend (HP-filtered trend) as a conditioning variable that links the required level of the capital buffer with financial and economic conditions.[33] More precisely, the credit-to-GDP gap is computed using one-sided HP-filtering with a large smoothing parameter of 400,000 for quarterly data.[34]

In a practical use of the aforementioned scheme, however, I emphasize that it is difficult to adequately discern the long-term trend of credit on a real time basis.[35] The procedure proposed by the Basel Committee on Banking Supervision (2010d, e) considers the information availability on a real time basis by using one-sided HP-filtering, not the standard two-sided HP-filtering. Still, we should be concerned that the estimated series of the credit-to-GDP gap is likely to suffer from an endpoint bias for trend measurement on a real time basis.

Figure 10.8 plots Japan's credit-to-GDP ratio and its HP-filtered trend based on both the two-sided and one-sided procedures (in the upper panel) and the computed credit-to-GDP gap (in the lower panel).[36] In spite of using a large smoothing parameter, the one-sided HP-filtering is deemed still vulnerable to

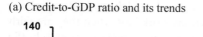

(a) Credit-to-GDP ratio and its trends

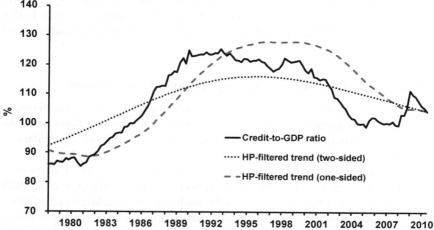

(b) Credit-to-GDP gaps

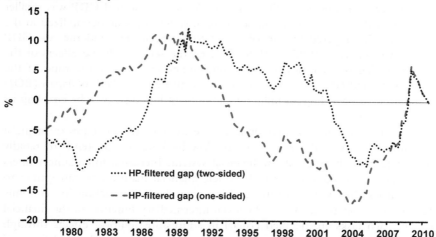

*Figure 10.8* Credit-to-GDP ratio in Japan

Sources: Bureau of Economic Analysis, National Economic Accounts; Board of Governors of
the Federal Reserve System, Flow of Funds Accounts of the United States.

Note: Hodrick–Prescott filtered trends for both one-sided and two-sided procedures are computed using a smoothing parameter of 400,000, as proposed by the Basel Committee on
Banking Supervision (2010d, e).

the effects of data accumulation, as shown by the significant differences with
the estimates of the two-sided HP-filtering.

The above observation suggests that it is difficult to rely solely on a rule-based
mechanism for setting countercyclical buffer levels. As mentioned earlier, however, macroprudential policy tools are most likely to work well when implemented

as automatic stabilizers, based on simple rules and guidelines, and experience with monetary policy suggests that policy actions work best when they are fairly predictable and transparent. A scheme for a countercyclical capital buffer thus needs to be designed so as to balance discretion with predictability and transparency.

### 3.3. Measures to deal with spillover effects in the financial system

A sharp contraction in economic activity is likely to occur when the financial system becomes destabilized and malfunctions through spillover effects of shocks within the financial system, typically triggered by the failure of a financial institution.

In the recent global financial crisis, the real GDP in advanced economies registered the largest decline during the period from the fourth quarter of 2008 to the first quarter of 2009 (Figure 10.9). Such a massive decline was attributed to a malfunction of the financial system, particularly interbank money markets, triggered by the failure of Lehman Brothers. By contrast, Japan did not take an abrupt liquidation measure for its failed financial institutions during the financial crisis in the late 1990s, and the decline in the real GDP was smaller in Japan at that time. The Japanese financial system became destabilized in the fall of 1997, triggered by the failure of Sanyo Securities, and the real GDP declined most from 1997 to 1998.[37] Given the serious adverse effects of the failure of Sanyo Securities on interbank money markets, at the time of the subsequent and larger failure of Yamaichi Securities, the Bank of Japan (BOJ) committed to providing an unlimited amount of liquidity, thereby enabling its orderly resolution.[38]

A complex and highly interconnected network of various types of financial institutions, as typically seen in the shadow banking system, tends to rapidly propagate risks throughout the financial system. Increased interconnectedness and exposure to common risks have left financial institutions susceptible to endogenous shocks, potentially resulting in a sharp contraction in economic activity. In order to maintain a financial intermediary function in the financial system, two tasks are deemed crucial in addressing spillover effects through the financial system: one is to enhance the robustness of individual financial institutions, and the other is to contain spillover effects resulting from such a failure.[39]

Regarding the first task, a number of approaches have been suggested to limit the systemic importance of large and complex financial institutions, recently called systemically important financial institutions (SIFIs). Those include capping the size of those financial institutions, keeping them from seemingly risky activities, requiring them to hold more capital, and reducing their odds of failure by requiring them to hold debt that automatically converts to equity in a crisis situation (contingent capital). In that context, blanket limitations on the size and scope of financial institutions do not seem to be effective measures, given that those financial institutions play an important role in promoting efficient financial intermediation on a global basis. Capital and liquidity surcharges need

(a) Output decline after the failure of Lehman Brothers

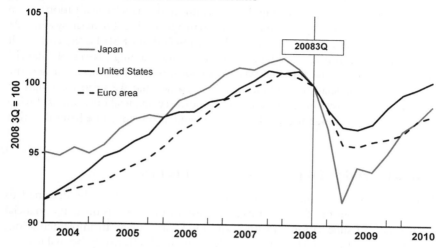

(b) Output decline in Japan

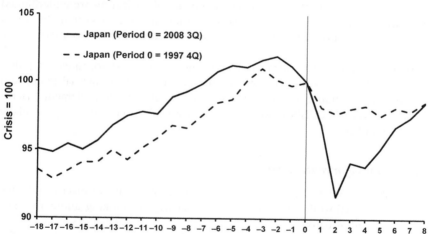

*Figure 10.9* Output declines after the crises

Sources: Cabinet Office, Annual Report on National Accounts; U.S. Bureau of Economic Analysis, National Economic Accounts; Eurostat, National Accounts.

Note: Crisis = 100: Index number indicating that the figure at the beginning of a crisis is equal to 100.

to play a central role in enhancing the robustness of individual financial institutions against systemic risk, while, in implementing such surcharges, there remains a difficult question regarding how to set the level of surcharges by striking a balance between the costs and the benefits of limiting the size and scope of financial institutions.

Concerning the second task, it is essential to devise an effective scheme to resolve a failure of large and highly interconnected financial institutions in an orderly manner, thereby minimizing the damage to the financial system. As recent events attest, in the case of an abrupt resolution of SIFIs, the end result can be market turmoil, cascading declines in wide-ranging classes of financial assets, and panic in the financial system. In addition, as I discussed earlier, the prevalence of the shadow banking system suggests that we need to design an orderly resolution scheme that covers nondepository financial institutions. Living wills and some contingent capital schemes would also seem to be helpful in that regard.

## 4. Macroprudential policy and central banks

As discussed so far, a macroprudential policy regime needs to be designed to integrate contributions from various policy authorities, such as those for financial regulatory and supervision and fiscal and monetary policy. In implementation, macroprudential policy tools are considered to work effectively by making use of their nature as automatic stabilizers of boom-and-bust cycles. In that respect, it is important to note that incentives for a financial institution are underpinned not only by a framework for financial regulation and supervision at the micro level but also, importantly, by the financial and economic environment at the macro level.

In this section, given such an understanding of a macroprudential policy regime, I will discuss the role of central banks in macroprudential policy and explore a policy framework for central banks to effectively implement macroprudential policy in collaboration with other areas of central banking, particularly monetary policy.

### 4.1. Missions of a central bank

As a starting point for discussing the role of central banks in macroprudential policy, it is worthwhile to examine a practical way of thinking about the missions of a central bank.

In general, a central bank is assumed to have the mission to achieve price stability as well as financial system stability, thereby laying a solid foundation for sustained economic growth.[40] On the one hand, price stability is generally defined as a state where various economic agents may make economic decisions without being concerned about fluctuations in general price levels.[41] On the other hand, financial system stability can be defined similarly as a state where various economic agents may make economic decisions without being constrained by the state of the financial system.

There has been a repeated debate about whether a fundamental trade-off exists between the two objectives.[42] Even though a trade-off between the two may exist in the short term, it is clear that both continue to be an important basis for sustained economic growth. Japan's experience since the late 1980s

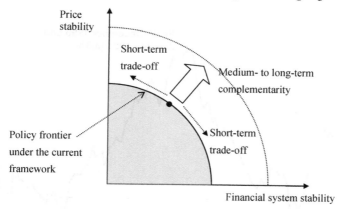

*Figure 10.10* Policy frontier for the two stabilities: illustration

clearly shows the importance of achieving sustained stability in monetary conditions, supported by both price and financial system stability, as an indispensable basis for the sound development of the economy in the medium to long term. In that sense, such trade-off arguments seem to be a matter of time horizons, and price and financial system stability are complementary to each other in the medium to long term. Central banks need to map out their policy framework, from a medium- to long-term viewpoint, to expand the policy frontier for price and financial system stability with a short-term trade-off (Figure 10.10).

Shiratsuka (2001) elaborated on the concept of price stability by differentiating between "measured price stability" and "sustainable price stability". Measured price stability expresses price stability in numerical terms to set a tolerable target range for the inflation rate, such as a rate of inflation from 0 to 2 percent. Sustainable price stability emphasizes the importance of achieving a stable macro-economic environment as a fundamental condition for sustainable growth, rather than merely pursuing a specific level of inflation measured by a specific price index at a particular point in time.

If we look back at Japan's experience since the bubble period, the Japanese economy experienced a decline in inflation and faced the risk of tumbling into a deflationary spiral in the aftermath of the bubble economy (Figure 10.11).[43] Okina, Shirakawa, and Shiratsuka (2001) concluded that "Japan's economy did not succeed in sustaining price stability after the bubble period" and emphasized the importance of evaluating the sustainability of price stability over a fairly long period.

The above arguments suggest that the two objectives for central banks, price stability and financial system stability, can be considered as complementary and inseparable in the medium to long term, in the sense that one is a precondition for achieving the other.[44] A central bank can contribute to economic growth by simultaneously achieving the two objectives.

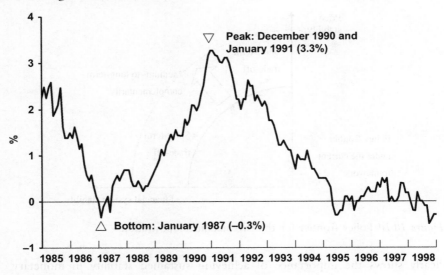

*Figure 10.11* Price development since the mid-1980s

Source: Ministry of Internal Affairs and Communications, Consumer Price Index.

Note: Figures are adjusted for the impact of the consumption tax.

### 4.2. Central bank policy responses to an asset-price and credit bubble

Given that the two objectives for central banks, price and financial system stability, are complementary and inseparable in the medium to long term, one often-asked question is what should be the central bank's policy responses, including both monetary and macroprudential policies, to an asset-price and credit bubble and a potential build-up of financial imbalances under benign financial and economic conditions.

That issue is often debated simply as whether monetary policy should lean against the wind, i.e., against excessive asset-price increases. Before the recent global financial crisis, the majority view could be summarized in two points.[45] First, before the burst of an asset-price and credit bubble, monetary policy should respond to asset-price fluctuations, whether driven by the fundamentals or not, only to the degree that those movements have implications for future inflation and economic growth. Second, after the burst of a bubble, central banks should carry out "mop-up operations" aggressively and swiftly against its adverse effects.

The above line of argument is generally premised on the assumption that a bubble is very difficult to identify on a real time basis. Thus, it seems fair to follow the principle that monetary policy should respond to asset-price movements, whether driven by the fundamentals or not, only to the degree that those movements have implications for future inflation and economic growth.

However, the real issue here is how to understand the expression "only to the degree that asset-price movements have implications for future inflation and economic growth" in implementing monetary policy. From our experiences of the recent crisis as well as Japan's asset-price and credit bubble, it is apparent that if we allow an asset-price and credit bubble to expand massively, that is most likely to make *ex-post* policy responses extremely difficult. Asset-price movements potentially have implications for inflation and economic growth over a fairly long term beyond the boom phase of asset-price movements.[46]

Monetary policy needs to address asset-price fluctuations considering their long-term implications for prices and economic activity. In that regard, preemptive monetary policy actions are needed anyway to contain excessive asset-price increases, even though the build-up of excesses cannot be contained by monetary policy alone and needs to be addressed by a combination of policy measures. It should be noted, however, that such preemptive policy actions are not aimed at pricking a bubble but attempt to prevent asset prices from increasing to excessively high levels.

### 4.3. A comprehensive policy framework for central banking

As repeatedly emphasized in this chapter, central banks have the medium- to long-term goal of maintaining price stability as well as financial system stability. In addition, those two objectives are closely interlinked and complementary in the medium to long term. Given increasing macrofinancial linkages, neither objective can be achieved without maintaining the other over a fairly long period.

From the viewpoint above, it is crucially important for central banks to evaluate risks to the economy at an early stage from a system-wide and long-term perspective and to deal with them in a preemptive manner. Of course, it is impossible to totally eliminate a build-up of financial imbalances in a boom-and-bust cycle. But it is possible and desirable to contain risks associated with a build-up of financial imbalances by carrying out both monetary and macro-prudential policies in a sufficiently preemptive and consistent manner, thereby making economic fluctuations smaller.

In that context, I suggest extending the framework of constrained discretion for monetary policy, proposed as the conceptual basis for flexible inflation targeting, to an overall policy framework for central banking.[47]

Constrained discretion for monetary policy is designed to pursue price stability in the medium to long term while responding flexibly to shocks in the short term.[48] More precisely, central banks retain some discretion over the use of monetary policy instruments to respond to economic shocks, financial disturbances, and other unanticipated developments. Such discretion, however, is constrained by a firm long-term commitment to keeping inflation low and stable. That approach is expected to strengthen the overall policy performance of central banks in achieving price stability in the long term, thereby promoting the sound development of the economy.

Similarly, constrained discretion for central banking attempts to pursue price and financial system stability in a consistent and sustainable manner. As examined earlier, a central bank needs to make some discretionary judgments in implementing macroprudential policy tools. In doing so, a central bank needs a more pragmatic approach in implementing policy measures from a long-term perspective while explaining the intention and rationale to society. Such a policy framework, although an abstract concept, provides central banks with a basis for achieving sustained stability in monetary conditions, supported by both price and financial system stability.

The above direction of practice can be observed in some central banks through the incorporation of assessments of the long-term risks to price stability into a monetary policy framework. The BOJ, for example, examines its monetary policy from two perspectives. The first perspective examines the baseline projections for one to two years in the future, and the second perspective examines, over a longer horizon, various risks, including of a low-probability event that entails extreme costs.[49] Similarly, the European Central Bank takes the monetary policy strategy of a "two-pillar approach": economic analysis and monetary analysis. Economic analysis assesses short- to medium-term price developments by focusing on economic activity and financial conditions. Monetary analysis serves as a means of cross-checking the economic analysis, from a longer-term horizon.[50]

## 5. Conclusions

In this chapter I have explored a policy framework for central banks from a macroprudential perspective, to pursue price and financial system stability in a consistent and sustainable manner. In that context, I have emphasized the importance of a "macroprudential perspective", not just "macroprudential policy". This is because such a framework needs to bring together contributions not only from financial regulation and supervision but also from macroeconomic policy, particularly monetary policy.

Macroprudential policy, combined with monetary policy and other macroeconomic policies, is expected to address a build-up of financial imbalances in upturns and their subsequent unwinding in downturns from a more system-wide perspective. To make such a framework workable, it is deemed crucial for central banks to implement monetary and macroprudential policies in a preemptive and consistent manner. From the above viewpoint, central banks need to evaluate risks to the economy at an early stage from a system-wide and long-term perspective, thereby dealing with them in a preemptive manner. Constrained discretion for central banking, while still an abstract concept, provides central banks with a basis for pursuing price and financial system stability in a consistent and sustainable manner.

It should be noted that no concrete rules exist regarding how to recognize risks associated with financial imbalances. Kindleberger (1995), for example, notes that there are no cookbook rules for policy judgments against asset-price misalignments, and it is inevitable that central banks will have to make discretionary judgments.[51] It is thus crucially important for central banks to have a good track record and credibility regarding their policy actions. In that case, a good track record should include decisive actions by central banks with a high degree of transparency, which would support good economic performance.

It should be also noted that achieving higher financial system stability purely by more stringent microprudential regulations tends to result in lower efficiency in financial intermediation. Crises are fundamentally endogenous to the financial system and arise from exposure to common risks among financial institutions, underpinned by complicated incentives at both the micro and macro levels. It is thus deemed crucial to map out a macroprudential policy framework in order to strike a balance between the efficiency and the stability of the financial system as a whole.

## Notes

1 This chapter was prepared for the Pacific Economic Outlook (PEO) Structure Specialist Meeting on "Macro-financial Linkages and Financial Deepening" in Osaka, September 11–12, 2010. The author thanks Akira Kohsaka, Helen Chan, Robert Deckle, Toshiki Jinushi, Kazuo Ogawa, Kunio Okina, participants of the two Pacific Economic Outlook Structure Specialist Meetings in March and September 2010, and staff at the Bank of Japan for their comments. The views expressed in the chapter are those of the author and do not necessarily reflect the official views of the Bank of Japan.
2 According to Clement (2010), the origin of "macroprudential" can be traced back to the late 1970s, in the context of work on international bank lending carried out by the Euro-currency Standing Committee (currently Committee on the Global Financial System [CGFS]) at the Bank for International Settlements (BIS). Since then, that term has always denoted concerns over financial system stability and its link to the macroeconomy, although the specific focus has changed over time.
3 Shirakawa (2009a) points out that "liquidity" and "macroprudence" are the two most important keywords in examining the lessons from the crisis and measures to prevent a recurrence. He then emphasizes the importance of a macroprudential perspective in various areas related to central bank policy, including monetary policy.
4 As explained later, an economy-wide bubble is generally characterized by three things: not just a rapid rise in asset prices but also the over-heating of economic activity and massive expansion in monetary aggregates and credit. To clarify such an understanding of a bubble, I use the term "asset-price and credit bubble" in this chapter.
5 The term "financial imbalances" is used in a vague manner, but it basically describes unsustainable developments in the financial system, typically observed as substantial and persistent deviations of various financial variables from the long-term historical trends.
6 Shirakawa (2009c) emphasizes the importance of analyzing the incentives of financial institutions from the viewpoints of the macro as well as micro level.
7 Regarding the recent policy discussions on financial regulatory reform, see the Financial Stability Board (2010b). The Basel Committee on Banking Supervision (2010b, c) presents the details of global regulatory standards on bank capital and liquidity requirements.
8 The Group of Thirty's Working Group on Macroprudential Policy (2010) provides a comprehensive review on macroprudential policy, such as the definition, necessity, tools, and implementation. It should be noted that a big practical challenge still lies ahead concerning how to make a macroprudential policy

framework operational. Research on macroprudential policy is still in an early stage to provide an analytical underpinning for such a policy framework, in contrast to research on monetary policy. For an overview of research on macroprudential policy, see, for example, Galati and Moessner (2010).

9 A cross-sectional dimension of the externalities in the financial system is also used in a slightly different manner. Borio (2003), for example, points out that a macroprudential approach to financial supervision has implications for the design of the framework with respect to both the time dimension (procyclicality) and the cross-sectional dimension (addressing common exposures across financial institutions).

10 The recent policy discussions seem to narrow down the issues on spillover effects through the financial system to those on systemically important financial institutions (SIFIs). It should be noted that spillover effects need to be examined from the broader perspective of a cross-sectional amplification mechanism in the entire financial system, including the working of the "shadow banking system".

11 Shirakawa (2009b) argues that central banks need "one large toolkit" to achieve the two inseparable long-term objectives, price and financial system stability. Yellen (2009b) also points out the importance of reexamining the previous understanding of separation between monetary and financial regulatory policies.

12 In response to the outbreak of the recent financial crisis, the U.S. Federal Reserve has naturally taken credit-easing measures to intervene aggressively in the credit products markets and related markets. Such policy responses can be regarded as an extension of conventional measures for liquidity provision to the commercial banking system to a broader range of the financial system, or the shadow banking system. For the details, see discussions in Shiratsuka (2010).

13 See, for example, Bernanke *et al.* (1999) for details on the constrained discretion for monetary policy as a conceptual basis for flexible inflation targeting.

14 Okina, Shirakawa, and Shiratsuka (2001) define the bubble period as the four years from 1987 through 1990, based on the criteria of the coexistence of three fundamental symptoms for an asset-price and credit bubble: a marked increase in asset prices, an expansion of monetary aggregates and credit, and an overheating of economic activity.

15 If an increase in asset prices is caused by a rational bubble, an evaluation of economic fundamentals will remain unaffected. On the contrary, euphoria is certainly associated with a recognition that economic fundamentals have shifted upward. Such a difference between a rational bubble and euphoria is crucially important in considering the implications of asset-price fluctuations for monetary policy.

16 Okina, Shirakawa, and Shiratsuka (2001) point out that, in retrospect, a wide range of industries had exposure to the common risk of skyrocketing commercial land prices during the bubble period. For example, the high profitability of computer-related industries at that time was primarily a result of large computer-related investments by financial institutions. Such investments, triggered by financial globalization and the progress of technological innovation, were also closely related to a rise in asset prices. Under such circumstances, the economy tended to be influenced by asset prices more than was generally thought.

17 Okina and Shiratsuka (2004) pointed out that the Bank of Japan had to conduct monetary policy amid a significant and unforeseen slowdown in potential growth, which differed significantly from a standard stabilization policy around a stable growth trend.

18 Okina, Shirakawa, and Shiratsuka (2001) point out that during the bubble period in Japan, loosening external financing constraints and seemingly rising productivity

and profits in many sectors were interconnected and became amplified through rising asset prices, especially land prices.

19 As discussed below, the traditional banking sector, although it has a limited share in the overall asset size of the financial sector, also took a substantial amount of risk by engaging in operations related to the originate-and-distribute business, such as the provision of credit and liquidity enhancement to off-balance sheet investment vehicles.

20 Some investment vehicles intentionally generated maturity mismatches between their assets and liabilities by investing in structured credit products with longer maturities against short-term funding in asset-backed commercial papers. That behavior suggests that investors and financial institutions behind such investment vehicles were taking highly leveraged positions with significant credit, liquidity, and interest rate risks, thereby pursuing higher returns.

21 Pozsar *et al.* (2010) provide a comprehensive review of the shadow banking system. Adrian and Shin (2008) propose an analytical framework for a risk transfer mechanism by modeling a balance sheet interaction between various financial intermediaries, called a "financial system perspective". Hattori, Shin, and Takahashi (2009) apply the perspective to analyzing the fund flows behind Japan's asset-price bubble in the second half of the 1980s.

22 In addition, we also need to address the issues related to, for example, the governance of the institution, the incentives of its executives, and the enhancement of market discipline.

23 As mentioned earlier, the Basel Committee on Banking Supervision (2010b, c) presents details of global regulatory standards on bank capital and liquidity requirements.

24 The Basel Committee on Banking Supervision (2010a) quantifies the benefits from stronger capital and liquidity requirements and compares them to the long-term costs. The Macroeconomic Assessment Group (2010a, b) estimates transition costs for raising capital adequacy requirements and introducing liquidity requirements. A basic conclusion appears to be that the benefits outweigh the costs in the transition phase as well as in the long term. It should be noted, however, that such cost-benefit comparison depends crucially on the structure of the financial system and the composition of banks' balance sheets.

25 Bank of England (2009), Committee on the Global Financial System (2010), Group of Thirty (2010), and Hanson, Kashyap, and Stein (2010) provide a more detailed examination on a broader range of macroprudential policy tools.

26 Hanson, Kashyap, and Stein (2010) emphasize the social costs of excessive balance-sheet shrinkage, in the form of credit crunches and fire sales, stemming from a common shock to a wide range of financial institutions.

27 It should be noted that a macroprudential perspective is also important in implementing microprudential regulation and supervision, given the interaction of incentives between the micro and macro levels.

28 In this context, there is heated debate on how to design a systemic stability regulator, especially whether to keep monetary policy and systemic stability regulation separated or not. In practice, however, the financial reforms in advanced economies share a common direction that central banks need to be involved in a macroprudential policy framework.

29 For further discussion on unconventional monetary policy, see Shiratsuka (2010).

30 The tendency of market participants to behave in a procyclical manner has been amplified through a variety of channels, including through accounting standards for both mark-to-market assets and held-to-maturity loans, margining practices, and through the build-up and release of leverage among financial institutions, firms, and consumers. The Financial Stability Board (2010b) provides an overview of the progress of a broad range of financial reforms.

31 Caruana (2010) points out the importance of designing macroprudential tools so as to function as automatic stabilizers.

32 Time-varying capital requirement is also considered as an alternative measure to dampen procyclicality in the financial system. That scheme requires financial institutions to hold higher ratios of capital to assets in good times than in bad times. In designing such a scheme, it is important to note that the regulatory capital requirement is often not the binding constraint on financial institutions even in bad times.

33 Drehmann *et al.* (2010) deliver a comprehensive review of the candidates for conditioning variables and conclude that the credit-to-GDP gap shows the best performance. They note, however, that no conditioning variable provides perfect signals, and a strict rule-based measure does not seem possible at this stage.

34 A one-sided HP-filtered trend is computed by running a loop over time and retaining the final value from the HP-filtered trend at each point in time. Regarding a smoothing parameter, Hodrick and Prescott (1997) propose to set it at 1,600 for quarterly data, which corresponds to the duration of business cycles ranging from four to eight years. Drehmann *et al.* (2010) make a guess about the duration of credit cycles as being three to four times longer than that of business cycles, and recommend using a smoothing parameter of 125,000 (= $3^4 \times 1,600$) or 400,000 (= $4^4 \times 1,600$).

35 Okina and Shiratsuka (2002) emphasize that continued economic expansion gradually makes it difficult to decompose a rising growth rate into cyclical and trend components. They then point out that that makes assessment of inflation pressure on a real time basis crucially difficult, since the level of the output gap varies depending on the estimates of potential GDP. In addition, we should be concerned about the effects of *ex-post* data revisions, especially regarding nominal GDP in Japan. It is well know that Japanese GDP data tends to be revised significantly from the initial estimates to the final ones.

36 The data for the credit-to-GDP ratio in Japan is complied by basically following the description in the Basel Committee on Banking Supervision (2010e), except for making seasonal adjustments using X-12-ARIMA, considering the significant seasonality in the end-of-month series of credit aggregates. The data for the credit-to-GDP ratio starts from 1970, and two-sided HP-filtering is computed using data for the full sample. One-sided HP-filtering is computed from 1978, which is the starting point for the figure, to obtain enough time-series for the initial loop.

37 The failure of Sanyo Securities in 1997 led to the first default in interbank money markets in the postwar period in Japan. That triggered a sudden liquidity contraction in the interbank money markets, immediately spilling over to a wide range of the financial markets.

38 Yamaichi Securities played an important role as one of the four big securities companies in Japan and actively conducted overseas businesses. Because of massive off-book liabilities, the so-called stock shuffle (loss compensation), Yamaichi's funding became increasingly tight both at home and abroad. Yamaichi finally decided to go into voluntary closure of its securities business in November 1997. When Yamaichi failed, the BOJ provided uncollateralized liquidity in order to support the orderly wind-down of its transactions, some of which turned out to be irrecoverable at the conclusion of Yamaichi's bankruptcy procedures in January 2005.

39 The Financial Stability Board (2010a) proposes asking for higher loss absorbency for global SIFIs (G-SIFIs) and improving a resolution scheme for SIFIs in an orderly manner. It should be noted that spillover effects through the financial system need to be examined from the broader perspective of a cross-sectional amplification mechanism in the entire financial system, including the working of the shadow banking system.

40 Of course, it is still difficult to say that a global standard has been established with respect to the role of central banks in promoting financial system stability, especially in the field of financial regulation. In practice, it is also true that central banks certainly play various roles in achieving financial system stability from a system-wide perspective, regardless of their assigned roles in financial regulation.

41 Greenspan (1996), for example, refers to price stability as a state in which "economic agents no longer take account of the prospective change in the general price level in their economic decision making". That definition can be interpreted as indicating the importance of attaining the state of a "classical dichotomy" in which price fluctuations do not affect the decision making of economic agents regarding resource allocation.

42 For issues on the separation of monetary policy and financial supervision, see, for example, Goodhart and Schonemaker (1995).

43 At the time of the bubble period, consumer price inflation had been extremely stable until around 1987 before starting to rise gradually in 1988, and the year-on-year increase in the consumer price index was still 1.1 percent in March 1989, immediately before the introduction of the consumption tax. The year-on-year increase in the consumer price index, adjusted for the impact of the consumption tax, continued to rise after April 1989, reaching 2 percent in April 1990 and 3 percent in November 1990, and then peaking in December 1990 and January 1991 at 3.3 percent.

44 As mentioned earlier, Shirakawa (2009b) argues that central banks need "one large toolkit" to achieve the two inseparable long-term objectives, price and financial system stability.

45 See, for example, Bernanke and Gertler (1999) and Kohn (2008). White (2009) argues against such views and emphasizes the necessity of extra operations in advance.

46 Kohn (2008) points out the importance of making economic projections over the long term, even though he maintains a skeptical attitude toward preemptive monetary policy actions against asset-price and credit bubbles. In light of the recent financial crisis, Yellen (2009a) and Dudley (2009), who used to stand up for the majority view before the crisis, have revised their position to be more supportive regarding preemptive monetary policy responses to asset-price and credit bubbles.

47 The Bank of England (2009) also points out the importance of constrained discretion in a macroprudential policy framework. From the viewpoint of a monetary policy framework, White (2009) emphasizes the importance of integrating a macroprudential perspective into monetary policy implementation, thereby establishing a new macrofinancial stability framework. He asserts that such a framework enables a central bank to respond to an asset-price and credit bubble in a systematic and symmetrical manner.

48 See, for example, Bernanke *et al.* (1999) for details on constrained discretion for monetary policy as a conceptual basis for flexible inflation targeting.

49 Shirakawa (2010) argues that the BOJ's monetary policy practice based on examinations from the two perspectives can be regarded as an innovative approach of implementing "flexible" elements of inflation targeting in a systematic manner.

50 See European Central Bank (2010a, b) for recent advances in monetary analysis to assess long-term risks to price stability.

51 Kindleberger (1995) comments on this point as follows: "When speculation threatens substantial rises in asset prices, with a possible collapse in asset markets later, and harm to the financial system, or if domestic conditions call for one sort of policy, and international goals another, monetary authorities confront a dilemma calling for judgment, not cookbook rules of the game."

## References and Further Readings

Adrian, Tobias, and Hyun Song Shin. 2008. "Financial Intermediaries, Financial Stability and Monetary Policy," in *Managing Stability in a Changing Financial System*, Kansas City: Federal Reserve Bank of Kansas City, pp. 287–334.

Bank of England. 2009. "The Role of Macroprudential Policy," Discussion Paper.

Basel Committee on Banking Supervision. 2009. "Strengthening the Resilience of the Banking Sector," Consultative Document, Bank for International Settlements.

Basel Committee on Banking Supervision. 2010a. "An Assessment of the Long-Term Economic Impact of Stronger Capital and Liquidity Requirements," Bank for International Settlements.

Basel Committee on Banking Supervision. 2010b. "Basel III: A Global Regulatory Framework for More Resilient Banks and Banking Systems," Bank for International Settlements.

Basel Committee on Banking Supervision. 2010c. "Basel III: International Framework for Liquidity Risk Measurement, Standards and Monitoring," Bank for International Settlements.

Basel Committee on Banking Supervision. 2010d. "Countercyclical Capital Buffer Proposal," Consultative Document, Bank for International Settlements.

Basel Committee on Banking Supervision. 2010e. "Guidance for National Authorities Operating the Countercyclical Capital Buffer," Bank for International Settlements.

Bernanke, Ben S., and Mark Gertler. 1999. "Monetary Policy and Asset Price Volatility," in *Achieving Price Stability*, Kansas City: Federal Reserve Bank of Kansas City, pp. 77–128.

Bernanke, Ben S., Thomas Laubach, Frederic S. Mishkin, and Adam S. Posen. 1999. *Inflation Targeting: Lessons from the International Experience*, Princeton, NJ: Princeton University Press.

Blanchard, Olivier J., and Mark Watson. 1982. "Bubbles, Rational Expectations and Financial Markets," in P. Wachtel, ed., *Crises in the Economic and Financial Structure*, Lexington: Lexington Books, pp. 295–315.

Borio, Claudio. 2003. "Toward a Macroprudential Framework for Financial Supervision and Regulation," Bank for International Settlements Working Paper 128.

Borio, Claudio, and William R. White. 2003. "Whither Monetary and Financial Stability? The Implications of Evolving Policy Regimes," in *Monetary Policy and Uncertainty: Adapting to a Changing Economy*, Kansas City: Federal Reserve Bank of Kansas City, pp. 131–211.

Caruana, Jaime. 2010. "Macroprudential Policy: What We Have Learned and Where We Are Going," keynote speech at the Second Financial Stability Conference of the International Journal of Central Banking, Bank of Spain, June 17.

Clement, Piet. 2010. "The Term of 'Macroprudential': Origins and Evolution," *BIS Quarterly Review*, March issue, pp. 59–67.

Committee on the Global Financial System. 2010. "Macroprudential Instruments and Frameworks: A Stocktaking of Issues and Experiences," Committee on the Global Financial System Papers 38, Bank for International Settlements.

Drehmann, Mathias, Claudio Borio, Leonardo Gambacorta, Gabriel Jiménez, and Carlos Trucharte. 2010. "Countercyclical Capital Buffers: Exploring Options," Bank for International Settlements Working Papers 317.

Dudley, William C. 2009. "Remarks," The Eighth Annual BIS Conference, Basel, Switzerland, June 26.

European Central Bank. 2010a. "Asset Price Bubbles and Monetary Policy Revisited," *ECB Monthly Bulletin*, November, pp. 71–83.

European Central Bank. 2010b. "Enhancing Monetary Analysis," *ECB Monthly Bulletin*, November, pp. 85–99.

Financial Stability Board. 2010a. "Progress since the Washington Summit in the Implementation of the G20 Recommendations for Strengthening Financial Stability," Report of the Financial Stability Board to G20 Leaders.

Financial Stability Board. 2010b. "Reducing the Moral Hazard Posed by Systematically Important Financial Institutions," Financial Stability Board Recommendation and Time Lines.

Galati, Gabriele, and Richhild Moessner. 2010. "Macroprudential Policy – a Literature Review," DNB Working Paper 267, De Nederlandsche Bank.

Goodhart, Charles, and Dirk Schoenmaker. 1995. "Should the Functions of Monetary Policy and Banking Supervision Be Separated?" *Oxford Economic Papers* 47(4), pp. 539–560.

Greenspan, Alan. 1996. "Opening Remarks," in *Achieving Price Stability*, Kansas City: Federal Reserve Bank of Kansas City.

Group of Thirty, Working Group on Macroprudential Policy. 2010. *Enhancing Financial Stability and Resilience: Macroprudential Policy, Tools, and Systems for the Future*. Washington, DC: Author.

Hanson, Samuel, Anil K. Kashyap, and Jeremy C. Stein. 2010. "A Macroprudential Approach to Financial Regulation," mimeo.

Hattori, Masazumi, Hyun Song Shin, and Wataru Takahashi. 2009. "A Financial System Perspective on Japan's Experience in the Late 1980s," Institute for Monetary and Economic Studies Discussion Paper 2009-E-19, Institute for Monetary and Economic Studies, Bank of Japan.

Hodrick, Robert J., and Edward C. Prescott. 1997. "Postwar U.S. Business Cycles: An Empirical Investigation," *Journal of Money, Credit, and Banking* 29(1), pp. 1–16.

Kindleberger, Charles P. 1995. "Asset Inflation and Monetary Policy," *BNL Quarterly Review* 48(192), pp. 17–37.

Kohn, Donald L. 2008. "Monetary Policy and Asset Prices Revisited," speech presented at the Cato Institute's 26th Annual Monetary Policy Conference, November 19.

Macroeconomic Assessment Group (established by the Financial Stability Board and the Basel Committee on Banking Supervision). 2010a. "Assessing the Macroeconomic Impact of the Transition to Stronger Capital and Liquidity Requirements," Interim Report, Bank for International Settlements.

Macroeconomic Assessment Group. 2010b. "Assessing the Macroeconomic Impact of the Transition to Stronger Capital and Liquidity Requirements," Final Report, Bank for International Settlements.

Okina, Kunio, Masaaki Shirakawa, and Shigenori Shiratsuka. 2001. "The Asset Price Bubble and Monetary Policy: Japan's Experience in the Late 1980s and the Lessons," *Monetary and Economic Studies* 19(S1), pp. 395–450.

Okina, Kunio, and Shigenori Shiratsuka. 2002. "Asset Price Bubbles, Price Stability, and Monetary Policy: Japan's Experience," *Monetary and Economic Studies* 20(3), pp. 35–76.

Okina, Kunio, and Shigenori Shiratsuka. 2004. "Asset Price Fluctuations, Structural Adjustments, and Sustained Economic Growth: Lessons from Japan's Experience since the Late 1980s," *Monetary and Economic Studies* 22(S1), pp. 143–167.

278   *Shigenori Shiratsuka*

Pozsar, Zoltan, Tobias Adrian, Adam Ashcraft, and Hayley Boesky. 2010. "Shadow Banking," Federal Reserve Bank of New York Staff Reports 458.

Shirakawa, Masaaki. 2009a. "Macroprudence and the Central Bank," speech at the Seminar of the Securities Analysts Association of Japan in Tokyo, December 22.

Shirakawa, Masaaki. 2009b. "Preventing the Next Crisis: The Nexus between Financial Markets, Financial Institutions and Central Banks," speech given at the London Stock Exchange, May 13.

Shirakawa, Masaaki. 2009c. "Some Thoughts on Incentives at Micro- and Macro-level for Crisis Prevention," remarks at the Eighth Bank for International Settlements Annual Conference, Basel, Switzerland, June 26.

Shirakawa, Masaaki. 2010. "Roles for a Central Bank – Based on Japan's Experience of the Bubble, the Financial Crisis, and Deflation," speech at the 2010 Fall Meeting of the Japan Society of Monetary Economics, September 26.

Shiratsuka, Shigenori. 2001. "Is There a Desirable Rate of Inflation? A Theoretical and Empirical Survey," *Monetary and Economic Studies* 19(2), pp. 49–83.

Shiratsuka, Shigenori. 2010. "Size and Composition of the Central Bank Balance Sheet: Revisiting Japan's Experience of the Quantitative Easing Policy," *Monetary and Economic Studies* 28, pp. 79–105.

White, William R. 2009. "Should Monetary Policy 'Lean or Clean'," Working Paper 34, Dallas: Globalization and Monetary Policy Institute, Federal Reserve Bank of Dallas.

Yellen, Janet L. 2009a. "Closing Panel Presentation," at the Federal Reserve Board/*Journal of Money, Credit, and Banking* Conference on Financial Markets and Monetary Policy, Washington, DC, June 5.

Yellen, Janet L. 2009b. "Linkages between Monetary and Regulatory Policy: Lessons from the Crisis," FRBSF Economic Letter 2009–36.

# Index

For Product Safety Concerns and Information please contact our
EU representative GPSR@taylorandfrancis.com Taylor & Francis
Verlag GmbH, Kaufingerstraße 24, 80331 München, Germany